Once Upon a Time
in Hollywood

Once Upon a Time in Hollywood

Moviemaking, Con Games, and Murder in Glitter City

ROD LURIE

PANTHEON BOOKS   NEW YORK

Copyright © 1995 by Rod Lurie

All rights reserved under International and Pan-American Copyright
Conventions. Published in the United States by Pantheon Books, a
division of Random House, Inc., New York, and simultaneously in
Canada by Random House of Canada Limited, Toronto.

Library of Congress Cataloging-in-Publication Data
Lurie, Rod, 1962—
Once upon a time in Hollywood : moviemaking, con games, and
murder in glitter city / Rod Lurie.
p.   cm.
Includes index.
ISBN 0-679-43522-0
1. Emr, Jon.   2. Swindlers and swindling—California—Hollywood—
Biography.   3. Murder victims—California—Hollywood—Biography.
I. Title.
HV6698.H6E475   1995
364.1′63—dc20   94-42319
CIP

Book design by M. Kristen Bearse

Manufactured in the United States of America

First Edition

2   4   6   8   9   7   5   3   1

To Tamar, my mom, from whom
I learned the lesson of perseverance

To hell with the truth! The history of the world proves that the truth has no bearing on anything. It's the lie of the pipe dream that gives life to the whole misbegotten mad lot of us, drunk or sober.
—Robert Ryan in John Frankenheimer's *The Iceman Cometh*

CONTENTS

BOOK ONE

The Producer and the Cop

Hmmm. Amazing. It's absolutely amazing, but, under the right circumstances, a producer could make more money with a flop than he could with a hit. Hmmm. Yes, it's quite possible. If he was certain that the show would fail, a man could make a fortune.
—Gene Wilder in *The Producers*

A Murder in Culver City:
July 11, 1991

We'll start with a few murders—big man, little man—
just to show we make no distinction.
—Claude Rains in James Whale's *The Invisible Man*

Culver City traffic cop Mike Roth was issuing a speeding ticket at the corner of Slauson and Jefferson at precisely the moment that the Lincoln full of corpses sped past him.

It was the long, steady drone of the horn that got him to spin around. Roth was unable to see the Lincoln's backseat passengers because the car's rear windows, already tinted black, were spattered with a coat of blood. But he certainly could see the two men who were seated in front, because those windows were rolled down. There was the passenger, stocky and bearded, his head arched backward on the headrest. He was clutching a blood-soaked poodle which was yapping away in poodle hysteria. The driver, a much younger man, was slumped slightly to the right, atop the other victim.

Within the split second that the 1991 white Lincoln town car was directly in front of him, Officer Roth was also able to see a black-haired woman, lurching from her position in the back of the car and trying like all hell to steer the out-of-control vehicle. She wasn't having much luck. Her hands were slipping and sliding on the blood that had covered the steering wheel. The only thing she succeeded in doing was banging her fist on the horn.

The Lincoln was barreling down Slauson Boulevard. Roth dropped his bulging pad of tickets, hopped his two-hundred-pound-plus frame on his still-running motorcycle, made a quick U-turn, and began his pursuit of the makeshift hearse, which for some reason did not have a license plate.

This was a new experience for Roth. This type of road-warrior stuff was hardly endemic to Culver City. Roth's primary duties centered on traffic and jaywalking citations and on rare occasions sending prostitutes on their way. But today here he was, sucking in the fumes of the Lincoln as it made its aimless journey down this typically wide Southern California street. Eventually, Roth pulled alongside the Lincoln and yelled futilely to the black-haired woman to put the car into "Park." From inside the Lincoln, Roth could hear the old lady screaming, "Oh my God! Stop the car!"

The Lincoln swerved to the right and careened over a grassy tract between the sidewalk and the street. *Bam!* The Lincoln rolled over a small tree. *Bam!* Down went another. Then a third.

The vehicle slowed down. Roth got off his bike, laid it on the pavement, and chased the car on foot. When he got to the driver's-side window, he dove into the car. With his feet dangling out the window he reached in and slapped the gearshift into Park.

The car screeched to a halt. The two bodies in the front seat jerked forward violently and then, just as quickly, backward, spraying blood on the windshield and Officer Roth's black leather jacket.

The black-haired woman and another, much older lady were in the backseat screaming. Roth begged the women to calm down. He told them that everything would be all right and he would call for an ambulance right away.

Roth jogged back to his motorcycle, still catching his breath, hoping he would remember the precise procedures required of him in a situation like this. He lifted his bike, took a solid breath, and called for the ambulance and, goddammit! more police! Now! He told the dispatcher that there had been a shooting! A "187"! A murder! A double murder! He took off his helmet and thick sunglasses and wiped away the sweat and blood that left his dark curly hair soaked and pasted against his forehead. Then he returned to the women.

The old lady was already out of the car by the time Officer Roth had gone to call for the paramedics. She had opened the passenger-side door and cradled her son, a 215-pound man of forty-five. He was still wearing his black aviator sunglasses. The right lens had a small bullet hole in it, through which one could see that his eye had popped out and was hanging by the optic nerve. There was, the old lady thought, a small pulsation in his neck, coming in periodic intervals, a little spasm of life, a spasm of hope. She held on to his head, stroking his blond hair, now sticky and clumped together. She cradled him so that he was facing her. She didn't want the man to turn and see that the driver was dead.

Roth, holding a small spiral notebook in the palm of his hand, needed to get some information from them. What were their names? The old lady said she was Renee Emr and the younger, black-haired woman next to her was Sue Fellows. Between frightened gasps, Renee explained that the driver was her grandson Roger. The passenger was her son, Jon. *Roland* Jon Emr, to be exact. Sue was Jon's girlfriend.

Roth then asked them if they'd got a good look at the shooter. Sue Fellows said that she hadn't seen a thing, that she had ducked the very second she heard the first shot fired. But Renee, still clutching her son to her chest, said that she knew exactly who the killer was. His name was Robert Suggs and he worked for her son. She noted that, for some reason, there had been something different about Suggs's appearance, though she couldn't quite nail down what it was.

Roughly a dozen police cars arrived on the scene and formally secured the area. An enormous traffic jam—even by the outrageous standards of Los Angeles County, began amassing. It certainly didn't help that these murders occurred at precisely the hour when most Los Angelenos started heading home from work.

A radio-news helicopter hovered above, rubbernecking along with the rest of the traffic, issuing a warning—a SIG alert, as it was commonly referred to in California. There was dramatic "police activity" in the area, the reporter announced, and commuters should do their best to avoid this intersection altogether.

Within a few minutes, another helicopter had converged on the scene, and then another, this one flying low enough that the gold KABC logo was visible to everybody on the ground. The three machines made a terrific whooshing noise and caused gusts of wind to rip through this section of Culver City and the smog-stained palm trees to whip violently about. The activity didn't shock anybody on the ground. The sight and sounds of several helicopters flying at once was as natural in Los Angeles as was its smog. The commuters didn't seem to mind.

But the cops minded. Especially when they heard a fourth copter coming. A fourth copter that had smelled blood, a potential news story.

The supervising officer stood on the ground and waved off the intruders. Slowly, each of the four copters rose, higher and higher, each slowly circling the chaos below, canvassing the situation, until, soon, the steel vultures were out of sight, searching for more delicious prey on these ugly gray streets.

Sergeant Hank Davies and his partner, Steve Yoshida, were having a grand old time at the Culver City Police Department, bullshitting with Chief Ted Cooke, a thirty-seven-year veteran of the force. Only a few days earlier Davies had been appointed head of the Culver City homicide division. For the past four years he had been an undercover narcotics officer. Davies had viewed it as the fun stuff: the job where, out of nowhere, you got to pull out badges and smirk like a son of a bitch at all the dopeheads and dealers you had fooled for months. Now, running a homicide division—especially at the young age of thirty-four— had to be considered something of a step up.

There was, however, one problem. There had not been a murder in these parts for nearly two years. Davies felt that he might as well have been appointed head of the flood commission in the Sahara. The predominant crimes in Culver City were auto thefts. Car thieves were attracted to this particular town, located just a few miles outside Hollywood, because Columbia, MGM, and Tri-Star Pictures were all headquartered here—as well as the ostentatious vehicles of their wealthy employees.

Murder was so uncommon in Culver City that on this particular day Davies and his right-hand man, Yoshida, were making a convincing case to the Chief about reopening a 1985 murder investigation. A young woman had been strangled and beaten to death and nobody had ever been busted for it. In looking over the records, Davies felt he had a pretty good idea who the killer was and had been begging his boss to give him a crack at bringing in the perp. But then Davies heard his name over the intercom. He picked up the phone and contacted the dispatcher.

After the dispatcher told him about the 187, Davies began drilling for all the data he could get. There was very little concrete information available: There had been a shooting. From one car into another. Two men were down. Nine, ten, eleven shots. Something like that. The incident had occurred in the vicinity of the Fox Hills Mall. The Mall was Gangland. The Bloods and the Crips. As a narc, Davies used to make the Fox Hills Mall one of his premier hangouts.

"Sounds like a drive-by shooting," Yoshida said.

"Yeah," said Davies. He had to respect Yoshida. Although Davies technically outranked him, Yoshida was quite a few years older, a far more seasoned police officer, and certainly had more experience in the area of investigating homicides.

Davies tucked his pistol in the back of his pants and put on his jacket. He hated jackets. He wasn't used to them. Not after spending all that time dressed like a drug dealer with hair down almost to the small of his back and pendant in his left ear. Yoshida was dressed sharply but without flair. Just like a Japanese businessman.

The two men got into the olive-colored Chevy Caprice that had been allocated to both the robbery and homicide divisions of the department. Yoshida was holding on to a cup of steaming black coffee. This was Yoshida's M.O.: coffee. Any time. Any place. Even in a swift-moving vehicle. Yoshida had become an absolute master at coffee cup manipulation and balance.

Davies and Yoshida arrived on the scene within five minutes. Davies must have suspected the very second that he laid his eyes on the spectacle before him that he was about to kiss good-bye not only to the golfing vacation that was supposed to begin when he got off that day but to almost every day off between this moment and the day that he would exchange vows with his bride-to-be, Julie, in eight weeks. All that he could see before him were paramedics, squad cars, motorcycles, fire trucks, about twenty police officers, and siren strobes still whirling.

Officer Mike Roth galloped over to the two detectives. "Hey, Hank," he said.

"You fuck the scene up?"

"Nah, it's nice and cherry, Hank." Then Roth began a rambling explanation of the events as he understood them. Davies and Yoshida scribbled furiously in their small department-issue notebooks. Some son of a bitch in a white Toyota had pulled up and opened fire . . . Hit the men sitting in the front seat . . . Killed them, he thought . . . One of the bullets had grazed one of the women . . . the younger one . . . The victims were a man named Jon Emr and his son Roger.

Roth started banging the back of his hand on his own notebook. The shooter's name was Robert Suggs. His friends called him Suggsy. Renee—she was the mother—had fingered the killer. The old lady was dead-on sure about it! Roth even had a physical description of the perp.

And there was something else. According to Renee, the victim Jon Emr was a producer. In fact, Jon Emr had just left his office at GMT Studios, just up the road on Buckingham Parkway, when Suggsy blew him and his boy away.

When Davies asked Roth what Suggs's relationship was to Jon Emr, Roth told him he thought he was Emr's bodyguard. Hank lifted an eyebrow and glanced at Yoshida. A bodyguard?

One thing was intuitively clear to Sergeant Hank Davies. This would be a real "PI," a "Press Interest" case—which was the vernacular used to describe a case *that mattered* . . . even if the press didn't *really* give a damn about it.

From the information that Officer Roth had given him, it now sounded to Davies as if the murder had been a Mob wipeout. The Mafia tended to exact their punishments precisely in the manner portrayed in a thousand permutations of *The Godfather* and *GoodFellas*: brutally and publicly, bloody calling cards to anybody who was even thinking of crossing the line with them. But if the murder of Jon and Roger Emr was Mob-related—and the apparent precision of this Suggsy fellow indicated that he may well have been a professional—why had the two women been spared? Even if they were not the intended victims, they were certainly witnesses. That was reason enough to waste them. Why had the killer, this Suggsy, not bothered to disguise himself, even with something as simple as a black stocking?

Davies and Yoshida next directed their attention to the paramedics, who were cool and collected when they told him that, sadly, both victims had "expired" upon their arrival at their respective hospitals.

Davies walked to the squad car in which Renee Emr and Sue Fellows were sitting. Their clothes were stained with blood. Renee was quiet and contemplative, her eyes still moist. Susan Fellows's face was still bleeding slightly from the one bullet that had grazed it. The paramedics had already treated the wound, cleaned it up, and decided not to cover it with a bandage so that it would be able to breathe.

Renee's head hung low as she petted the dog sitting comfortably on her lap. Davies noticed that the poodle had a broken leg. The detective stuck his head through the open window. "I am Sergeant Hank Davies with the Culver City homicide division. Are the two of you okay? Do you need to go to the hospital?" They both shook their heads. He turned to Sue Fellows. "Do you want the paramedics to look at that?" he asked, not aware that they had already done so.

Sue shook her head.

"Mrs. Emr, we'd like to try and catch this guy as soon as we can," Hank said to Renee. "I know that it's a very difficult time for you. But I'm going to need all the details that you can give me."

It was difficult for Renee to speak. As Sue Fellows held her hand, she tearfully recounted the story that she had already given to the uniformed officers and would give many, many times again. It was simple. Roger was driving. Jon was in the passenger seat. She and Sue were in the back. Roger had stopped at a red light. Suggs pulled up next to them on the passenger side of the car, and started shooting, just like that. There had to have been a dozen shots. When he was done firing up the two men, Suggsy turned the gun on her. For some reason he decided not to fire. After whipping off a quick smile, Suggs rode off, going north on Sepulveda.

At the end of her story, Renee gave Davies a physical description of Suggs and the white Toyota that he was driving. She also told him that she knew for a fact that the white Toyota did not belong to Suggsy.

Davies asked Renee how sure she was that the killer was Suggs.

"He was two feet away. It's a sure thing," she said.

Davies leaned in to pick up the mouthpiece of the radio in the squad car. He gave the dispatcher additional details about Suggsy for the all-points bulletin that had been put out about ten minutes earlier.

Davies never had the stomach to tell people that their loved ones had died. His composure was always mentioned in his efficiency reports. But when it came to things like next-of-kin notification, Davies would just as soon designate the duty away.

Steve Yoshida walked over to Davies's side, conferred quietly with him, and then turned toward the women. "I'm very sorry, ladies. Neither one made it." He said it softly and with feeling. Davies was surprised. For the most part, Steve Yoshida's voice never wavered from the monotone, his eyes never flashed with anger or excitement.

Both women began to cry. Yoshida stroked Renee's hand.

After a short while Renee Emr spoke to Hank Davies. She told him that there was some material she needed in the trunk of the Lincoln Continental.

Davies nodded. "We'll take care of everything," he said.

Davies got the keys to the vehicle from Officer Roth. He walked over to the Lincoln, which was still in the same place it had been when it came to its abrupt halt at the intersection of Slauson and Segrelle. He put the second key on the ring into the lock of the trunk. When he lifted the door, he saw a huge pile of paperwork and a briefcase. In the briefcase lay a document that had a cover page which read, "James Dean: The Legend."

Next to the papers was a shiny black .22-caliber pistol. Davies checked and saw that it was loaded. He let the bullets drop out into the palm of his hand and then deposited them in his jacket pocket. He placed the gun in the back of his pants and then returned to Yoshida.

Davies asked Steve Yoshida to drive the two women in a "black and white" to the police station, about a mile and a half away. He told Yoshida that he would catch up with them later. Then Hank Davies got down to the business of investigating what would come to be known as "The James Dean Murders."

There are many things that are required to be done at a murder scene: searching the car, dusting for fingerprints, recovering shell casings, putting out more crime broadcasts, speaking to any eyewitnesses, and so on.

Even though this was his first murder case with Culver City, Davies knew he was up to the task. He had graduated several years earlier from the Police Academy, after obtaining a sociology degree from Wake Forest University in Winston-Salem, North Carolina. The recession that rocked the nation in the late eighties and early nineties had brought an infusion of college graduates into the police force. About 50 percent of the Culver City cops boasted some kind of advanced degree. Davies nevertheless managed to rise above most of the competition. In his class at the academy, Davies was number three out of about seventy-five rookies. He was at the very top in academics, but was done in by some gazellelike cadets on the running track. His record beyond the Academy was spotless. He had even earned the coveted Medal of Valor when he got caught in mortal combat with a crazed and armed junkie and finally managed to subdue him. But what confronted him now was different. This double-murder investigation was going to be a bear. He could just feel it. Feel it in his cop bones.

Davies's first determination was that .22-caliber bullets had been used in the murder. He had actually spotted one of the bullets in the backseat of the white Lincoln. Apparently that bullet had gone completely through the passenger-side victim, proceeded to graze Sue Fellows's cheek, and then came to a dead stop on the backseat.

Determining the type of bullet used was not exactly groundbreaking stuff: the .22 is the favorite bullet of assassins and gang members, primarily because it is so inexpensive. Almost all hardware stores sell federal-issue bullets for under two dollars a box. Any gun that fires off a .22 has almost no recoil because the low density of the bullet requires little gunpowder. The .22, due to its shape and weight, is capable of traveling great distances. The boxes that contain the bullets carry a warning that the bullets can travel up to one and a half miles.

Nobody was immediately able to tell Hank how many bullets had actually hit the two men. For that, he would have to wait for the autopsy results. But, certainly, enough bullets had connected with enough flesh to make things mighty messy inside the Lincoln. Blood had found its way to every nook and cranny of the vehicle like butter on an English muffin. There was spatter on both armrests, a gory little puddle had formed on the driver's seat, and blood had already coagulated on the carpeting. Small chunks of brain were lying on the passenger-side floor. Brain fluid was sticking to the inside of the windshield and the vinyl seats, and was dripping like sap from the inner roof of the car. One tooth, belonging to the driver, had somehow found its way to the passenger side. Tufts of hair were scattered throughout the car. A bone fragment was on the backseat.

Jesus, Hank thought to himself. Jesus Fuckin' H. Christ. What had Jon Emr and his teenage boy done to deserve this punishment?

Davies pulled out a pair of surgical gloves from his inner jacket pocket. He put his tie over his shoulder so that it wouldn't dip into any of the blood puddles. Using a pair of tweezers, Davies lifted the brain sections, bones, and hairs and deposited them into plastic Baggies. In the glove compartment Davies found a contract with a local car-rental agency. In addition, there was a black fanny pack on the passenger-side floor. Among other items, the pack contained an unregistered .38 Special revolver, a small bottle of the prescription drug Zovirax (used to contain genital herpes), and nitroglycerine pills that were apparently used to help Jon Emr with a serious heart condition.

Davies also found a fake ID for Roger. The name on the card was John Roger Shane. The imaginary Mr. Shane was twenty-five years old, four years older than necessary to make him "legal" to drink. In reality, Roger was only nineteen and, because of his baby face, couldn't have passed for twenty-five if his hair had been gray. Also in Roger's wallet was his father's business card. It read: "R. Jon Emr. Producer. 'James Dean: The Legend.'"

A Gathering in Culver City:
July 11, 1991

Insanity runs in my family. It practically gallops.
—Cary Grant to Priscilla Lane in *Arsenic and Old Lace*

It was not until two hours after he initially met Renee Emr and Sue Fellows that Hank Davies was able to return to the Culver City Police Station. The bureaucratic-looking building, red brick and two stories tall, with a flagpole and a dying patch of grass in front of it, was located just a few blocks away from the corporate headquarters of both MGM studios and the lot for Columbia/Tri-Star Pictures.

Davies immediately ascended to the second floor of the building and met with Steve Yoshida, who was busy with the grunt work of running the killer's name through the computer and putting out bulletins to the various bus stations, cab companies, airports, seaports, and train stations in the Los Angeles area. So far, there had been no luck. With every passing minute, the chances of snatching the killer became more remote. It is a commonly accepted fact among criminologists that after twenty-four hours on the lam, a perp is close to home free.

"There's something else," Hank said to Yoshida. He pulled out Renee's .38-caliber pistol. "This belongs to the old lady. Found it in her briefcase. Can you fuckin' believe it?"

Yoshida wrote down the serial number. "I'll run it through the computer."

Davies waited a few minutes as Yoshida's whirring computer came up with the information that the gun was unregistered. Davies walked down the hall to the conference room where Renee and Susan had been sequestered. Also in the room was a man named Alan Hauge, who was Jon Emr's last business partner; Alan's wife, Lanette; and their partner, Frank DiPasquale. A female detective named Pamela Graves was there to provide comfort to the two women.

Renee and Susan were wearing the same clothes they had on when they were attacked. The blood on their blouses was now dried and flaky. Davies asked if they wanted a change of clothes and offered to send a cop to their apartment in Torrance to pick out a couple of outfits. Neither accepted Davies's offer. When he asked them if they wanted to eat, nobody in the room confessed to having much of an appetite.

It was the first time that Davies got a real good look at the women. Sue Fellows had a dark, pockmarked face and an elongated nose. This surprised Hank Davies. He had examined Emr's driver's license photo and thought Emr was handsome. Surely a good-looking hotshot in the movie industry could have a looker by his side. But many people who worked with Sue Fellows had a nickname for her. They called her "Monkey-face."

Renee resembled Golda Meir, only with whiter and straighter hair. She had a bulbous torso that was supported by swollen legs shaped like fire hydrants. Her face was wrinkled and grandmotherly. A sweet old lady, Davies thought for the first and, perhaps, last time.

Davies approached Alan Hauge, a small, gentle-looking man who bore a strong facial resemblance to George Bush, and asked him about his connection to Jon Emr.

"Well, I worked with Jon. We were working on the Dean project."

"You were making, what, a movie based on the life of James Dean?"

"That's right. That's what I was doing with Jon. At the studio."

"Studio?"

"GMT Studios."

Davies wrote the initials in his book. It seemed bizarre that a movie studio existed in town and he had never heard of it. "What do those letters stand for?"

"GMT? It stands for Great and Mighty Things."

"Pardon me?"

"It's from the Scriptures."

Hauge went on to feed Davies more information. He claimed that there had been considerable interest in the James Dean project. One of the principal parties was a reputed organized-crime figure in Santa Monica who had offered to pay $1 million for the rights to the project, an offer that Emr had refused. Hauge said that Jon had become increasingly paranoid about the mobster, even saying that he had threatened his life. In any case, Jon had claimed that he had lined up an entirely different group of investors, who were prepared to write checks "any day now."

When Davies asked him if there was anybody else who might be interested in seeing Jon dead, Hauge said that perhaps the "Texas boys" had hired Suggs to kill Jon. The "boys" were investors from a few years back who claimed that Jon had bilked them of their life savings by convincing them to invest in one of his failed film projects.

"I see." Davies tapped his notebook. "Listen, Mr. Hauge, what we'd like to do is send some people over to your studio to gather up any material connected to Mr. Emr and Suggs."

"Ooooh, sure," Hauge said, genuinely cooperative. "You take whatever you need, Sergeant Davies."

Davies thanked Hauge and then instructed a few uniformed police officers to head over to GMT Studios.

Davies did not yet have the authority to put out a warrant for the arrest of Robert Suggs. An official warrant would require that the case be filed with the district attorney's office. So far, all he had was Renee as an eyewitness. Sue Fellows was still insisting that she had had her head down and thus had not seen a thing. The six other witnesses whom Davies had rounded up at the scene had yet to participate in a photo lineup. Davies would schedule that as soon as he was able to get a photo of the killer. All that Davies was legally able to do right now was to put out an order that the killer, if found, be detained for questioning.

Later in the evening, Davies asked Renee Emr to join him and Yoshida in the offices of the juvenile bureau, the only place available where they could interview her in private.

"I just want to repeat to you that we know this is a tough time," Davies said. "It couldn't be worse. But you do understand that if we're going to catch this guy we're going to have to do it fast. So we need your full cooperation."

Renee nodded.

"But first, we have a bit of a problem." Hank laid the weapon he had confiscated from her briefcase on the table. "Do you recognize this gun?"

Renee said it was her gun without giving her answer the merest thought.

"Well, Mrs. Emr, I need to ask you what you're doing with a weapon on your person."

The question seemed rhetorical. She told him it was for "protection."

"You do realize that the gun is not registered."

"Oh, you know, Jon handled all those things," Davies remembers her saying.

"Legally, you don't need to have your weapon registered. But you are certainly not allowed to carry a concealed loaded weapon."

"Like I said," Renee repeated. "Jon used to handle all those things."

"Why did you feel the need to carry a weapon? Had Suggs intimidated you, threatened you?"

"No, not Suggs. There were others."

"Others?"

"Jon had many enemies," Renee volunteered. "You make many enemies in this business."

"Jon had enemies?"

"There's a man named Scott Barnes. He'd threatened our lives on many occasions. That was the reason for the gun. That's why we first hired Suggs. Jon wanted him to bring me to and from the set."

The detectives spent forty-five minutes listening to Renee and taking notes. They did not want to tape-record her. That would be an unnecessary intimidation. After she told them a little bit more about this Scott Barnes, Renee very calmly, very deliberately began to list Jon's enemies.

Renee also explained that, independent of Scott Barnes and all her son's other enemies, Suggs might have had his own personal motive for killing her son. She claimed that Suggsy had entered their lives in early 1990. He wanted to offer them his services as a private investigator. They took him on, hiring him to provide "security" for their film projects, including their latest one, a feature film based on the life of James Dean. Renee said that recently Jon had begun to have an "uncomfortable" feeling about Suggs. For one thing, they had discovered some misrepresentations on his résumé. They had made the decision to phase him out of their lives. A month earlier they had actually fired him, and the breakup was especially acrimonious.

By the end of the interview session, Davies and Yoshida had a number of questions: For example, according to his driver's license, Jon

Emr lived in an apartment complex in the lower-middle-class community of Torrance, a few miles outside Los Angeles. If Jon Emr was a big hotshot producer, why didn't he live in Beverly Hills or Bel Air or Malibu?

Why had Hank never heard of a Jon Emr? Davies had developed a good knowledge of the players in the industry. His future father-in-law, who had retired from the police force years ago, was now working as a producer on the ABC action series *MacGyver*. Davies himself had made many industry friends by working security for various film crews when they shot in the Culver City area.

What "business dispute" could possibly have driven somebody to execute a man if, as Renee insisted, there was very little money involved?

Had Renee taken out life insurance on her son?

Then came the big one: Was it possible that Emr was the victim of a conspiracy? Could Suggsy have been commissioned to commit this murder by one of the members of the "enemies list" that Renee Emr had provided?

Davies and Yoshida realized that they would have to contact each of the people who Renee insisted were openly hostile to Jon Emr.

Early that evening, Renee had left a fervent message for her other son, Art Emr Jr. She had rambled into his answering machine that they had been caught in a "drive-by shooting" and that Jon and his son had been taken to separate hospitals. She left him the phone number of the detective's desk at the Culver City Police Station.

When Art finally called in to the police station, it was Detective Pamela Graves who answered the phone. She tried answering Art's panicked questions. "Well, I can't say, sir, I'm not a doctor . . . No, they're at different hospitals . . . No, we haven't caught—"

Renee snatched the phone from the policewoman. "They're dead, Art," she said. Then she began babbling, crying, screaming. Pam Graves could hear Art yelling at Renee to "Be quiet, Mom, I can't understand you!" Eventually, Renee handed the phone over to the police officer.

"I'm sorry about my mom," Art said quietly.

"It's understandable. But, you know, she needs you here."

"Is it true? Are they dead?"

"Yes, sir."

"Okay. I'll be there right away. Where are you located exactly?"

Alan Hauge, Jon's business partner, was on the pay phone in the lobby of the Culver City Police Station when Art walked in with his wife, Jenny. Art bore little resemblance to Jon. Art did not have any facial hair, and he was many pounds lighter. As Art and his wife waited to be buzzed into the well of the police station, Art tried listening to Alan Hauge's conversation. It was strange to Art that Hauge seemed so very businesslike. Hadn't Hauge just learned that his business partner had had his brains blown all over Slauson and Sepulveda?

"No, no, I'm in charge," Art Jr. thought he heard Hauge saying.

Art walked up the stairs and was greeted with condolences by Hank Davies. Then Art pulled Davies aside and told him a thing or two about his family, his younger brother, Jon, and, most of all, his mother, Renee. They had been imposing on him for years. They were into "a lot of stuff," he insisted. They associated with real lowlifes and they were both in *way* over their heads. He gave Davies a list of the people who he thought would benefit from Jon Emr's death or be delighted to hear about it.

Many of the people whom Art named as Jon's enemies were the same people Renee had listed. There was one name in particular that Art wanted Davies to consider very carefully. *Scott Barnes.* Art repeated the name over and over again. Scott Barnes—Scott Barnes—Scott Barnes! Art described Barnes as "this Vietnam crazy" who had had a pretty nasty falling-out with Jon over a failed movie deal. He told Davies that Scott had been embarrassing and harassing Jon for years and that an evil and dangerous rancor existed between these two men.

Davies took all of this in, nodding during various points of Art Jr.'s dissertation. Davies wrote Barnes's name down, underlined it, gave it an exclamation point, and then circled it. Given all the enemies that Jon Emr had, Hank Davies could not rule out the possibility of a conspiracy.

The last point that Art wanted to make was that he himself was not part of the Jon Emr business world. Completely disconnected, he insisted. He claimed that he was a legitimate film producer and that he

was certainly not attached to this absolutely "absurd" James Dean project. Davies said he understood and then suggested to Art that he go
and see his mother. She needed him. Davies would later learn that Art
indeed was a legitimate, albeit struggling, producer.

Art entered the conference room, which, at this point, had filled up
to capacity. Even Alan Hauge's minister, Ralph Moore, had arrived to
offer his moral support. Art approached his mother and said only a few
words to her. It was clear to everybody in the room that the two of them
were estranged. After a few minutes, Art went to the corner of the room
and started making phone calls, "the busywork," as he saw it. He telephoned his aunt. He telephoned his children. He wanted to make sure
that they were safe.

Alan Hauge walked back into the conference room after finishing his
series of phone calls from the lobby. He announced that he had just
called GMT Studios to see how things were being handled there. He
said that a man named Bill Finch, yet another business associate of
Jon's, had called the studio earlier and had been informed by some
young, dazed secretary that Jon had been murdered.

For a moment, Renee seemed to split into another personality. The
grieving mother became a cool businesswoman. Renee ordered Alan to
call Finch "right now!" and tell him not to speak to anybody—anybody
at all—about the murder. She said that she had a meeting coming up
with a potential investor named David Jackson. He was supposed to
put $1.5 million into the James Dean project. If Finch called Jackson
with the news that Jon was dead, he would destroy the deal.

Before Hauge could respond, Art leaped into the fray. "You're not
calling anybody!" Art said to Hauge. "Just keep the hell out of this."

The two men got into a shouting match over who could tell whom
what to do. In the end, Hauge did not call Finch. But he did contact his
other partners at GMT, assuring them that there was no need to panic.

Later that night, Art would later recall, Renee asked her son if she
could speak with him in the hallway. She wanted to talk to Art about
"the deal" with the James Dean project that she and Jon had pending.

And that was about all that Art Emr could take. For years now he
had watched his brother and his mother try to become movers and
shakers in the film industry. He knew that her futile drive to succeed in

the film business had taken a kind of demonic hold of her. And now, this obsession of hers had gotten his brother and his nephew blown to Kingdom Come. Art slapped his forehead. "OH GODDAMN IT, MOM!" he screamed. "You don't know what you're talking about! Please! Just get out of town! Go back to your husband! Just get out of town!"

When they were finished, Davies reluctantly gave Renee her weapon back. He figured that it would almost be an act of cruelty not to allow her to be armed under the circumstances. He told her to leave the weapon at home. She was forbidden by law to carry it.

By two in the morning, Hank Davies had completed his interviews with the assembled crew. Under protective custody, Renee and Sue were driven to Art's home. A caravan of patrol cars followed Alan Hauge and his wife to their son's home in Malibu.

Sitting alone in the office, with bland, cooling coffee by his side, Hank Davies began knocking out his police report. He finished by four-thirty and then went to his new home by the airport. Davies picked up some fresh clothes and went back to the station an hour and a half later. He worked out in the department gymnasium for about an hour—lifting weights and climbing three miles on the StairMaster.

When Hank got back to his cubicle he found a pile of documents sitting on his desk. On top was the résumé of Robert Suggs. It apparently was among the documents confiscated during the search of GMT Studios. The résumé was full of very valuable information:

Suggs was born on January 19, 1960, in Lynwood, California. That fact would help Hank track down Suggs's birth certificate and, subsequently, the names of his father and his mother.

He was six feet tall and weighed 175 pounds. Davies would be able to add that information to the all-points bulletin that had been issued for Suggsy. However, Renee had insisted that Suggsy had become quite the fat boy, having ballooned to some 220 pounds.

Suggsy had owned two private-eye firms: one in Arizona and, for five years, another one in Tacoma, Washington. That would help Davies track down Suggsy's associates and employees.

But there was bad news. The four-page, crudely typed résumé was crammed with courses and seminars that Suggs had taken throughout the eighties: Differential Diagnosis of Equivocal Death, Forensic Dentistry, Sexually Motivated Homicides, Serial Murders, Blood Spatter Interpretation, Asphyxia, Crimes of the Antisocial Personality, General Crime Scene Problems, Electronic Surveillance, and Narcotics Raids.

Suggsy even claimed to have been the student of an Israeli intelligence agent. Furthermore, Suggsy had sat in on a class at "The G. Gordon Liddy Academy of Private Investigation, Corporate Security, and Executive Protection."

It was now clear to Hank Davies that there was little if any chance that he or anybody else would be able to take Suggsy—at least alive.

The Cons of Jon Emr:
Rex Ravelle, 1980–1983

I'm not just talented. I'm geniused.
—Rita Tushingham in *A Taste of Honey*

From all available accounts, Rex Ravelle had been the first victim. Over the three years that he knew and did business with Jon Emr, Rex became a walking embodiment of how the lure of the Hollywood dream could lobotomize even the most intelligent among us. Many people who have heard the story of Rex Ravelle have openly wondered how any man could be so credulous, such a sucker. But, then again, many of those people would someday tell their own Jon Emr stories.

Rex Ravelle can't remember who it was who introduced him to Jon Emr in 1980, who it was that invited Jon to one of his world-famous, Ritz-style parties. What Rex does remember—and he'll recall every last, single, solitary conversation, transaction, and contract—is how Jon Emr drove him into becoming indigent.

Rex once owned a chain of physical fitness centers in Honolulu. He lived in Kahala, one of the richest suburbs of Honolulu, just a few houses away from Clare Boothe Luce. Rex was such a fine physical specimen that he had been Johnny Weissmuller's stand-in for the Tarzan films. When Johnny was called on to do anything physical, Rex was the man: diving, falling, fighting. *Everything but the loving, dammit.* He also appeared in a few movies of his own, including *No Time for Love*, with Oscar winner Claudette Colbert. But what had made Rex wealthy was the fitness centers. Nine of them. Then there were his beauty college and modeling agency.

"*Don't Exercise . . . Rexercise.*" That was his motto. "*If you rest . . . you rust.*" That was another one. Rex asserts he is the strongest man in the world for somebody his age. "I weigh two hundred five pounds and I can do things that very few men of any age can do—including Jack LaLanne." Rex's body is still outlined with the muscular definition of his youth and he still wears a neatly trimmed goatee, now flecked with a few gray hairs.

There was a time when Rex was worth $6 million, the majority invested in real estate. His home in Hancock Park, California, was valued at over $1 million in the mid-seventies. He owned a home of greater value in Encino a few years later.

By the time Jon Emr was murdered, Rex had become a pathetic version of what he once was. When I met him, he was living in Van Nuys in a grimy apartment complex on Fulton Street, the main drag. His place was not air-conditioned and in the summers Rex lived with his clothes perpetually sticking to him. The pool in the middle of the complex was unusable because of the infestation of algae. He pays $700 a month for the apartment. He had gone through four roommates by the time we met. They covered $300 of the monthly rent plus, of course, their own phone charges and their share of the maintenance.

Rex moved to this apartment not only because it was affordable, though his Social Security is all that he had left to pay for it, but because it was mere blocks from the local courthouse. Rex is in court nearly every day because of Jon Emr, a dead man. His apartment became an adjunct of the courthouse. Everywhere one looked there were piles and piles of documents, all pertaining to Rex's whammo case against Jon Emr.

Years ago, Rex kicked Emr's ass in court. Actually, Emr never even showed up. The judge ordered Emr to pay Rex some $2.6 million. Now, Rex's problem was getting the Emr estate—whatever that was—to pay up.

Rex has become something of a legal scholar in the past few years. Ever since his attorneys told him they could no longer represent him because of financial considerations, Rex has been representing himself *pro per*, that is, without counsel. He's pissed off many judges over the years. He's slowed up the process.

"Get an attorney, Mr. Ravelle."

"No can do, Your Honor."

Once, Rex even irritated America's living room Solomon, Judge Wapner of *The People's Court*. Rex had lost his complaint against a young girl who had once worked for him. She charged sexual harassment. When Judge Wapner, erudite and wrinkled, asked Rex if he was attracted to her, Rex gave the judge an answer he'd never heard before. "No, but I think you are."

Wham. End of case. Next thing you know poor Rex is in the hallway talking to Doug Llewelyn about how unfair the judge was. That didn't stop Rex Ravelle. Rex sued *Judge Wapner*, stayed on his back until the station said the hell with it, and gave him $3,000 to go away.

In 1992, shattered by years of getting nowhere with his lawsuits against the Emr family, Rex wrote a letter, actually several letters, to the Los Angeles district attorney Ira Reiner and to California attorney general Dan Lundgren:

> . . . I retired a multi-millionaire—today I am indigent and classified as a felon because I cannot afford insurance and licensing. Why? Because the Van Nuys court is infested with judges that are corrupt, tyrannical, racist, arrogant, and biased. They break laws right and left, and since they are unregulated and not accountable to anyone, they do it with impunity. . . .

In the margin of the letter, Rex Ravelle promised to "kill" three judges if he did not get satisfaction. He also included newspaper clippings of the murder of Jon Emr. Rex knew the murderer, had even had recent contact with him, he claimed.

That is when Rex Ravelle finally got some action from the authorities, though it probably was not what he had expected. One day, Rex answered a knock on his door. Six marshals burst in, one of them holding a shotgun up in the air. As Rex demanded to know what the hell this was all about, he was handcuffed and taken away. Rex does not remember whether or not his rights were read to him.

Rex was held without bail in the violent, overcrowded Los Angeles county jail. He was placed in a cell with five other men, all being held for felonies. The first thing Rex noticed when he entered his cell was a puddle of vomit.

A few days later, Ravelle was kicked in the groin by a guard—"A little Hitler" as Rex described him—with such intensity that Ravelle passed out. Weeks after his release from prison, Ravelle still had blood in his urine stream.

"I don't know why I would be made to live this hell. I think that if I ever got sent to jail again I would ask them just to kill me! Give me the death penalty. I am in fantastic condition for a man of my seventy-six years. But, it is too much for me to endure. Why put me in with these people! Murderers, rapists, drug dealers? I couldn't kill anybody. Put a gun to my head and I am not capable of killing anybody." There is a pause at this moment, a pause of either reflection or dramatic effect. "I might, however, make an exception if I had had the chance to have killed Jon Emr."

When Rex first saw Jon Emr in the fall of 1980, his first thought was, Damned if that sonofabitch doesn't look exactly like the goddamn, spittin' image of Clark Gable. Rex noted this as he saw the stranger coming through his front door for one of his infamous parties. Emr immediately shook a hand or two, though not Rex's, and then he headed right to the liquor cabinet.

For most of the evening, Emr gripped a goblet of Scotch like it was his life force and clasped a huge, smoldering cigar in his right hand. He was relaxing by the bar, his shoulder blades resting on the mirrored wall, his hips gently swaying back and forth to the big band music scratching on Rex's phonograph, as geriatric retirees and country club denizens walked past him. All the while, Rex noticed that Emr was talking, barking greetings to anybody sauntering up to the bar. Emr's eyes were zigzagging around the room, examining every corner, every guest, every couple. Rex was sure that he was stoned. He decided not to approach Jon Emr, not to impose conversation on him.

Rex noticed that whenever Emr downed one glass, he would grab the bottle and pour himself another. He repeated the process until the bottle was empty. When *that* happened, Jon was apparently ready for business. He slapped his hands together, and trotted out to the center of the room, where the action of the party was, where the faded beauties were mingling, where Rex was entrenched and standing his ground.

"Jon Emr," the Gable-lookalike said, extending his hand to Rex Ravelle, the world's healthiest man. "How are you?"

"Thank you for coming," Rex said, not having any real idea who Jon was and who had brought him here.

Jon slapped Rex on the back. "No problem. Glad to be here. Gorgeous place, simply fuckin' gorgeous."

Rex told Jon a bit about his home, a $1 million estate that covered more than 9,000 square feet. "It's haunted, you know," Rex told Jon.

"I didn't know," Jon said to him, his eyes popping open just a millimeter. "Tell me about it."

And so Rex did. "When I go to bed at night there is this rattling all through the walls, like somebody is running through them. All I have to do is yell 'stop' and it stops. Later it begins again."

Jon nodded politely, excused himself to get a drink, and then returned to the host, who was quick to tell Jon about his riches. Then, Rex just stopped and asked Jon what he did for a living.

Jon downed the Scotch. "I make movies."

"Oh really?"

Jon lied to Rex that he had starred in *The Adventures of the Wilderness Family*, a film that had grossed "boffo" dollars at the box office. Jon told Rex that he had played the father in the film. He had used a pseudonym back then—Robert Logan—for "security reasons." Jon claimed that he had been involved in hundreds of television productions and had even run an actors' workshop in Palm Springs.

"Look, Rex," he began. "I'm here because a buddy of mine told me all about you. I've seen your work, and frankly, I think that you'd be great in a project that I am putting together."

Rex was stunned. "Is that right?"

"Yeah, That's right. It's a karate movie. I'll be in it as well."

"What's it called?"

Jon smiled. "You're going to like this. It's called"—there was a pause—" 'Magnum Thrust.' "

"I was a good actor," Rex said with a queasy grin. "I was in some of the Tarzan films."

"So, I hear, Rex." He stopped and put his arm around Mr. Health. "So I *know*. You could become a part owner of the film."

By now, Rex had drowned out the rest of the party. He had not been before a camera in years, but, *goddamn*, now he was going to get his chance all over again. "How so?"

"Well, there's room for another investor. Rex, my friends tell me that you've always been a man of honor. I want you to be in this film. I think that it's the right thing to do."

Rex was no dummy. "Can you get me a script?"

"A script? No fuckin' problem."

Jon got one last stiff drink before heading out the door.

Jon stopped by the next morning, unannounced. The first thing Rex noticed, as he would do almost every time that he met with Emr, was the overpowering stench of alcohol combined with cigar residue on his breath. Jon was carrying a brown grocery bag filled with papers.

"Rexy!" Rex hated being called Rexy. Jon steamrolled into the house and headed for the liquor cabinet. "You don't mind, do you, Rex?"

After he poured himself a drink, Jon explained why he was there. "Here's the script." He handed over the paper bag.

"Why thank you, Jon," Rex said. "Let me get dressed and—"

"NONSENSE, REXY." Jon pointed to his couch. "Have a seat."

Rex smiled. The sixty-three-year-old fitness guru was impressed by the arrogant gesture, the booming, ostentatious confidence of youth. Rex sat down, crossed his long legs, and ran his fingers across his beard. "Go ahead, Jon."

"I wanna show you something." Jon started giggling. "You're going to love this." He started pulling out sheets of paper from his bag. "Once you read all this stuff over, Rexy, you're going to be begging me to let you invest in this movie."

Rex looked over the documents. Included were some clippings from *Variety*, the Hollywood trade publication, about the recent successes of martial arts films, a rundown of projects that were "in development" at Emr Productions, a Xerox copy of an ad for a movie called "Feet of Death," starring the "Four Amigos of the martial arts" (one of whom was Jon Emr), and the synopsis for his newest project, "Magnum Thrust."

For days after he gave him the synopsis, not the actual script, to "Magnum Thrust," Jon consistently badgered Rex about becoming an investor in the film. Eventually, a browbeaten Rex invited Jon to come to his home to discuss the terms of his becoming a financial partner in the project.

When Emr arrived at Ravelle's home, he made his traditional trek to the liquor bar, grabbed a bottle of Scotch, and plopped himself down on Rex's couch. "Rexy, I'm glad you called me."

"Well, Jon, I like the script."

"And, I'll tell you, Rexy, you belong in the industry! You belong in it! You've paid your dues. You're a real talent!"

Rex slapped his thick hands together. "Okay, what do we do?"

"Here's what I need from you—" Jon said as Rex leaned forward in anticipation. Jon offered a small, inviting, Buddha smile. Then he whispered, letting the following word pop out of his mouth. "*Nothing!*"

"Nothing?"

"Well, no money anyway. I understand that you have filed a lawsuit against a pal of mine. A guy named John Anderson."

John fucking Anderson! Rex knew him all right. Anderson had screwed Rex in a botched film deal and owed him at least $70,000. Rex had filed a lawsuit against Anderson and was prepared to make his case against him in court in a few weeks.

"I know the guy," Rex said with a growl, squinting critically. He grabbed the bottle from Jon and took his own swig. "Don't tell me this crook has anything to do with 'Magnum Thrust.' "

"Nothing, Rexy," Jon said. "He's just a friend. The offer that I am going to make to you should give you an indication of the type of friend that I can be."

Jon handed Rex a one-page contract, which had been typed on a manual typewriter and was only three paragraphs long. Rex read it several times. As far as he could tell, there was no downside for him at all. Jon had already signed his name to it. Rex took a blue ballpoint that was on his coffee table and affixed his signature to it. He handed the document back to Jon. "Mr. Anderson is lucky to have you as his friend."

The two men hugged.

AGREEMENT BETWEEN JON EMR AND REX RAVELLE,
SIGNED MARCH 17, 1981

Jon Emr has agreed to giving Rex Ravelle 1/3 of the profits from the film, "Magnum Thrust" and a small part in the film, providing Rex Ravelle refrains from pursuing John Anderson.

Jon Emr further agrees to assuming full responsibility for the return of $70,000.00 that is owed by John Anderson to Rex Ravelle.

Upon the performance of the foregoing, Rex Ravelle agrees to drop his lawsuit against John Anderson.

Rex Ravelle never heard another word about "Magnum Thrust" after he signed that contract. Jon Emr never paid off John Anderson's $70,000 debt.

Over the next year, Jon was still a consistent presence in Ravelle's home. Each time Jon left, it seemed that he had extra cash in his pocket. He would tell Rex that he needed money to feed his mother, his father, his two boys who had been, according to Jon, abused, molested, and abandoned by Jon's ex-wife. Rex would routinely go to a cabinet in the house and retrieve a wad of bills, which he would turn over to Jon. Rex would do this over his wife's vigorous objections. She warned him that Jon was a con artist, a charlatan. Rex waved her off. "We're millionaires," he would tell her. "What does a few thousand bucks matter? Besides, Jon is going to get us into the movies. He promised me and I believe him."

One day, Jon told Rex that he desperately needed a car. His own set of wheels was worn and torn into oblivion. He needed an impressive car to drive around prospective investors in his films. Rex had seven cars, including a Maserati and a Lamborghini. The auto collection was given to him as part of a swap for his property in Hawaii. Rex, understanding as always, gave Emr a late-model white Cadillac. A grateful Jon wrote out a $7,000 promissory note.

Between his giving up the $70,000 for which he had forgiven John Anderson, the car, and various loans and "gifts," Rex Ravelle had easily dumped over $100,000 into Jon Emr's lap. Rex's relationship with Jon Emr was now seriously damaging his marriage. Rex was convinced that his wife just did not get the nature of the film business. "Things take time, baby." That is what he'd tell her. "Once Jon makes his first movie we're going to be swimming in it, baby."

Rex's wife asked him exactly what movie would be the first one produced, when it would be made, who would direct it, who else had invested money in Jon, and what were Jon's true credentials?

Rex had no answers for her.

■ ■ ■

In late 1982, Rex got the sign that he was waiting for . . . the sign that Jon Emr, God bless his soul, was for real; the sign that he was just months away from being a major league player in Hollywood; a sign that his marriage was about to be saved.

Jon told Rex that he had bagged some "serious elephants" who wanted to invest in his film ventures. He explained to Rex that there was a group of Taiwanese who were prepared to put serious bucks into any—*repeat any*—films that Jon Emr, master of the martial arts film, wanted to make.

According to Jon, the group in Taiwan very much wanted to meet with Jon Emr. Jon confided in Rex that he was too scared to fly and would instead be sending an attorney. Rex was excited to hear about this momentous advance.

There was just one thing, Jon said. He did not have the money to send the attorney over. He wondered if Rex would lend him the cash. In fact, he wondered if Rex would accompany the attorney to Taiwan. Rex agreed. In fact, he was delighted. This couldn't be a con, could it? What could Jon hope to gain? Would he *really* scam Rex into giving his attorney a free vacation? Not a goddamn chance!

This better not be a scam, Rex's wife warned him.

Trust me, Rex told her. I know people. We're just this far from producing our first film.

Rex pretty much figured the Taiwan deal was dead as he flew with the attorney. On the flight over the Pacific, Ravelle felt that the attorney was rude and boorish and, furthermore, was neither knowledgeable about nor interested in the various movie deals that they were allegedly going to present to the Taiwanese investors.

When they got to Taiwan, the attorney essentially disappeared. As far as Rex could tell, he was out sightseeing or conducting some other business. Only one brief meeting was held with some Taiwanese businessmen. What Rex did know to a certainty, as he sat steaming in his hotel room, was that the attorney was *not* there selling movies, was *not* there protecting Rex's investment, was *not* there protecting Rex's marriage.

When Rex Ravelle and the attorney returned home after a ten-day stay in Taiwan, no deal had been cut, no film had been sold. When Rex called Jon to complain about the attorney and his lack of professionalism, Emr was shocked. "Jesus, Rex," he said. "Do you think that he took us for a ride?"

A few weeks after the Taiwan fiasco, during which both Jon and Rex commiserated over how they had both been taken by this "miserable motherfucker," Jon had some more exciting news for his friend and perpetual adviser Rex Ravelle.

"Rex, Michael Whitney is in town. He is Twiggy's husband. Do you know who Twiggy is?"

"Sure," Rex said. Who didn't know who Twiggy was? Years ago, she was the world's leading model, a blond waif so slim and tiny that she could have been the poster child for an anorexia movement.

"Well, Michael has written a script. It's a western called 'Jonah.' I read it and I loved it."

"You know how much I respect your opinion, Jon."

"It's not just my opinion, Rex. I gave it to Kirk Douglas—"

"Spartacus?"

"Yeah, yeah. Kirk says that it's a cinch. He says that it's going to make a goddamn fortune. He says that it's a real first-class western."

Rex sighed. "And you want me to invest?"

"Nooooooo," Jon said. "I'm real sorry, Rex. There's no room for any investors. But I do need a favor. Michael Whitney needs a place to stay. Is it possible that you could accommodate him? You've got a six-bedroom house over there and all. It would be for about ten days. I need that time to get him to lower his price. I'm going to try and romance him."

Rex agreed and Michael Whitney, who looked frail and sickly, moved in within a few days. During the visit, the two men became quite friendly. Whitney would not go into details about his deal with Jon, except that Emr needed to come up with $15,000 in option money and then, within a specified time, $100,000. They had even signed an agreement on June 7, 1982. Whitney also confided that he questioned Jon's credibility, that he seemed too slick and to have too many answers.

On the ninth day of Whitney's stay, an agitated Jon Emr rang Rex's doorbell and asked him to step outside. He didn't want Michael Whitney to hear what he had to say. "Rexy," he said. "I am desperate for this script."

"I thought you had investors."

"Things fall through," Jon said with a philosopher's guarded wisdom. "This is what happens in this business. Look, it's simple. I need fifteen thousand dollars."

Rex ran his fingers up and down his goatee. "Jon, I could invest the money. But I would have to mortgage my house." Of course, that was just a line of bullshit. What Rex wanted to see was whether or not this realization would make Jon crumble, would turn Jon into somebody compassionate.

Emr smiled. "Rexy, Rexy. I don't want you to invest. I want you to loan me the money." He pulled a crumpled note out of his jacket pocket. "Tomorrow morning I am going up north to San Francisco to collect a hundred thousand dollars. I have some interest in land up in Idaho that has just been sold." He shoved the paper into Rex's hand. "See, look for yourself. I'll let you have all the money."

Rex didn't even read it. "Jon, you mean to say that if I give you fifteen thousand dollars you will pick me up tomorrow morning, we'll drive up north, and you'll collect one hundred grand? Shit, Jon, why don't you just give Michael the fifteen thousand out of that money tomorrow?"

Jon shook his head. "No, no, no. Michael told me that he has to have the money today or the entire deal is off."

Rex wrote out a check to Jon Emr. Then he went indoors to set his alarm clock for early the next morning. Rex told his wife that he was absolutely sure that Jon Emr would be there the next morning to take him to Idaho. "You don't understand, sweetie," he told his wife. "This is a fabulous script. A western! Kirk Douglas is going to be in it."

Jon Emr never showed up the following morning. Rex couldn't phone him because Jon had never given him his phone number. Jon had told him he couldn't for "security reasons." Rex couldn't drive to Jon's home because he had no idea where Jon lived. "Security reasons." When Rex called his bank, he learned that the check he had written to Jon Emr had been paid out in cash. That was probably for "security reasons" as well, Rex thought.

Michael Whitney never received the money that Jon promised him. Rex, realizing that his ailing friend was in desperate shape, wrote out a check to Michael Whitney for $15,000. Whitney then wrote Rex a letter, warning him about Jon Emr, and promising Rex the rights to "Jonah" if Jon did not pay him back.

Six months later Michael Whitney died. Within a few weeks, Rex's wife left him and took him for $2.6 million. Rex began his legal quest against the Emr estate. He had only one thing left. In his mind he felt that he was the rightful owner of Michael Whitney's script "Jonah."

Bad News from Paradise Valley:
July 12, 1991

When a man kills, it's the one act he does totally alone. The world isn't with
him. Therefore, his convictions must be tremendous.
I admire people with convictions.
—John Mills to Deborah Kerr in *The Chalk Garden*

"Listen," Davies said to Renee when she arrived at the station the following day. "Is there anybody else that you need to have notified? Any family?"

She slowly nodded her head. There was her husband, Art Emr Sr.

"Your husband doesn't know?" Davies asked, incredulous. He made a mental note to explore the marital relationship of the elder Emrs.

Renee shook her head. She said that she didn't want her husband to hear about the tragedy over the phone. She told Davies that Art Jr. would drive out to their home in Paradise Valley, Arizona, just outside Phoenix, the following day. She demanded that Hank not call Art Sr. with the news.

"I won't, Renee," Davies agreed. "What about the mother?"

Renee was confused. What "mother" was Davies referring to?

"Roger's mother. Has she been contacted? I think—"

Renee insisted that the mother, Gloria Farrens, had not seen the boys in years. She wanted nothing to do with them. Renee said that she had no idea where Gloria was and would be delighted to leave it exactly that way.

"Well, we can find her for you," Davies said helpfully.

Renee insisted that Gloria had put the family through so much. There was no way Gloria could be notified!

"What are you talking about?" Hank said, trying his best to be gentle, soothing. He quietly pulled out his notebook as Renee explained.

Renee claimed that Gloria was a Satanist who had allowed her two boys to be abused and molested. In any case, Renee claimed that technically she, not Gloria, had custody of Bobby. Years ago, the courts had given her and her husband the care of the two boys while Jon and Gloria fired horrible allegations at one another.

It sounded a little bit fruity to Hank, but, anyway, in the end, it was just not his business. *What the hell.* "Okay, Renee. I'll let this be your call."

Something did not feel right to Hank Davies. He wanted to hear Art Emr Sr.'s voice. *Just to make sure.* And so Davies called the Paradise Valley phone number. Nobody answered. Davies made several more calls to Arizona over the course of the next few hours. Still no luck. During their interview, Renee told Davies that Art Sr. was a bit of a homebody with a set schedule who could almost certainly be found at home. But not only did Art not answer the phone; Davies never got so much as an answering machine, which Renee said Art would have set had he for some reason left the house.

Throughout the day, Davies and Renee got down to business, going over the ever-growing list of Jon Emr's enemies. To Hank, the whole situation was bizarre. Jon Emr was a producer. Not a drug dealer, not a gun runner, not a bookie. What could he have done in his life to amass this army of adversaries?

This time around, Renee was prepared with more complete biographical sketches and the phone numbers of the people she said had an interest in seeing Jon dead.

Once Renee had left for the day, Davies placed a call to the Paradise Valley Police Department. He wanted to take one last stab at determining the welfare of Art Emr Sr.

When Davies had the dispatcher on the line, he asked if it was possible to send a team out to the Emr house to check things out. "Just give him some kind of story about why you're looking in on him," Hank said. "The mother wants her husband to find out about the murder of her boy from his other son. So please make sure that you don't tell him anything."

Because the call came after five in the afternoon, which is exactly when the entire government of Paradise Valley dies for the night, the dispatcher did not contact any detectives. A patrol car was sent over to 9322 North 68th Place to make a "welfare check."

REPORT OF OFFICER DENNIS DODD,
JULY 12, 1991

At approx. 1915 hrs. I was dispatched to the residence of 9322 N. 68 Pl. to check the welfare of the resident, who was known as Arthur Emr. The call came in from California, as a relative had been attempting to contact Mr. Emr by telephone and was unable to do so and was concerned for his welfare due to a poor physical condition and medical problems that Mr. Emr was suffering from. I arrived at the residence and parked in front of the residence on the street. The residence is located at a cul de sac area and faces an easterly direction with the rear of the house toward the west. It is a brick home with a sidewalk leading up to the front door and a gravel driveway leading to a covered carport on the north side of the residence. I rang the doorbell and knocked on the door but did not receive a response. I checked the front door and it appeared to be locked. I walked to the south of the house, then through an opened wooden gate, to another wooden fence where I opened the latch and entered the rear yard of the house. At this time I was checking the doors and looking in the windows to see if I could see any sign of the individual.

In the rear of the house I saw an Arcadian door. The glass part of the Arcadian door was open but the screen appeared to be locked, as I tried to open the screen door and could not do so. I continued through the wrought iron fencing that separated the pool from the doors to the house and found that a door to a game room type area was unsecured. I opened the door, stepped into the residence and loudly identified myself as a police officer. I asked if anybody was home but got no response. I stepped out on to the rear patio and notified the dispatcher that I found an unsecured door. I asked the dispatcher to telephone the relative in California and inquire as to whether they wanted me to go into the residence and check on Mr. Emr. As I waited I noticed a white two-door in the carport with a flat right front tire.

A short time later Officer Seay arrived at my location and informed me that an on-going investigation was being conducted in California and the relative felt Mr. Emr could be in danger. Officer Seay and I entered the residence and began searching room to room throughout the residence. At that time it was daylight outside but the residence was dark. As I was checking the rooms, I would open the closet doors and look in the closets and then close the door. As I was checking a room on the west side of the house, Officer Seay advised me verbally that he had found a dead body in the closet of a room, which appeared to be an office located at the far south side of the residence.

While the Paradise Valley police were checking in on Arthur Emr, Hank Davies passed his time placing as many calls as he possibly could to associates and enemies of Jon Emr. Most of the conversations were quick, with very little information given out. But two things stuck out. First, many if not all of the people whom Davies phoned gave a little whoop of joy at the notion that Jon's brains were spattered unceremoniously all over downtown Culver City. Second, it seemed that everybody was already aware of the murders, despite the fact that there had not yet been a single news report. The loop had closed on the anti-Emr circle.

There was, for example, a Texan named Aubrey Brothers. Renee had told Davies that in 1986 Jon Emr convinced Aubrey, a building tycoon, to invest in a television movie that Jon was making called "A Chance to Live." It was a film about American soldiers still being held in captivity in Vietnam and Laos.

Like many projects in Hollywood, this one never got a distributor, was never picked up for syndication or by a network, and thus never aired. In short, Aubrey Brothers and all the other investors lost their money. There were lawsuits on both sides, angry letters and phone calls, and, Renee claimed, all sorts of devious behavior on the part of Aubrey Brothers.

"So, what I hear is true? Jon Emr's dead, huh?" Aubrey Brothers said when Davies contacted him. Brothers's accent was so deeply Texan that it was almost comical.

"Yes, sir," Davies said. Then he asked him if he knew this Suggsy.

Brothers said he didn't. "Is he the guy who killed Jon?"

"That's what we think, sir."

"Well, goddamn, I gotta be honest with you. I'd prefer if you didn't catch the guy."

"I see," said Davies.

"You'd say that too if you knew Jon Emr," Brothers said. "I'll tell you what. If you catch the guy, gimme a call. I'll pay for his defense."

After finishing his conversation with Aubrey, Hank turned to others on the list. What he found especially interesting was how they had found out about the deaths:

JEAN JOHNSON, the sixty-year-old owner of a video production company, heard about the murders from Scott Barnes. "Did you hear the news," Scott had asked her excitedly. "Jon Emr's been killed!"

Jean turned to her son Tim who was her partner in the video company. "It's Scotty," she said with a chirp. "He says Jon Emr's been killed." Then, with a small grin and a soft sarcastic voice. "Isn't that too bad?"

RANDY COLLIER, a reporter for the *Arizona Republic* who had written a damaging article about Emr, cut short an investigative assignment in Memphis. Randy had called his wife and learned he had a message from Gloria Farrens, Jon Emr's ex-wife. Jon had been killed! Almost as soon as he walked in the door of his home, Randy received a call from Scott Barnes. Randy remembered that Scott acted "like a kid who just got some electric trains for Christmas."

RANDY PIKE'S WIFE found a note on the door of her home at the Palm Springs Country Club. It had been left there by Randy's former business partner, Alan Hauge. The note told them to meet him at a local Denny's restaurant.

When Randy and his wife met Hauge, he was pale and shaking and almost at a loss for words. But he did get out the big news. Jon Emr was dead and the killer was Suggsy. They drank coffee and ate for the next thirty minutes, Randy and Alan recalling that they had thought all along that Jon was a con artist. His evil had simply caught up with him, that was all.

On the ride back home, Randy Pike told his wife, "Now that this motherfucker is dead, maybe our movie can get made."

ED GOLD, a television movie producer, was watching the local news when he received a call from Bobby Garwood. Garwood was a former Vietnam-era prisoner of war who had sold the rights to his life story to Jon Emr and his mother, Renee. Bobby, full of tears, gave Ed the news. The first thing Ed did was call George Stanford Brown, a onetime regular on *The Rookies* and now Ed's producing partner. "Think we should throw a party?" he asked George.

JANE FAVOR, an investment broker who had once worked for Jon, heard the news from Aubrey Brothers. She thought back to the hateful final conversation that she had had with Renee Emr. At that moment, she recalled a prayer that she said that night. "Dear God, I've not asked for much in the past. But please, bring me vindication on the Emrs. And, please, God, let me be able to see that vindication."

JOHNNY BOND, an illiterate, Philadelphia-based ex-con who had turned over the rights to his life story to Jon Emr, got a phone call from a former radio promoter named Bill Romero. "Did you do it, Johnny?"

"I'm sure I did," Johnny said, laughing. "What're ya talkin' about?"

"Jon Emr's been killed. Was shot in Culver City. He and his son."

"Sheee-iiiiiit!"

"C'mon, Johnny, did you do it?"

"I wish I did! That motherfucker! Say, did I ever tell you about the time that I chased the prick with a hatchet?"

Bill wasn't buying into this. "Jesus, Johnny! I think that you did this! I think that you did. Johnny, it was a Mob-style hit."

Damn! Johnny was eating all of this up. The whole damn thing. He laughed hard. "I don't know any mobsters! I don't know any."

Davies's curiosity about Arthur Emr Sr. had now turned into genuine concern. The Arizona police still had not gotten back to him. He placed another call to Paradise Valley and was transferred from switchboard to switchboard, until finally somebody got on the phone with him.

"Can I help you?"

"Yeah, I called a few hours ago. I wanted you to go out and check—"

"The Emr house?"

"That's right. I did. Is everything okay?"

The answer was slow in coming. "Not exactly, sir."

"What do you mean?"

"Arthur Emr's been murdered." There was a short pause. "Also, there is a flat tire in his car. There's a nail in it."

The officer on the Paradise Valley end sounded a bit stunned. Murder in Paradise Valley was an even greater rarity than it was in Culver City. There is not even a homicide division in the Paradise Valley Police Department. The small and wealthy town had averaged only one murder every five years since the town had been incorporated in 1962. With the exception of the post office, police station, and courthouse (which are all in the same tiny building), a private boarding school called Judson (which Roger Emr and his younger brother, Bobby, attended), four major resorts, a flower shop, and an antiques store, every building in the town is residential. There isn't even a gas station. For those types of services, Paradise Valley residents depended on next-door Scottsdale, another wealthy community in Arizona. A local ordinance requires that every home in Paradise Valley sit on at least one acre of land, thus ensuring that no unsightly tract housing will pop up.

Detective Alan Laitsch, a boyish, handsome thirty-five-year-old, had just arrived home from a full day's work when he received word that he had to return to Paradise Valley. He jotted down the address of the Emr home and kissed his wife good night. It looked like it would be a long one, he told her.

Actually, when Laitsch arrived at the Emr home, he and all the other police officers were legally forbidden from even stepping on the property. To gain entrance, the police would have to obtain a search warrant from one of the judges who were on call that evening. The police sealed off the property with yellow tape and waited patiently for the warrant to be hand-delivered to them.

As Laitsch and a good chunk of the police force stood ready for action on the cul-de-sac in front of the home, young Bobby Emr, the blond, long-haired son of Jon Emr, appeared on the scene. He asked one of the police officers what was going on. Bobby was told that there was some kind of "problem" inside the house and that he could not enter. They were not permitted to give out any more information than that. Of course, it did not take any elaborate deduction to figure out exactly what had happened.

Bobby asked Detective Laitsch if he could be taken into protective custody. Prior to placing Bobby in the patrol car, Laitsch told him that he had to be searched for weapons. That was when Bobby told him that he was armed with a .38 pistol in his jacket pocket.

Laitsch talked with Bobby as they both sat in the patrol car. Over and over, Bobby asked for the specifics of what had happened to his grandfather and, over and over, Laitsch was not able to satisfy his curiosity. However, Laitsch did have several questions for Bobby, who, after all, had just walked onto a murder scene with a lethal weapon. As far as Laitsch was concerned, Bobby was as much a suspect as anybody else. He asked Bobby if he lived in the house. No, he had an apartment not far away, where he had been residing for the past four months. He asked Bobby who actually lived in the house. His grandfather, he answered. While questioning Bobby, Laitsch looked over the teen's clothes for spattered blood. He found none.

Laitsch asked Bobby if his grandfather had any enemies. Bobby, who was calm and collected, said that Arthur had no enemies. However, his father, Jon, was a different story. "Scott Barnes should be a suspect if Grandpa is dead," he told Laitsch.

Laitsch thanked Bobby for his cooperation and then sent him on his way to the police station, where he would be fingerprinted and asked a few more questions. It was clear to Laitsch that Bobby knew nothing about the murder of his father, Jon, or his brother, Roger.

The search warrant did not arrive until almost midnight. Laitsch and an evidence technician entered the home at exactly "0000 hrs." In order to get to the body, Laitsch walked along the walls since he wanted to keep his footprints off the carpet. Later, using an electrostatic dust lifter, they would be able to ascertain the exact movements of Arthur and his killer.

Any police officer, like any battlefield veteran, can confirm that there is no odor quite so pervasive and wrenching as rotting flesh. Laitsch recognized the stench as soon as he walked into the Emr house. Although he had never investigated a murder as a detective, he had come across "hundreds and hundreds" of dead bodies when he worked on the West Side of Chicago as a young cop on the beat.

When he saw the body, Laitsch came to some immediate conclusions. From the condition of the corpse, he surmised that the elder Emr had been in that hot coffin of a closet for well over twenty-four hours. Nature had begun to pound the hell out of Art's feeble, seventy-four-year-old body. He was essentially a piece of rotting meat.

Art's skin had begun to blister and his toes and fingers were now fully affected by a death phenomenon called lividity. Gravity was forcing Art's blood to settle in his extremities. His fingers were now coal black, as were his feet, starting at the area of his white socks. His tongue, swollen with blood, was protruding from his mouth, hanging slightly to the right. Art's bodily fluids had poured out of him, his pants stained with feces and urine.

Laitsch noticed two sets of shell casings on the floor. The first group was made up of four individual casings, arranged in a half-moon shape on the ground by the closet. That indicated that the killer was moving in a circular motion, like a wolf on patrol, while executing Art. The second group of casings was found closer to Art and in a pile. The killer had apparently moved in, stood over the body, and pumped three more bullets into the old man's body for good measure. Nothing like finishing off the job.

There was one other bullet lying on the bookshelf above Art. It was sitting peacefully next to a lucky floral horseshoe. Apparently this wild bullet went through the bottom of the shelf, hit a tape cassette, then a wall, ricocheted off another wall, and then came to rest on the shelf. Now, as he looked at that bullet, Laitsch could say with absolute certainty that it was a .22.

A few minutes later, Laitsch instructed the photographer to shoot everything in every room in the house, even the girlie posters in Roger's room. One thing Laitsch noted was that the house was full of stuffed animals. In Jon Emr's room, which had one half of a twin bed set, there was a big stuffed Bugs Bunny.

The photographer systematically took shots of all the bullet casings. He also photographed the various footprints, even those not discernible to the naked eye. The photographer also took shots of the Lincoln with the flat tire.

It was not until seven the next morning that Laitsch was able to get out of the house. Only he didn't go home. Instead, he went to the coroner's office to attend the autopsy. Laitsch was required to be physically present when the coroner was dissecting Art's body. In any case, it seemed like a good idea. If the doc found some major "hold-the-presses" kind of surprise, then Laitsch wanted to be there.

The "mortuary of the month" selected to pick up bodies for the police delivered the corpse to the coroner's office where the autopsy was to take place. The whole affair turned out to be quite boring. The only excitement came when the coroner shaved Art's head, took a sharp object, made a long incision across the forehead, and then peeled off Art's skin from the top of his skull and then over the mouth. That was the easiest way to examine bullet holes in the skull.

After the examination was over, the coroner concluded that Art Emr Sr. had died as a result of multiple bullet wounds to the head. A total of seven bullets had penetrated Art Emr, all in a cluster over the left eye. It was true precision shooting. For the record, the coroner noted that Art had atherosclerosis: his coronary arteries were severely clogged.

After the autopsy, Laitsch drove to his home half an hour away and slept for six hours. He would be up for the next two days going through the entire Emr house. Laitsch collected so much evidence, so many documents, videotapes, cassette tapes, and photos, that he needed a truck to transport everything. In fact, so immense was the quantity of material that a small building had to be erected to contain it all.

By the time Hank Davies was getting ready to leave the office to deliver the news of Arthur's death to Renee, the old lady walked into the police station, shaking and crying. Apparently her son Art Jr. had been contacted by his nephew Bobby. "Uncle!" he screamed into the phone. "They got Grandpa! They killed Grandpa!"

Art Jr. thought it best not to tell him: Guess what else, your father and brother are dead as well. As he had planned to do with his dad, he wanted Bobby to hear the news from him in person.

That night, as Art Jr. was driving to see his nephew in Scottsdale, the reality of it all hit him. Now that his father was dead, there was actually *somebody* to mourn. The terrible thing, he thought, and he would repeat it time and time again, is that it was his father and not his mother who had been murdered a day or so earlier.

For the past two weeks, Arthur Sr. had been confiding in people close to him that he was considering "ending it all." His health had been quickly deteriorating. In fact, he had awakened one morning and for several minutes had not been able to move his legs. But even more important was that Arthur felt he had been abandoned by his son Jon and his wife, Renee, who had trotted off to Hollywood where they had planned to make themselves famous and wealthy, and had left him to fend for himself in Paradise Valley. The only reason Arthur did not take his own life was because of the trauma he was sure it would cause to his grandchildren, Bobby and Roger.

As Art Jr. sped down Interstate 10, the highway that connects Los

The Cons of Jon Emr:
Tim and Jean Johnson, 1985

I don't mind a parasite. I object to a cut-rate one.
—Humphrey Bogart to Peter Lorre in *Casablanca*

Tim Johnson was young and had an air of incorrigible naiveté. When he graduated from college in 1983 he made the decision that Hollywood was his for the taking. For years he had watched television program after television program, film after film, commercial after commercial, with the absolute conviction that he could do better. Much better.

In 1983, Tim convinced his mother to invest with him in a complete inventory of video equipment: three cameras, switchers, editing bays, reel-to-reel taping systems, lights—the works. The mother-and-son team incorporated themselves as CSI Video. Tim's idea was that the two of them could be all-purpose independent entertainment contractors. They could edit, light, film, and tape with the best of them.

Tim and Jean's first gig was with a Burbank-based company called the Oceanic Cable network, run by a man named Peter O'Neal (not his real name). The network, located across the street from NBC Studios, was an absolute start-up operation. The Johnsons had enough equipment to get Oceanic Cable completely on the air.

The shows that Peter O'Neal put on his network were all "bullshit programs," Tim now says. There were six hours of programming during weekdays, usually local citizens putting on cooking shows.

O'Neal's hopes of creating a major cable network, a CNN or an HBO or an MTV, were quickly quashed. The company attracted almost no significant advertisers and O'Neal's cash was slowly getting burned. Things got so bad that the Johnsons were not paid for two months. When Tim threatened Peter O'Neal with withdrawing his equipment from Oceanic Cable, he found himself locked out of the studio. His equipment also stayed behind.

Tim and Jean retreated to some rented office space. They had no work and they had no equipment. Nevertheless, Tim was still dreaming. He told several of his friends that he and Jean were going to start their own cable network. Although Oceanic Cable was an obvious bust, Tim was astonished at how easily the network actually got on the air in the first place.

One day, a friend of the Johnsons introduced them to a man, "some sleazebag," as Tim puts it, who told Tim that he could hook him and his mother up with a television "genius" named Jon Emr.

Jon Emr, wearing a floral shirt, chains hanging around his neck, a cigar clenched in his teeth, showed up at Tim and Jean's offices the following day. Jon immediately presented them with his credentials. He had once owned his own network called "MV3," a music video station that preceded MTV. He claimed to have been involved in hundreds of television programs. He talked about studying with the great acting tutors. He talked about his pals Robert Redford and Jan-Michael Vincent. Throughout it all, Tim Johnson sat in awe. He was almost certainly in the presence of a "player."

Tim explained to Jon his dream of owning his own cable network. Jon nodded in understanding as Tim gave him some of his ideas for programming. Jean was impressed as Jon gave them some of his own concepts. Diversity, he insisted, was the key. If they hooked up as business partners, they would spend weeks and weeks creating "pilots" before they went "on line." In fact, he suggested with a wink, they might be able to convince his pal Michael Douglas to throw his support to the fledgling network.

By the end of the one-hour conversation, Tim and Jean were hooked. But there was a problem, Tim said sadly.

"Let's hear it," Jon said.

Tim explained his crisis. He would be ready to rent space and get on line, but Peter O'Neal and Oceanic Cable were holding his equipment hostage.

Jon took a calm puff on his cigar, completely unimpressed. "So? Why don't you just steal it back?"

"Steal it back?" Jean said.

"Well, fuck, it wouldn't actually be stealing. It is your stuff. You do own the equipment, do you not?"

"Yeah, yeah."

"Well, then," Jon said, primed with confidence, "let's go get it back!"

It was with considerable joy that Peter O'Neal took a phone call from a big-time producer named Jon Emr who was interested, *very, very interested,* in buying out Oceanic. "In fact," Emr told him, "I want to invite your entire staff out to lunch in a day or two. I want to get a feel for how your company is run. There is no better way to do that than to talk to all of your employees."

O'Neal told Jon Emr that he considered this a splendid idea. Anyway, a free lunch at this point was more than welcome. O'Neal told all of his employees that they would be having lunch on Wednesday with the white knight whose name was Jon Emr.

On Wednesday, a slick-looking Emr walked into the studio, shook hands with Peter, and then, like the Pied Piper, marched all the employees to the nearby Smokehouse Restaurant. Even the janitor. "From the bottom to the top!" was how Jon put it. Nobody thought it peculiar or odd that this man who had an interest in their company did not bother even to take a peek at the studios.

At precisely the time that Emr left with the crew, Tim Johnson was entering the Oceanic Cable studio through a window that he knew was broken, never taking into consideration the very strong possibility that somebody looking down from another building might just call the police. He entered the building and snapped open the dead bolt.

Two massive trucks carrying a dozen workers and his mother, Jean, rolled on to the property. As quickly as they could, they began to load the equipment onto the trucks.

Tim felt a tap on his shoulder. He turned around.

"What are you doing?" the police officer said.

"Oh, just relocating. Is there a problem, Officer?"

The cop looked Tim over. "Who's in charge here?"

Tim pointed to his mother, who, at age fifty-seven, was the oldest person in the group. She certainly did not look like a cat burglar. "She is."

The officer had a chat with Jean, who gave him the same story as her son. Eventually, the cop shrugged and walked away.

The Johnsons had set a limit of forty-five minutes to get everything loaded and out of there. They didn't want to be caught. As a result, they left $80,000 worth of equipment behind.

When they were a few blocks away, Tim got to a pay phone, called the Smokehouse and asked for Jon Emr.

Emr excused himself from the table of revelers, telling them that he had to take a call from Michael Douglas. A great deal of liquor had been bought and nobody bothered to eat lightly. Peter was impressed. This bill was easily coming to over $400 and this Emr fellow wasn't batting an eye.

Emr went to the phone, "Yeah?"

"Jon," the conspiratorial voice said. "It's okay. We're done."

Jon laughed. "Good. Let me pay for the meal and I'll meet you later today."

Then Jon hung up the phone and walked out the door, keeping in his pocket the $350 that Jean Johnson had given him to pay for the meal.

An hour later, Tim Johnson responded to a call on his beeper. It was Jon. Apparently he had punctured one of his tires and was out of money. Could Tim please come down to the Chevron station and buy him a new tire?

"No, problem, Jon," he said. "I'll be right there."

The next day the Johnsons signed a contract with Jon Emr. Together they would form 21st Century. Tim and Jean would provide the equipment and the financing. Jon Emr would provide his "talent."

A Missing Person in Manhattan Beach:
July 15, 1991

I'd give my soul to take out my mind, hold it under the faucet and wash away
the dirty pictures you put there today.
—Kirk Douglas to Eleanor Parker in *Detective Story*

"There's somebody here to see you, Hank."

Sergeant Davies walked out into the waiting room and saw a detective waiting for him in the sparse lobby. "I'm Sergeant Zea" he said, showing his Manhattan Beach ID. "Can we go to your office?"

"Cubicle," Davies laughed. "C'mon."

When they sat down, Zea got right to the point. "You know anything about GMT Studios? I think it's located in your jurisdiction."

"Yes, I do. Why are you asking?"

"Well, we got a missing persons case down here. Girl by the name of Susan Lynn Calkins. Know her?"

"Never heard of her."

"Well, this may be nothing, but, you know, I thought I'd follow up on it."

"Go ahead."

"Well, the girl's missing. Her sister reported her—"

"What does it have to do with GMT Studios?"

"She was living with a guy that worked there. They break up. He's grief-stricken, really loves the girl. He calls her up and asks her to go on one last fling with him, a Fourth of July vacation. He doesn't tell her where they are going, so the girl can't tell anybody else. She agrees and then, boom, that's the last we hear of her. We can't find the boyfriend and we can't get anybody at GMT Studios to call us back."

Davies was sure that he knew the answer to his next question. "What was the boyfriend's name?"

"Robert Suggs."

■ ■ ■

Kathy Calkins, a thirty-year-old transplant from Michigan, called her answering machine from her Mercedes. Mingled with the messages left by the clients of her financial advice company was one left by a Sergeant Zea. He needed to see her right away.

Kathy phoned him. "What's going on?"

Sergeant Zea would not say. "I want to talk to you in person" was all that he would offer.

Kathy redirected her car toward the police station. She had been there a few days earlier to report that her sister, a gorgeous blond named Susan, was missing. She had left for a "getaway" weekend with her on-the-outs boyfriend on July 3 and was scheduled to have returned three days later at around noon. When she had still not shown up the following day, Kathy called her parents in Michigan. Her younger brother answered the phone. Kathy told him that their sister had vanished. "Mike, I'm really scared. I'm really scared that he's done something to her."

"Don't say anything to Mom and Dad," Mike told her. "Let's just wait and see what happens. Maybe their plane is late. Maybe they're in Mexico and she can't call."

That struck Kathy as a reasonable possibility. She remembered that Susan had taken her passport with her.

The next day, when there was still no word from or about Susan, Kathy stormed into the police station and demanded an investigation. The officer who took her report was unimpressed. "Maybe she got caught up in the moment," he said with a wink and a knowing smile.

"My sister doesn't get caught up in moments!" Kathy yelled. "I know that my sister would call me. Something is wrong."

"Well, lady, in any case, she is an adult and I am sure everything is just fine. But we'll take a report anyway."

When Kathy got home she began calling all the airlines. No planes had been delayed out of Mexico. Then she called the bartender who was always on duty with Susan at the Airport Hilton. Susan was a very popular cocktail waitress, one of the biggest tip earners, and had never missed a day of work or even been late. He too was worried.

Now, less than a week later, this Sergeant Zea was calling her in for a face-to-face talk. Kathy consoled herself with the fact that at least there was no sense of urgency in Zea's voice.

When she met Sergeant Zea her first impression was that, with his "beady dark eyes and his tattoo" he looked like a criminal, a "Charles Manson type." He barely let her speak. "Ms. Calkins," he said in a voice that was cold and near monotone. "I want to let you know that Jon Emr and his son have been killed." She winced. She knew exactly who Emr was. He then told her that a man they called Suggsy had been fingered as the killer. Not much else seemed to sink in after that. "Emr's father was killed yesterday in Arizona. We are waiting for a ballistics report to see if the same gun was used." He could have served the next unemotional line on ice. "We do not hold much faith for your sister."

We do not hold much faith for your sister.

That was the end of the meeting. Sergeant Zea did not even bother asking Kathy any questions about Suggsy or Jon Emr. Kathy numbly shook hands with Sergeant Zea, walked slowly to her car, and drove home on automatic pilot.

As soon as she got home, Kathy threw on some running clothes and went out for a long jog. Like her sister, Susan, she was especially athletic. When she returned home she opened up a bottle of wine, cuddled in the corner of her couch, and began drinking. In her blank state, she made a few phone calls to close friends. She was supposed to go see the Arnold Schwarzenegger film *Terminator 2* that night. Her friends understood when she canceled.

Later, four of her closest friends came over to console her. They sat in her elegantly decorated one-bedroom apartment, the one she had been sharing with Susan, and they talked about the problems that her sister had had with Suggsy, and about the weird conflict that Suggsy had been having with his boss, Jon Emr . . . something to do with James Dean.

When her friends left for the night, Kathy tried phoning Suggsy's best friend, Benny. But, the line had been disconnected. She didn't know whether or not to be shocked and disturbed. Could this mean something?

Two hours later, midnight Michigan time, Kathy decided that it was time to call her parents. She sat curled up atop her office chair, weeping. It was the first time that she had cried since she began to suspect Susan was in trouble. She asked both her parents to get on the line. She told them that Sue was missing and that she was last seen with Suggsy. That was dreadful news to the parents. They had never trusted

The Cons of Jon Emr:
Aubrey Brothers and Bob Franks, 1985

*If we've told lies, you've told half lies. And a man who tells lies—like me—
merely hides the truth, but a man who tells half lies
has forgotten where he put it.*
—Claude Rains to Peter O'Toole in *Lawrence of Arabia*

Aubrey Brothers lives in Tarrant County, in the town of Arlington, a few desolate miles outside Dallas, Texas. Aubrey, who was in his sixties when I met him at an old-fashioned sawdust-on-the-floor barbecue joint, lives with his girlfriend, Louise, and her daughter, Tina, in a home that they rent. At the time Aubrey, who is twice divorced and once widowed (his third wife was murdered, the assailant never captured), lived almost exclusively on a $700-a-month Social Security check. Now and then he'd take a job digging dirt in the Houston area for a couple of bucks above minimum wage. He did that to maintain some of that famous Texan pride. But, basically, it was the Social Security and Louise's commissions from her job at a real estate firm that kept him from having to turn to food stamps.*

It was not always this way. There was a time when Aubrey Brothers was a local building czar, with a liquid worth of about $4 million. Brothers Construction was one of the most successful privately owned small businesses in the Dallas–Fort Worth area. Aubrey also ran a successful chain of beauty schools, just as Rex Ravelle had in Honolulu.

Aubrey is classic Texan, huge of girth and resonant of voice. Everything about him smells of excess, from his ten-gallon hat (which seems to be permanently affixed to his balding scalp), to the

---

*Aubrey now owns a liquor store outside Dallas.

massive mustache that looks like a thick white wafer above his sun-cracked lips.

One day in October 1985, Aubrey Brothers and his partner, Bob Franks, met Jon Emr, forked over a nice chunk of his fortune, and stood by helplessly as his bank account and credit vanished.

There is a fact one must take into account when considering Aubrey Brothers, one which Jon Emr almost certainly did. At the time that he and Emr initially made contact, Aubrey had not set foot in a movie house since 1969. Drill him intensively and still he can't recall the name of that last film. He's sure it was a western, for those were the only kind of movies he tolerated and certainly the only type he would shell out good money to see. Maybe, he says with a light rub of the chin, it was *True Grit*, the movie that finally won John Wayne his Oscar. *John Wayne*. Now there was a real man, Aubrey felt. Was there even a reason to go to the movies after the Duke died?

There are two different versions of how it was that Jon Emr became a fixture in Aubrey Brothers' life. Jon Emr claimed in an affidavit that there was only one reason Aubrey Brothers had any interest in him at all: Aubrey felt that Jon would be able to give him a "guided tour of a real-live Hollywood studio."

Emr's claim was that Aubrey was little more than a movie star groupie who saw Emr as the key to having a good time in Hollywood. It was only after they became "friends," Emr insisted, that he even "considered" allowing Aubrey and Bobby Franks the privilege of investing in one of his new movies.

That was Jon's story. Aubrey's is much different.

Jane Favor would never have heard of Jon Emr had it not been for Violet "Vi" Hower (not her real name). Looking back on it, Jane acknowledges that she never should have trusted Vi. Jane was an employee of an entertainment firm that had hired Vi because she had claimed to be "well connected" in Hollywood. Jane claims that Vi was fired when it became clear she had overstated her abilities to get entertainment power czars kowtowing to her. But one day Vi phoned Jane with information about a "great deal" that had fallen into her lap.

Vi told Jane that on January 22, 1985, she had met this charming gentleman at a Sheraton hotel in Dallas. He had flown in all the way from California to listen to a singer named Sonny Martin whom he was thinking of promoting. The promoter was a real looker, she said, a Clark Gable type who, and here came the kicker, was a *very* powerful player in Hollywood. "His name is Jon Emr," Violet said with excitement, "and he is heavily, heavily connected with the Douglas family."

"The Douglas family?" Jane said. "You mean as in Kirk Douglas? Michael Douglas?"

Yes, yes, Violet said. Those very same Douglases! Jon Emr was their emissary, their man in the field, the creative genius behind a film production company that was called, appropriately enough, Emr-Douglas Productions. He even had business cards emblazoned with "Emr-Douglas" on them. Imagine! Business cards!

But there was more.

Though Emr was in town to listen to and consider this singer, he was also trying to drum up investor dollars for his new movie. It was going to be a modern western called "Jonah," one that would explore the recent savings and loan crisis that had decimated Texas. Emr had assured her that "Jonah" was going to star Kirk Douglas himself. Indeed, there was an excellent chance that Kirk's old buddy and frequent costar from the old days, Burt Lancaster, might also appear in the film. And, if they played their cards right, Robert Mitchum might also get a role. Joe Don Baker, who was known to Texans as the celebrated star of the *Walking Tall* series, was absolutely, deliriously eager to get a role in the film as well.

And here was the exciting news! Jon Emr had asked her, little old Vi Hower, to be his broker in Texas. Her responsibility was to raise pre-production investment dollars—just enough so that Jon Emr and his partners—the Douglas family—could get the project prettied up in order to raise the actual production funds.

Vi Hower signed her deal with Emr on February 13, 1985. She would get 10 percent of the money that she herself raised and, on top of that, 1 percent of the producer's fee—whatever that was. She had already attempted to land some investors for Jon. She had introduced Jon to Maria Elena Holly, the widow of the late rock star Buddy Holly. The big question that Vi Hower had for her former boss, Jane Favor, the question that would soon change dozens of lives from there on, was this: "Would you like a piece of the action?"

"What do I get?" Jane wondered.

Vi promised her 10 percent of whatever *she* got. Jane smirked to herself. That meant that she would just get 1 percent of all the cash that she was bringing in. "We'll talk about the money later. Why don't you just send over whatever material this Jon Emr gave you. I'll check it out. Then we can talk business."

The package that Violet Hower sent to Jane Favor arrived a couple of days later. It was an amateurish portfolio filled with sloppy and loose photocopies of some newspaper clippings that were themselves un-impressive. But what jarred Jane and what she kept reading over and over again was that the Douglas family was behind the entire project. Among the newspaper articles was a small blurb from *Variety*, Holly-wood's oldest and most respected trade publication, announcing that Jon Emr and Joel *Douglas* had bought the script of "Jonah" from a man named Michael Armstrong.

By 1985, the Douglas family had indeed established themselves as one of the most powerful institutions in the entertainment industry. Kirk was the grandpa of the old guard, widely regarded as one of the great "tough guys" in film history. He had been nominated for an Oscar for *Champion* and had solidified his legendary status with his turn in Stanley Kubrick's epic *Spartacus*.

Of course, the Douglas of the moment was Michael, the eldest of Kirk's children. In the early seventies, Michael played second fiddle to Karl Malden in a television series called *The Streets of San Francisco*. Though Michael had appeared in a few films, it was his first shot out as a producer that made him a power player in Hollywood. For years, Kirk had been trying to make a film out of Ken Kesey's modern classic *One Flew Over the Cuckoo's Nest*, to which he owned the rights. Eventu-ally, Kirk turned over the rights to Michael, who hired Milos Forman, a brilliant but unknown Czech, to direct, and Jack Nicholson to star. The film won five Oscars, including producing the Best Picture prize for Michael.

In the early eighties, Michael Douglas became a full-time pro-ducer/actor. His major accomplishments were *Romancing the Stone* and its sequel, *The Jewel of the Nile*. In both films, Douglas played an ad-venturer saddled with a romance-novel writer played by Kathleen

Turner. Both films were enormously successful and both gave a producing credit to Michael's brother Joel.

After holding on to the "Jonah" package for about a week, Jane Favor received a surprise call from Jon Emr on July 19, 1985. He asked her if she had had a chance to look over the package and if she thought there was any chance that they could do business.

Jane told him that she would have to see more. What she saw was "impressive," she told him, but would surely not go a long way toward selling an investor who had any kind of business savvy. For example, there was no script. Emr agreed to send another packet of information.

Then Jane brought up another issue. "I think I can round up some investors for you," she said. "But the thing is, I am not happy with the deal Vi offered me."

"Well, we'll give you ten percent of what *you* bring in. We need three hundred fifty thousand for preproduction costs. That means thirty-five thousand for you. Not bad," Jon said. Then he added, "You really don't have to worry about Vi Hower. She'll be my responsibility."

The new package that Jon promised arrived in the mail several days later. It contained the hefty script for "Jonah." Oddly, there was no writer credited on the cover page or anywhere else in the script. There was also a budget included. It called for a total of $10 million to be spent on the production of "Jonah," although all Emr wanted out of her was $350,000 for "preproduction." The proposed budget for "Jonah" actually made it a relatively low budget effort. The industry average for a major motion picture, at the time, was hovering in the $21 million range.

Remarkably, Emr had included a letter that bore the signature "Kirk Douglas." There it was! Right in front of her eyes! Kirk's big, bold, beautiful signature. Nobody would be so bold as to forge a signature, would they? And what was Jane supposed to believe Kirk was promising? If, within two years from the date of receiving the $350,000 development money, Emr and the Douglases could not raise the $10 million budget from other sources, then, according to the Emr document, Papa Kirk would personally put up his own cool millions to make the film.

The day after she received the amended package, Jane decided that the man for the job was Mr. Aubrey Brothers, who had recently become acquainted with her father's best friend, Roy Ashton.

Roy had shared a jail cell with Jack Favor in the state lockup in Angola, Louisiana. Both men were serving time for felonies, Jack for murder and Roy for armed robbery. The difference was that Jack was innocent (a new trial would eventually prove that) and Roy was guiltier than hell. Jack felt that Roy was responsible for having saved his life two or three times while they were in the slammer. Jack was retried on the order of a federal judge and was acquitted. When Roy finished out his term, he moved to Texas so that he could be close to his good buddy Jack and Jack's daughter, Jane.

From what she had heard about him from Roy, Jane knew that Aubrey, with his gambler's instincts, might just cotton to the idea of becoming a Hollywood tycoon. So she asked her father to take the package to Aubrey. She made it clear to Roy that she would give him 25 percent of any funds that would emerge from the deal that Aubrey might make with Jon Emr. In this case, Roy stood to make over $8,000.

With Jack Favor sitting on a couch reading *Texas Monthly* magazine, Aubrey looked over the prospectus. From his point of view, the thing looked impressive. Real impressive. Even though he was a fish out of water when it came to the film industry, he damn well recognized the names of the people this producer Jon Emr was promising would star in the film. Burt Lancaster and Kirk Douglas. Hadn't they been in a bunch of westerns? Yup, Aubrey thought to himself, he was sure that they had. God, he loved westerns. Why didn't they make them anymore? If he got involved in "Jonah" he could be involved in bringing back this dead form of cinema art.

He told Jack Favor that he was very, very interested in the project and that he wanted to send it over to his pal and fellow Texas mogul Bob Franks.

In his résumé, which was included in the package, Emr had written that he had worked on three hundred television programs and six major motion pictures, though he did not name any of them. Nevertheless, as far as Aubrey was concerned, "workin' on three hundred of anything makes you an expert on that thing."

According to his résumé, Emr's first-ever job in the entertainment industry was producing a television special starring the great black singer Dionne Warwick (Emr incorrectly spelled the singer's name as *Warwik*). Brothers could not at the time have known that that was a lie, that in fact it was Jon's older brother, Art, who had produced the show. Jon even let it be known through Jane that he was a personal friend of Robert Redford. *The Sundance Kid!* In fact, Redford was his brother Art's contact. Jon also claimed that he was once partners with Jan-Michael Vincent, the famous Young Star of Tomorrow. To press the point, Emr even provided Xerox copies of stationery emblazoned with Emr/Jan-Michael Vincent stationery. Actually, the stationery heading read "Art Emr/Jan-Michael Vincent" but somebody had simply whited out his brother's first name.

With Aubrey Brothers clearly interested in "Jonah" and with what appeared to be a Kirk Douglas warranty in hand, Jane contacted Jon Emr at his home in Torrance, California, on September 27, 1985. She told him that she was sure she could get things moving.

Jon asked Jane if she and her two potential investors might fly out to Los Angeles to meet with him and his mother, Renee, who was also his partner and, he added, quite the creative genius. "Everyone calls her Granny," Emr said. Jon was convinced that if he had a chance to go eyeball to eyeball with the Texans it would greatly enhance their chance of success. He guaranteed Jane that if she brought Aubrey Brothers and Bob Franks to Los Angeles, he would introduce them all to Kirk Douglas.

Jane phoned Bob Franks. "Mr. Emr is trying to encourage me to move this along," she told Bob. "He wants to know if you guys have any interest or not. If you do, he and his mother would like us to come out and meet with him."

Franks told Jane, "Tell Mr. Emr that we'll be happy to come out if he pays for it."

That sounded very reasonable to Jane and she relayed the request to Jon Emr. Emr became angry. "These guys are businessmen and I am a businessman," he screamed into the phone. It was the first time that she'd heard him raise his voice. "Let them live in the real world! They pay their expenses and I'll pay mine!"

When Jane brought Jon's answer to Aubrey and Bob the investors guffawed. "I guess we should go out there and see what this guy is all about," Bob said.

"Hell," joked Aubrey, "if anything, we'll get to meet Kirk Douglas." At that moment, that was all that seemed important.*

Before leaving for the airport, Bob Franks wanted to get together with his attorney, an avuncular man named Earl Rutledge, to discuss some real estate matters. That was the first time that Earl had met Aubrey, who came into the office late in the meeting, ready to pick his friend up for their trip to California.

Bob explained to Earl that they were flying west to see about investing in a movie. A Kirk Douglas film! At that time Earl felt an obligation to warn his client against investing in the film business. "They'll pencil-whip you!" he warned them.

Bob asked Earl if he would consider handling the negotiations or the contract should they decide that they indeed wanted to proceed. Earl laughed as he shook his head. "I know just enough about the movie industry to be dangerous. Look, you boys just be careful. You probably won't need me, but if you do, I'll be here."

Jon Emr was there to pick up Aubrey, Bob, and Jane at the airport. Jon was dressed in a floral shirt that was unbuttoned to his navel. The Texans were a bit put off by Jon's unbusinesslike appearance. However, this was Los Angeles and they had heard their share of stories about the fast-and-loose Californians. They would reserve judgment until later.

When they arrived at the Century Plaza Hotel in Los Angeles, where Presidents Ronald Reagan and George Bush routinely stayed on their West Coast visits, Aubrey, Bob, and Jane went straight to the

---

*Jon Emr wrote the following in an affidavit on October 18, 1988: "On September 27, 1985, Jane Favor called me and said she was coming to Los Angeles with Aubrey Brothers, who she said was interested in a project involving Dirk Benedict. I was not in any manner involved in the Dirk Benedict project . . . later Brothers apologized and admitted that Favor indicated Brothers' interest in my projects was only to induce me and my mother, Renee Emr, to take Favor and Brothers on a tour of the studio.

register and checked themselves in. As Jane pulled out her pen, Jon stopped her. "Oh, no, no. You're not staying here. You're family. You're coming home to stay with us. We wouldn't think of allowing you to stay in a hotel."

Family? Jane thought to herself. What was Jon talking about? He had assured her that he would pick up her airfare and hotel bills. "Oh? Well, that's not necessary. I really would rather stay in a hotel."

"You'll stay with us." He put his arm around her and gave her a knowing squeeze and a small grin. Jane decided not to argue. That might have compromised Aubrey and Bob's faith in her.

A half hour later, Jane was at the apartment of Flora "Genie" Jousett, Jon Emr's aunt and Renee Emr's sister. It was a one-bedroom apartment without air-conditioning. It was about ninety degrees outside. Jane looked at the bed that was made up for her. Actually, it was not quite a bed. It was a hard, cheap, turquoise Naugahyde couch with a big crease down the middle.

Before Jon Emr left, he told Jane that he would be by the next morning to pick her up and he would treat her and the Texas investors to a big California-style breakfast.

That night, Jane could not sleep. The same thought kept rolling through her mind. Was Jon Emr for real? Could a man who placed her in these squalid accommodations be an honest-to-goodness producer?

The next morning, Jon Emr never arrived. There was no answer at Aubrey and Bob's room nor was anybody picking up the phone at Emr's home. So Jane just sat watching game shows, perspiration rolling the makeup off her face.

The doorbell rang at about noon. When Jane answered the door, there was Jon with the two Texans standing proudly behind him, each with string ties dangling loosely around their necks. As angry as Jane was, she didn't want to be responsible for blowing a deal, especially one that promised to net her some $35,000. When Jon, his eyes and teeth twinkling, asked her how she'd slept she gave him a quick stare and muttered, "Oh, just fine, thank you," and then walked to the car. In the backseat, sitting quietly and grandmotherly, was Renee Emr.

Renee expressed her profound disappointment that Jane had not been able to join them for breakfast. Aubrey turned to Jane, "Do you know Renee?"

■ ■ ■

Jane knew Renee. Boy, did she ever.

Jane had met Renee in late July of that year, when she had come to California on other business. Renee had invited her to a little restaurant by the ocean. She told Jane that she had a great idea. A wonderful concept. One that would make them all rich. She wanted to make a movie out of the life story of Jack Favor, rodeo star extraordinaire and Jane's dad. In fact, Renee said, she would write the script.*

Jane looked at this old, fat woman who had never had a single one of her lines uttered on-screen and wondered to herself who this woman thought she was kidding. Renee had pulled out a script, one with her byline on it. It was titled "In his Shadow" and was about the son of Sherlock Holmes.

Renee had made Jane read the script right then and there, while her shrimp scampi cooled off. Jane finished it after an hour and a half and smiled. "Very nice."

Renee wanted to make sure that Jane expressed her positive opinion of her work to Aubrey Brothers and Bob Franks.

For some reason, the subject of Jack Favor, rodeo star, never arose again during that meeting.

As the group drove off, Jon Emr told some amusing anecdotes about his experiences with Hollywood's elite. He talked about life with Michael Douglas. With Kirk. With Bob Redford. With Jan-Michael Vincent. With Robert Conrad. All the while, Aubrey hee-hawed loudly and Bob Franks sat quietly, contemplating Jon's stories. It was good to know that Emr was so well connected. Slowly and surely both men began to dismiss the notion that Jon Emr was anything but a credible knight of the Hollywood Round Table.

An even more sterling show of his credibility came when Jon drove his Lincoln through the unassuming gates of Twentieth Century Fox on Pico Drive, right next door to the corporate headquarters of the Los Angeles Rams. Towering above the vehicle was a huge poster for the James Cameron film *Aliens*, which starred Sigourney Weaver and which would be opening in a few weeks. Jon rolled down

---

*Renee claims it was Jane who tried to get *her* to make a film of her father's life.

his window when he came to the security gate. "Emr-Douglas Productions," he said to the sparkling guard, who practically popped into a salute.

"Certainly, Mr. Emr. Go right on through."

Certainly, Mr. Emr. Go right on through. Those were magic words. Magic to Aubrey and Bob anyway, who looked at each other and nodded with satisfied assurance. This man *had* to be a player. Jon didn't bother to tell anybody in the Lincoln that getting within the Fox studio gates was not exactly like gaining entry into the Pentagon. A few years later, security would clamp down tight and hard after a deranged, obsessed fan arrived at the studio in pursuit of the British actress Tracey Ullman, who filmed her weekly television series on the lot.

As soon as they rolled past the gate, Jon pointed to his left, where there stood the familiar facade of 1940s New York City. "That's where they filmed *The Sting*," Jon told them. Actually, the 1973 Paul Newman–Robert Redford Oscar winner was made at Universal and had been set in 1920s Chicago.

When the troupe got out of the car, which had pulled into a visitor's parking space, Renee pulled Jane over.

Renee asked Jane to walk alongside her good ear. Then she began talking about nothing much at all. Just girl stuff. In the meantime, Jane was agonizing to hear what lines Jon Emr was laying on her clients, for they were now several feet in front of her and Renee.

Eventually, they came to a small building. When they entered, they walked a few yards down the hallway until they came to a door. "Here it is!" Jon bellowed.

The *here* he was announcing was the alleged offices of Emr-Douglas Productions. There was, however, no sign on the door at all. Jon opened the door and stuck his head in. Then, without inviting anybody in, he slapped his hands together and abruptly shut the door. "Let's move on."

And off they went.

"What's going on here?" Jane asked Renee. "Why didn't we go in?"

Renee scurried up to Jon and briefly spoke to him. Soon she was back with Jane. She explained that Jon looked inside and the IRS auditors were in there. They were auditing the books from *Jewel of the Nile*, Renee said, referring to the Michael Douglas sequel to the very popular film *Romancing the Stone*. Jon didn't want to take them in there because it might scare them off.

"JESUS, RENEE! WHY WOULD THAT SCARE THEM OFF? As much money as that film has made, they ought to be glad. I would think it a positive thing they made so much in total earnings."

The group's next stop was at CSI Studios, which Jon Emr claimed he owned. The studio was located in Domingas Hills about a half hour outside of Los Angeles in Orange County. When they walked into the studio, which seemed to be filled with the requisite camera and sound equipment haphazardly strewn around, Jon introduced the group to the mother-and-son team of Tim and Jean Johnson, who happened to be the real owners of the studio. During the drive over, Jon had explained to Aubrey and Bob that Tim and Jean Johnson were two of his most prized "employees." He loved hiring people who were related to one another. "Family!" Jon said. "Nothing more important!" Then he gave his mother a sweet smile.

"You like westerns?" Jon asked Aubrey as the group walked along the inside perimeter of the studio.

"SURE DO!" Aubrey said.

Jon slipped a tape into a VCR that they had just then come upon and pointed to a television screen. "This is a western that we are working on."

An image appeared on the screen: A man was riding a white horse, wearing a cowboy hat, and talking into the camera about some kind of film project. His words were hard to make out because the wind had been blowing into the microphone when this "footage" had been shot. To Jane, the footage looked rather rough and amateurish. But she decided that she should not be judgmental. After all, she had never been involved with any film from this angle before. In fact, she had never been involved with any Hollywood film at all. What Jane did not realize, what her clients Aubrey and Bob certainly did not realize, was that the video was of Jon's brother, Art Jr., riding his horse.

Jon then popped in tape after tape, explaining to the Texans that what he was showing them were "pilots" for a brand-new television network that he was creating with the Johnsons. Tim Johnson later described these "pilots," as Jon referred to them, as "strictly high school bullshit. They didn't even come close to being professional."

Eventually, Jon showed them a few minutes of footage from a project he said was called "A Chance to Live." This was *the big one*, the series that would propel Emr-Douglas Productions to an even *higher* level in the entertainment stratosphere. This was to be the great Vietnam epic, a season's worth of documentaries on the greatest scandal that has ever rocked the world: the fact that Americans were still being held captive in Southeast Asia. All that the Texans saw in the footage was a few minutes of official-looking people being interviewed. Neither Aubrey nor Bob was impressed with what they saw. But, hell, what did they know about Hollywood? Right now, they were in the hands of a pro, Jon Emr, a man who would not dare to steer them in the wrong direction.

That night, after going to dinner, Jon Emr dropped Jane off at Aunt Genie's one-room, un-air-conditioned apartment. When everybody was out of earshot, Jane pulled Jon alongside of her and quietly growled at him. "Jon, I want to tell you something. The only reason I haven't yanked this whole thing out from under you is because everything I see shows this to be real. But you'd better never leave me cooling my heels again."

"I don't know what you are talking about." Jon was quite aghast at being the object of scorn.

"I'm not an East Indian and I don't want to sleep on a bed of nails," Jane said. "Plus, there is no air-conditioning in here. I hate to be ungracious, but my agreement was that you would take care of my airfare and my hotel room. If you all have a money problem I would have preferred it if you had just told me so."

"We're real upset that you are unhappy about this. It's just that we don't think about air-conditioning out here in California," Jon said, as he gave Jane a hug and a pat on the back. "Trust me. *Nobody* has air-conditioning. Besides, we almost have these Texans hooked."

It came as more than a mild disappointment to Jane when Renee showed up at the apartment the next day—*sans* Jon Emr—and told her that there was nothing of note planned for that afternoon. "I'll tell you what," Renee told Jane, "let's you, Genie, and I, just us girls, go shopping! We'll go to the malls. Let the boys go out and have some fun and, why, we'll just shop till we drop!"

In reality, quite a bit of business had gone on that day. Jon took Aubrey Brothers and Bob Franks to meet with his attorney, Ira Miller. Miller wasn't a specialist in entertainment matters, but Jon had long ago decided that Ira would be his man in the foxhole. He had become associated with Ira through his brother, Art Jr., years ago. He had grown to like Ira, with whom he had no complaints, and of whom he was personally fond.

The meeting lasted well over three hours. For the most part, Jon pleaded his case to the Texans. "Jonah" was sure to be a success. Not only would the very experienced Joel Douglas be his partner on the deal, but Kirk was as good as locked into the project. Jon also stated that he had managed to secure an "original" song called "One of These Days" from Paul McCartney. Aubrey had no idea who this McCartney fellow was, but he took Jon's word for it when Jon explained that the ex-Beatle was arguably the hottest rock star Planet Earth has ever known.

The meeting consisted of almost no business negotiating other than the acknowledgment that the Texans would have to come up with $350,000 if they wanted a piece of the action. At one point Aubrey asked when they could expect to see the money they were going to invest in "Jonah."

"Well," Ira began, "the contract that we will ask you to sign says that you'll get your money back when the budget for the film is raised—"

"How much is that?"

"We need to raise ten million. When that money is raised you get back your initial investment and then you get ten percent of the producer's share."

"What does that mean? What's a producer's share?"

"Look, somebody comes into a theater and he pays his five dollars. The theater can take anywhere up to fifty percent of that five dollars. Then from that, there would be X percent of the five dollars available, of which the distributor will get anywhere from twenty-five to fifty percent. From what is left there, the investor who put in the ten million will get their money back. Then, what's left is shared between the production investor and the producer. And the part that goes to the producer is the producer's share."

Aubrey didn't get it. Not one goddamn word of it. It sounded like a bunch of fast-talking Hollywoodese to him. But that didn't seem to matter. Here is what he did know: Douglas, McCartney, Lancaster, a good old-fashioned western.

"We'll take all of this back to our attorney," Aubrey told Miller and Emr at the end of their meeting. Nevertheless, Aubrey knew in his heart, as did Bob Franks, that the two of them were mere inches away from handing over the money. It would just be a matter of time before they would be trading quips late at night with David Letterman.

After the meeting, Jon Emr had a special treat for Bob and Aubrey. It was time for them to finally sit at the foot of royalty. Their enthusiasm had earned them that privilege. They were all going to have lunch with Joel Douglas. Son of Kirk. Younger brother of Michael. In fact, Jon insisted, Joel was the true talent of the family, the brains behind the Douglas operation. All the success that the Douglases had had in recent years could be attributed to Joel. Aubrey and Bob were so excited about the lunch that they completely overlooked the significance of a rather audacious part of the contract they had predetermined to sign:

> The method and the manner of expenditure of the preproduction budget shall be at the sole discretion of the producer.

In other words, as soon as they turned over their $350,000, they would have not a single word as to how the money would be spent.

Aubrey, Bob, and Jon met Joel for lunch at a Japanese restaurant. Joel laid out for them his plans for "Jonah." The more that Aubrey and Bob heard about this movie, the more it sounded like a sure thing. Joel had explained to them that he was the money man and that Jon was going to be the talent behind the project. They need not be worried. Had they read Jon's credentials? Why Jon was some kind of creative genius!

After lunch the men had trotted up to Joel's office, the one on the Twentieth Century Fox lot. Actually, they thought, technically, it might have been Michael's office. They weren't sure. But, really, what did it matter? Aubrey and Bob saw posters on the wall for movies like *Jewel of the Nile* and *Romancing the Stone*.

These guys are for real, Aubrey and Bob thought. In reality, they were in an office that Twentieth Century Fox had set aside as the headquarters for *Jewel of the Nile*. The production company formed to oversee the day-to-day business of that film was called El Corazone. As soon as that film no longer needed any kind of postproduction and posttheatrical release staff, it would be shut down permanently. That was exactly the course of action taken on almost all major motion pictures.

Later that day, Aubrey, Bob, and Jon met up with the ladies. Jane blew her stack when she heard that she had been excluded from the meeting with Joel Douglas. "Why did you tell me there was nothing going on!" she screamed at Renee. "They met with Joel Douglas!"

Renee recoiled. Nobody had ever raised a voice at her like that. Jon interceded, putting his arm around Jane. "Now, don't you jump on Granny. The truth is, we couldn't have you there. It would be very unwise. Trust me. I know this business."

"Jon," she said, words escaping from between her clenched teeth. "What in the world are you talking about?"

"If you were there we'd have to explain who you are."

"Well, Jon, what's wrong with telling them I am the investment broker?"

"Look," he began with a grin. "You'd just blow the deal. That would hurt all of us."

At least Aubrey looked happier than all hell, Jane thought. At least, she said to herself, she could finally begin seeing her commission sitting over there on the horizon.

On their Delta flight home, Aubrey was whooping it up as Bob sat silent and dreamily content. If things went right, it would not be long before he'd be a movie mogul. He could probably see himself on the slopes of Aspen. Jack Nicholson on one side, Cher on the other.

On October 30, 1985, Brothers and Franks flew to Los Angeles for their final meeting with Ira Miller, Jon's attorney. By the time they arrived at Miller's office, their own attorney, a man named Ronald Mankoff who was specifically hired for this one contract, was already there. Over the course of the meeting, lawyers for both sides worked on the text of the contract. Renee and her husband, Arthur, eventually joined the get-together.

It was at the end of the long meeting that Miller said something that almost made Jon fall off the windowsill where he was sitting. Out of nowhere, Jon Emr's ace attorney began trying to convince Aubrey and Bob to back out of the deal.

"Look," he said, "from what I have read independently, if you take a hundred projects that are conceived independently in somebody's mind, something like seventy percent of them never have any money raised at all, which leaves something like thirty percent. And then if they get some money to look for a budget, probably seventy percent of those never have the budget money raised. And then if they have the budget raised, something like half of those movies produced don't get released. From there, you have those that are successful and those that are not. By 'successful' I mean just getting the money back."

Aubrey and Bob nodded their heads in understanding.

Ira Miller made an additional point. "Look, you only have one protection. According to this contract, if we cannot raise the ten million in two years, then you guys get the rights to this script. But, in all honesty, I cannot see that doing you any good. You guys are simply not producers."

Jon walked over to Miller and slapped him on the back. "Okay, old buddy. Don't scare these boys."

The "boys" were not scared at all. Hell, they were from Texas, where "risk" was everybody's favorite hobby. In fact, after the meeting, Ira Miller received a certified check from Bob Franks. Aubrey Brothers sent his half of the money two days later. Both checks were for the amount of $175,000.

Now it was time for Bob and Aubrey to see how Hollywood really ticked.

That night, Jon invited Jane Favor to have some drinks with him at a hotel bar. He told her that he wanted to talk to her about his buying the rights to the life story of her father. Jack Favor was a rodeo star who had become a cause célèbre after he was convicted for a murder he did not commit and who was later released after years of lobbying for a new trial in which he was found not guilty.

Jane agreed to meet with him, although she felt in her heart that Jon's real purpose was to try to get her to give up part of her fee for locking Aubrey and Bob into "Jonah." Sure enough, at the bar, Jon spent almost no time talking about Jane's father.

"Joel is really impressed with you," Jon told Jane.

"Well, that's lovely, Jon." Joel had never met her.

"Jane, we have another project; it's called 'A Chance to Live.' I don't know whether or not your guys are going to do it, but we certainly are going ahead with it."

"What do you mean? Have you spoken to Bob and Aubrey?"

Jon sucked some smoke out of his cigar and smiled. Yes, he told Jane, and they seemed quite interested. He explained to her that "A Chance to Live" was his dream project. It was going to be a twenty-six-part documentary, an hour a segment, that was going to conclusively prove that there were American MIAs still alive and enslaved in Vietnam and Laos. He also told her that it appeared his pals Robert Redford and Michael Douglas had agreed to "star" in the "documentary."

Jane told Jon that she thought it sounded very interesting.

"I know that you feel that the deal on 'Jonah' was not handled well," Jon said. "I feel very badly about that. Joel Douglas and I feel that you have great potential. We want to continue doing business with you. Now, I'm going to make you an offer that I would make to nobody else."

"What is that, Jon?"

"I want you to be an equal partner on 'A Chance to Live.' "

Jane got right to the point. "And how much is this going to cost me?"

Jon laughed. "Believe me, not as much as it should . . . and certainly not as much as Joel and I already have in it."

"Come on, Jon. How much?"

"Thirty-five thousand dollars."

That was exactly the amount of money that Jon owed Jane Favor for her work on "Jonah."

"Well, Jon, I really appreciate the confidence that you've shown in me. I really wish that I could take you up on this opportunity. But I can't accept."

Jon was flummoxed. Had he heard her correctly? Had Jane Favor, this Texas plebeian, actually turned down an opportunity to be partners with him and the Douglas family? "Jane, this is a present. It's . . . it's a gift."

"I'm sorry, Jon."

Jon smiled and raised his glass to Jane and smirked. That night, Jon had conveniently forgotten his credit card and Jane had to pick up the tab.

As soon as attorney Ira Miller received the two checks from the Texans, the money was immediately dispersed.

A check for $4,124 went to a travel agency in Beverly Hills. This money went to pay for an airline ticket for Patty Douglas, Joel's wife, for first-class airfare between Los Angeles and Nice, France. In the memo section, the words "A Chance to Live Corporation" were typed in.

Another $105,000 went directly into the bank account of Jon's parents, Art and Renee.

Arthur and Renee were also paid (with a separate check) the sum of $93,000.

Ira Miller's law firm received $6,000.

A $6,000 check was made out to, yet again, Art and Renee Emr.

Miller cut a check for $5,000 exclusively to Renee.

Joel Douglas personally received two checks from Miller's firm, both in the area of $15,000.

Jane Favor received $33,000 for her work. The other $2,000 owed her had already been advanced. Jane turned over about $8,000 to Roy Ashton, the convicted felon who had arranged for her to meet Aubrey in the first place.

Miller wrote out a few other checks, amounting to about $5,000, for miscellaneous items that seemed to have nothing to do with "Jonah."

Perhaps the most interesting check was made out to the "Clerk of Superior Court" for the sum of $63,000. The memo at the bottom left corner of the check read "Emr vs. Armstrong—Interpleader."

Had Aubrey Brothers and Bob Franks seen that check and its

memo, it might well have set off an alarm. That $63,000 was placed with the court so that it could be collected by the estate of Michael Armstrong, aka Whitney, the man who had written "Jonah." In other words, when Jon Emr convinced Aubrey Brothers and Bob Franks to invest in "Jonah," he did not actually own the rights to it and had no business raising the cash to make the picture.

And what about Jon Emr's claim that Paul McCartney would perform an original song for the film? In this instance, Jon was relying on a letter that had been written on September 21, 1983, two years earlier, to the now deceased Michael Whitney from McCartney's managing director:

> This letter will confirm that Paul McCartney has granted permission for you to make a cover recording of the song "One of These Days" for use in a screenplay entitled "Jonah."

The letter demonstrated two glaring discrepancies in Emr's claims. First, the permission was specifically granted to Michael Whitney, *not* Jon Emr. Whitney, who had been married to the model Twiggy, had a friendship with the ex-Beatle. Second, the letter granted permission for a "cover" of the song. That meant that a singer other than McCartney would perform it. Third, "One of These Days" would not be an "original" song. In fact, it was one of the tunes featured on the McCartney II album released in 1980.

There was another small matter that would have been disturbing had Aubrey and Bob known about it. During the time that Jon had been negotiating with the Texans, cajoling them into living out their own personal Hollywood dreams, he had misled them into believing that his partnership with Joel Douglas was a done deal.

Joel and Jon had been introduced years before by their mutual hairdresser, Roger DeAnfrasio, who called himself the Celebrity Stylist for men. On April 15, 1985, Jon signed an agreement with DeAnfrasio giving the hairdresser permission to help him seek out investors for his films. For his troubles, DeAnfrasio would receive 10 percent of the fee paid to Jon Emr as a producer, 10 percent of any income derived from distributing the picture, and a finder's fee for locating preproduction investors. Not long after the signing of this agreement, DeAnfrasio matched Joel Douglas with Jon Emr.

The partnership agreement between Jon Emr and Joel Douglas was actually signed on October 11, 1985, long after Aubrey Brothers and Bob Franks made their initial visit to Los Angeles. In it, Joel and Jon were each to receive $45,000 from the Texas cash. However, Joel was to receive as much as three times more money than Jon, once the profits on "Jonah" started to roll in. While this did not seem a model of equality—hardly a real partnership—Jon Emr probably could not have cared less. For "Jonah" was never to see the light of day . . . and he knew it.

An Autopsy in Culver City:
July 18, 1991

Laddie, I've never gone anyplace peacefully in my life.
—Victor McLaglen in *She Wore a Yellow Ribbon*

Hank Davies would have liked to have been physically present at the autopsy of Jon Emr and his boy Roger. In most police stations across the country that is regarded as the most standard of standard procedures. If the examining coroner made some kind of stop-the-presses discovery, the case detective would learn of it instantaneously. In manhunts and homicide investigations, time was an enemy for the good guys.

However, attending autopsies was not part of the routine in Culver City. Chief Ted Cooke had put out the royal edict that his homicide detectives would not be permitted to attend a coroner's examination in their cases. That required time and manpower. Time and manpower, of course, translated to money, of which the Culver City Police Department was desperately short. In addition, several police officers noted that Cooke was simply pissed off by what he considered the exorbitant fees that the coroner was charging.

Despite his pleading with Chief Cooke to be present for the slicing and the dicing of the two Emrs, Davies was instructed to simply wait for the reports on both Jon and Roger to arrive on his desk. That happened several days after the executions. The two reports were each twelve or thirteen pages long. The first thing that Davies checked was the blood test section. In the case of both men, there was a negative reading for both drugs and alcohol. That somewhat surprised him since both Jon's drinking and use of cocaine were attested to by so many of the people that Hank had interviewed. Of course, cocaine was a narcotic that stayed in the system for only three days. It was certainly possible that Emr, who was scheduled for a cardiology appointment in a day or two, had decided to stay off the drug for a while.

The autopsy confirmed that Jon Emr indeed had had a bad heart. But otherwise, both he and his son were in good health at the time they were killed. It was not a big surprise to read the final analysis of Jon's condition by the medical examiner: "On the basis of the autopsy findings it is my opinion that the decedent died as the result of multiple gunshot wounds."

What the report did give Davies was his first real indication of how badly butchered Jon and Roger were. After all, by the time he arrived on the murder scene, both bodies had been removed. According to the report, Jon had been hit a total of six times. He was shot three times in the head and three times in his right arm. The first bullet, the fatal one, apparently ricocheted along the inner table of his skull and then finally came to rest between the brain and the left dura. The second bullet, which would have been just as fatal as the first, hit him in the cheek, bore its way through his sinuses, grazed his tongue, and then landed in the left eye globe.

Roger was hit five times: four bullets to the head and one to his right arm. He was hit in the forehead, the cheek, the mouth and the right eye, which was partially blown out.

Near the end of the reports, the examining doctors noted that neither of the police officers assigned to the case, Davies and Yoshida, had attended the sessions.

The Cons of Jon Emr:
Earl Rutledge, 1985

Stupid is as stupid does.
Tom Hanks in *Forrest Gump*

A few weeks after her return to Texas, Jane Favor developed a serious medical problem. As she describes it, "I had built a stone the
size of the rock of Gibraltar in my lower left submandibular parotid
saliva gland." That small problem cost her a five-and-a-half-hour operation, a lengthy hospital stay, and some extraordinary medical bills.

While she was at the hospital, Jane received the first of many panicked calls from Jon Emr. According to Jon, the two Texans were very,
very close to forking over a hefty amount of cash for his "A Chance to
Live" project, the one dealing with proving that American POWs were
still in Southeast Asia. All that he needed was for her to give a light,
friendly nudge to the Texans, to send the project over the transom.
Aubrey and Bob respected her, he insisted. They would listen to her.

Jon Emr sent Jane his packet for "A Chance to Live." It was a sloppy
and hastily put together spiral notebook of about thirty pages. It
mostly consisted of photocopied newspaper clippings about two men:
Colonel Jack Bailey and Bobby Garwood. According to the various articles, Bailey was a retired army officer who had made it his life mission
to search for and rescue Americans who were still being held captive in
Southeast Asia. Garwood was the last American to be released from
captivity in Vietnam. Garwood was found guilty of collaborating with
the enemy when he returned to the States. Both Bailey and Garwood
had "signed on" with Emr in 1985. "A Chance to Live" was going to
be their story.

The proposal packet also had a cast. Robert Redford was going to
play Colonel Jack Bailey, Gregory Peck was going to play General

Westmoreland, and Stuart Whitman would play a "POW." Never mind that, by definition, actors do not play roles in documentaries.

According to the packet, Emr himself had already filmed thirty-nine hours of footage and another fifty hours were forthcoming. In fact, Emr was such a talented documentarian that he claimed he had managed to convince former president Richard Nixon to sit for a no-holds-barred interview.

Finally, Emr had provided the Texas duo with a video. For the most part, the tape was a compilation of interviews that had already been conducted by Colonel Jack Bailey with various low-end government officials and former POWs. The footage was laborious, sloppily edited, and badly lit. Nevertheless, it was evidence that actual work had taken place on "A Chance to Live."

Eventually, Jane Favor agreed to broker the agreement. Again, she wanted 10 percent of any moneys that she raised from her investors. She, in turn, would have to pay off Roy Ashton, the convicted armed robber with whom she had had a brief and unfulfilling romance, for introducing her to the Texas investors. Jon happily agreed to the arrangement.

A few days later, Aubrey contacted Jane, who was back home. He had astonishing news. After considering the "A Chance to Live" proposal sent to them by Jane, he and Bob Franks had *already* sent Jon their money investing in the documentary. By the way, he added, they did this without a contract.

Jane was floored. "Are you fucked!" she screamed at Aubrey over the phone. "How could you give up that much money to anybody without a contract?"

Actually, a contract *had* been signed between the Texans and Jon Emr, although it was so slapdash that it was easy to understand why Aubrey did not consider it such. On December 2, 1985, Brothers and Frank signed an "agreement" that would require them to pay Jon Emr a total of $300,000, in three installments over the next month and a half.

In exchange for their $300,000, Aubrey and Bob were promised "... *1% of the gross revenues paid to us, Emr-Douglas Productions, by the distributors* ..." That meant that the Texans would make their money back only if "A Chance to Live" was bought by a distributor for $30 million. That was an almost unimaginably remote possibility. Consider, for example, that the average television movie (and this was to be a documentary)—even those that were huge ratings winners—cost under $2 million in 1985.

Jane herself had not signed a deal with Jon on the new brokerage deal. After hearing that Jon had received cash from her investors, Jane contacted Emr. "Jon, let's be frank," she said to him. "I've done my job. I brought to you people who are real, who have the money to invest. If you treat me and them properly they'll be around for a while and perhaps be repeat investors. Don't burn them and don't burn me."

"Oh, I would never do that," Jon said.

"When am I going to get my money?"

She could practically hear Jon smiling on the other end of the phone. "Oh, it's coming. It's coming. Maybe by Tuesday."

Jon Emr started to become a permanent fixture in Aubrey's life. He would call him once, maybe twice a day. As Aubrey recalls it, the calls were just to "bullshit" about nothing at all. Indeed, the topic that Jon most strenuously avoided was the two movies into which Aubrey and his partner had invested over three-quarters of a million dollars. Jon would persistently tell him, "We're working on it." On occasion, Jon would tell him that an investor had been hooked into the project. One time, Jon claimed that Budweiser was going to buy into the project. *Budweiser!* That was Aubrey's brew of choice. That was something to which he could certainly relate.

Often, Jon would fly to Dallas and stay with Aubrey. As Aubrey recalls it, Jon was in a constant drunken state and the stench of his cigars so infested the house that Louise, Aubrey's lover, threatened to leave him. But Aubrey had become quite charmed by Jon and enjoyed his visits. Aubrey didn't even object when Jon began to "court" his daughter. When Jon was in town, Aubrey had the opportunity to go "clubbing," which is something he had not done for years.

It was during one of these visits that Jon claimed that "A Chance to Live" had hit a major snag. Jon arrived at Aubrey's home with a face flushed with anger. He told Aubrey that he was *this* close—he placed his thumb and index finger almost one on top of the other—to landing the biggest elephant of them all—H. Ross Perot. Perot, the founder of Electronic Data Systems, had his own personal obsessions with Vietnam and POWs. Perot was a graduate of the United States Naval Academy and had an inbred sense of patriotism. Jon had thought Perot an obvious candidate to invest or even donate funds to the making of "A Chance to Live."

According to Jon, he had sent Perot the packet for "A Chance to Live" and the tycoon had been tremendously impressed. But then there was the matter of Colonel Jack Bailey. Bailey had had some kind of falling-out with Jon and Joel over money. Instead of "settling it like a man," Jack had gone to Perot and told the businessman that Jon was a con artist and that Perot would be an idiot to invest with him.

Aubrey was aghast. From everything he had read and seen about Jack Bailey, he seemed like a patriot. How could he bring a project like this to its knees? Aubrey suggested that they go see Bob Franks. Maybe Bob could figure out how to get Perot back on line.

Franks was not in his office when the two men arrived. Aubrey suggested that they go upstairs to the conference room of Earl Rutledge, Bob's attorney. Aubrey suggested that Jon might want to phone Perot and use that sophisticated Emr charm to settle the Bailey matter.

Attorney-at-law Earl Rutledge was passing by the conference room in his second-floor law offices in Hurst, Texas, a small bedroom community just fifteen minutes away from the Dallas–Fort Worth International Airport. Sitting there were Aubrey Brothers and a man, at the head of the table, who Earl thought looked greasy and sleazy.

Aubrey was sitting Aubrey-style: his chair balanced slightly on the back two legs, his left arm hanging over the side as if it were dead, and his gut proudly protruding. "Come on in," Aubrey bellowed to Earl. "I want you to meet my friend Jon Emr."

Jon seemed distracted as he shook hands with Earl.

"Jon's a producer from Hollywood," Aubrey said. "I'm thinking of investing in one of Jon's movies."

"Really?" said Earl.

Earl gave Jon Emr a once-over and decided that there was reason to be suspicious. The movie business was, after all, a business. And Jon looked nothing like a businessman. He was wearing a rayon shirt, unbuttoned to the navel, gold chains hanging around his neck, and enough rings to make Sammy Davis Jr. envious. And anyway, what the *fuck* was an important Hollywood producer doing in *fucking* Hurst, Texas, with *fucking* Aubrey Brothers? Then he remembered the time, months earlier, when Aubrey and Bob had gone on a trip to determine whether or not they wanted to invest in a Hollywood project. He now realized that the deal had actually been struck.

Jon barely acknowledged Earl's presence and then turned to Aubrey. "Motherfucker! He's a motherfucker!" Jon screamed.

For the next few minutes Rutledge stood in the doorway as Jon ranted and raved that this Colonel Jack Bailey had "fucked" his reputation with Mr. H. Ross Perot.

"Bailey is a no-good motherfucker! He's a liar. He's totally fucked every chance I have ever had of having Perot give his name to the movie!" Jon paused for a moment and turned to Earl. "Can I use the phone?" Then, with a sneer he added, "It's a local call."

"Go ahead," Earl said.

Jon dialed furiously. "Ross Perot, please. . . . It's Jon Emr. . . . WHAT THE FUCK! . . . Get Ross on the line! What? Fuck you! . . . I'll use whatever fuckin' tone I want. . . . Look, you want me to call Ross at home? . . . Fuck. . . . Okay, here's the message . . . I want to speak to Ross. Have him call Jon Emr . . . E . . . M . . . R . . . Tell him it's about Jack Bailey."*

Jon slammed the phone down.

Out of nowhere Jon turned to Earl, cocked his head slightly and said, in a voice seething with hostility. "I fuckin' hate lawyers." He paused and then spat out the next words. "They're deal breakers. Fuckin' deal breakers."

This wasn't a kind of good-natured anti-lawyer quip that Earl had been hearing since he graduated from the University of Texas a quarter of a century earlier. This was real anger. Real ignorance. "I'm sorry you feel that way," Earl responded, not at all interested in getting

*When I spoke with Perot in the winter of 1994, he acknowledged that he had received a proposal for "A Chance to Live" from Jon Emr. However, Perot insists that he never considered it at all, that he has never and will never invest in film projects. Perot would not discuss Colonel Jack Bailey. "I start talking about people and then they start lining up to sue me," Perot explained.

sucked into an argument. Instead, he got up and left the room, hoping Aubrey would have the sense to get this Jon Emr the hell out of the office.

A few days later, Earl was contacted by Bobby Franks. "I heard from Aubrey that you met Jon Emr."

"Yes, I did."

"We may be doing business with him." Of course, Aubrey and Bob had already invested their cash.

"I have to be honest with you, Bob," he said. "I just don't like this fellow. Didn't trust him. Doesn't strike me as being for real. I'd be real careful about jumping into a deal with a movie man."

"Well, could you be more specific?"

"Bob, I just found it kind of odd that a bona fide movie producer would conduct himself in the way that he did. He was very crude."

"Really?"

"I mean, Bob, really. What the hell is a big-time Hollywood producer doing in Texas?"

"Hmmm."

"And the way that he was dressed. He should have been dressed a bit better. Bob, the movie industry is a business. It is not a game. This man seemed to be playing a game as opposed to being a businessman. In any case, a banker and real estate investor—like the two of you— should not be investing in the movie industry, because you do not know the first thing about it."

There was a pause. "Earl, can I tell you what I think?"

"Sure," Earl said.

"The best that I can determine, from having gone out to California, is that Jon Emr's a bona fide producer. I'll tell you, I sat in this guy's of-fice. There were posters everywhere from movies I had heard of. This was on the lot of Twentieth Century Fox. Emr walked around there like he owned the damn place. Hell, Earl, I got to meet Joel Douglas. And, in any case, Kirk Douglas has signed his name to some papers on this film!"

"Okay, Bob," Earl said. Privately, Earl was getting pissed. Bob Franks was not one to judge people harshly. Bob was amazingly cred-ulous. It just was not his nature to write somebody off or be suspicious.

"Look, I disagree with you. But, I am not going to push this matter. You do what you want to do. If you need help, let me know."

At this point all that really mattered to Bob Franks and Aubrey Brothers was that Jon Emr had demonstrated not only his relationship to the Douglas family, but also one with H. Ross Perot.

In any case, even if "A Chance to Live" was running into difficulties, there was always "Jonah."

In the late summer of 1985, Aubrey Brothers received a rather disturbing phone call from a man named Rex Ravelle. For almost two years Rex had been searching for Emr. In his hunt, he had discovered that Jon had somehow finagled a couple of Texans into "Jonah." He had bad news for Aubrey. Jon Emr did not own "Jonah." He, Rex, did. Rex went through his entire history with Jon: the unreturned loans, the car he gave to Jon, "Magnum Thrust," the botched trip to Taiwan, and the entire Michael Whitney–"Jonah" scam.

"Aubrey, you sound like a nice man," Rex said. "But the truth is that this movie will never get made. Not by Jon Emr, anyway."

Aubrey told Rex that he was shocked and that he would check into the matter.

A few days later, Rex Ravelle heard from Jon Emr for the first time in about two years. He asked Rex if they could meet at a restaurant. Feeling that he had nothing to lose, that Jon Emr could not possibly suck any more money out of him, Rex agreed.

They met the next day for breakfast at a hotel restaurant off the 405 freeway on Sunset Boulevard. Rex refused to shake hands with Emr as they sat down at a booth by the window. Rex ordered a plate of eggs and bacon and a large glass of orange juice. Jon Emr ordered a "breakfast deluxe" and a large Bloody Mary.

Jon got right down to business. "Well, Rexy, you've got my investors in a bit of a tizzy. I don't know why you couldn't be a man and contact me directly."

"You're a son of a bitch, Jon. You betrayed me. You exploited me. You took advantage of my generosity and you broke a pledge to me. Do you remember when we were supposed to go up north to get that hundred thousand dollars? You left me high and dry. You're not just a flake. You're a predator."

Jon began to smoke a cigar, oblivious to the no-smoking sign at his table. "I'm not a predator. I'm a businessman. Anyway, this is all bullshit. I am here to resolve this whole thing."

"I'm listening."

"I'm going to give you fifteen thousand dollars. Then I want you to go away."

Rex was seething. "I must have put at least a hundred thousand in you. That's what I want you to give me."

Jon giggled. "I don't have it."

"Well, then, you may as well not make 'Jonah.' You'll never release it. I'll contest it in court. I have documents from Michael Whitney giving me the script."

Then Jon came up with a doozy. "I'm sorry you think I conned you. Rex." Jon downed his Bloody Mary and ordered another one. "I mean this sincerely. The truth is that I have plans for you."

"What are you talking about, Jon?"

"I'm sure, since you have a private investigator, that you know I now own a movie studio." Rex actually had no idea. Nevertheless, he let Jon continue. "It's small, but a real deal. It's called CSI Video. Starting next year we are going to own a cable station. It's going to be called 21st Century."

Rex could not believe what he was hearing. "Jon, do you mean to tell me that you want me to invest in your cable company? Are your balls that fucking big?"

"No, Rexy. I've come to realize something about you. I have come to realize that you belong in front of the camera. All this investing crap is beneath you. You're like me. We are victims of our own creativity."

Rex laid down his fork and his knife and seemed to forget that he was sitting with a man whom he had just minutes ago called a "predator." "Yes, I miss those days."

"Here's my idea. Rex, you are easily the most fit man I've ever met." Now Jon was talking Rex's game. "You should see my one-armed push-ups!"

"And, Jesus, you're almost seventy years old! Rexy, I want you to be the host of a physical fitness show for the elderly. We'll call it . . . 'Rexercise!' I'm willing to give you six thousand a month and six percent of all our health and fitness product placement. That should net you half a million in a year."

Rex was silent for a few moments. "You'll put this in writing?"

"I'll send you a letter today, Rexy. You just have to, you know, lay off of this 'Jonah' thing."

Rex nodded. Then with a sigh of resignation, he said, "It would be good to get back to work."

The two men discussed Rex's ideas for the show. After half an hour, Rex was hooked. Why get tied up in litigation for years? Why get into the muck and mire over a script he really didn't care about? Wouldn't it be great to be on a set again, to hear the clapboard snap, to hear a director call for action, to be recognized on the street?

Jon Emr got up and patted Rex on the back. "You made the right decision." Then he left Rex Ravelle to pay the breakfast bill.

That afternoon, Rex instructed his lawyer and private eyes to stop all actions and investigations against Jon Emr. A few days later the promised letter outlining the details of their "deal" arrived. Rex sent Jon a videotape of himself doing chin-ups and push-ups. A seventy-year-old exercise machine! That sure as hell would impress the investors!

Rex Ravelle never heard from Jon Emr again.

I could find absolutely no documentary, contractual, or testimonial evidence whatsoever to suggest that Jon Emr made any real effort to obtain financing for "Jonah" after he had gotten cash out of Aubrey and Bob. In a deposition he would later give on the matter, Jon's attorney, Ira Miller, suggested that there were about four individuals with whom he had made his own contacts, none of whom was serious about the project.

What in particular was baffling to all those involved was why the project did not get offered to any of the major studios. Had Kirk Douglas been as intimately involved as Jon Emr had claimed, it would have made sense that the actor's agent would have passed the script around to the various majors and, almost certainly, to Twentieth Century Fox, where Michael Douglas had set up shop.

During those two years, Brothers would frequently contact Ira Miller and ask him how things were going with the raising of the $10 million. Each time Miller's best answer was, "Working on it." Often he would add, "I don't know anything; Talk to Jon."

EXCERPT FROM THE DEPOSITION OF IRA MILLER,
Attorney for Jon Emr, Taken November 10, 1988

Q: How long a period of time did you talk to investors about trying to raise the $10 million on behalf of Mr. Emr [for "Jonah"]?

A: Two years.

Q: Were any of those efforts successful?

A: No.

Q: Can you tell me why they were not successful?

A: Because they didn't come up with the money.

Q: Why didn't this movie, which would star Kirk Douglas and be co-produced by Joel Douglas, get made? . . .

A: I have no idea. . . .

Q: What, if anything, had Joel Douglas done up to that point in time, if you know, to justify or earn a $45,000 producer's fee?

A: I don't know.

Q: What, if anything, to your knowledge, had Jon Emr done with respect to rewriting the script "Jonah" to earn or to justify him getting $30,000 out of preproduction funds . . . ?

A: I don't know.

It had been weeks since Aubrey Brothers and Bob Franks had told Jane that they had invested in "A Chance to Live," but she had still not seen a dime of her commission. She had racked up an impressive phone bill, making calls to Jon and his mother, Renee. Eventually, Jon simply laid the truth on her and explained that she was not going to be paid.

Jon explained that she would be "expensed" when the project was finished and sold. He told her that nobody was taking any money out of "A Chance to Live."

"I'm sorry, but that's the way it is," he explained to her. "I have no control over it. Joel Douglas is in control and that's the way it's set up."

Jane hung up on Jon and called Aubrey. He told her that *she-iiiit*, he and Bob had already invested their full three hundred grand.

Jane called Jon. "I frankly should have seen this coming," she said. "I am going to do everything I can to see to it that these people do no further business with you. I can also guarantee that I will send nobody else to you. There is a wonderful grapevine in the state of Texas. You won't get any more money out of here."

Emr seemed unimpressed. "That's not necessary, Jane," he said.

"Look, I got news for you," she said. "I've got a partner who is owed money."

"That's not my problem, Jane."

"It is your problem!" she screamed at him. "It is! This is the man that set me up with Aubrey. I promised him some of the action on 'A Chance to Live.' "

"So?"

"So, Roy just got out of prison for murder. He's a hit man!" she said, calmly referring to Roy Ashton. "He's really, really pissed. He already said that he wanted to kill me. I've had to move in with my father. All I have to do is tell Roy what you've done and then we'll wait and see what happens."

"Sounds like a threat."

"Fuck you, Jon!" Jane smashed the phone down.

There certainly was truth to what Jane had said. Roy had become plenty pissed and impatient when his financial cut of the "Chance to Live" money never materialized. He was convinced that Jane was keeping it from him. In fact, it took a good lecture from his old pal Jack Favor for Roy to become convinced that Jane was not holding back his funds. In fact, Roy's forgiveness of Jane became so complete that he proposed marriage to her. She turned him down, but not before convincing him that Jon had screwed both him and her.

Eighteen months later, Jane Favor found herself sucked into dealing with Jon Emr yet again. It seemed that Aubrey and Bob had become particularly despondent over the lack of progress of both "Jonah" and "A Chance to Live." They insisted that Jon needed a new infusion of cash, even though they personally no longer had the cash flow to provide it. They asked Jane for help.

Jane had come to truly despise Jon. If he was not a con artist, then he was certainly one of the very worst businessmen and/or producers she had ever known. In addition, she was unhappy with Aubrey and Bob. She was convinced that the two of them would certainly be able to squeeze some money out of Jon. But neither one had stepped forward to help her out.

Nevertheless, Jane did have what she perceived as a potential investor. In fact, it was a Goliath of an investor. Jane had managed to get business associates of tycoon Armand Hammer interested in a completely separate project: the life story of her father, Jack Favor. Over the past years, Favor had managed to foster a relationship with Sonja Katz (not her real name), a confidante and friend of Hammer's who had been discussing the project with her over the past year. Apparently Hammer had been developing a fund specifically intended for the financing of movies, which would be produced under the banner of Armand Hammer Productions.

When Jon heard that Jane might have Armand Hammer—*billionaire* Armand Hammer—in the bag, he became excited and called her with wonderful news. "Michael Douglas has agreed to act on behalf of the family on 'A Chance to Live.' "

"That's great. How did you manage that?"

"I didn't have to do anything. It just worked out that way. Now here's the kicker—"

"Oh, there's a kicker?"

"Well, Michael is in town for next week only," he said sadly. "Joel will be away. If you can get Hammer's people into town it will be a way of getting Michael to represent us on the front end."

Jane gave the matter some thought. Then she agreed: "On one condition Jon. I want your word of honor, cross your heart, hope to die, that absolutely, positively, you are not scamming me on this, that in fact this is real, and if I set this meeting up, Michael Douglas will be there in the flesh."

Jon gasped with his surprise. *Nobody* had *ever* challenged his integrity before. "My God, Jane. Yes. Yes. I swear on the lives of my children."

"Okay, Jon."

A few days later, Jane called Jon and told him that they would be meeting with Armand Hammer's contingent at four o'clock the following Tuesday. "Michael Douglas had better be there. And Jon, try wearing a tie."

Jane was very specific in not telling Jon the location of the meeting. That way Jon would have no choice but to pick her up from her hotel. Otherwise, he might just decide to wing the meeting on his own. Jon arrived twenty minutes late at Jane's hotel in a black Camaro. His girl-friend, Sue Fellows, was driving the car. Jon's hair was sopping wet and was combed straight back. He wore a navy-blue suit and a bright cherry-red shirt. He was not wearing a tie. Michael Douglas was not in the car.

"Jon, for Pete's sake, what is it with you? You can't take anything I say as real," Jane said as she lowered herself into the backseat.

He grinned widely. "Oh, calm down. Trust me. Everything will be just fine."

"What do you mean calm down! Jon, where the hell is Michael?"

Jon offered his explanation as Sue steered in the direction Jane was pointing. "Michael had a small family emergency," Jon said. "I'll call him from where we're going to and tell him where we are."

"Jon, if Michael is not going to show, then tell me now. I refuse to go in there and humiliate myself in front of these people with a no-show."

Jon leaned over and patted Jane on the knee. "Baby, I absolutely, positively guarantee you he will be there. Sue had him on the phone, isn't that right, Sue?"

"Yes. He'll be there," Sue nodded.

Eventually the car came to a T in the road. Jane pulled out a sheet of paper. "Jon, you don't know whether to turn left or right. This is the contract for my services. Sign it now or I don't give you directions."

Jon snatched it from her, read it hastily, and crossed out one section. "We can't make you associate producer. Joel Douglas would never go for it. You don't have the experience." Then he signed his name to the contract. Jane retrieved it and shoved it into her purse.

"I thought we were friends," Jon said with a pout.

"Fuck friendship, Jon. I can't afford your friendship. Now turn left."

■ ■ ■

They arrived at the Regency Club on Wilshire Boulevard, the private dinner club where the meeting was to take place. Apparently the lawyer who was to be in attendance was a member. Jon instructed Sue to go and wait at a restaurant across the street. As they walked into the lobby of the club, Jane saw Seth Jones (not his real name), the attorney representing Sonja Katz, Armand Hammer's representative. "I was just getting ready to go," he told Jane.

"I wouldn't have blamed you if you did," Jane said.

Jon jumped in. "I am so, so, so sorry. Michael had a family emergency. He'll be joining us shortly. I just need to call him on the car phone."

Because it was four in the afternoon, the club was almost empty, with maybe two or three businessmen taking off early from work hanging around. Because Jon had gone to make his phone call, Jane was alone with Sonja and Seth. "What's going on?" an irritated Seth asked her. "Where's Michael Douglas?"

Jane was straightforward. "He told me the same thing that he told you. I don't believe it, but we'll see."

"Well, I have nothing better to do," said Sonja, who was elegantly dressed, wearing a black hat and black veil. "Let's play along and see what comes of all this."

Jon returned and sat down. Actually, Jon sprawled down on a couch and lit his cigar. "Has Janey filled you in on 'A Chance to Live'? It's going to be a four-star winner—" And then Jon went into his spiel. A twenty-six-part documentary! It would become a part of history itself. There would be Oscars and Emmys all around. Redford! Douglas! There was no downside!

In fact, it would be almost fifteen minutes before Jon would stop talking. Or drinking. Or puffing on his howitzer cigar. Eventually, after nodding their heads in polite acknowledgment of Jon's ranting, Sonja asked, "When do you think Michael will get here?"

"I don't know, I don't know," Jon said.

"Well, as long as he's not here, would you put out your cigar?"

Jon smiled as he smashed his stogie into the ashtray. Then he started talking about his past credits. He'd launched Dionne Warwick. Jan-Michael Vincent was his discovery. He'd produced in excess of three hundred television shows, and—

"Jon, what the heck is going on?" Jane asked. "We have kept these people tied up for a long time now"—half an hour in fact—"and Michael is still not here."

That's when Jon grinned, picked up his half-a-cigar from the ashtray, put it between his teeth, and relit. "Jane," he said. "What's your problem? I have told you already. He's not coming."

All three heads jerked up. "Excuse me?" said Jane.

"How many times do I have to tell you that he's not coming?"

Seth stood up. "That's enough for me." He looked at Jane, who was mortified. "Call me later."

Sonja pulled out a cigarette. "I think I'm going to stay, Jon. You amuse me."

As they walked out of the club, Jane had her biggest showdown yet with Jon. "You tried to burn me in front of my own people," she said. "You made it look like I *knew* that Michael Douglas was not coming. What are you high on, Jon?"

Jon became defensive. "What makes you think that I'm high?"

"Well, I'd have to be blind, deaf, and dumb not to realize that you are flying on something. In fact, you just committed professional suicide."

That evening, Jane spoke with Sonja Katz on the phone. At that time, Sonja made a confession that as recently as that very morning Jon had already made contact with her. He had tried to find out the location of the meeting and had tried to convince them that Jane would just be a burden to the negotiations. If what Sonja said shocked Jane, what was coming next was an even bigger bombshell. She wanted "in" on "A Chance to Live."

"Let me tell you how it is," Sonja said. "If Michael Douglas is really a part of this project, we're in. But not with Emr. We do not want to talk with him and we do not want to hear from him. We don't even want to know him. I don't want Joel Douglas to show up representing the project, because he does not have the credentials to pull it off. Kirk maybe, but, let's face it, his prime has come and gone."

The two women then went on to discuss their true feelings about Jon. The last thing that Sonja said to Jane was, "You owe it to your investors to go to them and tell them that if they have any leverage, or any sort of control over the project, that they should get Jon off and Michael in. Otherwise, we simply wash our hands of it."

Jane phoned Jon the following day from Aubrey's home back in Texas. She explained to him exactly what had been told to her. Armand Hammer Productions was "in" on condition that Michael was, in fact, taking control of the project and that Jon would pull out.

Jon was stunned and hurt. "I . . . I don't understand."

"Jon, you are simply not acceptable to them. You do not have the professional credentials."

There was a long silence. Jane could tell that Jon was boiling. "Do you want to know what the real problem is, Jane?"

"What's that, Jon?"

"The problem is that Sonja wants to fuck Michael Douglas. That is the problem. That's all there is to it!"

"Jon, you and I are not going to have this conversation if you can't control yourself. Anyway, I'm afraid that this is the way that it is going to have to be."

"You're a fucking bitch! a whore! a slut!"

Jane remained calm. "Jon, you need to enter the real world. The person who controls the money is the deal maker. You don't have the money; you want the money. I have the people with the money. It's not a matter of trying to play games and say, I'm top man here! The fact is that I put you with them and you blew it. There were terms used like clown, carnival hustler, con artist, greasy. They don't want any part of you. You made a point to be late. You made a point of showing up without Michael Douglas. You didn't even show up dressed."

Jon began to scream so loud that he was unintelligible. Eventually Jane hung up on him. The entire conversation had been taped, as was the case with all calls at Aubrey's home. Aubrey turned a beet red as he listened to Jon calling Jane a "whore."

When it was all over, Aubrey buried his head in his huge hands. "Janey," he said quietly. "I think we got taken for all our money."

"Maybe, Aubrey," Jane said with resignation. "Maybe."

■ ■ ■

A few days later, Jane received a letter from Ira Miller, Jon's attorney. She says she was forbidden from having any more conversations with Aubrey Brothers, Bob Franks, the Douglases, the Emrs, or any money people. And, by the way, her fee was now very much in jeopardy.

Jon was also turning down Armand Hammer's offer and would not "back out" of the project. This was his baby, he claimed, and nobody but he was going to touch it.*

While Jon Emr had done next to nothing on "Jonah," he surprisingly did seem to be going through some motions on "A Chance to Live." His most significant progress was his hiring of Richard Nash, a practicing Mormon from Salt Lake City, to work on the "distribution" of the documentary. Nash had been one of the creators of a film distribution system called four-walling. In that system, an independent movie studio would create and promote a film, rent out a theater, and take in all the box office cash directly. It proved rather successful. Such films as *The Search for Noah's Ark* and *Where the Red Fern Grows* were four-wall projects.

RICHARD NASH:
NOVEMBER 1992

Jon always seemed to have projects. Once he wanted to do a project on Teddy Kennedy and the bridge deal. Jon had always maintained, "If I ever get anything together, you are my distributor." I told Jon that that was fine, as long as he was paying the way.

I had moved to Salt Lake City in 1981. Jon always maintained contact with me. I mean, it might be six months before I would hear from him again. I did not pursue Jon Emr; Jon pursued me because of my background in marketing. I knew nothing about his private life, and I didn't want to know. I could see that he was a fraud.

---

*When I spoke with Michael Douglas he claimed that he never agreed to become a principal on "A Chance to Live," never knew about the dinner meeting where Jon promised his presence, and certainly was unaware that his name was being bandied about as a producer to Armand Hammer.

One night I was at home and the phone rang and it was Jon. He said, "Do you know a fellow by the name of Jack Bailey?" I thought that I'd read his name before. Anyway, Jon told me all about "A Chance to Live" and he asked me, "Are you available to come to work with me on this? This is a done deal and it's ready to go." I told him that would be fine. I told him that it would cost him $1,600 a month and he said that was fine.

Jon told me that Joel Douglas was very interested in my kind of marketing. Joel was interested in four-walling "A Chance to Live."

By the time that I got down to Los Angeles, they were doing the editing on the movie. With what they had, I basically started to build the concept for ad campaigns and brochures.

One day they showed me all of their footage. I took one look at it and I said, "Jon Emr, you're going to die with this thing," because I must tell you, this was a real piece of shit. I felt now, that since they were paying me something, I had the right to voice my opinion. He would tell me that he was an experienced producer and I was just a distributor.

But it was odd. Jon seemed to think that he was, well, Michael Douglas. He had an ego that would not stop. But what he had was a disaster. First of all it was too long. Bunch of people talking. I told him that we had to make it into a bunch of segments like on "20/20." Then I told him, Jeez, we had to get some actual footage from Asia.

Well, they sent this guy over to Asia to do some filming. He didn't do anything. They couldn't keep this guy out of the whorehouses over there. Boy, I wish it had been me over there. I knew exactly what the film needed. But Jon didn't want to hear any of this. He'd just get pissed at me, scream and yell, tell me that he never wanted to speak to me again.

It was almost as though Jon wanted the film to fail. And there was something else. I was loaning Jon my credit card. He'd charge up meals and such on it. I was very uncomfortable, although basically Jon didn't beat me out of a dime. I wouldn't let him.

And Joel? Hell, the more I was around Joel, the more I could see that the only reason he was possibly in the position he was in was because of family. One day Jon told me that Joel would be nowhere were it not for daddy and big brother. Hey, I knew more about production than him.

I had to prove my point. So, I sent a copy of what we had to Fries Entertainment. I think that the guy's name was Harry Frederick. This guy told me, "It ain't gonna fly."

So, I met with Jon and Joel at the commissary. I told those two yahoos, "I'm ready to walk. You two can wallow in your crap if you want, but I don't want to get involved with it." And you know what? They looked at me and Jon was just kind of mellow. Couldn't care less. I told him he had a piece of shit that nobody wanted and he could not care less. How about that?

As shitty as this movie was, I figured that I had an obligation to do marketing on "A Chance to Live." Well, one day I say to Jon, "Why in the hell don't we get this thing geared up and done and go over to Cannes and get some foreign sales done on this?"

In March at about the time that Aubrey was beginning to lose all of his patience and all of his confidence in both the "Jonah" and "A Chance to Live" projects, he was contacted by Jon Emr, who had great news. "A Chance to Live" was finished and he, Aubrey, was invited to the invitation-only world premiere.

On Friday, March 14, 1986, the same day that Jon Emr had scheduled the very first showing of "A Chance to Live," a little item appeared in Army Archerd's column in *Daily Variety*. Archerd, famous for introducing celebrities as they walked down the red carpet into the Academy Awards, was the owner of the most potent column in town. In the modern film era, Army was the closest thing that Hollywood had to a Louella Parsons or a Hedda Hopper. Among his closest friends were the Douglases. So it was without reservation that he took Joel's word for it when "Kirk's boy" asked him to place the following item:

"After co-producing *Jewel of the Nile* and before starting 'Conquistador' [a project touted as 'the largest miniseries ever'] with brother Michael, Joel Douglas reveals an under wraps film he and Jon Emr have just completed, 'A Chance to Live.' It's the true story of the MIAs and 'live' American POWs, says Douglas. 'It's 21 years of work containing information there are live POWs.' The film was made in Vietnam, Cambodia, the Laotian border, Bangkok, DC, Georgia, and LA and was financed by a group in Texas including Aubry [*sic*] Brothers and Bob Franks. Douglas is talking to the nets and screening it tonight at Tony Bill's."

Jon was sure that Aubrey would be delighted to see the item in print, even if they had misspelled his name. In any case, even if Aubrey couldn't care less about the press that "A Chance to Live" was now getting, this would be a major clipping to hold on to. The kiss of Army Archerd was like the kiss of God.

Aubrey arrived at the screening via limousine, a big, long mother, that Jon had arranged for him. Aubrey was one of the first to arrive. There were no members of the press waiting at the doors, as Jon had predicted. That was okay with Aubrey. He didn't need to be in the public eye. Not now, anyway. Aubrey stood by the door, waiting, wanting to catch a glimpse of the power brokers, the savvy elite, as they made their way into the screening room for this major event, this first major screening of THE NEW JON EMR FILM!

He saw limo after limo make its appearance. Chauffeurs popped out of their doors like groundhogs and scurried around to the other side. And out came . . . well, nobody really. Nobody, that is, in the sense of who is somebody in Hollywood. Aubrey recognized a few of the people. There were a few of Jon's relatives and some of his buddies whom he had met in the course of the past year. But, mostly, Aubrey was in a fog over who was piling into the screening room.

The most famous person who Aubrey saw walk in was Colonel Jack Bailey. Aubrey had seen photos of Jack in the prospectus of "A Chance to Live." It seemed that for years Bailey had devoted his life to the search for Americans who were still being held captive in Indonesia. Wasn't Bailey the man who Jon claimed had "fucked" things with Ross Perot? Aubrey asked himself.

Colonel Jack showed up rather late. His ten-year-old Toyota had engine trouble along the I-10 freeway. Aubrey wondered why Jon had not ordered a limo for him. Tim and Jean Johnson, whom Aubrey had come to admire and grow quite fond of, did not arrive at all. They were not invited.

For the next half hour, Aubrey knocked back a few beers at the open bar that had been set up right outside the screening room. Aubrey talked with a few people who moseyed up to him. But he didn't know who they were and wasn't terribly interested in finding out.

Eventually, Jon found Aubrey. "Aubrey," Jon told him, "you are going to be resting very easily after you see this film."

"Well, good," Aubrey bellowed. "GO-OOOD!!" These were the words that he needed to hear.

"As a matter of fact, Aubrey, I've got some pretty terrific news." Jon slid his arm around Aubrey's shoulder and gave him a bit of a squeeze. "The networks are chomping at the bit to get this series. You're going to be making a great deal of money."

"Millions!" Aubrey said, as he hoisted his beer toward the ceiling. "Millions and millions!"

As Aubrey walked into the screening room, he, like everybody else, received a wristlet that was emblazoned with the name of an MIA. Aubrey was touched by the gesture. Before Aubrey took his seat in the relatively small screening room, Jon pointed out Kirk Douglas. Aubrey nodded. By God! There he was. Aubrey decided to remain cool. After all, despite Douglas's stature, Aubrey was a producer and Kirk an actor.

Aubrey was placed in a seat that was about three rows ahead of Kirk Douglas. Along with the other "VIPs," Aubrey sat in a comfortable chair and was musing over the honor of being among the first to witness one of the most important motion picture events of the century, a film that would perhaps alter the course of American history. A motion picture that was in the muckraking tradition of William Randolph Hearst. "A Chance to Live" was destined to open the eyes of Hollywood and the world—Washington in particular—to a national disgrace.

Aubrey was momentarily delighted when he saw his and Bob Franks's names as producers. He had to give himself a little congratulatory pat on the back for that. But, then, of course, came the rest of the film, which was a sad business indeed.

"A Chance to Live" simply went on and on. Talking head after talking head. Some of the talking heads were not even interviews. They were men and women at podiums giving speeches at fund-raisers. And the talking heads droned on for minutes at a time. Bobby Garwood, whom many had considered to be a traitor (he was the last prisoner of war released from Vietnam and was charged and convicted of collaborating with the enemy), was given a stage to drone on. Crazy Bob Dornan, a California congressman, went on and on, inarticulate as could be. And as hard as he looked, Aubrey Brothers could not find even a single shot of Robert Redford or Clint Eastwood, who Emr had claimed would be in the movie.

But Aubrey did see one recognizable face. Could it really have been who he thought it was? Could it be possible that up there on the screen was . . . Jon Emr? Yessir. That was Jon all right, portraying a weeping

POW. In the background, a preposterous melodramatic title song moaned along. In the same montage, Jon made a second appearance. In a complete non sequitur, he was kissing his girlfriend, Suzanne Fellows, on a pier.

As he watched the video, Aubrey kept reminding himself that he was, after all, no expert on the film business and that, hell, maybe he was watching some sort of nouveau artistic masterpiece. He'd wait to see how the Hollywood regulars in the screening room reacted to the film.

Jon's and Joel's families and friends *did* react. Cheers, clapping, whistles. This was an amazing ovation, truly stunning! Aubrey felt compelled to join in. Might as well. Aubrey just figured that he was wrong about the movie and that he should just leave things of this nature to the pros like Jon Emr and Joel Douglas.

As he got up to leave, Aubrey wiped away some imaginary dust on his jacket. He was still flummoxed. He nevertheless had to ask himself if he had pissed away all of his money.

As he walked up the aisle, he ran into Kirk Douglas. Joel made the introduction. "Dad, this is Aubrey Brothers. He's one of our investors."

Kirk shook his hand warmly. "Aubrey," he said in that familiar, gritty voice. "How are you?"

"Oh, I'm just fine." Motherfucker! Shakin' hands with Kirk Goddamn Spartacus Douglas! "So, what did you think?"

"Good. I think it's good. Real important stuff" is how Aubrey remembers Kirk's opinion.

Then Kirk Douglas smiled and he patted Aubrey on the back and moved along. Well, Aubrey thought to himself, if Kirk Douglas liked it, then, well, who in the name of God am I to argue?

He went back to the bar and knocked back a few with Emr. After a few minutes, Jon asked Aubrey for a favor. "My people tell me that we should take this film to the Cannes film festival. I was wondering if you would consider funding the trip."

"Absolutely!" Aubrey said with an explosion of warmth. "Why, I think maybe I'll join you."

"Uh, yes, well, see, Aubrey, I don't think that will work," Jon said. "I have already checked into this. I have spoken to the, uh, American embassy over there and they say that there are going to be just a shitload of riots and that they could not protect all of us. So, it's best if maybe it's just Richard Nash, Joel, and I."

Aubrey grinned. "How much you need?" he asked before writing Emr a check for $50,000.

A few days before Richard Nash and Joel Douglas were scheduled to leave for Cannes, France, Aubrey Brothers received a flyer in the mail. In a note, Jon explained that it was going to be distributed all over the festival. Here is a portion of that flyer allegedly quoting Kirk Douglas and also hyping the production:

> KIRK DOUGLAS said of the special "A Chance To Live," ". . . it will make you laugh, it will make you cry, it will make you angry. It is the most powerful film I have ever seen on the subject of the POW's/MIA's [*sic*]."
>
> After nine months of shooting and editing under tight security, producers R. Jon Emr and Joel Douglas (co-producer, with his brother Michael Douglas of "Jewel of the Nile") are now ready to market the first of 26 television specials, the pilot being on the highly controversial MIA/POW issue.

A Fiasco in Culver City:
Late July 1991

*I like persons better than principles—and persons with no principles
better than anything else in the world.*
—George Sanders in *The Picture of Dorian Gray*

What Sergeant Hank Davies of the Culver City Police Department really wanted was a funeral. Funerals were key to any homicide investigation. At the funeral, a detective got to meet all of the deceased's associates at once. At a funeral, it would be possible to spread out all of his business cards. For all he knew, he might even give his card to the killer. Killers often attended funerals. Maybe they went because they felt remorse. Maybe because they felt that their absence would be conspicuous. Perhaps they showed up because there were other people with whom they had a score to settle. Or maybe they just wanted to check out their handiwork.

Whatever, Davies wanted a funeral and a few days after the murders he began to consistently badger Renee Emr about what plans she had for the bodies of Jon, Roger, and her husband, Art. Each time, Davies got the same answer. "We're still trying to make plans. There's a problem with the coordination."

There was another problem. Her name was Gloria Farrens. Years earlier, Gloria had married John Emr, had his two children, divorced him, and then entered into an ugly sixteen-year custody battle in which the combatants traded charges of kidnapping and Satanism. Gloria Farrens heard about the death of her ex-husband and her son from her friend Jean Johnson, Jon's former business partner.

Davies began his phone relationship with Gloria when he called to question her about Jon Emr. When she asked Hank if he could help her reach her son Bobby, Gloria was told that that would just not be possible. Both Bobby and Renee were in seclusion. In any case, Renee claimed that Bobby did not want to hear from his mom at all. He hadn't really seen her since he was a baby and, after the things he had heard about her from Jon and Renee, he wanted to have nothing to do with her.

On the Monday after the murder, the coroner was ready to release the bodies from the morgue in downtown Los Angeles. For a full week, Gloria assaulted Davies with phone calls, wanting to know what was being done about the remains of her dead son, Roger. Every time, Hank would have to tell her that Renee had not made any decision.

Then word started to filter back to Gloria that Renee was broke and therefore unable to bury either Jon or Roger. So Gloria bit the bullet. She placed a phone call to Jon's brother, Art Jr., her former brother-in-law, and a man who she knew despised her. She left a message on his machine.

By Thursday morning, the coroner was starting to get in on the action. He wanted to know what the hell was going to happen with these bodies, which were taking up space in the morgue. There were about two hundred refrigerated caskets and they were all full. The only space available was in the hallway, which was itself starting to get crowded, and the ever-popular Decomp Room, used for bodies already rotted away. The absolute, categorical maximum amount of time the coroner normally kept a body was thirty days. Usually he'd have a body in and out in a couple of days. Now he wanted the rotting corpses of Jon and Roger out. Davies was, of course, unable to help him.

Eventually, Gloria called Hank Davies with a very good question. What would happen if *nobody* came forward to take care of the bodies? Hank explained to Gloria that if nobody from the immediate family did anything with the bodies, they would have to be placed in a common grave—a pauper's grave. The one that Jon and Roger would go to was in East Los Angeles. They would each get a little slab with their name and date of birth on it. A nondenominational clergyman would make sure that there was some dignity to their burial.

Gloria determined that just could not happen. Not to her son anyway. Frankly, whatever happened to Jon's body was not important to her. She was nonetheless terribly concerned about Roger.

So she came up with her own idea. Roger's body would be removed from the morgue to a mortuary, cremated, and then the ashes would be buried in her home state of Ohio. Gloria's family owned several plots in a very nice cemetery there. Roger could have one of them.

Of course, Gloria would be making a rather symbolic point. At last, she would be in union with her son, the one who she felt had been illegally pried away from her when he was a child. Gloria made all of the necessary arrangements and then left a message on Art's machine in Malibu. She told Art that she had made plans for Roger to be cremated and that she was eager for Bobby to come and view the body.

It did not take long for Renee to find out what Gloria was up to. She called the mortuary, full of fury, threatening to sue them if they allowed Gloria the privilege of burying her son. The next day Renee and Bobby marched right into the morgue, carrying a will—a will written by the late Roger Emr, a child barely out of his teens. Remarkably, the will dealt with, wouldn't you know it, the very issue at hand. If Roger actually wrote the will, then he had apparently insisted that it be his brother, Bobby, who would bury him.

Renee and Bobby demanded Roger's corpse. The coroner did not immediately turn over the body. He told them that he would get back to them shortly. Then he contacted Hank Davies and told him the wacky story.

"I understand that you have finally decided to take the bodies," Hank said to Renee when he called to question her about the incident.

Renee's claim was that Gloria had no right! No right!

"All right, all right. But, Renee, what is a young man like Roger doing with a will?"

Renee claimed that both of Jon's sons had wills. Her explanation was that the boys just wanted to make sure that if anything should happen to either of them, then the other would take care of things.

"Okay, Renee. Please contact me and let me know when and where the service will take place."

Renee assured Hank that she would.

When Hank contacted Gloria, she was grief-stricken but unwilling to fight. In the end, she concluded, it was indeed brother Bobby who had the right to bury his brother.

Davies told the coroner to release the bodies of the two men to Renee and Bobby Emr.

"I'll tell you what," the coroner said to Davies, "if you want a dysfunctional family, you've got a beaut right here. What happened to this family that got them to be such a mess?"

Davies thought for a second. "Hollywood."

The Cons of Jon Emr:
Robert Duvall and Richard Nash, 1987

There's a coup in the air!
—Jorge Luke in *Salvador*

FROM INTERVIEW WITH RICHARD NASH

So Joel Douglas and I went to Cannes. We used Aubrey's money, which I felt guilty about. Jon said business was business.

We set up a small booth. In the entire time, I don't remember one person stopping by and talking to us. Maybe that's because we had a VCR and a television and we were showing our movie, which was this piece of shit. I mean, I didn't want to show it, but Joel said, "Let's put it on!"

Look, I knew that it was an impossibility that we were going to sell this package. But, hey, my way was being paid and I was in France. Hell, we were staying at this place that was costing us—costing Aubrey $125 a night.

Well, I was running around and visiting the different booths and people that I knew over there, trying to sell our, uh, movie. I actually had a few people who were interested—people who hadn't been to the booth and actually seen it. In fact, I had a couple of contracts that were written up for Joel to sign but he wouldn't. I don't know why. I was so fed up, I was ready to leave two days before the whole thing was over.

I talked to Jon a couple of times. I told him, "Hey, things are not so good." He says, "That's not what Joel tells me." "Well, I don't care what Joel says. No sales!" So then, just like that, he says, "Okay, let's cut our losses." He's absolutely resigned to the fact that "A Chance to Live" is dead.

Now, I had one more hope. There was a fellow that I knew down at Turner Broadcasting in Atlanta. And you know what. He was willing to buy it. I mean, he knew it was awful, but there was footage that he could use in news broadcasts. The guy said to me, 10 grand, take it or leave it. I was excited. I mean, I was getting some money back for Jon. But, he said "no." Never understood that.

A few days after the Turner Broadcasting debacle, Jon Emr fired Richard Nash without paying him a huge chunk of the money still owed him. In addition, Nash was left holding the bag on several marketing bills—such as printing and design fees. Without anywhere to turn, Nash called Aubrey and asked him for some help.

Aubrey accommodated Richard Nash. But by now he and Bob Franks had just about had enough. What pushed them over the edge then was when Tim Johnson and his mother, Jean, told Aubrey about their own problems with Jon.

According to Tim and Jean Johnson, Jon had simply abducted many pieces of equipment from the studio and had brought them to his apartment. In addition, Emr had signed a letter guaranteeing the safety of the Johnsons' equipment when his "team" went to Thailand to do some shooting. That equipment was never returned.

Tim had personally gone to Joel Douglas's office on the Twentieth Century Fox lot to plead his case. Tim was crying as he explained that the equipment was everything he had in the world and that Jon had simply stolen it. Joel called Jon and essentially told him that he was disgusted with Tim Johnson and wanted him fired. Remarkably, Jon told Joel that he wanted to keep Tim on board. Joel told Tim that he would simply have to deal with the issue of Jon's having the equipment. Otherwise he'd be fired. As Tim recalled, Joel said to him, "There are at least twenty people who would love to be in your shoes right now."

Tim left with his tail between his legs. Tim would never again see his equipment.

It is a testimony to the complex lure of Hollywood that, even after all of their troubles and suspicion of Jon Emr, Jane Favor and Bob Franks extended their relationship with Jon.

On March 20, 1987, Jon signed a new agreement with the people whom he referred to as "my Texans." In broad strokes, the letter authorized Rutledge to form an escrow fund into which investors could deposit their cash. Specifically, Jon claimed to have a relationship with an Austin-based financier named Felix Ajebo. Though Ajebo never actually invested in "Jonah" or "A Chance to Live," he sparked up a positive rapport with Bob Franks. If he just found the right project, Ajebo promised Franks, he would be more than happy to invest. Ajebo, like everybody else, wanted to play ball in Hollywood.

Ajebo got his opportunity in the spring of 1987. Jane Favor had run into an old friend of hers. Brad Wilson was the son-in-law of an ancient country singer named William "Lefty" Frizzell. A few years earlier, Robert Duvall, who was researching his role as a Texas crooner in *Tender Mercies*, a role which would eventually earn him an Oscar, located Lefty's daughter. *Tender Mercies* director Bruce Beresford was interested in using a never-recorded or published Frizzell song called "It Hurts to Face Reality" over the credits of the film. During his stay in Dallas, Duvall became chummy with Brad Wilson and eventually hired him as his right-hand man.

One day, while Brad Wilson and Jane Favor were talking, Brad brought up the fact that Robert Duvall had written a screenplay called "The Apostle E. F. Hart." This was the actor's absolute dream project, one in which he would star and direct. The story deals with a southern evangelist out of Dallas who spends most of his time on the road. One day he comes home and discovers that his wife is having an affair with another minister. In a fit of rage, the evangelist beats the bejesus out of the minister and puts him in a coma. He then drives off, away from his wife and kids and the comatose minister, and moves into a small Texas gulf town and starts up a black church. The characters were based on several people whom Duvall had researched over the years.

Robert Duvall had directed only one film. Made in 1983, it was called *Angelo, My Love* and dealt with the twelve-year-old son of a New York City gypsy. Though a box office failure, the film nonetheless received widespread critical acclaim. Duvall was ready to tackle his next project and "The Apostle" was going to be it. As his costars, Duvall was looking at Wilford Brimley and Ann Wedgeworth, an eclectic actress who had appeared in small art films like *Scarecrow* with Gene Hackman and *Bang the Drum Slowly* with Robert De Niro. Duvall, Wilson, and a man named Robert Greenly (who was a friend of Duvall's assistant director on *Angelo, My Love*) formed a corporation called

Texanna with an eye toward making the film. The name was born of the fact that the film would be shot in Texas and Louisiana. The small group had already invested some $50,000 in their search for the film's production funds, mostly in legal fees and travel costs.

Greenly and Wilson had spent nearly every day for the past few months headquartered in Duvall's two-story apartment on West Eighty-sixth Street in New York City. It was a simple but large, wood-paneled place that was serving as Duvall's office and the headquarters for the Texanna Corporation. Years ago, the apartment had belonged to the great opera singer Enrico Caruso.

Jane Favor brought news of Duvall's dream project "The Apostle E. F. Hart" to Bob Franks who, in turn, contacted Ajebo. Ajebo was elated. Not only did the script appeal to him but Duvall's involvement seemed to guarantee the film would be in the black within a few days of its release. After several telephone meetings Ajebo told Jane and Bob that he would finance the movie with $7.5 million. The money would be wired to Bank Leumi in New York City the day after Memorial Day. Earl Rutledge would handle the legal matters for Bob Franks and Felix Ajebo.

Robert Duvall was ecstatic about the news. As a Hollywood veteran, he had witnessed firsthand the very slow process by which films are financed. But "The Apostle E. F. Hart" looked as though it was coming together swiftly and efficiently. For some reason, Duvall and his associates had faith in Earl Rutledge, Bob Franks, and this "mysterious" Felix Ajebo whom they had never met. In fact, Texanna had even rented out office space and opened a production headquarters in Dallas, Texas.

On Memorial Day, 1987, Earl Rutledge, Jane Favor, and Bob Franks flew into New York City to be there for what they hoped would be the closing of the deal. Throughout most of the day, the lawyers went through the "deal points" in great detail. Even though Duvall's group was spending quite a bit in legal fees, they were satisfied that their money would be repaid in spades. After all, since Earl Rutledge was an attorney, it was clear to them that Ajebo must *also* have been spending money to make money.

Duvall invited everybody to dinner at Le Cirque, where the mood was jovial and high-spirited. A few times Duvall whispered to his brother, who was also his attorney, "Now, this means it's for sure . . .

right?" Each time his attorney would nod in the affirmative. "That's what it means," he would say. By the end of the night, the champagne was flowing. Robert Duvall finally had the project that was born deep in his heart ready to roll. Bob Franks all of a sudden found himself as the mover and shaker he must have thought Jon Emr would make him.

The next day, Robert Duvall, Rob Greenly, Brad Wilson, Bob Franks, Jane Favor, and Earl Rutledge waited for the money transfer to come in. According to Ajebo's bank, $7.5 million had been wired. Nevertheless, it never landed in Bank Leumi. Throughout the course of the day both Rutledge and Rob Greenly made several calls to Ajebo, who kept stalling them. As Greenly would later say, "He was very evasive. He said he was very busy. It was one of those tomorrow, tomorrow deals."

Robert Duvall was the first to say to the dispirited group that there would be no tomorrow. "Something is fishy," Duvall said. "This money is never going to show up."

The next day the Texans went home, both shocked and embarrassed. According to the people on Robert Duvall's team, Jon Emr's investor Felix Ajebo had mysteriously fallen off the face of the earth. To this date, the money that allegedly left Ajebo's bank has never been recovered.

"The Apostle E. F. Hart" has "almost" been financed several times, but it still remains only in script form. The Texanna Corporation still exists.

With their suspicions and animosity toward Jon Emr having grown to their limits, Aubrey Brothers and Bob Franks did what they probably wished they had done two years earlier. They showed their contract with Emr and laid out their experiences to an expert in the movie industry, a man named Vern Nobles who had come recommended by Tim and Jean Johnson.

On March 2, 1987, Vern Nobles laid out his thoughts in an extraordinary six-page, single-spaced letter, which is excerpted here:

Dear Aubrey:

First of all, I'd like to thank you for your true Texas style hospitality. You made me feel right at home and welcome.

As a member of the motion picture community, I was appalled at the unprofessional, unbusinesslike treatment you obviously have received from someone who has claimed to be a part of that industry, First, let me say this, I can find no record that would indicate that he, Jon Emr, is in fact a part of this industry. And it is men like him who continually cast a shadow on those who are professionals in this business. . . .

Let's examine what Emr-Douglas did with your $350,000. First of all, there was no production budget to determine that, in fact, it would cost that amount. Standard industry procedures calls for a script to be written . . . and, from that, a production schedule and budget break-down is executed. . . . Unfortunately, it is written in your contract that you have no control over how that money is to be spent. When [Tim and Jack Johnson] asked why there was no budget available to them, they were told that it was none of their damned business. . . .

My estimate for the total production cost, everything included, would be approximately $185,000. I guess what I am asking is, one, if they did not pay all of the bills, and I can only account for $150,000, stretching the imagination, where did the rest of the money go???? . . .

A few days after they received the letter from Vern Nobles, Aubrey Brothers and Bob Franks went to see Earl Rutledge. It was obvious that Jon Emr had taken them to the cleaners. They wanted a little pay-back.

In his letter to Aubrey Brothers, Vern Nobles had asked a simple and very good question: "Where did the rest of the money go?"

Aubrey Brothers and Bob Franks had no smoking gun and no paper trail to suggest exactly where their money went. There was, however, a great deal of circumstantial evidence. First, there were the persistent claims that Jon was a cocaine abuser and that much of the cash may have gone straight up his nostrils and into his brain. Second, Jon was driving a white Trans Am during the "production" of "A Chance to Live" and he bought his girlfriend, Sue, a black model. Third, there was the matter of the Judson School, the expensive and exclusive pri-vate boarding school that Jon Emr's children attended. At the same time Arthur and Renee Emr bought an estate in Paradise Valley, Ari-zona, which came with a pool. The home, which was located about two miles from the Judson School, cost almost $200,000. When I met with

Renee Emr, she produced a document that indicated that the house was not paid for in full and that, in fact, a down payment of only $40,000 was the only cash she and her husband put out. Oddly, the document she gave me was undated, did not have the names of the Emrs on it, and was unsigned.

EXCERPT FROM THE DEPOSITION OF IRA MILLER
ATTORNEY FOR JON EMR

Q: [Jon Emr] told the whole world he was a producer?

A: Yes.

Q: What, to your knowledge, has he ever produced?

A: To my knowledge, "A Chance to Live."

Q: Now, he represented himself to be a producer before the "A Chance to Live" project came along, didn't he?

A: Yes, he did. . . .

Q: Did you ever check to see if he, in fact, had been a producer for 19 years?

A: No.

Q: At the time Mr. Emr first came to you respecting "Jonah," did you have knowledge of any documents or associations to whom you or anyone else could go to determine an individual's credits as a producer, director, or writer?

A: No.

Q: And "Chance to Live" is all you know of that he has credits to his name?

A: Personal knowledge, yeah.

Earl Rutledge walked into his office after a day at a civil trial and picked up his messages. Among the batch was one from a man named Scott Barnes. The note said that Barnes was a private investigator. Earl did not even consider returning the call. He did not know this man and, anyway, it was standard procedure for him to receive calls from P.I.s looking for work.

Two days later, Earl was working in his office. The phone rang and he picked up his own line. The man on the other end said that his name was Scott Barnes.

"I have some information that might be useful to you," Barnes suggested. "I understand that you represent some people who might be interested in suing a man out of California named Jon Emr. Well, I want you to know that I had a similar experience and from what I know he's not for real and you might want to advise your clients that if you are thinking of investing any more with him to be very careful."

"We certainly will."

"If you need any help, you know where to find me."

An Interview in Torrance:
July 13, 1991

Occasionally, we find a patient who can't wake up. He or she lacks insight, the ability to distinguish between what is real and what isn't. Now, that may be true in your case.
—Stanley Ridges to Joan Crawford in *One Man's Secret*

Although Sergeant Hank Davies could find no direct evidence that the mysterious Scott Barnes had anything whatsoever to do with the murder of the Emrs, he was still a suspect. His name had come up far too many times from too many different individuals to simply rule him out.

What really confused Hank Davies was that in his search through the files of the Culver City Police Department he had actually found a restraining order between Barnes and Emr. The order was dated March 26, 1991, a few months before the murder. Davies was beginning to get the impression that Scott Barnes was, if not directly involved in the murder, certainly a key to understanding what had happened. Strangely, Barnes was nowhere to be found. Even Scott's older brother, Craig, a Redondo Beach cop, had no idea where he was.

The much-sought-after Scott Barnes popped up in Southern California about a week after the death of the three Emrs. It was a telling point that Barnes had made contact with several journalists, myself included, before he ever met or even placed a call to Sergeant Hank Davies.

While I was setting up my interview with Barnes, he told me that, indeed, he considered Jon Emr a crook. "But nobody deserves to die quite like that," he added. "I'm no advocate of murder."

What Scott Barnes failed to tell me was that shortly after Jon Emr and his son Roger were murdered, he had called his younger brother, Brian, and said, according to Brian, "Jon Emr's dead and I'm sitting here with a glass of champagne and celebrating. Hee-hee-hee."

An hour after our scheduled meeting time at the Torrance Marriott, Scott Barnes came ambling into the lobby. He was wearing tight-fitting shorts, a well-worn safari shirt, and thongs. His beard needed some serious trimming and his hair looked mangled and unclean. He was carrying a brown paper bag that was filled with loose documents.

The first words of note that came out of Scott Barnes were these: "How am I gonna be compensated for my time?"

I explained to Scott that it was my policy, in fact the policy of all legitimate journalists, not to pay sources. It bastardized the journalistic process. Scott then asked me, "Will you mention my book?"

"Your book?"

Scott pulled out a massive tome from his bag. It was called *Bohica*.

"Sure," I said. "Does this book have any connection to Jon Emr?"

Scott giggled. "Hee-hee-hee. He tried to steal it from me!" he said.

After we sat down to eat, I turned on the tape recorder. "Okay, Scott. Just for the record, you are a private investigator?"

"I do international investigations. And I wrote a book called *Bohica*."

"And that's how you became connected with Emr?"

"That's correct. A *60 Minutes* producer had said that Jon Emr and his mother, Renee, had been trying to locate me, that they wanted to possibly sign a movie deal on my book."

"And *Bohica* is about what?" I wondered, staring down at the seven-hundred-page book that was sitting on the table next to us.

"It's about a prisoner of war rescue mission that I was involved in in 1981, on behalf of the United States government, the CIA, and the ISA [Intelligence Support Agency]. It was basically an intelligence-gathering team to confirm or deny the existence of American prisoners of war. Subsequently, we confirmed they were there and the team was ordered to stand down after an order to assassinate."

From there, I may as well have just let the tape recorder run. Barnes's basic claim was this: Jon was a con artist who preyed on two emotional issues, the Hollywood dream and the MIA-POW issue.

And there was more. He claimed Jon was a pornographer, a drug trafficker, and a drug merchant. He insisted Jon was a money launderer who had his millions stashed in the Cayman Islands. Hell, Jon had even *confessed* all of this to him. Barnes told me that he had begun to contact everybody he could find who had been connected with Emr in order to warn them off him.

Barnes wouldn't give me names of Jon's other victims, claiming that some of these people were very famous and powerful and a bit embarrassed. "I talked to the DEA, notified the FBI. They already knew about him. I found out from American Express that they had a major investigation on the whole Emr clan for credit card fraud." I subsequently learned that only Jon, not his family, was investigated.

Then Scott dropped an outrageous bombshell that I later learned was totally untrue. He said Frank Sinatra may have been involved in the murder of Jon Emr. Other celebrity names started popping out of Barnes's mouth: Kirk Douglas, Chuck Norris, Glen Campbell, H. Ross Perot, Martin Sheen, Ralph Macchio. That was just naming a handful.

Near the end of our conversation, Scott pulled out a whole packet of material that he would turn over to me and later to the police. "This was sent to me on July 8," he said.

I looked at the cover letter.

Scott:

You were right about Jon Emr. . . . Enclosed is evidence that Jon hired me to ruin you. . . . Yes! He screwed me too!

Then I glanced down at the signature. It belonged to Suggs.

Mere hours after my meeting with Scott, his brother, Brian, somehow having attained my unlisted number, phoned to tell me that I should be very careful of his brother. Brian said that Scott had ruined many of the lives with whom he had crossed paths. He faxed me Barnes's arrest record and some letters that Scott had written him from Chino State Prison. Brian also sent me some newspaper clippings from the Bakersfield *Californian* about Scott and his credibility, or lack thereof.

My conversations with Brian would continue for the next three years. For several charges that Brian made about Scott, his brother would retaliate. For example, Scott had faxed to me an arrest report which had *Brian* being charged with statutory rape. Scott even tried to convince me that Brian was actually the number one suspect in the murder of Jon Emr.

The feuding between the Barnes brothers seemed almost to be a Shakespearean tragedy. It made no sense to me at first. Then I learned something that put it all into perspective. Brian Barnes used to work for Jon Emr.

Nevertheless, given Brian's charges, I made several phone calls in the early days of my investigation to people who knew Scott Barnes. The most consistent thing that I heard about him was that he was a pathological liar and a meddler of the highest order.

Scott Barnes's book, *Bohica*, is a whopper. Not just in its seven-hundred-page length, but in the outlandish allegations made within it. Barnes claimed that in 1981, fully seven years after he was discharged from his duties as a "correctional specialist" in the United States Army for "failing to meet basic military standards," he was recruited by the Intelligence Support Agency to participate in a mission to track down Americans who had been held as prisoners of war in Indochina ever since the Vietnam conflict. The ISA, for years a phantom top-secret agency, was created in 1980 to deal with the Ayatollah Khomeini's hostage games.

Barnes claimed that he and his partner, Jerry Daniels, made an heroic trek, swam across a turbulent river into Laos, where, Holy Jesus! they saw not one—but two Caucasians wearing American military insignia. Americans doing hard labor with Laotian guards supervising them! There they were, larger than life, caught in the scope of their binoculars. Then, Barnes says, he and Daniels took four hundred photos, using a special zoom lens camera. Wait till they see these back home!

But nobody would ever see the pictures. In fact, if Barnes is to be believed, three amazing things followed the "sighting." First, the CIA destroyed all the photos, burned them to ashes. Second, Jerry Daniels died in Thailand under most mysterious circumstances—something about gas poisoning. And then—the grand finale—the CIA asked Barnes to "liquidate the merchandise." That is, kill the Caucasians.

The book, published by Daring Books in Canton, Ohio, is half Barnes's accounts of his adventures in Thailand (and the subsequent attempts of the government to silence him); the other half is filled with hundreds of documents: diplomas from various correspondence courses, certificates of merit, military records, photos, letters to Congress, letters from Congress, testimony transcripts, résumés, and newspaper and magazine articles.

One of the articles comes from *Soldier of Fortune*. Even this sensational, conspiratorial, ultra-right-wing magazine decided that they had to rip Barnes's claims to shreds. An *SOF* reporter was in Thailand at the same time as Barnes. The reporter hung out with him, even surveilled him. His conclusion? Barnes never crossed the river between Thailand and Laos during his time there. In fact, he wrote, there wasn't even a river to cross.

The press was not the only institution to call Scott Barnes's bluff. The United States government had its own two bits to add to the Scott Barnes credibility profile. The Defense Intelligence Agency, an organization that Barnes claimed to have worked for, conducted the investigation. In 1988, the DIA went public with their assessment of *Bohica*. They put out a four-page letter—addressed to the League of Families, an organization representing the loved ones of POWs and MIAs— which has since found its way to any journalist or law enforcement official interested in information on Scott Barnes. Appearing on DIA letterhead and signed by Colonel Joseph Schlatter, the memo was absolutely devastating:

> ... In going over Bohica, I find that virtually every page is rife with total fabrications and misrepresentations. As is his usual practice, Barnes packs his narrative with names of public officials and U.S. government employees in such a way so as to create an illusion of credibility for his claims. Another device he uses is to devote almost two-thirds of the book to reprinting "official looking" documents; again to lead the naive reader to believe he is credible and privy to sensitive intelligence information.

Schlatter goes on to dissect several of Barnes's claims and allegations and dismisses them. For example:

> Bohica also references an "Operation Duck Soup" where a so-called CIA special team rescued an American PW [prisoner of war] in Laos,

but gave him back to his communist captors. There was no such mission in Indochina under the name of "Duck Soup" or any other name. In reality, "Duck Soup" was a U.S. Government initiative which took place in 1949 in another part of the world. It had no bearing whatsoever on U.S. Citizens or American PWs. . . .

But the strange tales of Scott Barnes were not limited just to his *Bohica* claims. Ever since the famous mission into Laos in 1981, Barnes has been involved in countless "incidents."

Take, as one example, the case of the CIA Maniacs. It's well detailed in a book called *Kiss the Boys Good-bye*, written by former *60 Minutes* producer Monika Jensen-Stevenson, the woman who had introduced Jon Emr to *Bohica*.

Here is what Jensen claimed happened on one winter night in Kernville, the small Northern California town where Barnes lived. A BBC producer named David Taylor—one of the few journalists who had bought into the Barnes Laos escapades—got a phone call from Scott Barnes in the dead of night. Barnes claimed that he had been stabbed and shot at. "They're coming after me, David! They're coming after me!" Apparently, CIA hoodlums had come to his home. After trying to do him in with a knife, they blew the hell out of his house. Scott, of course, returned fire.

According to Barnes, the person who tried to stab him to death was a pro, a real smoothie. The knife was meant to nick the bottom of his heart. "I'd have bled internally because all you'd see would be a small external cut. It's a technique." That was how Barnes would later explain it.

Barnes frantically explained that an expert marksman had shot up the house from the bushes. The fact that he just barely missed Barnes was not an accident: it was a message.

But, there was something that both Scott and the book left out. Something that would blow to smithereens the veracity of the CIA Maniacs story. The bullets that Barnes had claimed had been fired *into* his house had actually been fired from the *inside out*. A police report filed by a detective with the Bakersfield police (Kernville does not have its own police force) seems to insinuate that it was Scott himself who fired all of the bullets. In fact, the only shell casings that were found came from Scott's very own .357 Magnum.

Then there was the Rewald story. A Barnes classic. It occurred when Scott Barnes was working as a prison guard in Hawaii in 1984. Not long into his tenure, he went to ABC News and told them a story that got their sweeps-week glands salivating: The CIA had hired him to assassinate a prisoner named Ronald Rewald. Scott told ABC that he was finking on the CIA as a matter of principle. Imagine that! Killing a man for no good reason! ABC did not bother to ask Scott why the CIA, whom he had betrayed when he wrote *Bohica*, would want him back on their side.

ABC ran with the story. The day after it aired, William Casey, the head of the CIA, made a call to Capitol Cities, owners of ABC. He announced that he was reporting ABC to the FCC. The story, he said, was utter bullshit. He assured ABC News that it could count on a lawsuit.

ABC developed an unfortunate complication when Barnes decided that he did not want to take a polygraph. He would later claim that the reason he refused to take the test was that ABC would not make the results of the test "public."

A few nights later, ABC News was forced to recant its story.

Exposing the conspiracies of the government—true or false—is a favorite Barnes activity. When he was a cop with the Ridgecrest Police Department he created enough waves to be dismissed. Barnes claimed that he was let go because he was conducting his very own investigation of the chief of police for illegal gambling.

Barnes also worked for the El Cajon Police Department. He was released from duty there as well. His dismissal was a direct result of civil charges being brought against him and the department by the Mongols motorcycle gang.

Then there is the matter of Barnes's criminal past. He spent time in jail for "electronic eavesdropping," that is, making illegal tape recordings of phone conversations, in this instance twelve conversations between himself and government officials. Barnes was sentenced to one year in jail, though after spending a "time served" of 109 days, the rest of the punishment was suspended for three years.

During that time, Dennis Bartow, the man who had published *Bohica*, tried to raise funds for Barnes's legal debts by putting out a two-page flyer under the aegis of the "Faith Foundation: Friends Advocating Integrity, Truth and Honesty." Among other things, Bartow wrote:

Napoleon once said he followed the sounds of the guns to the battle, Well . . . the guns are booming and the battle is raging in Bakersfield, Calif.

The big guns of the government are zeroed in on our friend and deeply loyal American—Scott Barnes. It is as if he were facing the firing squad daily—and alone. He needs your help now!

. . . Please! Please! Send as much as you can. Send it today! The situation is desperate. . . .

A few years later, Barnes was arrested and convicted for false arrest and battery. Apparently, Barnes took umbrage when a repo man tried to take his brother's car away. He knocked the man to the ground, sat on his back, and then handcuffed him.

The very dramatic and seemingly insurmountable questions regarding the believability of Scott Barnes were never a secret. What then did Scott Barnes have going for him? If he spent years as a ranting, raving lunatic it was only because people were listening. Perhaps the only solid "evidence" about Barnes's involvement in the Laos mission is that he passed a polygraph test that was administered to him in 1982 by Dr. Chris Gugas, an expert in the field. Gugas was a former CIA employee who had also tested James Earl Ray and Robert Vesco.

Barnes took the test at the insistence of Ted Koppel, the erudite, British-born *Nightline* anchorman who was thinking about doing a three-part series on Barnes's adventures in the jungles of Indochina.

Why did Koppel decide not to put Barnes on the air? Koppel contends that even after Barnes beat the polygraph, the whole Laos thing sounded, well, fruity to him. Koppel conferred with his boss who told him that he had to meet Barnes face-to-face and come to his own conclusion.

Koppel flew out to California and had a series of meetings with Barnes. After listening to Barnes rant for hours and hours, Koppel simply deemed it all too wacky and just not worth the risk.

In 1992, Scott Barnes altered the course of American history. On July 16 of that year, H. Ross Perot withdrew his name from the presidential race. At the time, Perot may have been the most legitimate third-party candidate in American history. His approval rating was higher than either of his potential rivals, George Bush and Bill Clinton, and several polls had him winning the three-man race.

Perot's withdrawal was a shocker. He claimed that he was backing out because he was sure that his presence in the race would throw the election into the House of Representatives.

A few months later, he reentered the race. Eleven days before the general election I was contacted by Scott Barnes. He told me that the CBS newsmagazine *60 Minutes* was doing a piece about him and Perot. That turned out to be a bit of an exaggeration. In reality, Perot made the claim to the show's Leslie Stahl that he had originally gotten out of the race because of Republican "dirty tricks." Perot said that he had been told by two high-level Republicans and a Scott Barnes that the Republicans had not only wiretapped him but were going to pass out doctored photos of his daughter in a compromising position.

60 Minutes briefly profiled Barnes and effectively discredited him. The point that kept being hammered home was that Ross Perot believed Scott Barnes—that this man, running for the highest office in the land, was placing his faith and his trust in the hands of a lunatic, whom he had never actually met.

The episode proved a disaster for Perot. A *Newsweek* poll found that 48 percent of the voters felt that Perot relied on stories that were not backed up by evidence. Perot ended up with 19 percent of the electorate.

In May of 1993, Barnes phoned me at my office with the confession that the whole Perot affair was a hoax. Of course, there was a twist even to that. According to Barnes, Perot orchestrated the whole sad affair.

During my last conversations with Scott Barnes, he claimed to be "involved" in the Heidi Fleiss, Hollywood Madam imbroglio. What he was doing for her, however, was "top secret."

Clearly, Barnes was a man with little, if any, credibility. It was lucky, then, that most of the story he told me about his relationship with Jon Emr could be corroborated by other witnesses to the events. In fact, he gave to Hank Davies, who went to interview him at his mother's house two days after he met with me, exactly the same scenario he had given me.

October 1987. As their car knifed northward during their three-hour drive between Los Angeles and Kernville, California, Jon Emr and his girlfriend, Yoko Wright, noticed that the smog just seemed to cut off, as if it had fallen over the edge of a cliff. They had left the polluted world and entered a clean one within a matter of seconds.

This phenomenon occurred when they were crossing the border into Kern County, traveling on Route 178. The mountains, which were actually visible to them (no small feat, as the residents of Los Angeles County would make quite clear), were green and red and looked as they would on a topographic map. The deeper they got into the county, the more dense the foliage became. When they descended from the mountains, they found themselves in the flattest of flatlands. Great farming territory. As they drove, makeshift signboards, with advertisements for hay rides and indoor shooting ranges and guns at a 20 percent discount, drifted by them.

It was in the town of Bakersfield that they saw their first actual sign for Kernville. KERNVILLE, HOME OF THE WILD AND SCENIC KERN RIVER.

They cut through the mountains, the Sequoia Canyon of the sequoia National Forest, swerving over roads that appeared to have been laid out by an epileptic. This was a place that had seen a million rock slides. As the road narrowed, it seemed like the kind of location where Alfred Hitchcock would film an out-of-control car carrying Jimmy Stewart and Doris Day. A sign read DO NOT SWIM IN KERN RIVER. 158 DEATHS SINCE 1969. The numbers were on removable placards so that they could be changed at will, like the numbers on the McDonald's arches.

Before they entered Kernville, they first passed through the town of Wofford Heights (pop. 2,112), which is actually a major center for Kernville residents because it has the only movie theater for miles around. On the border between Wofford Heights and Kernville, there was yet another sign. WELCOME TO KERNVILLE. HOME OF WHISKEY FLAT. GOD BLESS OUR ARMED FORCES.

People have described Kernville as a one-horse town. That's an insult to horses across the world. It looks so much like those desolate towns in movie westerns that several episodes of *Bonanza* were filmed here. It's a town where people know exactly who has moseyed in, and what their business is once they have.

There is no real crime in this town, at least none that gets any attention anymore. There is an occasional burglary, though nobody remembers anybody being robbed at gunpoint or knifepoint. There was once a black woman from Bakersfield who spent a few hours in the Kernville Inn with a local resident and it became an immediate scandal. Had prostitution eked its way into town? The answer after investigation was no. At its most intense level, crime here is relegated to a store or warehouse being broken into late at night. But that's a real rarity. For the most part, people leave their keys in the ignition of their cars—almost all of them pickups—when they go and run their errands. Kernville doesn't even have a police station. When they need the police they have to call up the good folks in Bakersfield—the "big city" as they call it.

What keeps the economy of Kernville floating is the tourism. Before the river begins to run low during the late summer months, Kernville is the place to be for water sports enthusiasts. The locals will tell you that the Kern River is the fastest river per cubic foot in the entire United States. Great for rafting. Then, just a couple of miles up the road there is Lake Isabella, a massive body of water where windsurfing is the main order of business. During the week, the streets of Kernville are mobbed with tourists. The locals refer to downtown during the summer as "Bikini Alley."

Then there is the Sportsman's Inn, the hangout, the place to be, mostly because there is no other real bar (unless you count Ewing's, which, in reality, is a country-western dance joint). On the doors at the inn, there are signs written in longhand announcing that anybody under the age of 21 will be asked to leave. Not a major deal since the average age in the town is almost fifty.

In the back section of the inn there is a pool table standing on a slightly elevated platform. On the wall next to it is a mirror, which allows everybody to monitor the progress of whatever game is on. That's the entertainment. There isn't a television set in the Sportsman's Inn. The mountains surrounding Kernville make the cost of good reception prohibitive.

Jon Emr and Yoko Wright entered the bar and ordered a couple of drinks. Because there was no phone in the place, Jon had to travel a few hundred yards to get to the nearest and only pay phone in town, which was right by the post office. Jon felt lucky to have brought an umbrella with him. He'd never seen it rain so goddamn hard!

Emr dialed the number that he had for Scott Barnes. Scott was groggy when he answered the phone. But that didn't faze Jon. "He-ey, Scott Barnes! Jon Emr here!"

"Yeah, Jon," Scott said.

Jon explained to Scott that he was "trapped" in this bar and had no idea how to get to Scott's house. He asked Scott if he could come pick him and his "partner" up at the bar.

As Jon waited for Scott at the Sportsman's Inn he learned something about this kid Barnes. He learned the same thing as all journalists who had come to Kernville to investigate Barnes. Scott Barnes was not somebody to talk about. Mention the name and people move two or three barstools away, carrying their Bud Light by the bottleneck with them, thank you very much. It wasn't fear that caused this sensation. At least not the type of fear one gets when he's ratting on, say, a Mafioso. It was more a fear of getting involved in what was sure to be a complicated, sticky, and inescapable web. People who had tangled with Scott in Kernville eventually lived to regret it. The only group of people in Kernville who seemed to like Scott, really like him, were the waitresses at Cheryl's Diner, who loved the fact that Scott used to tip them ten bucks at a pop when he had cash. Scott had been the town "fat cat" for a while, running a very successful private eye business. He lost his license after his arrest and conviction for electronic eavesdropping.

Scott Barnes refused Emr's offer of a drink when he arrived at the bar. He told Jon he did not partake. Jon pointed to the pretty, middle-aged Japanese woman next to him. He told him that she was his partner Yoko Wright and that she was in charge of his foreign distribution.

Yoko nodded her head. "Hey," Scott said.

Barnes was not at all what Jon Emr expected. Instead of a beefy, Rambo look-alike, Barnes had a cherubic, Casper the Friendly Ghost look to him. A few months earlier, Emr had become aware of Barnes's account of his heroic mission into Laos. Could this actually be the hero of *Bohica?* It seemed unlikely. But, like he had always said, truth was often more interesting than fiction.

"Let's get out of here," Barnes said. "That's my car outside. Where are you guys staying?"

Jon explained that all the motels were booked solid. He said that he sure would appreciate it if they could spend the night at his place. Scott knew that Jon was lying. This was simply not the season for tourism. Still, Scott agreed and Jon Emr and Yoko Wright followed him up the winding roads to his home.

There is a world of difference between the homes in Kernville's valley and those that are either on the river or in the mountains. Scott's home was in one of the higher elevations, in a remote part of Kernville. About five years earlier he had bought it for $54,000, which seems like a bargain to most Los Angelenos, but is an outright fortune for the residents of Kernville. It has three bedrooms, a large living room–kitchen–eating area, and a garage that has been converted into his office.

The first thing that Scott pointed out to Jon and Yoko were bullet holes in the doorway. "We had quite a firefight here some time back," Scott said, referring back to his alleged altercation with the CIA Maniacs.

Jon rolled his thumb along the hole. "Is that right? Hmm. Motherfucker!"

Scott pointed out into the darkness. "They shot into the house from right over there. Good thing my kids were not here."

"Hmmm." Jon seemed oddly nonplussed. "Well, where can we stay?"

"You guys want to stay in the same room?"

"Sure."

"You're gonna sleep with your business partner?"

"Sure."

"Oh," Scott rolled his eyes. "Follow me."

Scott took them to a room that was bare save for a box spring, a mattress, a few blankets, and a couple of pillows. Jon pulled the mattress to the ground and told Yoko that she would be sleeping on the box spring.

A few minutes later, Jon came out into the living room where Scott was waiting for him. "Where's Yoko?" Scott asked Jon.

"She will be leaving us alone during the business negotiations. It's the Japanese way," Jon explained to Scott. Jon then unsnapped his briefcase and pulled out a gun and some cocaine, which he laid across a coffee table. He told Scott that sharing his cocaine was a sign of his goodwill. "I find that it is very relaxing before negotiating any sort of business."

"Well, not for these business negotiations." Scott slapped his knees and stood up. "We'll talk in the morning. I don't want to see any of that shit here tomorrow."

The next morning it didn't take long for Scott Barnes and Jon Emr to come to an agreement.* Scott plumb forgot about the cocaine and gun crisis from the night before. Maybe that had to do with the fact that Jon was calling him an "American Hero" and a model for his own children. Or maybe it was the fact that Jon told him that he'd love to buy the rights for his book for a deal that was worth $100,000. That was a mighty nice figure for Barnes, a man who right now had no food whatsoever in his fridge. However, what really impressed Scott Barnes, as it had impressed many before him, was the fact that Jon Emr was in partnership with Joel Douglas, he of the fabulous Douglas family!

Jon had brought with him at least five versions of a contract, each worded just a little bit differently. When Scott picked out the one that he wanted to sign, Jon told him that he had to just double-check with another one of his partners, a woman named Renee.

After he got off the phone with this Renee, Jon pulled out his checkbook. "Show time!" he said. He wrote Scott a check for $10,000. More money than young Scott had seen in years.

The first thing that Scott noticed was that the check itself had no company name, address, or imprint on it. Scott asked Jon what the hell that was all about.

"It's a new account." Jon smiled. "Here, this is what will make you happy." Then Jon simply wrote in "Emr-Douglas Productions" at the top left-hand corner of the check.

Talk to people in Kernville about the famous Barnes brothers and they will refer to Brian Barnes as "the good-looking one," "the kind one." On this day, Scott phoned the good-looking, kindhearted one at a restaurant that Brian owned called Inland Seafood, which had become

*Renee claims that Scott zealously pursued her and Jon to buy his film rights.

the favorite of the locals in Kernville. "I got somebody I want you to meet," Scott said to his little brother. "This is important. Real important. Can you whip up something nice?"

When the group got to the restaurant, Brian had already cooked and sautéed some scallops and bay shrimp and a little of every type of fish he had in the place. Scott introduced Brian to Jon and then took his brother to the side. "This is the guy that's buying my rights," he said. "He's a producer. A big-time producer with Emr-Douglas Productions." Scott grinned. "The guy just gave me ten thousand dollars." Then Scott showed his brother the check. "Can you fuckin' believe it?"

Before the dinner was served, Brian signed all the contracts as a witness.

During the meal, Jon started talking about his experiences in the martial arts. That was when Brian realized that he and Jon had something in common. They were both black belts and both had trained with the world's foremost judo expert, Gene LeBelle. In fact, both of them claimed that they had taken classes from Chuck Norris, the action superstar.

As soon as Jon learned that Brian was a martial arts enthusiast, the conversation quickly turned to the topic of the oriental fighting art. Brian claimed that he was a combative fighter, not an artistic one. "My whole idea is to get the fight over with. Boom. Shouldn't last more than a few seconds." Brian explained that one of his favorite moves is called oblique kick, which is a method of taking out an aggressor's knee.

Brian invited Jon to get up and they'd compare moves. Jon smiled. This was his kind of thing. Especially after the few beers and white wines.

And so there were Brian and Jon, leaping, kicking, punching, slamming the shit out of each other and loving it like a pair of sadomasochists. If Brian was combative, then Jon was more into stances and katas, which was all flowery movements and a little bit of footwork. Scott remained at the table, sipping on beer and white wine. Yoko, obedient Yoko, was doing the same. Every once in a while Scott would repeat the same joke, "I think a .357 Magnum does a better job." He was referring to the type of weapon that he owned.

When they sat back down, the conversation turned to business. Jon turned it on. He explained how his partnership with Joel Douglas worked. "This is the big honcho of the film industry," Emr assured everybody at the table. "The big honcho. Do you know the movie *Romancing the Stone?*"

Everybody did.

Jon put out his arms and enunciated every word. "A-Joel-Douglas-Production."

After some two and a half hours the night ended exuberantly. Jon Emr had made himself a new and close friend in Brian Barnes. Nobody knew it then, but it was the moment that the clock started ticking away on Roland Jon Emr's life.

A few days after his trip to Kernville, Jon gave a copy of Barnes's book *Bohica* to his brother, Art, to read. Jon respected his big brother. He felt that Art had instincts about the movie business that were right smack on the mark. Jon asked Art to peruse the seven-hundred-page opus just to see if he felt it was commercial.

"Well, what's your opinion?" Art asked his little brother as he took the book.

Jon laughed. "Fuck, I haven't even read it," he said. "I don't have the time for reading."

A few days before Thanksgiving, Jon invited both Scott and Art over to dinner at Yoko Wright's condominium in Rancho Palos Verdes, a wealthy suburb of Los Angeles. It would be an old-fashioned, brainstorming, motherfuckin' creative marathon session. They would all gather around and see what Art had to say about the book. It would be beautiful. By the end of the night, if everything went smoothly, *Bohica* would be ready to roll.

The meeting was to take place on Thanksgiving Day. By the time Art Emr arrived at the condominium, Jon and Scott were already there. It was clear to Art that Jon had already downed several drinks—probably Bloody Marys. As soon as Art walked through the door with his wife, Jenny, Jon wanted to know what he thought about the book.

Art did not come right out and say that Scott Barnes was a goddamn liar. All he said was that *Bohica* was a hell of a good story . . . if it was true. Earlier that evening, Art had determined that his questions would not be confrontational. In fact, one of the first things he said to Scott was, "Look, I've got to ask you a few questions, I'm curious about a few things. I want to ask you some of the same things that the hard-liners will ask . . . and these guys won't be on your side."

Over dinner, sitting around Yoko's splendid round glass table, Art laid into Scott, asking him about every discrepancy that came to mind. And Scott always had an answer to fire back with. He had notes! Phone numbers! Documented evidence! How about the photographs? If the photos published in *Bohica* were not good enough, then he had more.

Occasionally, Jon, who was guzzling away on Bloody Marys, would chastise his brother for being so skeptical. Each time that Jon would raise an objection, Scott would insist that it was intellectually healthy for him to be challenged. At one point, Yoko, who had remained quiet—"in the traditional Japanese way"—turned to Jenny Emr and suggested that it would be a good idea if the ladies went to the back room while the men discussed business. Jenny smiled and shook her head. She wasn't going to miss this.

Scott never wavered on answering any question. He dumped mounds and mounds of information on poor Art, who started to feel bad for ever disbelieving Scott.

After a couple of hours, Art was on his last questions. "Scott," he said, "you say that you saw two Caucasians in Laos. How do we know that they were Americans? Couldn't they have been say, Germans, who had been tried and convicted of, oh, rape or something?"

All of a sudden, Jon burst into the conversation, his words were swishing around in his mouth along with the Bloody Mary. "C'mon Art! You don't have to hound Scott!"

Scott was very gentle. "It's okay, Jon. Art's asking a very fair question." He turned to Art. "The answer is that I recognized some insignia on them. Still, the scenario that you paint is possible though not probable."

Art was ready with his last question. In *Bohica* Scott had reprinted an article called "My Favorite Flake," which had appeared in *Soldier of Fortune* magazine. The writer, Alan Dawson, did everything he could to dismantle Barnes's credibility. "How could a guy get away with this?" Art wondered. "It's such an intense attack on you."

Scott nodded slowly. "It's a tough article, Art. But, really, it is not out of line with all the forces that have been pitted against me. It's part of a bigger picture."

Now Jon Emr was in a tizzy. Art had already told him to be quiet several times, that his drunken stupor was breaking the flow of the conversation. But Jon was now in the mean-drunk state that was typical of him. He put his arm around Scott and squeezed tightly. "You wanna know somethin'," he said. "You're not my brother anymore. Scott here is my real brother." Then he gave Scott another little squeeze to serve as the exclamation point.

"You know, something, Jon?" Art said. "You're the one who wanted me to drive all the way up here! You're the one who wanted me to read—this! You asked me to do this! So, fuck you!"

And then Art and Jenny left.

Later that night, Art told his wife that he didn't believe Scott Barnes's story after all. His answers were just too perfect. There were no holes anywhere. No flaws. That just wasn't realistic.

In the end, whether or not Scott Barnes was a fabulist became a moot point. For Barnes's relationship with Jon Emr came to a crashing halt only a few weeks after Scott was paid by Emr. That is the only thing that Barnes and the Emrs, Renee in particular, can agree on. The substance of their rift is hard to pin down.

According to Renee Emr, Scott Barnes immediately started to hit her son up for money. In a letter, Renee wrote, "Barnes asked Emr for an additional $8,500 to pay an attorney to represent him in [a] felony case and said he would go to jail if he didn't pay his delinquent child support. . . . There was no money due on the contract, Jon refused to advance more money."

Renee claims that on March 7, 1988, she received a call from a man named Cliff Kincaid, a reporter with a journalistic watchdog organization based in Washington, D.C., called Accuracy in Media. Kincaid was calling Renee because he had just finished interviewing Barnes. The reporter asked Renee to confirm that they had, in fact, optioned the rights to *Bohica* and that Michael Douglas was all set to play Scotty. Renee could not confirm the part about Michael Douglas.

According to Renee, she chastised Scott for lying to Accuracy in Media. After that, she and her attorneys received a plethora of mailgrams from Barnes, the first demanding money, the rest saying that the deal was off.

For example, here are two mailgrams with Barnes's name in the signature block:

. . . I have a contract with this production firm in which I have not been paid the $100,000.00 as stipulated in said contract. This is to notify you that unless my $100,000.00 is paid by March 18, 1988, this contract shall become null and void.

. . . There is no contract between myself and Mr. Emr and Joel Douglas of Emr Douglas Productions. They have failed to pay the promised sum. I will now proceed with legal action. There will be no further contact between myself or any of you. And as previously advised all contracts are hereby rescinded and declared null and void.

Barnes says that he does not recall sending the mailgrams and insists that Jon Emr must have forged them.

Scott Barnes's version of events is far more colorful. He says that in mid-December he received a call from an elated Emr. Jon told him that *Bohica* was now fully funded and that Scott would receive the balance of his fee "any day now."

Emr claimed that *Bohica* had been bought by Menachem Golan and Yoram Globus, the Israeli "Go-Go Boys" of Cannon Pictures. Cannon was famous for its pioneering ultraprofitable schlock, karate and horror films that were made for minimal budgets. The company also had a small library of films that had been nominated for Oscars, like *Runaway Train* and *Cries in the Dark*, with Meryl Streep.

Cannon's most valuable commodity was a contract that they had signed with Chuck Norris, the karate champion whose all-American good looks and easygoing demeanor made him an obvious candidate for movie stardom. For years, Norris's inexpensive films had been earning millions for Golan and Globus. *Missing in Action*, a film about Americans still being held captive in Vietnam, was their biggest moneymaker at the time (a title that would eventually become *Bloodsport* starring the Chuck Norris protégé Jean Claude Van Damme). In the film, Norris plays the tough-as-nails Colonel Braddock (in one scene, the Vietnamese torture him by putting a bag over his head that contains a rat. When the bag is removed, the captors see that Braddock has the rodent clamped dead between his teeth). Norris went on to be the star of a few more *Missing in Action* films.

Given Cannon's obvious interest in the issue of Vietnam MIAs, Jon Emr told Barnes that it was a natural that they should be the company that produced *Bohica*. Emr explained that Chuck Norris had already signed on to play Colonel Bo Gritz, the man who led Scott Barnes's expedition into Laos. Emr told Barnes that he would soon be sending him the script of *Bohica*, which had been commissioned only a few weeks earlier and was now registered with the Writers Guild.

Barnes claims that he waited and waited for his money and the script, but that neither arrived. Jon just shrugged him off and refused to tell him who had written the script to *Bohica*.

Barnes says that in late December he spoke with an assistant to Chuck Norris. She acknowledged that a Jon Emr had peddled *Bohica* to them, but that they had simply not acted on it. In fact, absolutely no deal had been made with either Chuck Norris or Cannon Pictures.

Barnes made calls to the Screen Actors Guild, the Directors Guild, the Producers Guild, and the Writers Guild of America. Nobody anywhere had ever heard of a Jon Emr.

Scott then located Joel Douglas, who was now living permanently in Nice, France. Barnes's notes seem to indicate a long conversation in which Douglas appeared perplexed that Jon was saying they were still partners. According to Douglas, his relationship with Jon Emr had long since dissolved and that he was in no way involved with the purchasing of *Bohica*.

In fact, Douglas had questioned a memo that Jon had written in regard to *Bohica*:

We feel this true story of POWS still being held, will be the Power Picture of the century. My Partner, Joel Douglas has read the book, BOHICA and will Co-Produce the Film with me. His brother Michael Douglas has also read the book and desires a leading role in this Major Production. . . .

On top of this memo, Joel wrote a note to Emr: "Jon, What the Hell is this."

It was at this time, Barnes says, that he informed Emr that their deal was off. "All he was doing," Barnes would later explain, "was using my script to con people into investing in a project that would never have gotten made." Of course, Barnes had no intention of giving back the advance he had received from Jon Emr.

When Scott was done with his story I asked him where he was at the time of the murders. His answer? Halfway between the Bahamas, where he was on a vacation, and Los Angeles. The police would corroborate his claim.

The Cons of Jon Emr:
Yoko Wright, 1987

Love means never having to say you're sorry.
—Ryan O'Neal quoting Ali MacGraw in *Love Story*

E arl Rutledge decided that the best course of action before actually filing a lawsuit against Emr was to go and meet with some of the California-based people who had gripes with Jon. There were Tim and Jean Johnson, who claimed that Jon had stolen thousands of dollars' worth of video and editing equipment from them. There was, of course, Scott Barnes, who claimed that Jon had tried to "steal" his life story from him. Who knew how many others were out there?

Scott Barnes had it on good authority that Yoko Wright, the woman who had visited him in Kernville with Emr, felt Jon had ripped her off for thousands and thousands of dollars. Scott had only gotten bits and pieces of Yoko's story from her, but he was quite sure that her testimony and the documentary evidence of some of Jon's "other illegal extracurricular" activities would be valuable to Earl Rutledge.

Earl Rutledge, Bob Franks, Aubrey Brothers, and Earl's co-counsel George Flanagan decided to fly into Los Angeles International Airport, which is where Yoko had requested that they meet. Yoko had refused to have the meeting take place at her estate in Rancho Palos Verdes. Despite the fact that she had recently installed a full security system, she was nonetheless still terrified of Jon Emr. In their relationship she had seen him both drunk and violent. She also knew that Jon liked to carry a gun. Furthermore, she was more than keenly aware that Jon's penchant for cocaine accelerated his instability.

It was at the airport lounge that Yoko, speaking in a soft, stilted English that charmed all of the gentlemen, told her story. It was coming difficult to her, she claimed. Yoko said that she had tried to block out most of her experiences with Jon Emr, that the mere thought of him made her feel "dirty."

Jon had been her lover and she had not been able to date any man, let alone get into a long-term relationship, ever since she severed her ties to Emr. She said that she had come to realize that she was too trusting a person and, frankly, a perfect foil. Aubrey and Bob nodded their heads. They knew exactly what Yoko Wright was talking about. As her tale unfolded, they were both embarrassed and elated that they recognized so much of it.

Yoko met Jon at a Redondo Beach restaurant and club named Papa Gato on August 10, 1987. For some reason, Jon told Yoko that he already knew of her and that he had wanted to get together for some time. Yoko may have found it a little odd, for she had done only minor acting in the United States. Nevertheless, she was impressed. She never stopped to consider that maybe, *maybe*, Jon had taken a glance at her fingers and noticed the largest single diamond he had ever seen.

Yoko found Jon handsome and oh so debonair and was quite awed by his tales of conquest and creative dragon slaying in Hollywood. He told her about a film that he had just finished called "A Chance to Live." He told her that he was in partnership with the powerful Douglas family. By then, Michael Douglas had soared to heights greater than anybody would have conceived of even two years earlier. For one thing, Douglas had starred in the unequivocal hit of the summer, *Fatal Attraction*. For another, the buzz of the town was that he was a lock to win an Oscar for his portrayal of the Donald Trumpish businessman Gordon Gecko in Oliver Stone's *Wall Street*. Quite simply, Yoko was blown away.

When she was done with her meal, Yoko walked with Jon to her car. When they got to the shimmering white Mercedes, Jon said good night to Yoko. He looked at her with drunken, loving eyes and then leaned over to kiss her gently on the lips. She allowed the kiss to happen and then blushed like a high schooler. This was not the Japanese way.

"Can I have your phone number?" Jon said to her with a boyish grin that she found just too charming for words.

She nodded and then lifted her purse to get out a piece of paper, her hands shaking with nervousness. Imagine! A Hollywood producer was courting her.

"Here," he said clutching his Hawaiian shirt. "Write it on this."

Charming, Yoko thought. Charming, charming, charming. And original. She wrote her number on his shirt. He kissed her again. "I'll call you tomorrow."

Yoko was in heaven.

Jon Emr did call Yoko the next morning. And that afternoon, and every day between that evening and their first date. Jon had promised Yoko a great night on the town. The type of night that only a Hollywood player could provide. Finally, Yoko would get her chance to actually become a fixture among the stars. Emr told her that he would pick her up at 9:00 from her swank estate and then the evening would belong to them.

Jon was over an hour late arriving at her Rancho Palos Verdes home. When Yoko saw headlights through the window she went to take a look. Jon was arriving in what she thought was a black Camaro. Her immediate thought was to consider why this wealthy and successful movie producer, this man who could enrich her own life and career, this man who was the secret to the success of the fabulous Douglas family, was arriving in a car that she deemed substandard. Where was the BMW? The Jag? The Rolls-Royce? Even a Range Rover?

Yoko was even more taken aback when she saw how Jon was dressed. He was wearing shorts, thongs, and a T-shirt without any sleeves. He was dressed differently from everybody Yoko had ever dated in her life. In his hand he held a bottle of cheap wine. Yoko knew that Jon intended for them to stay in for the night. Well, she thought to herself, Jon was simply not like all those other producers. He was driven by the pistons of his creativity and not his wallet. He was modest. There was something delightfully *real* about him.

That night, they didn't talk business at all. Jon tried to get romantic with her that night, but she spurned him, telling him that she certainly did not know him well enough to get sexually involved. As well, Yoko told Jon that she knew that he had a girlfriend, referring to Sue Fellows. Jon laughed and told her that Sue was "only for sex."

Jon and Yoko began to date furiously. They became sexually involved almost immediately. Like many women who dated Jon Emr, Yoko was not impressed with his lovemaking abilities. After one quick

THE PRODUCER AND THE COP   135

session, she criticized Jon for his inability to perform in the sack. He spent the next hour or so locked in the bathroom pouting. One day he told Yoko, "You'll never know how much I love you. Every time I love somebody, God takes them away from me."

Yoko would normally pick up the tab on their dates, including trips to Laguna Beach and a ten-day vacation at Park City, Utah, which also included Jon's boys. That did not bother her too much. For most of her life, she had played the role of the servile Japanese daughter or wife. Now she was able to be in control. The only thing that troubled her was that Jon refused to tell her where he lived. He explained that it was a simple security precaution. He had been working on several sensitive projects. He told her about "A Chance to Live" and showed her his portfolio of clippings.

A couple of weeks into their relationship, Jon asked Yoko for a $10,000 loan. Jon told her that he needed the money to pay an option fee for the film rights to a property called *Bohica*, the book written by Scott Barnes. He told her that as collateral he would give her a $1 million certificate of deposit that was set to mature in three years. As a form of personal insurance, Yoko contacted Columbia Security and Transfer, the Canadian bank which had issued the CD, and spoke to Louis P. Mirando, the president who had issued it. After he confirmed the legitimacy of the CD, Yoko happily agreed to the deal with Jon.

On August 23, 1987, Jon introduced Yoko to two friends of his, Brad Diller and Herman Taylor (not their real names). Jon told her that he and these two gentlemen were shareholders and directors of a company called the Pentex Oil Corporation. He explained that the company was based in San Antonio, Texas.

Over the course of the meeting, the three men pumped up the investment possibilities with Pentex. The company was on the verge of something that was absolutely gigantic! It had created an oil well downhole airlift pump that would effectively reduce operating costs by some 80 percent and reduce the capital investment by 75 percent of hydrobearing fluids from oil wells.

Yoko didn't grasp a word of what was being rattled off to her. What she did understand was that her lover, the undeniable genius Jon Emr, was a believer. In fact, Jon told her that he owned 25 percent of the capital stock of Pentex. He told Yoko that he wanted to make her the deal of the century. He was doing this only because he loved her:

he was willing to sell her 5 percent of Pentex for the sum of only $16,500. He told her that the beauty of it was that she would be receiving dividends on the money for the rest of her life.

Yoko took very little time deciding to accept the offer. By the way, Jon recommended, maybe the easiest way for her to make an investment would be for her to purchase a delightful Jeep vehicle that he had his eyes on. And, what a coincidence, the Jeep happened to cost $16,500 . . . almost to the dollar.* Yoko thought it a bit strange, but who was she to argue? The Jeep was delivered to Jon Emr a short time later.

What might have surprised Yoko Wright was that Pentex Oil did not exist at the time that she bought stock in it. The company had been incorporated on July 10, 1986, and was dissolved by order of the secretary of the state of Nevada on June 1, 1987, for "failure to file the required list of officers."

In addition, Yoko might have been interested to know that Louis Patrick Mirando, the bank officer who had told her that Jon's $1 million CD was legit, had recently been indicted on several counts of fraud, most dealing with the uses of phony certificates of deposit.

As their courtship progressed, Yoko began to learn more and more about Jon's business. She was especially impressed with "A Chance to Live." In October 1987, Jon explained to Yoko that his first real love, the modern western "Jonah," was in grave trouble. He explained that in a few weeks the rights to the film would be transferred to Aubrey Brothers and Bob Franks, two "sons of bitches" who had invested in the project two years before. He told Yoko that he needed to pay them cool hard cash in order to gain an extension.

Jon had been partly honest with Yoko. It was true that he had requested an extension from the Texans. Aubrey and Bob told him that it would cost him $50,000. However, he told Yoko that he needed $120,000. Between October 7 and November 6, Yoko came up with the cash: half from a CD that had been maturing in her safety deposit box and the other half from taking out a second mortgage on her home.

Aubrey Brothers and Bob Franks never received a dime of Yoko Wright's money.

At the same time, Yoko was also afforded the "honor" of working for

---

*Jon Emr told several people that while Yoko did buy the Jeep for him, it was a birthday gift and not a business transaction. Renee Emr supplied me with an affidavit from the car dealer who confirms that the Jeep was a gift.

Jon Emr. On September 3, 1988, Emr signed a letter of agreement with her in which she essentially became his investment broker. Emr gave her his "permission" to represent herself to investors as the broker for three Emr Productions: "All It Takes Is Money," "A Musical Plea for Freedom," and "In the Shadow," the Sherlock Holmes film written by Renee. Two weeks later, Emr signed another contract with her, this time authorizing her to raise $700,000. On October 15, Yoko and Jon signed an agreement for her to raise $10 million for any Emr/Douglas film. None of these projects and contracts actually amounted to anything, but they sure did make Yoko feel like a player.

Jon would have kept right on going, conning her out of every last asset she owned, had it not been for his carelessness. In December of 1987, two months after she had gone up to Kernville with Jon to meet Scott Barnes, Yoko began to notice some "heavy activity" on four of her credit cards.

According to Yoko, all the excessive charges—in full totaling over $40,000—could be attributed to Jon Emr. In addition, Jon had made an application for an American Express Gold Card using her credit to get himself one of Yoko's secondary cards. It was only after she got billed for an R. Jon Emr's credit card no. 3728-261597-7201 for the amount of $22,308.88 that Yoko Wright brought her love affair with Jon Emr to a screeching halt.*

Yoko may have felt like a fool, but she was quite sure that she was not the only one who had ever been taken for a ride by Jon Emr. One day she collected her phone bills, which included the numbers of all the people whom Jon had called from her home, and brought them to Scott Barnes. She asked him to find out what he could. One of the first people whom Scott spoke with was Aubrey Brothers, who directed him to his attorney, Earl Rutledge.

As Yoko finished her story, she came up with an idea. She said that the real person they ought to be talking to was a man named Scott Barnes. "He is the one that has the most information," she insisted.

Earl nodded his head. "I know exactly who you're talking about. I'm real interested in meeting him."

---

*American Express acknowledges conducting a major credit card fraud investigation into Jon Emr.

"Well, damn, then," Aubrey said. "Let's do it!"

And so Yoko dialed Scott Barnes. Scott offered to come down to Los Angeles to meet with Earl Rutledge and the group. But Earl had another idea. He wanted to see this animal that was Scott Barnes in his own environment. And so he made Scott a generous offer: he'd drive up there with the rest of the gang.

Yoko then phoned Tim and Jean Johnson and asked them if they would like to be included in the meeting. Tim and Jean were enthusiastic and even volunteered to bring up Vern Nobles, the established Hollywood producer who had written Aubrey the advisory letter about his contract with Jon Emr.

And so Earl, Aubrey, Bob, George Flanagan, Earl's law partner, and Yoko all rolled into the dark station wagon that Earl had rented and began the three-hour ascent to Kernville. Given Aubrey's bulk, it was a mighty tight squeeze. Earl was happy that he had the privilege of driving the vehicle, with only tiny Yoko by his side and George Flanagan next to her. The conversation had nothing to do with business. Instead, Yoko was jabbering away about her life, about how she had once been a model for Neiman Marcus and how she used to live in Houston with her former husband.

Rutledge was becoming more and more impressed with Yoko as the ride progressed. She's a real lady, he thought to himself, a person of intellect, taste, and integrity. She'll make a good witness someday.

When they got to Kernville, Yoko directed Earl to Scott's house. They arrived at about three o'clock.

The first thing that Earl thought when he saw Scott was how clean-cut he was. He was not yet overweight and did not have the mustache and beard that would eventually become his trademark.

As the group entered his home, Scott asked everybody what they wanted to drink. "I can offer ice water or iced tea. I'm out of Coke."

"I'll have a beer," said Aubrey predictably.

"I don't have any beer," said Scott. "I don't drink."

Aubrey agreed to have iced tea.

Scott showed the group around the house and even showed them the bullet holes that were made by the CIA hit men who had tried to have him offed. They were impressed.

The group, everybody with some kind of beverage in hand, launched almost immediately into the discussion. Earl wanted to interview everybody about Jon Emr. But he was most interested in Barnes, the mystery man who had called him out of nowhere. Scott told him his story, slowly and assuredly. Earl was happy to see Yoko nod in agreement whenever Scott told a section of the story that had to do with her. Scott also talked about some of his experiences in Laos, and, again, Earl was content. Scott either knows a lot or he's cooking up a hell of a believable lie, Earl thought.

But when it was all over, Earl Rutledge was nevertheless skeptical as hell. As he saw it, that was his job as a lawyer. Never believe a damn thing until it is conclusively proven to you.

That night Earl Rutledge and Aubrey Brothers shared a Holiday Inn room in Bakersfield. Earl didn't get much sleep. It didn't have to do with his impending case. It was just that the big man Aubrey Brothers was snoring up a storm, literally rattling the windows.

The next day, the group met at Scott's home again. After several more hours of questions and answers with the various players (by now Tim and Jean Johnson had arrived with their own tales of woe), the decision was made that the gang would collectively sue the pants off Jon Emr and, while they were at it, his mother, Renee, and Joel Douglas as well.

Once the decision was made that the group was going to sue Jon Emr, Scott Barnes made it clear he couldn't pay Rutledge and Flanagan their fee, which at the time was in the neighborhood of $200 an hour. He was totally destitute. But he offered his considerable investigative skills if the rest of the group carried his share of the financial cost. Nobody in the room disagreed with the idea. And so it was settled.

On May 18, 1988, Jon Emr received a phone call from a reporter for the *Dallas Morning News*, asking him for a comment on a lawsuit that had been filed that day against him, his mother, and Joel Douglas by the plaintiffs Aubrey Brothers, Bob Franks, Yoko Wright, Tim Johnson, Jean Johnson, and Scott Barnes. Being completely blindsided, Jon Emr had nothing to say to the reporter. He did, however, have a great deal to say later that night.

Late in the evening, Jon Emr began making forty-one separate phone calls to Aubrey Brothers. Since Aubrey happened not to be at home, each of the calls was recorded on Aubrey's answering machine. Each message was rougher in tone and more slurred in diction than the one that preceded it. Clearly, Jon began drinking early in the evening and didn't stop until he fell asleep or passed out.

A sampling:

Beep . . . If Aubrey thinks he's ever had a nightmare, he's got to talk to me. He can fly in here and prepare the lawsuit!

Beep . . . Instead of my trying to make your investment hold, you want to destroy every chance I have of making your money back, 'cause I'm getting letters from Orion Pictures, I will pull and do a letter of intent with all the other distributors and tell them you don't want the film made!

Beep . . . Why don't you come in and serve the papers in person? You want to see a nightmare?

Beep . . . DON'T PLAY GAMES WITH THE DOUGLAS NAME!

Beep . . . THIS IS THE LAST CALL! I have tried to warn you guys. I tried telling you who you're dealing with. But you're not listening. You'll see it all in black and white.

Beep . . . Any judge in the land is going to look at the lawsuit and say, "You destroyed your own project and the ability of the man to repay you. I think we have a serious problem here and a lot of slander!"

Beep . . . These are the last words you'll hear if you don't talk to me tomorrow. I feel like calling you a big, dumb shit 'cause you're being used. I'm the big dumb shit for trying to save your fucking ass, so good-bye.

Beep . . . By the way, Barnes was your enemy long before you met him. I have the paperwork to prove it.

Beep . . . AUBREY, YOU'RE IN BIG FUCKING TROUBLE AND YOU ARE IN OVER YOUR HEAD.

Beep . . . Whatever you're doing, whatever's going on, it is always worth seeking the truth. Call me. Seek the truth.

Eventually, Aubrey Brothers's tape machine simply ran out of room.

On May 19, 1987, Earl Rutledge received a two-page fax from Jon Emr. Here is an excerpt:

Apparently, you would rather destroy "Jonah" and my ability to get distribution so we all could have made money.

The press release from the Fort Worth newspaper was cut out and delivered to one of the distribution companies I had "Jonah" in with, therefore, rather than be embarrassed by these gutter tactics, I am pulling "Jonah" from all the companies I gave it to for distribution today.

The courtesy of a phone call to tell me that you wanted to destroy the potential of making "Jonah" I guess was asking for too much integrity.

Best wishes as your new playmates are going to bury you.

In the end, the lawsuits between Jon Emr and his enemies would amount to nothing. His death would have something to do with that and so did the fact that Earl Rutledge made a mistake that he regrets to this day. His lawsuit against Emr was filed under RICO, used for the racketeering charges that are normally brought to bear by the government against the Mafia. In Dallas, where the suit was originally filed, it might have worked. But Emr's attorneys managed to get the case transferred to Los Angeles, where judges have a reputation for frowning upon RICO.

Aubrey Brothers, Bob Franks, Yoko Wright, Tim Johnson, Jean Johnson, and Scott Barnes were never to see a dime from Jon Emr, nor he (or his mother, Renee) from them. The importance of the lawsuit lay in how it came to be used as a sword to hack away at any credibility that Jon Emr might have been able to develop with any future business partners. In particular, Scott Barnes was able to transform the lawsuit into a tool of categorical destruction against Jon Emr's business endeavors.

False Leads in Culver City:
August 1991

*You know, a dozen press agents working overtime can do
terrible things to the human spirit.*
—Cecil B. DeMille in *Sunset Boulevard*

T he murders of Jon Emr, his son, and his dad were perfect fodder
for the tabloid television shows. First of all, this was one of the
most spectacular murders to have hit the West since Sharon Tate and
company were massacred by Charles Manson's gang of zombies. It was
a Mob-style hit, a broad-daylight execution that seemed more suited
for the trenches of Philadelphia and New York City than the laid-back
sunbathing beach cities of Southern California.

The victim was a producer. And we are not talking about your ordi-
nary, run-of-the mill moviemaker here. We are talking about a man
who was in the process of making a movie about James Dean.

Add to all this the fact that the alleged killer was the producer's
bodyguard and then, just for good measure, throw in the fact that the
bodyguard's gorgeous—just look at *them* photos!—girlfriend was missing, and, folks, those ratings were sure to light up.

Only a few days after the murder, Hank Davies, wearing a sharp suit
and having gotten his hair cut, appeared on *Larry King Live* on CNN.
Kathy Calkins appeared along with him. Since the show was broadcast
live from Washington, Davies and Calkins had to settle for being on a
satellite feed.

Davies and Calkins's national television debut was brief but explosive. Rather than concentrate on the murders, King kept playing
up what he knew he wanted his viewers to see—an emotionally distraught—though terrific-looking—blond begging for the safe return
of her sister. While Kathy cried, Hank remained cool and rational. He

figured that this would be the first of many appearances on television, and he was quite correct.

Next up was the enormously popular syndicated show *A Current Affair.* The producers titled the segment on the murders "Night of the Assassin," apparently oblivious to the fact that the murders occurred in the daytime. *Inside Edition, Hard Copy,* and *America's Most Wanted* all did their own versions of what happened during Suggsy's killing spree.

There was a common denominator to all the shows. First, they all used actors to re-create the events, a "dramatization," as it was commonly called. Second, all of the shows portrayed Jon Emr as, well, less than fully credible. *A Current Affair* even went as far as calling Jon Emr a con artist. Or at least they interviewed a few people who said he had swindled them out of their cash, told them he could make them movie moguls even though he knew full well he did not stand a chance. In fact, there was Scott Barnes, looking as ragged as the day that I met him, telling America how evil Jon Emr was.

Without a doubt, the most important show—as far as the Culver City and Paradise Valley police were concerned—was the successful FOX network program *America's Most Wanted.* If you looked closely, you could see Hank Davies, his hair demonstrably grayer than it had been when he went on *Larry King Live,* answering phones as the show's host, Adam Walsh, instructed audience members how to contact the police or FBI if they had spotted Suggsy.

A total of four hundred tips came in as a result of the show. The odd thing was that many of them seemed mighty credible.

A man bearing a striking resemblance to Suggsy was arrested in the Seattle area for stabbing his next-door neighbor in a trailer park.

When he was brought in, one of the police officers recognized him as being the very same Suggsy from *America's Most Wanted.* He pulled up the wanted photo and—damned if there wasn't a resemblance! Furthermore, Seattle was Suggsy's old stomping ground. If he was a creature of habit, then it was inevitable that he would return to his old hometown. The cop called in Officer Edward Casey, who was once Suggsy's brother-in-law. Ed Casey stared into the cage and said, "Yup, that's him! We got our man."

Then, just to make sure, the cops brought the booking photographs to Carol Casey, Suggsy's ex-wife, who said, "Hmm, that could be him . . . but he'd have changed some of his features."

The man was read his rights. He looked baffled when he was told that he was being arrested for the murder of three men and for the kidnapping of his girlfriend. "I don't know what the fuck you're talking about!" he said to the cops. The cops laughed and looked at each other knowingly. They sure did not expect him to confess right there and then.

Hank Davies got the word at about six in the morning on a Saturday. It was wonderful news to wake up to. He got on the phone and called Renee Emr and Alan Hauge and Kathy Calkins. He was off to Seattle and would be personally escorting the bastard back. He had even made his flight arrangements on Alaska Air.

About five hours after he had gotten the good news, Seattle police contacted him with the bad. The fingerprints did not match. Despite the positive ID they could not hold him for the murders. In fact, after reexamining the photographs of the real Suggsy, they were quite certain they had really botched this up.

There was also a sighting of Suggsy down in Reno. When Davies heard about this his heart quickened. One thing that he had learned about Suggsy was that the guy loved to gamble. And there was more good news. The man's California driver's license had Suggsy's name and birth date. The Reno cops asked Davies if he wanted to come pick up the perp. He had been arrested the day before for drunk and disorderly conduct.

That's when Davies knew that they had the wrong man. Suggsy was a famous teetotaler. He had never had a drink. He made it an annoying habit of preaching against the sin of drinking, of this absolute desecration of the human temple. There was no way that Suggsy would be found in an alley with an empty bottle of Scotch in his hands.

Furthermore, Suggsy did not have a California driver's license. He asked the Reno police to send in a photograph of the man. When Davies received a fax of the photo it was clear that—despite the incredible name and birth date coincidence—this was not his prisoner.

Another tip came from New Hampshire. Again, there was potential here. Sue Fellows, Jon's girlfriend, had moved to Dover, where her family lived, immediately after the shooting. As far as Suggsy knew, she was a surviving witness.

It was two girls who made the report. They insisted that the man whom they saw on *America's Most Wanted* was the very same person who had just moved into the trailer park near their neighborhood. Davies asked them to send in a video they made of the man. When they did exactly that, Davies again realized that he was no closer to finding Suggsy.

The shows also generated speculation about Susan Calkins. At one point, Sergeant Zea of the Manhattan Beach police contacted Kathy Calkins with some nauseating news. "I think we found your sister," he told her over the phone. "We found a body in the desert outside of Las Vegas."

This made sad sense to Kathy. Suggsy was a madman for Las Vegas. It was entirely possible that Suggsy would take Sue to casinoland for his final fling. Kathy Calkins might even have described Suggsy as a compulsive gambler had she had the professional knowledge to diagnose him as one. "Do I need to identify the body?" she asked Sergeant Zea through sobs.

"No," he said coolly. "The body has been eaten by animals. It is pretty much unidentifiable."

Kathy hung up the phone, cried soundly, and then proceeded to wait for more information to come in. It never did. So, after a full day of incessant nightmares of her sister's body having been ravaged by coyotes and such, she decided to take matters into her own hands. She contacted the Las Vegas police who, in turn, connected her with the coroner's office. "I understand that you have the body there of an unidentified female . . . Please, could you . . . Could you tell me anything? Like, could you tell me what she might have been wearing?" It was an important question. Kathy remembered precisely what her sister was wearing the last day that she saw her.

"The only thing that I can tell you is she had breast implants."

"Thank you very much," Kathy said. She knew for certain that the body in the desert was not her sister Sue. And she held on to the faint hope that her sister, her best friend, was still alive. . . . Out there . . . somewhere.

With him.

The Cons of Jon Emr:
Gloria Farrens, 1988

*I always thought I could give them life like a present, all wrapped in white
with every promise of happiness inside.*
—Dorothy McGuire in Delbert Mann's *The Dark at the Top of the Stairs*

There was one person on the planet whom Earl Rutledge wanted to find above anybody else: Gloria Farrens, Jon's ex-wife. For two years Earl's clients Aubrey Brothers and Bob Franks had their ears filled with Jon Emr's horrific stories about the woman that he had divorced years earlier. They had heard that Gloria had been an unfit mother and had a severe psychological imbalance. They had heard that she was a Satanist or, at the very least, was involved in a religious cult. They had heard that she had been unfaithful to Jon. They had heard that her lover was a mentally unbalanced man who had spent time in a mental hospital and had molested her and Jon's two boys, Roger and Bobby.

According to Jon Emr, he had won custody of the two boys by order of an Indio, California, court in 1975. So complete was Jon's alleged victory that Gloria was given no visitation privileges whatsoever. On October 15, 1975, Jon and Gloria were divorced. The custody battle, Jon had claimed, was especially brutal. Jon wanted the boys because he loved them and Gloria wanted them for her own nefarious reasons. On May 25, 1976, Renee and Arthur Emr Sr., the grandparents, were awarded custody of the boys. The judge saw that as the most Solomonesque way of dealing with the issue.

Earl assumed that much of what Jon had said was as trumped up as most of the other fantasies he had imposed on Earl's clients Aubrey and Bobby. A few weeks after he had filed his lawsuit against Jon Emr and Joel Douglas, Earl flew to Sherman Oaks, California, in order to, one, look into the divorce files of Jon and Gloria Emr and, two, actually locate Gloria. He assumed that her hostility for Jon would be especially intense and she'd be happy to turn over anything incriminating she might have or know about her ex-husband.

Earl was amazed to discover that, according to court documents, Jon had technically been truthful when describing the legal machinations of his divorce from Gloria and the awarding of the children to their grandparents. In the papers, Earl even found the hint of a molestation allegation written by the Emrs' attorney before the divorce was even finalized: "An emergency exists in that said children have been subjected to and continue to be subjected to mistreatment and abuse."

The one thing that Jon apparently never told Aubrey and Bob was that he had been accused of kidnapping the children shortly after Renee and Arthur had been awarded custody of the children. In late December 1976, Gloria filed a complaint with the court that Renee, Arthur, and Jon had "absconded with said minor children" in violation of a court order allowing Gloria visitation. According to the documents, Gloria had no idea where the boys were. The courts could do nothing to help her because the family had moved the boys out of the court's jurisdiction.

Now Earl *really* wanted to find Gloria. If he was reading things correctly, Gloria was a classic tragic figure, a woman whose children were torn from her bosom and whose minds and emotions were poisoned against her. Surely, if Earl could tell her that he knew where the children were located she would feel forever indebted to him.

Earl asked Scott Barnes to meet him in his hotel room and assigned him the task of tracking down Gloria Farrens. Earl sat back in awe as he saw Barnes weave his investigative magic. Within an hour, Gloria Farrens was on the phone, agreeing to meet with Earl.

A few days later, Gloria was sitting in a restaurant facing Earl, Aubrey, and Bob, who had flown in for the occasion. All of them wanted to be present for the encounter, for they felt that the meeting would be a momentous one. Gloria could take them back further into Jon Emr's life than anybody else, could help them understand how the beast inside Jon Emr was born.

Gloria was much more attractive than they had expected. She had auburn hair and a nicely chiseled face. She was lithe and elegant, her voice smooth and sweet. The men had been expecting a dark monster. Instead, they found themselves across from a more or less typical all-American woman. Gloria had brought her fiancé, Joe, a muscular man with an angular face. Joe was a cop. Gloria, who was in school getting a degree in psychology at the time, conceded that her marrying a man of law and order might have been subliminally driven as a result of her disastrous relationship with Jon.

The first thing that Gloria wanted to know was how her kids were doing. Aubrey and Bob, who had seen quite a bit of the boys during their relationship with Jon, told her that they were doing just fine, that neither one seemed to be following in the footsteps of their father. Gloria breathed a sign of relief. Earl told Gloria that Bobby and Roger were living in Paradise Valley, Arizona, with their grandparents. They lived in the home that Aubrey and Bob claimed was bought with the money that they had forked over to Jon Emr. The boys were attending a private school called the Judson School. Again, the men made the point that they felt their money was being used to fund the kids' education.

None of the participants of this meeting can recollect verbatim what was said. Here, however, is how Gloria relayed the essence of her marriage to Jon when she met with me in 1991 and 1992.

GLORIA FARRENS

I met Jon when we were in college in Ohio. I was nineteen. Jon was studying to be an architect at the time. He seemed to be there more because his parents wanted him there than having a personal desire about becoming an architect. He cut classes a lot. He was always getting involved in barroom fights off the campus; he always claimed he was coming to the aid or defense of someone else. He always portrayed himself to be very heroic, but I was never there to really see it.

Jon was very persistent in pursuing me. At first, I wasn't impressed with him. He'd follow me around campus, but not in any kind of inappropriate way. Like, if I'd go to a drugstore to buy something—he would just nonchalantly walk in and start a conversation with me. I became infatuated with his constant attention to me. One thing led to another and we began dating and, obviously, eventually got married. I was very gullible. I was raised in the Midwest, a very small farm town in Ohio. I basically took people at face value. I was not psychologically astute back then. Had I made a selection of a husband even two years later, it would have been somebody very different from him.

We moved to L.A. Jon hoped someday he'd be an actor, but it never panned out for him. So he started doing some screenwriting, but that never panned out for him either. Eventually we wanted to raise a family, and we went to Palm Springs to get out of the smog.

Jon wanted to keep his hand in the acting world. He started, I think, something like a summer playhouse. He came in contact with people who wanted to put on a play. He got himself more or less in position of directing that, though I don't think it ever came off.

In the midst of all that, a lot of people started expressing an interest in honing their acting skills. Jon said, "Well, I'll start an acting school." He was able to get enough people to pay him some fees and to rent out some space. Remember, Jon was a guy who could never make it as an actor.

Early on, I started to get quite concerned that he was in the incipient stages of alcoholism. He was also hypoglycemic and the doctor advised him to stop drinking.

Renee and Art were living in New Jersey and we were living in California. As soon as I became pregnant with Roger, they decided they wanted to move back out to the West Coast. Well, they came out without money to their name and they moved right in with us. We lived in a one-bedroom apartment. Four adults trying to live in a one-bedroom apartment with one of them being an alcoholic is not the best of conditions. I wound up sleeping on a cot in my living room for the entire length of my pregnancy. Jon and I literally went head-to-head on arguments about getting his parents out of the house. I went into labor on the cot, with Art and Renee sleeping in my bed in the bedroom.

It started to become clear that Jon was fooling around on me. One day one of the girls who was taking one of his acting classes said to me, "I hear that you and Jon have an open marriage." I started thinking about Jon's behavior prior to that and put two and two together. For example, Jon wouldn't come home until two or three in the morning. It got to be so frequent, even the neighbors made comments to me. I would never get a straight answer from Jon. He'd say, "This girl's been chasing me." Our sex life was nonexistent. That is typical of most marriages when they're going downhill.

Jon began to have a lot of what appeared to me to be very unscrupulous business dealings. He was getting involved with his brother doing some movie negotiations, which I can't substantiate, but they didn't seem like they were on the up-and-up. Renee started getting her hands involved in some of the stuff and was encouraging Jon to get more deeply involved in those things. It was quite distasteful to me. My family background was, you know, we're honest.

Rather than forcing Jon to stand on his own two feet and be financially responsible, pay his own bills, Renee and Art kind of condoned the fact that it was okay to get in arrears, it's okay to file bankruptcy. We didn't have to have good credit.

I didn't believe in divorce. I had two children, so I hung in there for as long as I could, until I lived with a daily fear for my life. Jon initially was only violent toward things in the house, breaking things, but when I started to indicate that maybe we ought to separate, then he began to get physically violent with me. Once, he got me on the floor and got on my back with my face toward the floor, then shoved my face into the floor. It was so hard that it shoved my jaw into my ear. My jaw was locked shut for six weeks. I wound up going to the hospital one time.

Eric Masterson was a young man who was a friend of Jon's with whom I wound up having a relationship after I divorced Jon. He came into the picture in the last six or so months of my marriage. Eric, as an outsider, could see what was going on. He said Jon was going to get real violent. He was in the house that day Jon was slamming my face on the floor.

I finally made the decision to leave Jon. I asked Eric if he could drive me and the kids up to my sister's house. My mother had flown out from Ohio. Jon and Renee were trying to convince my mother I was crazy or something. They told her I needed to be committed to a mental hospital. They were telling the same thing to my parish priest. Jon and Renee were trying to paint this picture of this crazy devil worshiper. In reality, once I had gone to a tarot card reading and the woman told me to do a blessing on the house using salt and bread. It seemed a harmless thing. In fact, the parish priest told me that I should get out. That was the blessing I needed to go and file for divorce.

I moved into a rental house. Jon constantly bothered me. He'd shine lights into the windows at night.

The custody battle was pretty intense. I found myself on the receiving end of a lot of accusations, specifically abusing my children. They had to submit to whole-body X-rays. Renee became furious when the pediatrician would not agree with her that I injured the children. She said my children were so bruise free that I must have kept them in a padded cell.

What really hurt me was my relationship with Eric. I desperately needed somebody for comfort and he was there. Jon and Renee had gone to a judge when they had the kids and told him I was living with a man out of wedlock. He was a very religious judge and I lost the kids.

I had moved out of Palm Springs at the end of 1975 when I had lost custody of them—I had to find a job. I didn't have a car, I was traveling by bus and couldn't come out that often. I came out about once a month and stayed with a friend. When they disappeared in 1976, I was living in Los Angeles. The judge basically said that since nobody lives in Riverside County anymore there was nothing he could do.

Through my company's employee assistance program, I hired a good set of lawyers and private eyes. We located them out in Thousand Oaks, California. I got them into court immediately, within three days. There were stupid accusations again. They said they had proof I was a member of the Satanist Satanic Church in San Francisco, and that the "church" was paying my legal fees. It was ludicrous. The judge kind of laughed at them.

At that point, my kids had been sent out of state. Jon refused to produce the kids. All the judge could do was threaten Jon and say, I demand you produce the kids. Jon laughed and walked out of court. He'd won. Because the kids were out of state—Arizona now, they were out of the court's jurisdiction.

And that was it, I lost the last chance to get or see my kids. Jon had abducted them and I had no idea where they were until I met Earl Rutledge.

When their meeting with Gloria was approaching its conclusion, the men gave her a copy of the résumé that Jon had provided them. They asked her if she could go over it, study it, and report to them any inaccuracies that might exist therein. Earl made it clear that one of their most important tasks ahead was proving that Jon Emr had grossly misrepresented himself when he initially approached Aubrey about investing in both "Jonah" and "A Chance to Live."

In a letter dated August 31, 1988, Gloria fulfilled her obligation to Earl Rutledge, picking apart Jon's résumé. By the time she was finished with it, Earl was astonished. He simply could not fathom the extent to which Jon had seemingly lied. He was also perplexed and saddened by the naiveté that his clients had displayed, for the credentials that Jon had claimed would have been easy to check out. For some reason, Aubrey and Bob had never done a due diligence of Emr and his claims.

IN EMR'S RÉSUMÉ he claimed to have *studied architecture at the University of Toledo and studied theater arts at UCLA.*

FROM GLORIA'S LETTER: Gloria said Jon attended the University of Toledo, but did not receive a degree. Jon's claim that he studied theater arts at UCLA was a distortion and exaggeration, she wrote. In September 1967, Jon enrolled in a writing course through the UCLA extension program, but did not complete the course.

IN HIS RÉSUMÉ Emr claims to have been a *film and television producer for 19 years.*

FROM GLORIA'S LETTER: Gloria called this an "outright lie." She gave the following timeline: "[I]n 1966, Jon was a student at the University of Toledo studying architecture. In December 1966, we both left the University of Toledo, and lived with his parents in New Jersey, until we moved to California in August 1967. While in New Jersey in 1967, Jon worked for Fairchild Camera in . . . Paramus, New Jersey. [From 1967 to 1969] Jon was an architectural draftsman for E. F. Hutton and Company. . . . In late 1971 or early 1972, Jon filed for bankruptcy. In spring of 1972 we moved to Palm Desert. Jon worked as an architectural draftsman until we divorced in September 1974. . . . Jon also got involved with a local acting group in Palm Springs. He began to offer 'acting lessons' to a few individuals."

JON'S RÉSUMÉ reflects that the *first show produced was a Dionne "Warwik"* (sic) *Musical Special in 1967–1968.*

FROM GLORIA'S LETTER: Gloria called this "another complete falsehood." In 1971, Jon's brother Art did produce a Thanksgiving special with Dionne Warwick (which he was unable to sell to the networks). Jon, Gloria wrote, was not involved with this program at all.

FINALLY, JON ASSERTED that he had *produced family G-rated west-erns and a rock video T.V. show which aired for 1½ years, 5 days a week. He also claimed to have produced over 300 television shows and 6 major motion pictures.*

FROM GLORIA'S LETTER: Gloria assumed that [Jon] produced no television shows or motion pictures while married to her.

A Letter in Culver City:
August 15, 1991

Since this show was the only thing I had going for me in my life,
I have decided to kill myself. I am going to blow my brains out
right on this program a week from today.
—Peter Finch in *Network*

After following a steady train of irrelevant leads, including those four hundred phone tips that had come courtesy of *America's Most Wanted*, Hank Davies knew he was on to something big. Real big.

Kathy Calkins had gone through a brown paper bag that she had found in her office, which is where Susan had set up a futon to sleep on. The bag was filled with receipts, probably in anticipation of the upcoming tax season. Also in the bag was an envelope addressed to Susan at her mail drop. On the left-hand corner was printed Suggsy's name. On the bottom of the envelope, handwritten in big bold letters and underlined were these words: "DO NOT OPEN UNTIL JULY 10." On the back of the envelope was the same message. July 10 was the date that the police and the FBI determined Suggsy had killed Art Emr Sr.

Kathy opened the envelope and found two typed pages. At the end of the letter was Suggsy's familiar signature. She began to read the single-spaced letter but was too emotionally overwhelmed to finish it. She faxed the note to Sergeant Davies.

Only *after* she had sent the letter off to the police did Kathy finish reading it. When she was done she felt nauseated. That night was the first time that Kathy had too much to drink in a long time.

My sweetheart Susan,

If you read this letter, it is because I am not coming back. I wanted to write you a letter that was not too dramatic but truthful; not an easy thing to do. At this point in my life, I really don't have the desire to keep my nose to the grindstone, I want all or nothing!

I love you more than you will ever know. A reasonable person would say, "If he loved her that much, he wouldn't have done what he did." This is true to a point.

However, there is not a doubt in my mind that we would have eventually failed because of our living arrangements and circumstances that we talked about. I cannot say how much of what [Benny] and I are going to do is for money, and how much is for the thrill of it. I would say 80% money, 20% thrill. I knew for sure that if I had a reasonable option, I would probably take it. Right now, my desperation for money combined with my low zest for life, add up to my actions.

Do not let anyone try to tell you that you should have talked me out of it. For one thing, you had no idea what we were going to do, the other is that you couldn't have changed my mind anyway. I had made up my mind that I was going to give it a week of surveillance, then, decide if it was possible. If you read this, it is because I was wrong.

Please tell my mother I am sorry for my selfishness. Suicide, or any other action that could cause an untimely death, is probably the most selfish thing a person can do to those close to him. I wish I did not have any relatives that would have to grieve. Susan, I know if we did not make it, I would end up like my father . . . lonely and alone. I cannot grow old like that. Unless I am able to get out of my "mental rut" NOW, it would soon be over for us. This thing that Benny and I have done was my way of getting out of the rut; obviously, it did not work and I ended up deeper.

If you read this, by now I know that I made the wrong decision. I am so sorry that the people that care about me have to suffer. I would give anything for it not to be this way. If anyone wonders why I let myself die before I was captured, it is because I will not go to prison. I cannot bear the thought of coming out in 10–20 years starting my life where I left it in 1991. I really would rather be dead. If I kill anyone during the "job" it is only because I wanted to get away to be with you; I do not want to hurt ANYONE. I hope we get away clean so there is no chance of anyone getting hurt. Give this to my mother after you read it.

Please don't ever forget me. Take care of our little man. He adores you as much as I do. Whenever you look into his eyes please look for me, I'll be there. Together, Joe and I will love and protect you. And, just like the movie, "Somewhere in Time," we will be together again someday. I love you my baby.

■ ■ ■

"Who's this Benny guy?" That was the logical first question Hank Davies had for Kathy Calkins after having read the letter for himself.

According to Kathy, Benny was Suggsy's best friend, somebody she considered a dim-witted moron, a real weird character. There was something else that was kind of interesting. Benny was a Catholic who, at the age of thirty-one, already had something like seven children. Benny and his wife, Jennifer, had one set of twins in the litter.

There was one more question that Davies had for Kathy. In Suggsy's letter there was mention of a guy named "Joe." A "Joe" who would take care of Susan "forever." Who was he?

"Oh," Kathy said. "Joe was his dog. A big German shepherd. That dog loved Susan more than he did his own master. Is this important?"

"Maybe. Okay. Do you have Benny's phone number?"

"Yes," she said. "But it's been disconnected."

Davies dialed the number anyway and, sure enough, he had his ear blown away by a shrill recording telling him that Benny could no longer be reached at that particular number.

"Do you think that it's significant that his number has been cut off?" Kathy wanted to know.

"It might be," Hank said. "Do you have an address on this guy?"

The Cons of Jon Emr:
Houston and Scott Barnes, 1988

We're not quarreling! We're in complete agreement! We hate each other!
—Nanette Fabray to Oscar Levant in *The Band Wagon*

In July 1988, Earl Rutledge hired a private detective to look into Jon Emr's business dealings in Houston, Texas. According to Aubrey, who often hosted Jon's stays in the Lone Star State, Jon often bragged that his connections in the Houston area were *"not to be fucking believed."* Because Aubrey allowed Jon to use his phone freely, it was possible to track down several of the people with whom Jon associated in Houston using Aubrey's phone bills.

When Earl read the official report from his private eye, he could hardly have been surprised. For the pattern of behavior and deception that Jon Emr displayed in Houston could only be described as absolutely consistent with the modus operandi that he himself had borne witness to. The italicized comments are mine.

PRIVATE INVESTIGATION REPORT

Ronnie Niday of Admiral Limousine Service [*whom Emr had commissioned to serve as his chauffeur*] took me by a lot with a vacant, gray two-story house on it, which was surrounded by a five-foot chain-link fence, had a large gravel parking lot with Johnson grass approximately three feet tall over it. It is located on Telephone Road in Houston, south of downtown and a few blocks north of Hobby Airport. There is a real estate "for sale" sign clamped to the fence. . . . According to Niday, he took Jon Emr to that location many times in the middle of the night. Niday was never allowed to go in and would wait long periods of time in the limousine while Jon Emr was in that building. Niday says that Jon Emr told him he was visiting that building for the purpose of business conferences to raise money for movies. It looks to me like a classic crack house, although it obviously has not been used in some time. . . .

According to Niday, Jon Emr frequented a [topless] nightclub . . . almost every night in the more than three months he was in Houston. When they first went there Niday would go in with Jon Emr and his assistant. . . . Drinks were charged to [the assistant's] credit card, until one night the club refused to accept the credit card. For the following two weeks Jon Emr would not go there. After a length of time Niday quit going into the club and would simply wait several hours in the limousine while Jon Emr frequented the club. . . .

Randall Marino is a hairdresser in Houston who somehow made contact with Jon Emr and introduced Jon Emr to a lot of people in Houston whom Marino had given haircuts to over a period of time. . . . Marino accompanied Jon Emr a great deal when Jon Emr was in Houston. On one occasion they told Niday to pull the limousine over, discussed how frightened they were of something, went into a gun shop and bought four guns. One gun was a rifle, two were handguns; Niday cannot remember what the fourth was. Randall Marino quit cutting hair approximately two weeks ago and went to work for . . . a ticket service. Recently, after over six months of no contact, Marino called Bob Miller [*who was a man-about-Houston who served as Earl Rutledge's primary Houston contact*]. He told Miller that he had been hired by the F.B.I. to conduct an undercover operation relating to Jon Emr. Marino told Miller that if he wanted to make money the F.B.I. was willing to pay him as well, and then proceeded to try to pump Miller for information. The evening of August 18, 1988, the first evening I was in Houston, the owner of Marino's ticket service called Aubrey Brothers, at his residence, talked for over forty-five minutes and asked Aubrey a lot of questions. It is apparent that the owner found out that I was in Houston and was trying to find out why. Marino also told Miller that one of Jon's favorite nightspots was one of the focal points of the F.B.I. investigation and suggested that they could have a lot of fun doing the investigation by patronizing it. Miller declined on all fronts.

According to Miller and Niday, Jon Emr first stayed at the Holiday Inn downtown when he was in Houston. According to the hotel's manager, who was the sales representative there at the time, Jon Emr was at the Holiday Inn on two occasions. The first time was for approximately two weeks, during which time he was comped his room, meals and drinks. The second time he was there almost three months and was comped some portion of the cost of meals and drinks and a large portion of the cost of rooms. He was provided rooms at $25.00 a day rather than the regular rate. Jon's assistant was there for a large amount of that stay and so was Felix Ajebo. [*Jon Emr had been given complimentary or discounted service because he had convinced the hotel that he would be filming a major movie in Houston and that the production company would stay in the Holiday Inn—where they would pay full price.*] . . .

When Emr's bill at the Holiday Inn got large enough that they began to become concerned, he then moved to the Four Seasons Hotel in downtown Houston. He was steered to the Four Seasons by a Chinese businessman in Houston known by the nickname "Bobo." Bobo is very civic minded. Bobo is well known in Houston to be the Godfather of Houston's China Town. He was steered to Jon Emr by Randall Marino. Bobo is good friends with the owner of the Four Seasons Hotel and asked the Four Seasons, as a favor, to treat Jon Emr as a V.I.P. since he was a movie producer. Jon Emr ran up a $3,200 bill at Four Seasons and as he tried to walk [out on] the bill, the Four Seasons called the police, had Jon Emr arrested. Before booking could be completed and charges formally lodged the next day, Bobo agreed to pay the Four Seasons bill by putting it on his own credit card.

While in Houston Jon Emr displayed a large number of the Columbia Security and Transfer phony certificates of deposit. He represented to several people that he had one million dollars worth of CDs. At one point, Jon Emr was to allow the CDs to be pledged as security for a forty-million-dollar loan that a bank in Houston was going to make to build a luxury hotel. It is not clear what blew the transaction apart. [*That hotel was never built.*] . . .

While in Houston, Jon Emr showed Bob Miller the original of a CD. . . . Miller was suspicious of Emr and asked a venture capitalist named Bruce Strunk to look at the CDs. Strunk pronounced them phony and advised Miller to have nothing to do with Jon Emr. . . .

Paul Bernstein and his wife, Sandy, are the owners of the Presidents Health Club located at 2100 Travis in the Central National Bank building. It is approximately three blocks due west of the Holiday Inn. Bernstein is a body builder and has acted in films. His wife is very intelligent and is gathering a number of documents having to do with a purported transaction whereby Jon Emr was going to buy that health club. Jon Emr said he was going to rename it "The Spa of the Stars," was going to arrange for a large number of Hollywood stars to come to Houston for the opening of the center and the promotion of it. The Bernsteins have an original bank commitment letter to make a loan to be backed up with the CDs which apparently the bank learned were phony. By his appearance, his conduct, Jon Emr blew the proposed loan transaction all to hell.

While in Houston Jon Emr met a Houstonian named Don Goldman who is supposedly wealthy and interested in movies and is the person who supposedly provided the production funds for *A Tiger's Tale*, co-produced by Goldman and Peter Douglas and starring Ann-Margret. The movie company that made that movie stayed in Houston and a large part of the movie was filmed in Houston and a little town called Sealy.

While all the bad actors [from *A Tiger's Tale*] were in Houston, Jon Emr was put in touch with a man named Dave Nwamo, a Nigerian who was backed up by Felix Ajebo. Nwamo walks with a limp and looks like a Mexican. Ronnie Niday chauffeured Jon Emr to [Nwamo's] residence north of downtown Houston that Niday describes as "ratty." Nwamo is the one who put Jon Emr in touch with Louis Mirando of Columbia Security and Transfer.

According to the manager of the Holiday Inn, Jon Emr traveled from Houston to Canada on at least one occasion. He asked the manager to make the hotel reservations and arrange for him a reservation at a Holiday Inn in Canada. Her recollection was that it was in Toronto. Jon returned to Houston and told the manager that he would be receiving an important Federal Express from Canada. If it arrived in his absence, she was to sign for it. She was to carefully guard it and give it to him as quickly as possible. She followed his instructions and immediately upon handing it to him, he opened it, and showed her the CDs which were for several million dollars and said, "Now baby, do you believe I'm a really wealthy man and a movie producer?" . . .

I interviewed Scott Peyton, he is a bartender and is the only one I could locate who worked in the bar when Jon Emr was there who is still employed by the Holiday Inn. He remembered Emr very well. He said, "Tell that son-of-a-bitch to kiss kiss, and I hope he's in the penitentiary by now." Scott vividly remembers Jon Emr as being extremely obnoxious, loud and fond of spending most of his waking time telling people what a big movie producer he was. He also clearly remembers that Jon Emr represented himself as being close to the Douglas family and that he was a partner of Joel Douglas. I then showed Scott a photo of Joel Douglas and said, "Do you ever recall seeing this man?" Scott said he looked very familiar. He then said he remembered seeing him in the bar of the Holiday Inn. He is the only person who positively asserted that he recalls seeing Joel in Houston.

Jon told chauffeur Ronnie Niday and Bob Miller that if they ran into any of the Douglas clan during the filming of *A Tiger's Tale* they were not to mention his name. Kirk Douglas and his wife came to Houston and stayed at the Four Seasons Hotel. They arrived on Continental Airlines flight #44, leaving LAX at 9:55 Pacific Time. . . . The production company of *A Tiger's Tale* employed Ronnie Niday's Admiral Limousine Service to chauffeur Kirk and his wife around Houston. According to Niday, Kirk left earlier than planned because he had a viral, flu-like infection and didn't feel well. On October 10, 1986, he chauffeured Kirk and Mrs. Douglas from the Four Seasons to the Texas Commerce Bank in downtown Houston. They were there for six and a half hours. He does not know the nature of their business. The following day, Niday chauffeured Kirk Douglas and his wife from Houston to Sealy, Texas, to the location where *A Tiger's Tale* was being filmed. Kirk Douglas made a very brief on-camera appearance, then left the scene and was taken to his lawyer's office in Houston. . . .

Sandy Bernstein says that several people saw Kirk Douglas when he was in Houston and all reported that Kirk came to Houston to "rescue Junior"—whatever that means.

According to Sandy Bernstein, she knew of a makeup artist and some casting people who said that Jon Emr lied so much [*about the movie he was going to make in Houston*] that he actually had them on standby ready to begin work and the casting people actually had ads answered and people show up for casting interviews and auditions. She does not know what film it was supposed to be but will check with these people and give us more information in the near future. . . .

In a letter dated April 21, 1987, a lawyer representing the Admiral Limousine Service demanded $14,262.25 from Jon Emr that he claimed Emr owed his clients.

While Earl Rutledge was in the business of trying to build a case against Jon Emr, Jon and his mother began to assemble their best defensive arsenal. At the center of their defense would be a wholesale debunking and Satanization of Scott Barnes.

Renee and Jon wrote several lengthy letters, some addressed to their own business associates and some to law enforcement officials, claiming that they had been harassed to their wits' end by Scott Barnes. The letters that the Emrs wrote are consistent and paint a horrifying portrait of Barnes. If the Emrs were to be believed, Scott Barnes was the moral equivalent of Max Cady, the character who was played by Robert Mitchum and later by Robert De Niro in the thriller *Cape Fear.*

Here are a few of the things that the Emrs claimed Scott Barnes had done to them:

On March 8, 1988, Renee contacted Scott and informed him that she had registered a script of *Bohica* with the Writers Guild of America. She wanted to meet with him on March 17 for the purpose of further research. Scott told her that he had already contracted his services to a film company producing a movie based on the life of the alleged MIA hunter Bo Gritz. He told Renee that he was receiving $250 a day from that production company and would want at least that much from her.

On March 15, 1988, Barnes phoned the Emr household in mid-afternoon. He spoke with Renee, telling her, "I know where the boys and you are and if you don't pay, you'll all be dead." Renee had her phone number changed the following day.

On March 19, Renee's car was broken into sometime during the night. The glove compartment lock had been pried apart and the car registration had been taken out of its bag and spread along the front seat, as if to indicate that it had been read.

On May 17, the *Fort Worth Star Telegram* printed the small article on the lawsuit filed against the Emrs. Renee insinuated that Barnes himself delivered the article to Orion Pictures, where an Emr project was allegedly being considered. The article was also delivered to *The Hollywood Reporter* and *Variety*, the two local trade publications.

On May 20, 1988, Scott phoned Jon directly. "Your business is ruined," he snarled at him. "If you won't pay, then the Douglases will. You'll never make it to court alive. You, your mother, and the boys are all dead. Then I'll collect from the Douglases!"

On June 1, 1988, Barnes sold his option on *Bohica* to a small, independent film company for the sum of $6,000, even though the Emrs still maintained that they owned the rights to the book.

On July 29, 1988, Barnes called Sue Fellows's place of employment—Spectradyne, a video company. Barnes made claims to the owners that Fellows's boyfriend [Jon Emr] and Michael Douglas were in police custody for narcotics and that Fellows was their distributor through Spectradyne.

On that same day, Scott sent a letter to Joel Douglas in France and forged Jon's signature at the bottom. The idea was to create friction between the two men and thus divide and conquer.

On September 21, 1988, Scott Barnes called the Judson School, which Jon's two boys attended, and told personnel there that the kids were in porno films and that Jon was a drug runner.

On an unspecified date, Barnes contacted the Paradise Valley Police Department and accused the Emrs of making threatening phone calls to him in California. Jon Emr was indeed charged in 1989, though the case was subsequently dropped.

Through 1988, Jon Emr collected various affidavits from individuals who claimed to have been contacted by Scott Barnes. Typical was one filed by Barbara Wick, the wife of the president of the Judson School, which Jon's two boys attended. She wrote that Scott, posing as an FBI agent, called her with the misinformation that the boys were involved in porno films and narcotics. She also said that Scott forewarned her about an upcoming NBC special on Jon Emr. "He did not sound rational," she concluded.

Another affadavit was written by Louis P. Mirando, the president of the Columbia Security and Transfer Company, who was indicted for the distribution of fake certificates of deposit. He also claimed that Scott approached him, again playing an FBI agent. "He is alleging all kinds of illegal activity," Mirando wrote. He also wrote that other Columbia clients had been contacted by Barnes.

In September 1988, Brian Barnes wrote the following affidavit:

> When Yoko [Wright] returned from a ski trip she came to Scott's house with me present. Yoko told Scott that she would pay him what he wanted to ruin Jon Emr. At that time she and Scott were looking up phone numbers. . . .
> I know that he called Paris, LA, Oklahoma and spoke with a few people, saying Jon was a drug runner and he was with Douglas Productions.

He also said that Jon embezzled money from investors and left town. . . .

At several times I've heard Scott say on the phone that he is working for the FBI investigating Jon Emr.

The Cons of Jon Emr:
The *Arizona Republic,* 1988

My job is to teach these natives the meaning of democracy, and they're going to learn democracy if I have to shoot every one of them.
—Paul Ford in *The Teahouse of the August Moon*

R andy Collier would be your typical roll-up-your-sleeves, nose-in-the-mud beat newspaper reporter if he were actually capable of rolling up his sleeves. By most estimates, Randy weighs over three hundred pounds, is about five feet eight, and likes to describe himself as a taxi cab with the doors wide open. For the most part, Randy Collier would show up to work at the *Arizona Republic,* based in downtown Phoenix, in a short-sleeved shirt. In the winter he'd wear a sweater. However, he never, never wore a tie. There was once an edict put out at the newspaper that all male staffers must wear ties. *Ties!* Ties in blazing hot Phoenix. Randy proudly led the revolution against the tyrants who wished to control how he dressed. Randy went to the head tyrant and said to him, "If I didn't have feet would you make me wear socks?"

"No, of course not."

"Well, I don't have a neck," he explained with a twang. "So why are you making me wear a tie?" Randy was not a journalist to fuck with. More than one person viewed him as the Jimmy Breslin of Arizona.

The powers gave in to Randy. He was simply too valuable to lose over an issue that minute. This was a man who, along with a partner, was named "Reporter of the Year" in Arizona in 1991. He's considered one of the paper's SWAT reporters, specializing in short-term investigative pieces.

I met with Collier twice. Both times it was at Chez Nous, a dark bar that was his perpetual hangout after work. It was far enough away from the *Republic* that he didn't have to bother dealing with his coworkers, whose faces were easy to tire of. Collier loves his job. That was immediately obvious. At the time, he had been at his desk at the *Republic* fourteen years. "I'll be here until I retire," he says. Then, without hint of humor, "Or probably until I die. That's probably what'll happen."

Randy didn't go to a "real" college, just a two-year institution where he didn't study much but did work for the college paper, which was enough to land him a job with the Associated Press. He took a break from journalism and joined a public relations firm. Three years later, he was back with AP. A couple of years after that he joined the *Republic.*

"This is a great paper," Randy Collier said to me one of those nights at Chez Nous. "They send me wherever I need to go. I must've flown a hundred thousand miles in the past few years."

Several of those miles were made in connection with Randy's investigation into Jon Emr and his way of life. Randy regards the story as one of his biggest and most interesting. "I kicked his ass pretty good," Randy now says of Jon Emr. "Renee said that I was the sleaziest journalist in America. *That* made me feel like I had done something for mankind."

Randy even went as far as surveilling Jon in California. "The reason I did that was that he had been sending faxes to people saying that he was at a pool in Beverly Hills or something like that. Well, he had the crummiest goddamn apartment, driving an old motorcycle, living with his mother who dressed in these JCPenney–type dresses and old sandals. Jon was always wearing flip-flops. I don't know what he did with his money, but they sure didn't spend it on clothes.

"If I was a con man and a crook, I'd give Jon Emr a lot of credit 'cause I think he was a really good con man. But, I'm not. So I thought he was just an asshole."

On Sunday, October 9, 1988, the *Arizona Republic* ran a front-page story on Jon Emr by Randy Collier. The headline read: VALLEY FIGURE PROBED IN MOVIE FUND SCAM. The article was massive by *Republic* standards, running over 2,000 words. Collier detailed Emr's seduction of Bob Franks and Aubrey Brothers. He detailed Emr's theft of Tim and Jean Johnson's video equipment. He detailed Emr's game playing with Scott Barnes. He detailed Emr's romancing and conning of Yoko

Wright. He detailed Jon's kidnapping of his children from Gloria Farrens. Collier's articles also revealed that the Federal Bureau of Investigation had now begun to take a look at Jon because of his relationship
with Louis P. Mirando, the banker being indicted for issuing phony
certificates of deposit.

In short, the article was absolutely devastating. In retrospect the article did not probe that deeply into Jon Emr. With the amount of space
he was afforded, Randy could tell only so much. Nevertheless, in the
bedroom community of Paradise Valley, the article was especially embarrassing.

After the publication of the article, Renee called Randy's managing editor, essentially telling him that his reporter was a scumbag who
needed to be reined in. She told him that she and Jon intended to sue
the *Arizona Republic* for the damages that they had suffered from Collier's "malicious libel."

A few days later, Randy was notified by his assistant editor that Jon
Emr and his mother, Renee, were waiting in the lobby to talk with him.
Randy did not want to go and meet Emr. He had never met the man,
but he disliked him. Disliked him immensely. The truth was that after
he had published the article, Randy had become personally involved in
the story by helping Gloria Farrens get legal help in the Phoenix area
to take Jon to court. In fact, Randy even arranged for Gloria to get
photos of her children, whom she hadn't seen in years.

Randy's assistant editor told him that they had to go and confront
Emr. Randy called down to security and told them to go ahead and
search and frisk Jon and, if they wanted, the mother as well.

When Randy reached the lobby, Jon and Renee were red-faced at
having been searched. Also there was "Jon's attorney of the month," as
Collier described him. Jon was wearing flip-flops, a Hawaiian shirt that
was opened down to his belly button, and a gold necklace, and his face
had a sheen to it.

Randy looked at Jon and grunted. "I wonder why a guy your age has
to bring his mother along." Jon opened his mouth to respond, but
Randy cut him off. "You're a big boy, Jon. You also have your lawyer
with you, which makes me think that you're probably going to sue me.
I don't know anything about this lawyer. I don't know if he's any good

or not, but I'm sure that he knows how to write a letter of demand. So, I don't want to talk with you."

Randy pressed the elevator button. "I think you're rude," Jon said to him.

Randy shoved his heavy index finger into Jon's chest. "You're fuckin' right I'm rude. I'm not going to be nice to you! Why don't you get outta here!"

As Randy rode the elevator with his editor he said, "Screw 'em! I wrote a fair and impartial story. Anyway, it was accurate."

Neither Jon nor Renee Emr made an immediate response to the *Arizona Republic*'s Sunday exposé. Instead, the paper's publisher, Pat Murphy, had to contend with a letter written by Jon's son Roger. The letter was the ultimate nastigram, accusing Randy Collier of being an opportunist who would lie to get on his newspaper's front page. Roger told Murphy that he should be "ashamed" of having Collier on his staff. After demanding a front-page apology, Roger wrote: "I feel sorry for you and I am glad my dad and grandparents are not like you people."

What appeared to incense the Emrs more than anything else from the *Arizona Republic* article was the claim that they were being investigated by the Federal Bureau of Investigation. In truth, the Bureau was very much looking into Columbia Security and Transfer and, naturally, Jon Emr was part of that equation. He was ultimately never charged with any kind of securities fraud and the FBI has never formally acknowledged that Jon Emr or any member of his family had been the subject of a probe.

At this point, after suffering the indignity of an embarrassing and potentially career-devastating newspaper profile and a multimillion-dollar lawsuit that charged him with racketeering, Jon Emr must have felt that he had to go to work destroying Aubrey Brothers and Earl Rutledge. It was his only mode of survival. He would start by putting his own spin on the FBI matter. He assumed that his principal ally would be Jane Favor. After all, wasn't it true that Jane was on "the outs" with Aubrey's best friend Roy Ashton. She *must* be ready to turn on Aubrey and company.

■ ■ ■

When Jane got to her house one day, she was greeted at the door by her father, Jack, the old rodeo star. "You had a call that you have to return," he said to her with a big grin. Jon Emr had called.

Jane smiled and then called up Earl Rutledge. "I have a message here to call Jon Emr," she said. "And I need to know what it is all about. Do you have any idea?"

Earl told her that he did not. But then he got into the various aspects of their lawsuit against Jon and added that the FBI was investigating Jon for a number of things including drug running. That made sense to Jane. She had suspected it all along.

Jane got her thoughts together, sighed gently, and then slowly dialed Jon's number. When Jon answered, his voice conjured up a million and a half bad memories. But she remained composed. "Hello, Jon."

"Jane! God, it's good to hear your voice. How long has it been?"

Probably not long enough, Jane thought. "Jon, what can I do for you?"

Jon told her about the lawsuit that Brothers and company had filed against him. They were *bad, bad* people, he told her. They never should have gotten involved with them, he said. Then he dropped a bombshell on her. "Jane, they're planning to do you harm. They want to see to it that you never get your fee."

"Fee? Jon, you've had two years to pay me my fee. Why should I assume that you have any intention of paying me?"

"C'mon, Jane, calm down. The truth is that your fee will come upon the completion of the—"

"Give me a break, Jon. What is it that you want?"

"You may already know this. The FBI is investigating *Aubrey Brothers* for drug running."*

Jane shook her head. "Jon, you can't be serious."

"You don't believe me?"

"Of course not, Jon."

---

*In an attempt to discredit Earl Rutledge and Bob Franks, Renee Emr gave to me a *Dallas Morning News* article dated May 11, 1990, that began "[Bob Franks and Earl Rutledge] were charged Thursday in an eighteen-count federal fraud indictment. [They] are accused of defrauding the failed Metroplex Federal Savings Association." What Renee did not give me was an article of January 1, 1991, in the *Dallas Morning News* which begins: "A federal jury in Dallas has acquitted [Bob Franks and Earl Rutledge] on charges of bank fraud, conspiracy, and obstruction of justice."

There was a pause. "Would you like to speak to the FBI agent in charge?"

"Yes, Jon. I think that I would."

"I'll call you back with the number."

Within an hour Jon was back on the phone. "Unfortunately, that agent is gone now. I think that he may be back in Washington, D.C."

"Really?" Wasn't this ever a surprise.

"Here's what I'd like you to do. I'd like for you to write out the chain of events as you saw them regarding Aubrey and myself. Then I'd like you to send it to the FBI."

"I see."

"Would you agree to that?"

"Sure."

"And then, you know, Mother and I would like to read it . . . before you send it off. We want to make sure there are no mistakes or anything, you know, superfluous stuff. We don't want to bog down the FBI."

"Oh no, Jon. Heavens, no."

"So, you'll write it out, then?"

"Sure, sure."

"And give it to us?"

"Sure, Jon."

After Jane hung up the phone she had a good laugh and then pulled out her typewriter.

Jon would call two or three times a day for the next week wondering where the letter was. "We really need the letter, Jane." Need it, need it, need it.

Eventually Jane finished *her* version of events. She faxed it to Jon.

A few minutes later Renee called, saying that Jon was too upset.

Eventually Jane interrupted Renee. "Renee, I hate to break the news to you. But there is no way that I would even dream of helping you. It's an ego thing, Renee. You take me for an idiot. I'm not so stupid that I am going to fall in with you people all over again.

"Renee, let me put it to you this way." There was a pause. "Not only will I not write a letter in support of you and not only will I not allow you to edit it, but I will make it a point to support anybody— ANYBODY—who has some complaint against you. I will not rest until you people are brought to justice. That, Renee, is my pledge. You can go to the bank with that. And Renee, don't ever dial my number again."

Jane hung up. The phone rang on three separate occasions. Jane eventually picked it up. Sure enough, it was Renee on the other end. Jane did not let her get in a single word. "Renee," she said slowly and with enunciation. "You are pushing it. I know where you live."

"Is that a—"

"I'll tell you something. If I ever hear that you have used my name or my father's name in connection with any of your so-called projects, I'll kick your small gray butt all over Los Angeles."

Jane slammed the phone. To her recollection, that was her last conversation with anybody named Emr.

A Visit to Orange County:
August 23, 1991

*There are certain pleasures you get, little—little jabs of pleasure when—
when a swordfish takes the hook or—or—or when you watch
a great fighter getting ready for the kill, see?*
—James Mason on how Judy Garland sings in *A Star Is Born*

It took Hank Davies and Steve Yoshida almost an hour to get into Benny's neighborhood in Orange County. Davies had been itching for this moment ever since he read Benny's name in the letter that Suggs wrote to his girlfriend Susan. When they arrived on Benny's street, both Davies and Yoshida fell into a silent shock. The road was crammed full of paramedics, police cars, even a fire truck. It was as if an earthquake had just hit and dozens of people needed to be excavated from a collapsed building. Davies said it first. "My God. He's come and killed the entire family. Jesus."

"Wow," said Yoshida.

When they spoke to the paramedics they were told the ironic story. Benny's wife, Jennifer, had backed out of the driveway and didn't notice that one of her platoon of children had run right behind her. SLAM! She hit the little girl. The paramedics told Davies that the girl's condition was real iffy, that the injuries were considerable and very possibly life threatening.

"Maybe we should come back another time," Yoshida said.

"Fuck that," Davies said.

Davies did not need to be told who Benny was. He was the slight, sorry-looking son of a bitch in the T-shirt standing next to the woman crying hysterically. Davies walked up to the couple, his expression not betraying his feelings for them. With Yoshida dutifully in tow, he flashed his badge in Benny's face. "I'm Sergeant Davies. Culver City homicide, This is Detective Yoshida."

It struck Davies that the minute Jennifer heard the word "homicide," she must have thought they were there to arrest her for the murder of her child. Davies wasted no time saying, "We're investigating the disappearance of a Susan Lynn Calkins."

"Yeah?" Benny said nonchalantly, as if he didn't even know the girl.

Davies took a quick look around. "I know this is a bad time. I'd like to look through your house."

Benny nodded, "Go on."

Davies and Yoshida gave each other a look of subtle surprise. *Go on?* Is that what he had said? Obviously, this was no career criminal.

The two police officers could not find anything of relevance. When the search was over, Davies grilled Benny. But nothing he squirreled out of Benny proved helpful. Yeah, he admitted without much tugging and pulling, he was a pal of Suggsy's and, goddamn, was he shocked when he heard what had happened. In the end, the only thing that Benny was absolutely, dead-on sure about was that he knew nothing. At all.

It is standard operating procedure to run a credit check on any fugitive. The logic here is simple. A credit check will list all of the person's credit cards, which can then yield information on the exact location of the perp at specific points in time.

As it turned out, Suggsy's credit was surprisingly good. The only thing working against him was that he was overdue on $200 of his Visa card. In addition, he had missed his last several car payments, totaling about $1,500.

Davies collected the numbers of the various credit card companies from the Culver City fraud officer and dialed their security offices.

"Look," Davies told whoever was in charge, "we have a double homicide, maybe even triple or quadruple. The killer is on the loose, we have to track him down."

Within minutes, Davies would be transferred over to the business office where the young clerk would be instructed to be as helpful as possible to the nice sergeant from Culver City, California. At no time did any of the companies demand that Hank Davies produce a search warrant. Instead, they spent hours on the phone, going over Suggsy's credit activity from the weeks before the murders. Visa was apparently the most used card of the lot. Suggsy had not used any of his cards since the murder.

Davies was able to piece together that before the murders Suggsy had driven from Los Angeles to Laughlin, Nevada, to Las Vegas to Paradise Valley and then, finally, to Culver City where he offed Jon and Roger Emr.

Then came the Chevron card. The Chevron card was the kicker. The Chevron card would change the whole tenor of the investigation.

By the time he got to the Chevron card, Davies was beat tired. He was certain that all he was going to get from the Chevron security office was a confirmation that Suggsy had stopped for gas somewhere along the way, probably in some hick, remote town. As the young lady on the other side was giving him the details, giving him every purchase Suggsy had made in the past few months, Davies wrote robotically in his notebook.

"Wait a minute," the clerk said at one point. "This must be a mistake."

"What's that?"

"This is his credit card all right. But—"

Davies sat straight in his chair. "But what?"

"But it's not his signature."

"What's the name?"

It took her a few seconds to actually decipher the signature. But then she had it all figured out. "I can read the first name. The first name is Benny."

"Sh-iiiiitttt!"

"Excuse me?"

"Never mind. Could you drop all of those in the mail to me?"

"Yessir."

Then Hank Davies went to see Steve Yoshida and the Chief to tell them that they now had an accomplice in the murder of the Emrs.

The Cons of Jon Emr:
NBC News and Ross Perot, 1988

Mephistopheles is such a mouthful in Times Square.
—Robert De Niro in *Angel Heart*

Jon Emr met Robin Gregson in the winter of 1986 through a man named Major Mark Smith, a retired United States Army officer. Smith had made a name for himself by suing then President Ronald Reagan on September 4, 1985, for "abandoning" the issue of the MIAs in Vietnam. The lawsuit obviously went nowhere. However, Smith's passion on the topic and the rumor that he had dramatic "inside" information earned him at least the right to testify before a Senate subcommittee in late January of 1986.*

During the testimony, Smith claimed that a man named Robin Gregson, a shady and mysterious arms merchant who lived in Thailand, had in his possession a videotape that showed American soldiers still being held captive in Southeast Asia. Smith even claimed that he had seen it. According to Smith, the tape ran for 248 minutes. It included footage of thirty-nine Americans working in a logging camp with leg irons keeping them in tow. One American, apparently a trusty, is riding a horse.

For the next few weeks, Smith was bombarded with phone calls from this man named Jon Emr, who claimed to be a major Hollywood producer who was in partnership with Joel Douglas, "the brother of Michael!" Emr had gotten his number through Colonel Jack Bailey (the star of "A Chance to Live"), who was Smith's good friend. Emr told Smith he was making a movie about Jack Bailey's life called "Bai-

---

*Interestingly, at the same hearings, Scott Barnes told his *Bohica* story. The hearings were interrupted with the announcement that the space shuttle *Challenger* had blown up.

ley's Bandits." Emr wanted to meet Smith to discuss the possibility of their making a film together.

When Smith was on the West Coast, he sat down with Jon Emr and Colonel Bailey. Though Jon promised Major Smith a top-notch meal at a top Hollywood restaurant like the Polo Lounge—after all, he was a war hero who deserved the best possible treatment—the meeting took place at Denny's Restaurant. Smith immediately disliked Jon. He found him boorish and dressed inappropriately for the occasion. Smith came up with an immediate nickname for Emr: "The King of the Oilers."

Jon told him that he wanted to get the "rights" to the Gregson videotape showing the Americans still being held in captivity. Over the three-hour sitdown at a Denny's, Major Smith explained and reexplained that he did not have the right to speak for Gregson. He also told Jon that the videotape was under the control of the Israeli Mossad.

Jon began telling Mark Smith that he wanted to make a movie about his life. At one point, Emr turned to Jack Bailey and said, "You know who should play Major Smith, here? Michael should. Michael Douglas."

By the end of their session, as a favor to Colonel Bailey, Smith agreed only to being interviewed for "A Chance to Live." He also said that he would do what he could to introduce Gregson to Emr.

In February of 1986, Gregson was brought to the United States by Major Smith, who hoped that he would play the infamous videotape for the United States Congress.* However, the only "power player" that Gregson met was Jon Emr, who was presented to Gregson as a kind of big-time Hollywood producer. The two con artists took to each other right away. Before anybody knew it, they had a partnership agreement. Emr agreed to get Gregson's tape on the air for a huge amount of cash in exchange for a piece of the action.

The first thing that Jon did was bring Gregson to his brother Art's house. Art had plenty of video equipment and even a cameraman who worked for him. Jon wanted to have Art film some of Gregson's explosive "evidence." Art reluctantly agreed.

When Gregson arrived at Art's home, he made quite a show of it.

---

*Gregson made an appearance but would not produce the tape.

He asked to see everybody's "credentials" and then had his Iranian right-hand man "check the perimeter" for "assassins." As Art would later recall it, Gregson "was out of his fucking mind. He was a slob and a reprehensible pig. He was so full of shit."

Art videotaped Gregson sitting in his dining room and showing photos that served as "proof" of a modern massacre. The photos showed dozens of "prisoners" lying dead in a body of water. Art noticed that many of the corpses had their heads above water and were trying to breathe. At one point, Gregson instructed Art to "get a shot of my rings. The *people* will know what that means."

After the shoot, Gregson showed Art a photo of himself with a Laotian who was bound and gagged and lying on the dirt. Gregson's foot was on his face and he was holding an assault weapon to his ear. Gregson laughed. "Fucking wog," he bellowed.

"Someone's liable to shoot this asshole," Art Emr later told his wife. When Art told Jon that he thought Gregson was a fraud, Jon became angry. He told Art that Gregson was for real. He was a freedom fighter. A bona fide hero.

A few weeks later, Major Smith was summoned to a hotel in Los Angeles where Gregson was again being filmed, this time by Jon himself. Apparently Colonel Jack Bailey had gone crazy out of his mind and had brandished a .45, waving it around hysterically. When Smith arrived at the hotel, Gregson was sitting on Bailey, subduing him. It seemed that Bailey had lost it during the shooting of the footage wherein Gregson was allegedly burning "The Tape."

The next step for the illegal tape was an offer to the White House. Mark Smith's attorney, a man named Mark Waple, delivered a letter to Vice President George Bush demanding $4.2 million for a copy of the tape. Oh, and there was something else—$42,000 was needed to bail Robin Gregson out of a prison in Singapore.

Bush obviously could not use government funds to buy the tape from what might well have been a crackpot. Instead, Bush personally contacted H. Ross Perot, who, it seemed, was very much in the business of keeping crackpots in business. Bush wanted Perot to purchase the tape and, if he could, somehow get Gregson out of jail. If the tape turned out to be geniune, Bush promised Perot that he would be reimbursed.

Perot must have had an extra ounce of confidence in the Gregson-Emr tape. After all, it was no less than the vice president of the United

States asking him to buy it. The Goddamn Veep! Why, Perot even checked with his big honcho contact at the Defense Intelligence Agency who told him that, yes, there was a great deal of hope resting on this tape.

Perot did not bail Gregson out of jail but he did manage to get the charges against him dropped. Gregson had been incarcerated for allegedly rolling an Indian businessman for some $42,000. Perot simply remunerated the businessman and, bingo, Gregson was released.

Perot promised Gregson that he would give him the $4.2 million if he flew to Dallas and provided the videotape. When Gregson asked Perot for a plane ticket, the billionaire laughed and told him, "For this amount of money you can buy your own ticket."

Gregson never materialized in Dallas. If he had, his bluff would have been called. After all, there was still money to be made on the mystery tape. That's what Jon Emr assured Robin Gregson.

Today, George Lewis is NBC's man on the scene in Los Angeles. In the early 1990s, as Los Angeles lost its luster, that of George Lewis rose in proportion. When Rodney King was beaten to a pulp, it was Lewis on the scene. He was there for two subsequent King trials and the disastrous riot that was sandwiched in between them. He was there for the series of natural disasters that absolutely devastated Southern California, starting with fires, through mud slides, and finally with one of the biggest earthquakes in decades. He was there for Michael Jackson. For O.J. He was there for it all.

Lewis is a tall, burly man with wavy, normally unkempt hair, and a thick mustache out of a John Ford film. He's hardly a natty dresser. When he knows the camera will only catch him from the waist up he likes to wear jeans. There is not a real possibility of his getting a cute moniker like the "Scud Stud." Nevertheless, Lewis is about as trustworthy and professional as they come, a cut from the Edward R. Murrow school.

For years, Lewis's best friend and producer has been a veteran named Art Lord. Lewis and Lord met each other when they were two of NBC's four-man team of war correspondents in Vietnam in 1971. Since the war, both have taken up shop in the Burbank, California, offices of NBC. The stories that they have been proudest of have been those dealing with the Vietnam MIA issue. In fact, whenever the New

York assignment desk needed a team to cover a Southeast Asia story, it would invariably go to Lewis and Lord.

And so it came to be that in 1986, the team of Lord and Lewis came in contact with Jon Emr. What ensued was the single most bizarre journalistic experience either of them has likely ever had.

On July 16, 1986, Art Lord received a call from the security gate. "A Mister Jon Emr" was there to see him. Lord had made the appointment a day or two earlier. Jon Emr had contacted him with the exciting news that he and only he had the keys to the Nightly News Ratings Kingdom: he had a video that was proof positive that Americans were still being held in captivity in Southeast Asia. Lord received many such calls, but he was loath to disregard any of them. Who knew from what innocuous source the next great Watergate-style story might emerge? Lord told the security guard to admit Emr.

Lord could sense that Emr was a hack or a phony from the start. Jon was dressed in his classic uniform of a Hawaiian shirt, shorts, and sandals. Lord might have thrown him out, but he noticed that Emr was carrying a couple of videotapes and there would be no harm in checking them out.

After shaking hands, Jon explained that he had *the* footage of *the* "infamous" Robin Gregson tape. Lord nodded patiently without giving off any emotion. Inwardly, he was somewhat tantalized. Within the MIA hunter community, Robin Gregson, who also went by the name of John Obassi (he took the pseudonym from the code accorded him by the CIA: "The Obese Man"), had gotten a reputation as a kind of fly-by-night con artist and mercenary who had all sorts of dealings in Southeast Asia and the Middle East. Rumors had Gregson dealing in drugs and gold. The grapevine consistently had him involved with murky Chinese and Thai government officials who had knowledge of American soldiers being held in captivity.

Art took Jon into his office on the third floor of the building, one story beneath the news studio. Art shoved the cassette into the VCR and sat on the edge of his table as the tape began.

Lord was mighty disappointed when all he saw was an enormously fat, bearded Robin Gregson, wearing a suit that looked like it was ready to burst off him, sitting at a desk in what appeared to be a hotel room. On the tape, Gregson holds up a videocassette and starts unspooling the tape from it, dumping it in a wastebasket. Gregson then squirts the basket with lighter fluid and sets it on fire. All the while Gregson, in a clipped British accent, is explaining how the United States government did not deserve to see this tape and how many innocent people were now going to die.

When the tape ended, Jon smiled and explained that he was the one who actually videotaped the sequence they had just watched. "Don't worry, Art. What he burned was only a videotape. That was to make a point. But I can tell you, just between us, that the real thing is on film and I can get it for you." Art was ready to kick Jon out right then, but before he could, Jon had inserted another tape in the machine. This time it was a copy of "A Chance to Live," or at least those segments he had on tape. By the time that tape had concluded, Lord was ready to call it quits. He walked Jon to the door and told him that he would get back to him shortly. That night, Lord wrote in his journal, "had meeting with scuzball Jon Emr."

Art Lord was dead positive that Emr and Gregson were jointly running some sort of scam. When George Lewis came in from an assignment about, of all things, bike riding as a popular new sport, Lord told him about his odd encounter with Emr. They decided that there might indeed be a story in the relationship between the Hollywood hustler and the phony MIA hunter.

George Lewis contacted Jon at his home and asked if they could meet. In addition, Deborah Pettit, NBC's Washington-based field producer, flew in. Pettit, the daughter of former NBC vice president and general assignment reporter Tom Pettit, had been covering the Senate hearings before the Senate Veterans Affairs Committee in late January 1986 on the MIA issue. That included the testimony of the staunch advocate of Robin Gregson, Major Mark Smith. Deborah was on top of the topic and the NBC brass felt that she would be valuable to the segment.

As much as it irked Art Lord and George Lewis, NBC was now willing to purchase "A Chance to Live." Since Lord and Lewis knew that they would have to air at least a brief segment of the "documentary" as part of their broadcasts, they would have to legally protect themselves and buy the broadcast rights.

Art Lord began to research Jon's credentials. His calls to the various guilds in town and his talks with his substantial Hollywood contacts yielded absolutely no revelation as to who the hell Jon Emr actually was. "He had no credentials," Lord would later say. "He had never produced a thing in his life. We knew that we were dealing with a con artist."

What Art and George really wanted to see was just how far and in what direction the con would go. What truly fascinated Lewis, Lord, and the rest of the brass at *NBC Nightly News* was that, somehow, Jon Emr *did* have connections with MIA circles and he *did* have the Douglas family name to cling to. Lewis was dying to know what made Jon Emr tick.

At his first meeting with Jon, which took place at a Holiday Inn restaurant in Torrance, Lewis was hit right away with a demand from Emr for half a million dollars for the videotape that Robin Gregson had of American soldiers being held in captivity. Jon told George that this was a steal and that he'd better hop on it because every other "fucking" network in town wanted a piece of it. Emr also made the dramatic claim that both the United States government and the billionaire Ross Perot, who was heavily involved in the MIA/POW movement, had offered millions for the tape. Lewis, who had the meeting with Jon secretly videotaped, explained to Jon that all they wanted was the right to use a brief clip from "A Chance to Live." They would also buy the footage of Gregson burning the alleged MIA tape. There was not a chance in the world that NBC or any legitimate news organization in the United States would pay the kind of money Jon was asking.

That one meeting with Emr translated into several other such meetings. It was as if Jon were stretching out the negotiations so that he could get a few more free meals and drinks. Every meeting was the same. NBC indeed wanted the Gregson tape and "A Chance to Live," Jon wanted a ton of money, NBC told him it was out of the question. "At some of the points of our negotiations, when he'd get pissed off, he'd get drunk as a skunk and he'd call my house at night," Lewis now says. "Sometimes he'd get my answering machine and he would be totally blitzed and abusive."

Some of the messages that Jon left were threatening. He would promise to send his "buddies" over to George's house unless NBC gave him what he wanted. Eventually, George brought one of the tapes to one of their meetings. He played it for Emr. Although George had set himself up all along as the "good cop," with Art Lord the "bad cop," he nonetheless found himself compelled to say, "Look, Jon. I could turn these over to the authorities and have you arrested, so just fuckin' stop it."

Eventually, George Lewis and Art Lord agreed to give Jon $2,900. The understanding was that he would use the cash to fly to Cyprus, where he claimed Gregson was in hiding. When he arrived there he would facilitate a meeting between Gregson and George Lewis on September 18, 1986.

Near the end of August, George and Jon signed their deal at the Holiday Inn. The money gave Lewis the right to air a few seconds of "A Chance to Live" footage. According to their contract, Jon would be given an "air check," which was a recording of the broadcast as it had been broadcast.

Emr walked away with the cash and, essentially, vanished.

By the middle of September, when there was not a single phone call or postcard from Jon, Art and George made the reasonable assumption that NBC had been taken for three grand and that was that.

A number of times one of the NBC producers called Jon's home. Either there was no answer or Renee would pick up. When George Lewis suggested that her son had up and left with their money, Renee became indignant. "I raised my son to be honest," she said. "How dare you accuse my son of such a thing!"

A few days after Jon Emr's great disappearing act, a secretary at NBC received a phone call from none other than the mysterious, tape-burning Robin Gregson. He had been told that Emr was negotiating with NBC and he wanted to know what was going on. Gregson was gruff and rude and demanded to speak to "anybody fuckin' in charge over there." Eventually, Gregson would have a series of calls with both George Lewis and Deborah Pettit in the Washington bureau of NBC. Pettit's mission had been to tie up the loose ends on the Gregson story from the government's point of view, dealing mostly with the Department of Defense and the National League of Families. Both of those organizations derided Gregson's claims.

Over and over again, Gregson's point was essentially this: he had

unequivocally severed his ties with Jon Emr and was no longer affili-
ated with him. Jon Emr, that goddamn, cock-sucking, drunk-off-his-
ass, cocaine-snorting son of a bitch, did not speak for him.

"That's funny," George said during one of their conversations. "Jon
took some of our money and he was supposed to use it to set up a meeting between you and us."

"That bloody son of a bitch!"

"He even signed a contract."

"How much did you give the asshole?"

"I dunno, a few thousand."

"Well, he was supposed to split that money with me. Now I don't
even know where he is!"

"We understand," Lewis said. "Look, if there's anything to this
film of yours, we'd like to put it on the air. We'd like to be able to discuss it."

Gregson agreed to meet with Lewis in Larnaca, Cyprus. Art Lord convinced his superiors in New York that this was a story worth following.
On the one hand, there was the tale about a pair of wonderfully con-
trived con men. And then, of course, there was this one in a million
shot that there might be a picture of some of "our boys" digging
ditches in Laos. "You don't want to be remembered as the person that
didn't hire Elvis," he explained.

Before leaving for Larnaca, Lewis stopped off in Dallas. He wanted
to determine whether or not there was any truth at all to Jon Emr's
claims that both the government and Ross Perot had wanted to buy the
Gregson videotape. The mere fact that Ross Perot, the founder of
EDS and one of the nation's wealthiest men, had made the time to
meet with him was interesting enough.

Lewis showed up at Ross Perot's offices with a complete camera
crew. Perot told Lewis that he would meet with him on a "background" basis only. That meant that Lewis could use his information
but attribute nothing to him directly. There was, Perot added, no
chance in hell that he would agree to go on camera. He would not even
allow Lewis to tape-record him.

When the billionaire and the reporter were alone, Perot conceded
that Vice President George Bush had indeed asked him to purchase
this videotape that had footage of the American prisoners of war. Perot

said that, yes, he bailed Gregson out of a Singapore jail but withheld several million dollars until the video materialized. It never did, Perot said, and that was that. Just another Vietnam loony trying to squeeze him for some money.

Perot and Lewis both agreed that what Gregson and Emr had pulled was a "cruel hoax."

Lewis flew to Cyprus in late October of 1986. Before his arrival, Lewis had sent his crew in Greece the footage of Gregson burning a videotape. He asked them to find Gregson and secretly tape him.

On October 30, 1986, after a couple of days in the country, Lewis was picked up at his hotel by a bunch of bearded young men in a Land-Rover. Lewis's cameraman, an Israeli named Avi, begged him not to go. "If you get into that Land-Rover, you're dead," he said.

"I'm going, bye-bye," and that was that. George Lewis was off in search of one of the "great" stories of his career. Several minutes later, Lewis found himself at a dark and secluded beach. One of the men in the Land-Rover pointed due east and told Lewis to walk, simply walk. Lewis later described it as "ultra-melodramatic, with a cloak-and-dagger flair to it. It was something like a bad Robert Ludlum novel."

A few minutes into his stroll, Lewis walked over a chain that was draped across a road. In front of him he saw little thatched gazebos. Lewis walked into the first one and there was Robin Gregson.

The two of them shook hands. "Why are there no lights?" George asked.

"I don't want to be photographed," said Gregson, who, just months earlier, allowed himself to be filmed burning a videotape. "I've got to frisk you," which is exactly what he then did. "I just wanted to make sure that you didn't have any tape recorders or cameras with you."

Lewis found it all amusing and nodded in understanding. Lewis noticed that where they were was out of any reasonable view of somebody who might be filming from the road. In addition, the sounds of the waves crashing on the beach would have made taping their conversation difficult.

They sat down at a picnic table all by themselves. Lewis allowed his host to ramble on about a conspiracy between the CIA and drug run-

ners and how that was the reason why Americans were still not released. It was the same kind of loony MIA folklore that Lewis had been
hearing for years. As Gregson droned on and on, Lewis considered the
fact that he was about to have his ass chewed off for wasting NBC's
money on a plane ticket to Cyprus.

At the end of their talk, Gregson finally brought up the matter of
the footage. "Look, if you guys can put up the money—"

Lewis cut him off. "We already told Jon Emr that was not possible."

"Jon Emr's a fucking scumbag, let me tell you. This bastard screwed
me. You can't trust him."

Lewis smiled. "Well, we don't exactly trust him, either. He took us
for some cash. He said he was going to organize a meeting between us."

"Ha! Motherfucker!"

"Look, before I can negotiate with you at all I have to see this
footage."

Gregson rubbed his fingers through his prominent beard. "You
gotta understand that there are these powerful intelligence agencies
that have their finger on this thing. I would be fucking totaled if this
thing got out. It can only get out under the right circumstances, the
right place and time."

"In other words . . . what, Robin?"

"In other words the money has to be worth the risk." Gregson
leaned forward. "You know, it was the Mossad behind the film," he
said, referring to the elite Israeli secret service. "They're the ones."

"Jesus, Robin! What the hell does the Mossad care about Americans
in Southeast Asia?"

Gregson nodded his head omnisciently. "It's the drugs. The golden
triangle. It's the opium."

That was it. George Lewis had finally found a nut who could make
Jon Emr look like Honest Abe Lincoln. "Let me think about it. It's a
lot of money."

In fact, Lewis had no intention of continuing his negotiations with
Gregson. But he wanted to give Gregson an upside to letting him leave
the site unharmed.

The next day, Lewis received a call at his hotel room. It was Robin
Gregson, furious. "You were supposed to come alone!"

George was baffled. "I was alone."

"Bullshit!" Then Gregson gave him a physical description of the men in his camera crew. "We filmed you!" Gregson screamed.

"You must be referring to my film crew. We had three guys fly over from Israel. We're getting ready to cover the release of David Jacobson," Lewis said, referring to the American who had been held hostage by Iranian-backed terrorists for several years. "You're getting paranoid, Robin."

"Fuck you!" and with that the conversation ended. Lewis would neither meet nor hear from Gregson again.

Lewis had not lied to Robin Gregson. When George phoned Art Lord and Deborah Pettit with the news that the trip to Cyprus had been a bust, they were not terribly stressed. Since he was already in that part of the world, they assigned him to cover the release of the hostage Jacobson. The story would require him to travel to Frankfurt.

Before he left for Germany, George decided that he would tie up the loose end of Joel Douglas. He was now absolutely obsessed with nailing down the truth behind Jon Emr. While it was Emr's MIA connections that truly fascinated George, he knew, and more important, his producers knew, that Emr's Hollywood connections would appeal to his viewers.

Telexes went back and forth between Joel Douglas, who was alternately in Nice and Milan, and George Lewis in Greece and, eventually, West Germany. At first, Douglas consented to an interview. Lewis flew to Nice to meet him at his studios. When they got there, the place was closed down and Douglas was nowhere to be found. Later, Douglas formally withdrew the offer. Douglas was loath to even meet with George Lewis, on or off the record. Douglas's letters urged NBC not to connect him with Emr.

Back in Burbank, sitting at NBC headquarters, Art Lord and George Lewis sat back to analyze exactly what they had. As far as they were concerned, the story was about how Jon Emr had manipulated the emotionalism around the MIA issue for personal gain. "That was a hot-button issue with a lot of people at the time," Lewis explained in reflection. "I believe there was an ABC poll taken in 'eighty-five that showed seventy-three percent of the American public believed there were living American POWs in Southeast Asia. Here was a guy who saw the opportunity to manipulate. Well, when the group in Texas filed their lawsuit, we had a concrete event to center our story around."

Of course the Texas clan was only too happy to be helpful to NBC. In the spirit of cooperation, Earl Rutledge turned over to Lewis the name and the phone number in France of the mole that was working for him in Michael Douglas's production company, the Stone Group, the man who had been feeding Earl information about Joel Douglas. It was this man, Francis Levy (not his real name), who finally solved for George Lewis the big mystery of where Jon had disappeared to with NBC's cash the previous August.

According to Levy, Jon Emr bought a ticket to France, where he attended Joel Douglas's wedding. When he came back, Jon told people that he had been Joel's best man.* The two were now *that* close.

One day, weeks into their investigation of Emr, George Lewis phoned Jon and told him that he had been talking to a number of people who had rather nasty things to say about him.

"Why the fuck are you doing this to me?" Jon asked.

George was up front with him. He told him that he thought he was a hustler and a manipulator and that he hoped to prove it.

"Look," Jon said in earnest, "there are lots of things I can do for you."

George laughed. "Like take our money?"

"Robin and I had a falling out. It was basically his fault."

"Jon, you didn't even go to Cyprus."

"Ah, that's bullshit."

One day, George interviewed Gloria Farrens, Jon's ex-wife. After he had gotten her story, he decided that it would be only fair to speak to Jon about what she had had to say. Renee answered the phone. George said to her, "I've heard some rather astonishing things about Jon's past, and you and your husband, the bankruptcies and the long list of finan-

---

*When I interviewed Michael Douglas, he personally assured me that Jon was very much not the best man and that he, Michael, was.

cial dealings, going way back." He then went into what Gloria had told him.

When it was all over, Renee let him have it. "You're out to get us, you're out to do a hatchet job on us. You're trying to sensationalize this."

"Well, Renee, I want you and Jon to understand that there are people accusing him of defrauding them. They're suing him. If these changes are true, it seems like a cruel hoax."

"Oh, we're not trying to do that, we're just trying to get to the bottom of this thing. Jon's an upstanding and patriotic young man."

George paused. "Just have him call me."

Jon did indeed call George Lewis. After being barraged with insults and curses, George offered Jon an opportunity to tell his side of the story. Jon's response: "Fuck you, George."

"Okay, Jon. Just keep watching NBC News."

On December 5, 1988, the spot aired. It contained not only the amateurish footage from "A Chance to Live" and the footage of Gregson burning his videotape, it also featured surveillance footage of an overweight Jon Emr riding a motorcycle.

A Confession in Culver City:
August 23, 1991

---

*Listen, I don't want to be a sore loser or anything, but when
we're done, if I'm dead, kill him.*
—Paul Newman in *Butch Cassidy and the Sundance Kid*

B enny, we need to talk some more," Detective Sergeant Hank
Davies said when he showed up at his home the same afternoon he
learned that Benny might be an accomplice in the Emr murders.

Benny invited Davies in. "Okay, Hank," he said. "Come in."

Davies refused a cup of coffee, plopped down on a couch that clearly
had been at war with Benny's kids, and pulled out his notebook. "You
told me that the last time that you saw Suggsy was on the Fourth of
July."

"Yeah, yeah, the Fourth of July. You got it."

Davies nodded his head. "Hmmm. Are you sure about that? You're
not lying to me? That's not something you would do?"

"Jesus, Hank, how can you say that? No, man. I swear on—"

"Well, let's get real specific. Tell me exactly what happened."

"Okay, that's easy. I remember it exactly," he said. "Suggsy showed
up at my house with his U-Haul attached to a red Buick. He had come
to pick up his stuff that he had stored in my garage."

"Okay. Why was his stuff there?"

"Well, he had broken up with his girlfriend. So he didn't have his
apartment. He needed to store his shit somewhere."

"What are we talking about?" Davies asked. "What *shit?*"

"Things like filing cabinets and paperwork and he also had his computer here. Anyway, he just picked the stuff up and he left. He came
back the next day because he wanted to go see a movie."

"A movie? Which one?"

"We went to see *The Naked Gun 2½.*"

"Who was in it?"

Who was in it? This didn't seem relevant. "That guy with the white hair. Leslie Nielsen. It was real funny."

"Maybe I should go see it with my fiancée."

"Oh, yes, Hank. You should. It shows cops in a very funny light. I won't give any of it away. Anyway, the next day Suggsy showed up again and asked me if I wanted to get a hamburger. It was only five in the afternoon, a bit early for me, but, you know, what the hell."

"Benny, how is he looking during this whole period? Tired, sick, what?"

"You know, come to think of it, Suggsy did look very tired. Exhausted. I asked him about it, He told me that he was up all night talking with Susan. He told me that they were staying at a motel in Westminster. He told me that things would work themselves out.

"The next day, of course, was the Fourth of July. I wanted to stay at home. So I invited Suggsy over for a barbecue. When Suggsy showed up he brought some steaks with him and a few fireworks to light off. It was about six in the evening."

"Did he come with Susan?"

Benny shook his head. "He came alone. I asked Suggsy where Susan was. He said that Susan was staying with her sister."

"Kathy?"

"Yeah," Benny let out a long whistle. "Boy, Suggsy hated her!"

"Yeah?"

"Ooooh, Hank. He sure did. He thought that Kathy poisoned Susan against him."

"So, he stuck around. What did he do that night?"

"He was eating and setting off Roman candles for about three or four hours. Then he said that he was leaving to go and visit with Robert and Ellen, his other good friends in the neighborhood."

That got Hank's attention. "Robert and Ellen?"

"Yeah, Suggsy was in the service with Robert. They're good friends. Robert is a cop."

"A cop?"

"Yeah, yeah." Benny wrote down Robert's phone number and handed it to Hank. "Here. You should talk with him. Maybe he knows something. Anyway, the next day, Suggsy came back. It was early in the morning. When you have seven kids there is no such thing as anything but an early wake-up. Know what I mean?"

"What did he want, Benny?"

"He wanted me to go with him on a trip to Arizona to get some guns he'd pawned. I didn't go."

"You just stayed at home? Hmmm." Hank nodded his head and silently started examining his notes. He was silent for about five minutes as he pretended to read and then reread his entries. Eventually, he looked back up. Then, very quietly, "Benny, you're lying to me."

Benny looked hurt. "Me? No way. I've been straight with you."

"Bullshit. Benny, you made a mistake. Do you remember signing your name to Suggsy's Chevron card?"

Benny dropped his head and clasped his fingers together. "Jesus. Oh, Jesus."

Hank stood up, took off his jacket, laid it over a chair and moved back toward the couch. "Now, how 'bout telling me the truth, Benny?"

The Cons of Jon Emr:
Ed Gold, ABC Television,
and Bobby Garwood, 1989

I'm not a man that people overlook.
—Clifton Webb in *The Razor's Edge*

One day in early 1991, a producer named Ed Gold, a short man with a waft of red hair, ambled into the office of one of his partners at Interscope, a Westwood-based independent production company. As with any successful producer, the top of his desk was stacked with an array of scripts. As Ed perused them, he came across one for a project called "James Dean: The Legend." At the bottom of the cover page, written in bold black letters, were these words: "Produced by R. Jon Emr."

"What the fuck is this?" Ed said, picking up the script. "Are we actually thinking about doing this?"

His partner gave it a glance. "Oh that. No. I took a look at it. It's really quite awful."

"Just stay the fuck away from it!" Ed was like a parent who discovered a crack vial under his teenager's pillow. "We want to have nothing to do with this! Don't take any calls regarding this. Just kill it! Forget about it! You get involved with this in any way and your life will be totally, completely fucked!"

"Ed, I don't know why you're so zealous. Is there something about James Dean that—"

Ed slid into a wooden chair in the office. "It has nothing to do with Dean. It has to do with this man." Ed pointed to Emr's name. "Believe me! This guy, he's probably fuckin' Satan himself. George Stanford Brown and I got tangled up with him once and, Jesus, it was the worst experience of our lives."

■ ■ ■

Ed Gold, like many directors and producers in town, loved to play poker, a habit he had picked up from his days and nights on movie sets. He had been involved in a regular Wednesday night poker game for ten years, which was long enough for his wife to stop complaining about it. She came to realize that for Ed, poker was not mere recreation. It was a force of nature, as it was with several husbands around the globe.

On one Wednesday night in early 1989, Barbara Dean, another regular player, was about to change the fragile course of Ed Gold's life. Barbara was a psychic. Like everybody else who played in the game she was in the industry. Barbara's claim to fame came from being the psychic of wunderkind Fred Silverman when he was running the sinking ship at NBC. Barbara was the one who told him, begged him in fact—her premonitions were that strong—that he had better schedule Monday nights for women. It was the only way to counter the juggernaut that *Monday Night Football* had become. That is exactly what Silverman did, and the rest is programming history.

Years earlier, when Ed was told that a psychic had been invited to join the poker game, he was floored. Why don't we just play with all our cards exposed, he often wondered out loud. However, it turned out Barbara lost just as much as the next guy.

As they were playing one night, Barbara told Ed about "a guy." This guy with properties. Great properties. Properties that were provocative and could help make a name for anybody connected with them. Properties that could make everybody rich. The guy who owned these properties was a big-time Hollywood producer. His name was Jon Emr. Ed had never heard of him but, what the hell, he had never heard of many producers in town. Sure, he'd love to meet this Emr fellow, Ed said. That night Ed lost a couple hundred dollars. It was only the beginning of his problems.

The next day, Ed made an appointment to meet with Jon Emr at Ed's offices at Nexus Entertainment, which was located on the first floor of a rehabbed apartment building in Studio City, just over the canyon from Hollywood. Nexus was located across the street from the CBS/MTM complex in the valley.

Ed would never forget the first time that he saw Jon Emr, the first time that he saw "Satan." Through his window, he saw Emr walking up the path to his building, his stogie clenched between his teeth, puffing away. He strolled casually into Ed's office and flopped his ass on the chair in front of Ed. He didn't bother to ask if it was okay to smoke. Maybe Emr assumed it was all right. Because he smelled the remnants of cigar smoke held over from when George Stanford Brown had been in the office a few hours earlier. Stanford Brown, Ed's partner, was formerly one of the costars of the popular ABC series *The Rookies.* He had since become an Emmy-award-winning director for his work on the CBS cop show *Cagney & Lacey.*

Ed Gold had produced several "shows" with George, many Vietnam related. Their most recent was *Vietnam War Stories* for HBO, which had earned them several awards. Emr told Ed that he was an admirer of his work. In fact, he confided in Ed that he was a big, big believer that there were still MIAs left in Southeast Asia and that he was deeply connected with people trying to get them out. "I know this is a topic that you care about, Ed," he said. "So I'm here to give you the opportunity of a lifetime!"

"Opportunity of a lifetime?"

"A fuckin' lifetime!" Jon said, spreading his arms wide like a hawk.

Ed could tell right now that Jon was without a shred of real experience in the business—television, film, or otherwise. The only reason Jon was still in his office was that he had been recommended by a close friend of his whom he'd have to face that upcoming Wednesday. "Before we go on, Jon," Ed said gently, "can you tell me a bit about your background?"

The same stuff came out that Jon had been telling people for years. He had produced three hundred or so movies. He had been partners with Jan-Michael Vincent! Robert Redford! Joel Douglas of the Douglas family! "A Chance to Live"! Jon leaned forward. "I'm assuming that you have seen 'A Chance to Live'?"

"No."

Jon took out his cigar and blew out a stream of smoke. "Hmm. I would think that you, making the kinds of films that you do, you would surely have seen it. Okay, I'm going to get it for you. I think that you're going to be shocked. It's amazing. It's great. Me and Joel—Joel DOUGLAS—produced it. You sure you haven't seen it?"

"Positive, Jon."

"Okay, I'll get it for you."

"That's great, Jon. By the way, you said that you had been involved with—what—three hundred shows?"

Jon leaned back in his chair, his hands clasping the back of his head. "Something like that."

"What were a few of them?"

"We'll have a long talk when we're comfortable with one another." He pulled some paperwork out of the paper bag he was carrying. He dropped two "projects" on Ed's desk. One was a copy of the Scott Barnes book, *Bohica*. The second was a twenty-six-page treatment called "The Bobby Garwood Story." On the bottom of the cover page was Renee Emr's name.

"I assume this person is related to you?"

Jon smiled proudly. "My mom. She does all the writing."

Ed started thumbing through the material. "I see." Ed Gold knew exactly who Bobby Garwood was, as did any student of the Vietnam War. Garwood was the last POW officially released by the Vietnamese government. Instead of coming home a hero, as some believe he should have been, Garwood was widely regarded as a traitor, a collaborator. There was even a book written about him by Winston Groom called *Conversations with the Enemy*.*

He wasn't going to blurt it out right there, but Gold had no interest in doing a film about a traitor, a person whom he regarded as an unredeemable character. "Let's talk in a few days," Ed said to Jon.

That evening, Gold pored over *Bohica*. He was sure that the Garwood story was a bust. But the story of an adventurer ordered by his own government to kill American MIAs being held captive in Laos seemed to have potential. Big potential. But after doing some research of his own, Gold eventually arrived at the conclusion that the book simply did not ring true. Like many people before and certainly after him, Ed Gold decided that Scott Barnes was either a flake or a liar.

Gold phoned Jon Emr and told him that his production company was not interested in *Bohica*.

Jon hardly seemed fazed. "What about the Garwood story?"

Ed promised Jon that he would look at the treatment. But he also told Jon that he was predisposed to rejecting the project, if only be-

---

*Groom went on to write *Forrest Gump*.

cause he was not convinced that Garwood was anything less than a bona fide traitor to his country.

"Just read it," Jon said to Ed.

And Ed did. The quality of the treatment was atrocious. For one thing, it was about twice as long as it should have been. The length was a clear indication that the writer, in this case a seventy-year-old grandmother with not a single film or television credit to her name—was not a professional.* In addition, the "treatment" merely laid out the entire Garwood chronology. It made no effort to outline a script, which was the real purpose of a treatment. Finally, Jon Emr's proposed cast for this television film was laughable. For Garwood, Jon had "selected" Tom Cruise or Charlie Sheen. He wanted General Westmoreland to be played by Gregory Peck, who had recently portrayed Douglas MacArthur. Emr also wanted Gary Busey for an unspecified role. He spelled the Oscar-nominated actor's name "Bussie." Emr's proposed budget was $15 million, roughly five to six times more than the cost of most television films.

Nevertheless, Ed knew a good story when he saw one. And after doing a bit of research and more than a little soul-searching, he came to the conclusion that, hell, maybe Bobby Garwood had been railroaded after all. After conferring with George Stanford Brown, whose wife, Tyne Daly, had been directed by George in several episodes of *Cagney & Lacy*, he decided that this was a movie he wanted to be involved in. He would produce it and George would direct.

He contacted Emr. "Now, Jon, are you sure that you have secured the rights to Bobby's life story?"

Television was an interesting business. Producers buy "rights" even when it is not necessary to do so, as is the case with public figures like Bobby Garwood. Once you own "rights," the chances of your being sued and your time being wasted in a courtroom are greatly diminished.

"Yeah, yeah," Jon said. "What the fuck do you think?"

"I just want to make sure, Jon. I don't need any problems."

"Hey, you know, I can bring Bobby Garwood to you directly. Will that convince you? He can tell you that he sold us the rights."

Ed sighed. "No, Jon, that's not necessary. Your word is fine. But I will want to meet with Bobby. Research."

---

*Save for "A Chance to Live."

"Bobby's very shy. He's nervous about meeting people."

"You just told me that I could meet Bobby."

"It's not really necessary. All the research has been done already. We've got hours of Bobby on tape. Anyway, Renee is going to write the script. All we need you to do is set up the corporation where all of the money can be deposited."

Corporation? What the fuck was Jon Emr talking about? "I'm not sure the network is going to allow Renee to write the script."

"They can suck my fuckin' dick! Granny is writing the fuckin' script. That's the only way to be fair to Bobby. This movie has to be a tribute to Bobby! Bobby only trusts Granny."

"Look, Jon, this is just network politics." He paused, weighing how the next words were going to sound. "George and I felt that the networks were not going to take to Renee's treatment. I took the liberty of writing what I think will be an appropriate treatment."

"Motherfuck!"

"Jon, I—"

"Motherfuck! Granny's the one who knows Bobby! What makes you think that you can do a better job than Granny?"

How about fifteen years experience. How about dozens of real, honest-to-goodness shows under my belt. "We felt it would be in the best interests—"

"Never mind, just send me the treatment. Fax it to me!"

Ed groaned to himself. This was going to be a long relationship. "All right, Jon."

"Motherfuck!" Jon said right before slamming the phone down.

Ed faxed his treatment to Jon. The next day it came back with a multitude of "corrections," which Ed Gold chose to ignore.

The Garwood project was a tough sell to television. Movies of the week went through different fads. One year it might be diseases. The next year it might be true crime. After that, maybe adoption or divorce-theme films. The one common denominator with all of these movies was that the protagonists were almost all female. Women like Cheryl Ladd, Jane Seymour, Jaclyn Smith, and Donna Mills kept appearing and reappearing in the films.

"The Bobby Garwood Story," which was the title under which it was pitched to the three major networks, did not have a single major female character. It was a project that could not possibly have been more male-driven. And even men might rebel against it. No matter how he was portrayed in the script, a large contingent of the population would not be swayed from the notion that Garwood was a little punk who sold out his country to get a little extra rice while he was a prisoner of war.

Not surprisingly, the only success Ed Gold had in getting network interest for the film occurred over the poker table. One of the regulars in his Wednesday night group not only worked at ABC, he ran the movie department. Ed gave him his own treatment for a four-hour miniseries based on the experiences of one Bobby Garwood.

After a few days, ABC responded. There was no way that they were going to make "The Bobby Garwood Story" as a long-format movie. The depressing and controversial topic made it enough of a risk. However, ABC recognized the importance of the topic and if Ed could demonstrate through yet another treatment that it could be made as a two-hour movie, then they would be in business. They would finance it and put it on the air.

After the two other networks passed on the project, Gold agreed to the concept of producing a two-hour movie. He called Jon with the good news. Instantly, Jon had his own casting ideas. "Jan-Michael Vincent," he screamed into the receiver. "He's the one. He's our Garwood. I know Jan. He's a pal of mine. I've already talked to him about it and he's dying to do it. Dying!" Jon also said that he had the composer for the film lined up. His name was Kimo Mata and he had done the music for "A Chance to Live." Jon assured Ed that Kimo was a "fucking" genius!

It was right then and there that Ed knew to an absolute certainty that Jon Emr knew nothing—zippo—about the film industry. First of all, Vincent, who had made a slight name for himself playing rebellious heroes in the mid- to late seventies in such films as *White Line Fever* and *Hooper,* was maybe twenty years older than what the role called for (Bobby Garwood was in his late teens when he was taken prisoner). Second, any real producer would know that now was not the appropriate time to even consider casting. So many other things needed to be done. Third, it was naive to assume that you could plant whomever you wanted into your film. The network had its own list of contenders.

Eventually, Jon got on a subject that he would stay on forever: The

Corporation. Jon demanded that Ed, his partner, George, and he form a corporation into which all the money that ABC gave them would be deposited.

Ed Gold had already discussed the prospect of forming a Garwood Corporation with his partners at Nexus. It was certainly not uncommon for a film-in-progress to form a corporate entity. Once the corporation was formed, it would take the signature of all the partners to withdraw any money. Jon had made it clear to Ed that he wanted to have complete access to the funds, that he would have the right to withdraw money at will. Furthermore, as soon as ABC sent them a check, he wanted to be paid $50,000 for moneys he had already invested in the project. "First money in, first money out."

"What does that mean, Jon?"

"Granny and I put the first money in," he explained. "So, any money that comes we get the first money out."

First in. First out. First in. First Out. Ed would be hearing that for weeks and months to come, not just from Jon's lips but in faxes and correspondence. It was some kind of slogan with Jon.

It was very clear to Ed that he would not be able to form a corporation with Jon Emr. There was something about Jon's deal that had a horrible smell to it. Ed did not trust Jon, nor did anybody in Nexus. They would have dumped him in a second had he not "owned" the exclusive rights to the Bobby Garwood story. In fact, Ed told Jon that the four producers (Ed, Jon, Renee, and George Stanford Brown) would have to pay for costs and development fees not covered by ABC out of their own pockets.

"Huh? What the fuck are you talkin' about?" Jon bellowed.

Even the most green novice knew that. "The deficit financing, Jon."

"Deficit financing?"

Holy shit, Ed thought. This sorry son of a bitch doesn't even know what deficit financing is! Ed tried to soothe him. "We'll make our money when we sell our package overseas."

In fact, very few television movies make any money domestically. Small production companies almost always lose money up front. Even the cash paid by the networks is normally not enough to finance the making of a picture. The profits only start becoming a reality when the international market starts to buy the project for either television or theatrical release.

Jon was sucking on his cigar, burning it into one long ash almost instantly. "And how much will this cost me?" he said taking out his wallet.

"Oh, Jon, I'd say our end will run to two hundred fifty thousand. That means that you and Granny have to come up with about a hundred twenty-five thousand."

Jon could have swallowed the rest of the cigar whole. But he maintained his composure. "Okay."

"Okay, Jon?" Ed leaned forward. "You and Granny can handle that?"

Jon waved his hand. "That's not a problem." Jon slapped his hands together. "When are we goin' to form that corporation? We need a bank account . . . for all the money that ABC will be sending to us."

A few weeks later, Ed Gold arrived in Scottsdale to do some research with Jon, Renee, and Bob Garwood. Jon surprised Ed by offering to put him up. "You can't come to my home," Jon said to him with some sadness. "I'm having my father stay with me and he's just not well."

Yeah, yeah, Ed thought to himself. Jon put Ed up in a cheap motel—certainly not the Scottsdale Hilton, which is where Ed hoped he would have been placed.

Jon noticed that Ed was checking out some damage that had been done to Jon's car. There was a bent antenna and a scratch mark across the car that had clearly been made with a key. In addition, the door handles had been knocked off entirely. Jon shook his head. "Scott Barnes did this," he said between clenched teeth. "The sorry motherfuck!"

Ed was a little surprised. Wasn't Scott Barnes the heroic figure who had written *Bohica*, the very project that Jon had introduced to him?

Ed had always considered Jon dumb, but one evening he also came to the conclusion that he was potentially very dangerous. It was the night of the Gun-in-the-Briefcase incident.

Jon had asked Ed if they could get together for a meeting, only he wanted to schedule it at night. The meeting was scheduled to take place at the Nexus offices in Studio City. "It's the only time that I can get away," he said. Ed reluctantly agreed. He was the only one in the office when Jon arrived.

Jon was clearly drunk, his mouth reeking of Chivas Regal. Right away, he began to talk about the corporation. "The corporation goddammit! We gotta form the corporation. We have to have a bank account."

Ed was getting tired of the issue. He again explained that they could not acquiesce to Jon Emr's demands that he be able to withdraw money at will, nor would they accept the fact that Jon would be paid a huge chunk of the cash as soon as the money came in.

Jon dropped his head, changing the subject. "There are many people that want me dead."

"Right, Jon."

"They don't like this project. You and your family are also in danger. Here, look at this."

Jon clicked open his briefcase and withdrew a .38. He examined it lovingly and then pointed it toward Ed. "Do you have a gun? You definitely should get a gun."

Ed had many guns. In fact, he was something of a collector. But he left his weapons at home. He didn't carry them around with him. "Christ, Jon, put that fucking thing away," he said.

Jon giggled. "I don't really need it, you know." He lowered the weapon. "I can get a gun away from anybody at all. You wanna see?"

Ed could not care less, but he knew he had to humor Jon. "Yeah, sure. Do me a favor. Just take out the bullets."

Jon giggled again. He was so drunk that it took almost a full minute until six bullets fell out of the chamber. He handed Ed the gun. "Okay, now—you point it at me and, uh, I'm going to take it away from you."

"All right, Jon," he said. He walked over to Jon and pointed the gun at him. Jon's plan was to grab the barrel of the gun and twist it backward so that it twisted Ed's wrist. An old martial arts trick, one of the most elementary things taught. As Jon lunged forward, Ed simply stepped back and Jon missed him completely and fumbled forward a few steps.

"Shit," Jon said.

"C'mon, Jon. That's enough."

"Shit. You weren't supposed to move."

"What are you talking about?"

"You weren't supposed to move goddammit! Motherfuck!"

"Jon, you think a gunman is going to just sit there as you pull this martial arts bullshit on him."

Jon was steamed. "You're so tough!" he said. "Show me your best move."

Within a split second, Ed grabbed Jon's hand, and with two fingers applied pressure to the nerve housed between the thumb and the index finger. Jon buckled to his knees and jerked his hand away. "FUCK!" He shook his hand as if he could just dry off the pain.

Slowly, Jon got up and moved to a couch that was in the office. He sat in the corner, not facing Ed as he spoke. "Enough of this shit. Let's get to the meat. When are we going to form this goddamn corporation?"

The conflict over the "goddamn corporation" was threatening the entire project. ABC had a $2 million check they were prepared to deliver to the appropriate corporation, but one had not yet been formed. Despite Ed's protestations, Jon Emr was absolutely resolved to have a company in which he had complete and unilateral access to the money. Even if Jon did agree to the cosignature method of check cashing, it meant that Jon could prevent the production company from making purchases. This was an especially scary prospect given that Emr had been wildly territorial about "The Bobby Garwood Story." He wanted approval of everything, down to being able to pick the color of the toilet paper. Jon was demanding that he be made the chairman of the board of what was to be Garwood Productions. Ed and the rest of Nexus became convinced that no movie would ever get made because no corporation could be formed.

What was worse was that Nexus was now in preproduction on the film, spending money every day, money that would not be recouped until ABC was told what corporation to send the check to. ABC refused to entangle themselves in the mess. The attorneys for the network made it clear that no check was being delivered to Nexus, because that company could not supply the documents for the rights to the Garwood story. On the other hand, they were certainly not going to send funds directly to Emr.

Then came an unusual white knight: Chuck Fries.

One day, Ed Gold received a phone call from Fries. Fries, who owned a hugely successful television production company (best remembered for an expensive botched series called *Supercarrier*), had already been approached by Ed Gold and Nexus to take over as the project's foreign distributor. Fries had neither passed on nor accepted the partnership.

Fries told Gold that they were buying Jon and Renee Emr's rights from them. He would not disclose the terms of the deal. "I guess that we'll be making the film together," Fries told Ed.

There were two ways of looking at this. One way was that Jon Emr, who was serving only as a blockade, was out of the picture and the movie would get made. According to Fries, Jon would be given credit as an executive producer, as was in his contract with Nexus, and Renee would still be regarded as the film's coexecutive producer. But those credits were only window dressing, it didn't mean a thing. On the other hand, Fries had a fearsome reputation as one of the most unpleasant men in town and one of the most impossible to work with. "Of all the Germans you can hear from," Ed said later, "Goebbels [Fries] is not one of them."

There was another catch. Both Fries and Nexus agreed that it was absolutely essential that Bobby Garwood be on the set. The only catch was that Bobby would not agree to participate unless his pal Jon Emr could also be there. Both Ed Gold and Georg Stanford Brown ruminated over all the potential disasters that might occur if they allowed Emr on the set. They finally concluded that without Garwood, they might as well not make the movie. In late July, they invited Jon to bring Bobby Garwood to the set. Jon was told that he would have no creative control, and he agreed. The only thing that he cared about was that he be given two suites in the local hotel: one for him and one for "Granny."

A few months later, in the summer of 1990, filming on "The Bobby Garwood Story" started in Florida, which doubled for the jungles of Vietnam. Ed had gotten Ralph Macchio, the star of *The Karate Kid* series, to play Garwood. The role had originally been offered to Andrew McCarthy, the always twinkling brat-packer, via his agent. The agent did not even present it to Andrew, having made the assumption that his client would not do television. When McCarthy later found out what had happened, he fired his agent. It was the one role he gladly would have done for the tube. Martin Sheen, who was rapidly becoming well known less for his acting than for his activism, was given the small supporting role of a prisoner of war who had crossed paths with Garwood.

While he was on the set, Ed got a call from the van driver. "There's a guy name of Jon Emr here—"

"Yeah," Ed said, dreading to hear what he knew he was about to hear.

"He's demanding a limousine."

Ed slapped his forehead. Nobody was picked up at the airport by a limo. Not him and not the director, George Stanford Brown. Not even Ralph Macchio or Martin Sheen, the goddamn stars of the movie, had gotten anything better than a van when they landed in Florida.

"Try to work it out with him," Ed said.

A few minutes later the driver called again. "Mr. Emr told me to 'get the fuck outta here,' so that is exactly what I am doing."

"I'm sorry about this. How's he driving in?"

"He's going to rent a car."

About an hour later, Jon Emr, with Bobby Garwood in the front seat and his two kids in the back (and, notably, no Renee), rolled into town in a Lincoln Continental. "We're a big people family," he told Ed. "So, I need the Lincoln."

"Well, Jon," Ed began. "The budget only calls for you renting an economy car. The rest will have to come out of your pocket."

He patted Ed on the back. "No, problem, Eddie. No problem."

Ed Gold was surprised by how well Jon was taking this. Damn surprised. Until later. That is when he found out that Jon had paid for the use of the car with Bobby Garwood's credit cards.

Jon's jolly mood came to a crashing halt when he learned that the Holiday Inn where the crew and cast were staying was all filled and that he, Bobby, and his two boys would be staying in a hotel across the street. "No respect," he kept mumbling to Bobby Garwood. "No respect at all."

According to just about everybody who was there, Jon Emr did exactly what was expected of him on the set of the Garwood film: absolutely

nothing. "He sure would be there for meals," Ed Gold would later remember. During shooting, Emr stayed away from the central action.
Instead, he wandered the perimeter of the set. Occasionally, he would
pounce on Ralph Macchio or Martin Sheen. Jon befriended some of
the minor crew members, entertaining them with stories of his past
creative conquests. Jon was shocked—shocked—to learn that not one
person with whom he spoke had ever seen "A Chance to Live." The
person whom Jon most impressed was the show's propmaster, Kirk
Heinlen, a born-again Christian who saw it as his duty to have several
heart-to-hearts with Jon. But many considered Jon to be a tremendous
nuisance.

A few days into shooting, on August 15, Ed was pulled to the side by
his assistant. "We just got a call from Los Angeles. A guy named Scott
Barnes had called and asked a secretary if we were working on 'The
Bobby Garwood Story.' "

Scott Barnes? Why did Ed think this could not be good news? "And
what did she tell him?"

"She told him that yes we were."

"And—"

"And then Barnes laughs and says, 'I got you. I got you now!' and he
hung up."

Barnes was a kook, Ed thought to himself, just like Emr had told
him. There was nothing to worry about here.

The next day, Ed learned from the Nexus office in Los Angeles that
Winston Groom, the author of *Conversations with the Enemy*, was making a claim on their movie. His primary witness was Scott Barnes

When Jon walked on the set that day, his shirt unbuttoned, swag-
gering from too much booze and that perpetual cigar hanging lazily
from between his lips, Ed walked up to him and gave him the last bit of
news that he ever wanted to hear. "Scott Barnes called us yesterday. He
asked if we were doing the Garwood movie. Now, there's a claim
against us."

For the first time, Ed Gold saw Jon Emr at a genuine loss for words.
After a full minute, Jon said softly, "I . . . I . . . knew that this was going
to happen. I knew, I knew, I knew. Jesus. Fuckin' Barnes! Fuckin'
Barnes! I KNEW IT! Damn. Damn. I knew it. Jesus—"

Ed was quite certain that Jon was going to have a heart attack and
die right then and there. Literally. Jon had once confided in Ed that he

had something of a heart problem. Instead, Jon threw his cigar to the ground, grabbed his hair, jogged over to his Lincoln, hopped into it, and sped off, leaving a cloud of dust behind him. Ed Gold turned around and went back to work. He had a movie to make. Claim or no claim.

That day, Jon phoned Scott: "If you were in Russia you would be dead," he said. "You'd better stop fucking with our government or we'll kill you."

That afternoon, Ed was hand-delivered a long fax that had arrived for him at the hotel. The fax contained the *Arizona Republic* article written by Randy Collier and an article written in the *Calgary Herald* on November 19, 1989. The *Herald* article, which ran in the newspaper's Sunday magazine, was a lengthy analysis of how Jon Emr had nearly bankrupted the city government after he suckered them into allowing him to produce a television special based on a chess tournament that the city was hosting.

Also included in the stream of faxes was a letter that had been written over two years earlier. It came from the Putnam Publishing Group and was addressed to Joel Douglas and Jon Emr:

> It has come to our attention that one or both of you have acquired motion picture rights to Robert Garwood's life story. As the publisher of CONVERSATIONS WITH THE ENEMY: The story of PFC Robert Garwood, we may have a financial interest in the sale of motion picture rights to Mr. Garwood's story.
>
> On July 24, 1979, we acquired the exclusive publication rights to a work that was then entitled THE STORY OF BOBBY GARWOOD. The publishing agreement was with Winston Groom and Robert Garwood. . . . under the terms of our agreement, we have a financial interest in the sale or disposition of those rights. . . .

Ed was stunned. Stunned beyond all belief. Now, only now, Ed Gold figured the whole damn thing out. Jon never had the rights to the Garwood story and this letter was evidence of it. He had wanted a corporation, one in which he had complete access to the funds therein, so that he could take the money and run. After all, the cash could not be spent on the movie, for at some point Jon would have to come clean and say, sorry guys, we just don't have the right to make this movie. And getting the money back? Ha! Sue me.

Jon did not come back for several hours. As soon as Ed saw him, he pushed him up against one of the trailers. "Now's the time to come clean," Ed said. "Stop bullshitting us. Just tell us what the fuck is going on, Jon."

By now, Jon had apparently recovered. "It's taken care of, Eddie. Don't you worry about it."

A few days later, Jon stood at the edge of the set, arms crossed, fuming, with Bobby Garwood by his side, looking nervous and edgy. Jon motioned for Ed to come over. Ed rolled his eyes back. Now fuckin' what?

"Bobby has been telling me things."

Bobby had his head held low, embarrassed that he had created this impending rift. A few days earlier, Ed had told Bobby about the faxes. He told Bobby that his pal Jon Emr was a fraud. He told him that Jon did not have a penny to his name. Hell, he didn't even own a car.

"How do you know I don't own a fuckin' car," he said, jabbing at Ed with his cigar. "Maybe I do, maybe I don't. How the fuck would you know?"

At this point the various teamsters, led by Ed's brother David, got down from their vehicles and stood around the coterie of Jon, Bobby, and Ed, giving their tough looks to Jon. The teamsters, as much as anybody, had become fed up with this "producer" who was nothing but a pain in the ass and who clearly knew nothing about how to make a movie.

Ed would not respond to Jon. "I've got a movie to make, Jon. Why don't you go to the craft service table and eat a banana."

Jon started to scream at Ed. "Chickenshit faggot."

Ed stopped in his tracks. What went through his mind was whether or not he should attack Jon, finally have it out with him. Instead, he pointed at Jon from where he stood. "You're outta here. Get off the set!"

Jon looked stunned and opened his mouth to say something. But Garwood stopped him. "Maybe, you'd better leave, Jon."

Jon turned to Bobby.

"You hear what that asshole said to me?"

"Maybe you'd better leave, Jon," Bobby insisted.

Jon called his two boys over, piled them into his car and then tore away.

Ed went to George's trailer and made a call to the hotel. "Mr. Emr will be leaving tomorrow. If he insists on staying, then he will be paying."

Ed then called a representative at Fries Entertainment and told them that Jon's presence on the set was seriously jeopardizing morale and even the chances of the film's being finished on time and on budget.*

Jon Emr and the two boys left the next morning.

During the film's postproduction stages, as the credits were being put on in an editing bay, George Stanford Brown and Ed Gold left the editing room. They could not stand to see Jon and his mother, Renee, being given credit on the film. They were even toying with the idea of literally flashing their names on the screen. However, the lawyers told them that would not be advisable to do with people as apparently litigious as the Emrs. In the end, Ed and George arranged that their names would not appear on the screen simultaneously with the Emrs'.

The Garwood film did not air until the summer of 1993, two years after the death of Jon Emr. Lawyers at ABC claimed that they wanted to wait until a sufficient time had passed since the popular Gulf War before airing a film as controversial as this. In fact, what probably held up the airing was the lawsuit filed by Winston Groom. In 1993, the author settled with the network. Though the terms were not made public, it was rumored that ABC had to shell over in the area of $250,000.

*Renee insists this incident never occurred.

A Search in the Desert
August 25, 1991

I'm filthy, period.
—Dorothy Malone in *Written on the Wind*

The desert somewhere around Route 62, not far from the Arizona border. That's where Benny said Suggsy had buried his girlfriend's body. That dearth of information didn't feel right to Hank Davies, nor did it feel right to Steve Yoshida. Benny knew more than what he was saying. Davies and Yoshida were quite certain of it.

So, on Saturday morning, dressed in jeans and T-shirts, the cops drove out to see old Benny and informed him that they were going to the desert to begin searching for the body of the girl. They needed Benny's help. Benny was their lead.

Of course, neither Davies nor Yoshida thought that they had any chance of finding a body out there in the hundreds and hundreds of miles of desert. What they were hoping and gambling on was that Benny would break down, come to his senses, and take them directly to the body. It was a feeling in Hank's gut that Benny was there when the body was being buried, if not there when the girl was actually murdered.

The ride took a little over two hours. Benny sat in the backseat and the two cops were in front. During the whole trip, Hank bombarded Benny with questions, making him tell his story over and over again. Hank had to hand it to Benny. He was sticking to his story.

It was when they pulled over and began wandering around the desert that Hank thought Benny would crumple like a house of cards. There was nothing like the scene of the crime to motivate a confession. "Why don't you just walk around, Benny?" Hank told him. "You just go ahead. Tell us if anything strikes you."

That's what Benny did. He walked around, kind of aimlessly, taking in the sights. The two cops followed him. Nobody said anything for about fifteen minutes until Hank had just about had it. "You know what obstruction of justice is, Benny?"

"Yeah."

"Your wife is awful pretty."

Benny grinned. "I think I'll keep her."

"How long do you think it'll be before she's with another man. When you're in jail I mean."

"Hank, I—"

"How long do you think it will be before another man is raising your kids. Kids need a father."

"I'M THEIR DAD!"

"Yeah, Benny. Look, I gotta ask you—"

"Ask me what? Ask me what?"

"This is what I gotta ask you. Benny, have you ever been with a man?"

Benny's eyes widened a few millimeters. "You mean, like sexual-like."

"I'm only asking because, I think you probably already know this, you're exactly the kind of guy who becomes a punk in prison."

"What's a punk?"

Davies turned to Yoshida, who actually smiled. Davies turned back to Benny. "You'll belong to a few of the prisoners. You're a good-looking guy and all. You'd be worth like a whole fuckin' carton of cigarettes. Cell to cell, Benny. They're going to pass you cell to cell."

And that's when Benny did something awfully odd. Benny just began crying. Big damn crocodile tears. Hank thought he had him. "Benny, if you have anything else to tell us—"

"I told you everything I know, Hank!"

"If you had something to do with this you'd better tell me now. You'd better take me to the body."

Now came the real waterworks. Benny was an absolute blubbering mess. "I had nothing to do with it!" he said.

All of a sudden Hank realized that, at least from the point of view of killing Susan Calkins, Benny was telling the truth. Benny was just too dumb and slow to be manipulative, to have the ability to cry on cue, to feign this type of agony. Anyway, Hank Davies kept Benny walking through the desert for three hours. At the very least, he wanted Benny to keep thinking he was a suspect. That would keep him scared.

While they were out there, the August sun beating the bejesus out of them, Hank and Benny drank Cokes they had bought from a nearby 7-Eleven and Yoshida drank a cup of hot coffee. Davies looked at him with admiration. You had to respect a man who cut down a cup of hot joe in the middle of the summer desert.

In the end, they had found nothing and Benny had said nothing. On the drive back to Orange County, Benny fell asleep.

The Cons of Jon Emr:
Johnny "Bond" Carbonnara, 1991

When I get in a tight spot, I shoot my way out of it. Why, sure! Shoot first and
argue afterwards. You know, this game ain't for guys that's soft.
—Edward G. Robinson in *Little Caesar*

Journalists loved Johnny Bond and he loved them. When they flew into south Philly to see Johnny, which they did for years, he'd wait for them at the airport parking lot, standing like Rommel in front of his cherry-red Cadillac with the white vinyl top. It took exactly two minutes with Johnny Bond to understand why Jon Emr realized that the man's life story was worth a bundle. Two minutes is how long it took for Johnny to say to me, "You lookin' at the hole in the back of my neck?"

As he was driving me into town, he reached around with his right hand and poked at the back of his neck. There it was. A beaut. A hole. A perfect, circular indentation, about three centimeters in diameter. "Got that in the Atlanta pen. Standin' in line and a guy just pokes me with a knife. Luckily, I had a shank around my ankle. So, I fall down, and pick up my knife, and I popped the guy." He paused. "You want to kill me, you'd better finish the job. Finish it fast."

Mention Johnny Bond, aka Johnny Carbonnara, in the streets of south Philly and you are sure to get a reaction. He had been in jail ten, twelve times—he himself could not remember. He was not just a Damon Runyon character. It was as if he had been raised by Runyon.

There was a time when Johnny was the slickest record promoter in the country. Johnny ran his business with a baseball bat mentality. "We'd get a disc jockey whatever he wanted. Money. Broads. Booze. We'd take him to the track and make bets for him. Can you imagine? All we'd want is for him to play our music. Two, three times a night. It was payola, but it was the way. Most people knew better than to fuck us. If they did, I'd—" He stood up from his seat—still driving—and slammed his fist into his hand—"POW—fuck 'em right back."

And there were people who would fuck Johnny. Once. Take the case of Lew Brasil, a Philadelphia DJ in 1958. At the time, Johnny was promoting an all-black group called the Fabulous Dubbs. He had discovered them strolling down a grocery aisle and listened to them as they hummed an original tune. As Johnny remembered it, when he approached them they tried to rob him.

Johnny told them that there was no use stealing from him. "I have maybe fifty bucks in my pocket," he told them. "And if you guys stay with me, you'll be richer than God."

Richer than God? The Dubbs would have settled for being richer than Sam Jenson, who owned the soda jerk store in their community. Being richer than God, this sounded like a good thing. Within three days, Johnny produced a single from the Fabulous Dubbs and was ready to promote it.

In those days, Lew Brasil was step number one. Not the top-rated disc jockey in town, just the most easily bought. In exchange for $400 and a hooker, Lew was supposed to begin playing the single from the Fabulous Dubbs on a Monday night, just hours after Johnny and his partner had made plans to leave town. But Johnny's plane was late and he spent a few hours waiting in a bar. Imagine his surprise when his buddy Skeets came in and gave him the horrible news that the cocky Lew Brasil had decided to dump the Fabulous Dubbs' single in the trash. Just didn't like it. Wasn't going to give it airtime after all.

Johnny stormed over to the studio and burst into Lew's little booth. "Where the fuck's my single?" he demanded. He looked over and, sure enough, there it was in the garbage can.

Lew must have seen the veins percolating in John's forehead because he instantly went into the defensive. "Now, Johnny—"

Bam! Johnny Bond smacked Lew Brasil in the face and Lew went down like a great oak. Johnny took over the controls. "This is Johnnnnnny Boooond fillin' in for Lew Brasil who's off to the crapper. Now, ladies and gentlemen . . . The moment the city's been waiting for, the amazing new single from THE FABULOUS DUBBS!"

When the song concluded, Johnny buried his mouth in the mike. "We've had twelve requests already to replay this hit new single." And so he did. Ten times. And all along he had his foot on pathetic Lew Brasil's face, holding him down and giving him a swift kick every time he had the audacity to come to.

Then there is the great legend of the Alan Freed payola trial. Freed, a famous record promoter, was on trial for payola scams. Johnny and his pals were frightened that if Freed took the stand, he would rat them all out. So, one day, Johnny and a pal took Freed for a ride to the train tracks. They put Freed's head on the track as a train was approaching and gently persuaded him not to talk.

Once the trial of Alan Freed began and it was clear that the defendant was not going to turn Johnny over, Bond felt a certain obligation. He discovered the name and the address of one of the jurors. One night, he took a ladder, laid it up against the juror's house and climbed in through the bedroom window. Both the juror and her husband were asleep.

When Johnny woke up the juror, his hand was already over her mouth. He put his finger to his lips suggesting that she not wake up her husband. There was a long knife to her neck. He whispered, "You see how easy it is?" Johnny had a smile on his face. "Nobody better be convicted."

Nobody was.

Johnny has six tattoos running up and down the sides of both arms. For the most part they are the names of women. You can't make out the names and Johnny won't tell you what they are. They have been etched out. That Johnny was a ladies' man is now a piece of south Philly lore. In his black book you can find the phone numbers of Angie Dickinson and Dorothy Malone.

If you ask people for their favorite Johnny Bond story, chances are they will tell you about the great poker game.

Johnny used to live in Cherry Hill, New Jersey, next door to Muhammad Ali, the champeeeeee-on!!!! of the world. The way Johnny tells it, Ali would often come next door to see Johnny, "wanting to show me all his new toys," Johnny said. The two of them became such good friends that the champ wrote him a poem in which he described Johnny as the world's greatest record promoter.

One day, Ali brought by a pal of his, a cocky, Jewish "son-bitch" who immediately challenged the champ and Johnny to a one-hundred-dollar darts competition. Johnny Bond won.

Ali's pal did not take well to the loss and he said to Johnny, "I want your house. I'll play you in poker for it. I own an Ethan Allen furniture store. Here's what we'll do. We'll each get two hundred thousand in chips. We'll play until the other person is out of chips. I win, I get your house. You win, you get all the furniture that my store has."

The Great Poker match took two full days and nights to play. Standing behind Johnny were three of his pals. Behind his opponent were three of his own henchmen. "It was the Italian mob and the Jewish mob," Johnny explained. At the end Johnny had all the chips.

"Well," the defeated man said. "You'll have to rent the trucks."

Johnny jumped to his feet and—*pow*—slammed his fist right into the bridge of his opponent's nose. John's men drew their weapons first and gently suggested that the Jews take a seat on the couch. When they did, Johnny gave his new pal a few more swift blows to really make his point clear. One television set went to Johnny Bond's house. The rest of the furniture was divvied up among John's friends and relatives.

The first time that Johnny was ever convicted of a crime was in 1985, when he obtained fraudulent movie and television rights to the life story of Roberto Clemente and lured investors into giving him a cool half-million dollars. He went to jail, a country club in Pennsylvania called Allenwood. Johnny hooked up with the other wiseguys in the joint and lived the good life. Spaghetti and broads, all courtesy of the hacks, the guards.

One day, Johnny was pulled out of the barracks and told that the FBI was there to visit him. They sat Johnny down and they pulled out some photographs. There were pictures of him with some players in the Mafia. All of the photos were taken on the south Philly corner where the aging Mafia dons hung out, played the numbers, and made football bets.

"All you gotta do is talk about these folks and you can walk out of here today," the agent said.

Classic Johnny. He stood up and spat a luger into the face of the agent. Johnny was handcuffed, dragged away, and thrown into a tiny cell. A few days later he was sent to the Atlanta pen, which is largely regarded as the meanest such institutuion outside of Turkey.

Johnny Bond once wrote a script. Well, kind of. Johnny cannot read or write. So instead of actually writing everything down, he and his wife took a camera and made a ninety-minute movie called "The Other Guy," about a Frank Sinatra impersonator, that was intended to be a kind of script. Johnny made the film in three days, produced the soundtrack in three hours, and got all his Mafia buddies to act in the film.

The film never got off the ground. "Sinatra fucked us," Johnny told me. "Really fucked us. He got his people to say that we did not have permission to use his music. That fuckin' Sinatra. I went to the wiseguys and I told them about my problem and they told me that if I saw Sinatra, I had their permission to whack the bastard."

For the record, Johnny Bond had "no comment" when he was asked if he ever killed anybody. But he conceded happily, "I near beat some people to death. I can tell you that."

Johnny took me to a restaurant in town to conduct our interview. At the time, he had difficulty breathing and walking. In violation of his doctor's orders, Johnny started drinking beer and eating salty French fries. When the meal was over, Johnny asked me to get the car. By the time I got the Cadillac around front, the street was jammed with ambulances, fire trucks, and police cars. Johnny was on a stretcher, an oxygen mask over his nose and mouth. The frantic hostess of the restaurant told me that Johnny had had a heart attack.

I chased after the ambulance in the "Bondmobile." Once we got to the hospital, Johnny was moved almost immediately to intensive care. I was allowed to join him only because Johnny assured the nurses that I was his son. Over the next few hours, Johnny lapsed in and out of consciousness. Whenever he was awake, he would talk to me about his experiences with Jon Emr. At points, the interview seemed to take the form of a deathbed confession. Johnny copped to some things that I am sure he would not have had he not been staring death right in "the fuckin' eyeballs," as he put it to me.

Johnny lived for several months after the incident. However, during that time he never recanted his story and my research bore out almost everything that he told me.

It was Ralphy "the Finger" (not his real name), a thin, wiry man with a far less ominous presence than his name suggested, who was responsible for introducing Johnny Bond Carbonnara to Jon Emr. Up until the day he died, Johnny would hold a grudge against Ralphy, his onetime pal. Johnny would regularly phone Ralphy and sing into his message machine, a little song called "A Matter of Time" that he promoted. Johnny would sing the first few lines gently, "Some day, somehow . . ." Then the scream: "I'LL TELL YA WHAT, YA MOTHERFUCK! WHEN I GET OUT THERE I'M GOIN' TO GIVE YA THE BEATING OF YOUR LIFE, YOU SON OF A BITCH! OF YOUR FUCKING LIFE! I'M DREAMIN' OF IT, YA LOUSY FUCK!" Whenever Johnny was feeling down, a call to Ralphy helped relieve the tension.

Jon Emr was not the first person to realize that owning the rights to Johnny Bond's life story could be lucrative. That distinction belonged to Ruth Charney, an executive with the Mount Company, a fledgling production company run by Thomas Mount, a well-known producer.

Johnny loved the idea of a movie being made about his life, especially if he was going to get cash up front. Everybody seemed to buy into the notion that Sean Penn was the best actor to play Johnny. John's old photos, especially those taken during his days in the service, revealed that he looked exactly like Penn.

But one sad day, Ruth Charney told him that the movie company was going bust. Christ! Johnny thought to himself upon hearing the news. Son of a bitch! When the Mount Company had bought up his rights, Johnny had packed up a station wagon and moved from Philadelphia to Burbank.

Now that he was completely broke Bond decided to make sure that the rights to his life story would revert back to him. He decided to track down Thom Mount himself.

He drove to the Mount Company in the red-and-white Caddy, the Johnny Tank. He barged through the office doors, ignoring the secretary's plea to wait.

"Mr. Mount. I'm Johnny Bond."

"Johnny, I . . . I . . ."

"Mr. Mount, here's the situation—"

"Yes, Johnny?"

"I know ya got problems, see. I know! For two years since I signed with ya, there's been a lot of dickering going around and back and forth. This is like a game goin' on here. Like, uh, someone's playin' fuckin' basketball with me. Only, I'm not a fuckin' ball!"

"I didn't think that you were."

"So, here's the goddamn thing. I want you to know that if the rights do not revert to me without problem, I will get my lawyer all over you."

"Do I know your lawyer?"

"You do now." He planted his hand on the desk and leaned forward. "I'm my own lawyer. I never lose. And I take care of things differently than most lawyers."

"Well, Johnny, I don't think that we really have a problem."

"Well, if there is a problem, I'll handle things my way."

Mount nodded. He had read the synopsis of Johnny's life. Johnny Bond walked out of the office with the rights to his life story fully secure.

Johnny Bond told his Thom Mount story to Ralphy later that same day. Johnny had been advised to stay away from Ralphy by his pal Bill Romero, a onetime promoter of Freddy Fender. Bill warned him that Ralphy was one slick character. Johnny waved off Bill's fears. "This fuckin' guy isn't slick. He's an asshole, he's a fuckin' what ya call it, a stooge for Jilly Rizzo."

Jilly Rizzo, of course, was a name immediately recognizable to anybody in the music industry. Rizzo was the road manager and best friend of Frank Sinatra.

Ralphy listened with interest as Johnny Bond told him about the Mount Company. Then, later, Ralphy told him that Frank Sinatra himself was interested in buying the rights to his life story. He explained that Sinatra's point man would be Jilly Rizzo himself. Jilly wanted to meet with Johnny the following day.

"Fuckin' Sinatra! I almost had him whacked," Johnny said with a grin. "Someday I'll tell you about it. I don't got no problem with Frank Sinatra no more. No problems! Where do ya wanna meet?"

"Don't worry about it. I'll pick you up." Ralphy and Johnny shook hands. "Let's make some money, Johnny."

"Yeah! Yeah! That's what I'm talkin' about, Ralphy!"

Johnny knew Jilly Rizzo the instant he saw him. There he was, small and frail with a little hat, sitting in a booth at Matteo's. He knew Rizzo because he had that look. The look from the Mob candy store back home. But he didn't know who the much younger man sitting next to him was. He turned to Ralphy, who had come in with him, "Who's this guy?"

"That's a partner of Jilly's. His name is Jon Emr."

"Aw Jesus, Ralph, you didn't tell me nuthin' about this guy. You know this guy?"

"Don't worry about it. He's a good guy. I know him. He's okay."

Johnny Bond didn't like Jon Emr the very second he saw him. He was too slick. Cowboy hat, mustache, greasy face, shirt unbuttoned almost down to the navel. He looked like Clark Gable, Johnny thought to himself, only chunky and out of shape. And, Jesus Christ! What was this! Who was the old lady sitting next to this Jon Emr?

Jon stood up when the legendary Johnny Bond approached the table. The hand-grabbing lasted a few seconds. Jon introduced the fat lady to him. It was Renee, he said, his mother. For a split second, Johnny didn't believe this was his dear old mom. That was the type of thing Johnny used to do. Use an old woman to sucker a mark.

Jilly snapped his fingers and ordered the peppers—"You just gotta try the roasted peppers, Johnny, trust me on this." While they waited for the food to arrive, they talked and ate Italian bread. Actually, Jon was talking and Johnny was eating.

"I've heard all about you, Johnny—can I call you that?—and I'm impressed. These movie rights, the one about your life, I think that they are an important commodity. And I have been talking and we'd like to convince you to sign with us."

"That's why I'm here," Johnny said with clenched teeth.

"First of all, I don't think that you will find two people in all of Hollywood who are more aware of the stylistic needs of this film. Thing is, we're very well connected. You know about Jilly here and Mr. Sinatra?"

"Yeah, of course. Who doesn't?"

"Exactly! Now, I am one of the partners of Emr-Douglas Productions. As in Kirk and Michael Douglas."

"Kirk and Michael Douglas. No shit?"

"No shit. Emr-Douglas Productions. Notice what name comes first."

And so went the conversation. Renee remained quiet in the foreground as Jon spieled forth about his credentials. Three hundred movies he had produced! Dionne Warwick! Redford was a pal! "A Chance to Live"! The Douglas family!

This was all very nice, Johnny thought to himself. "What's the bottom line here, Jon? How much money can ya front me?"

It impressed Johnny that Jon Emr was not taken aback by the questioning. "Oh," Jon Emr said. "Good money." Then he paused for a second. "Johnny, tell me a little bit about your background."

As Johnny Bond told him a few of the stories—beating the shit out of the disc jockey, the poker game, all that good stuff—he knew full well that Jon Emr was keeping off the topic of money. That was ludicrous. The whole idea here was to make money. Not create art. When he was done with his story, Johnny wiped away at the edges of his mouth with a napkin and asked Emr what projects he had been involved with.

"Well, there's 'A Chance to Live.' Have you seen 'A Chance to Live'?"

"Yeah, you told me about that before. But you also said that you made three hundred movies—"

"Look, Johnny, have we got some kinda problem here?"

Johnny looked to Jilly and Ralphy for guidance. Who is this sorry-ass motherfucker? "John, all I wanna know, ya know, is some of your movies. I'm a big movie fan. I just wanna know."

"Aaawww fuck!" Jon burst into laughter. "Fuck, Johnny. It would take a whole fuckin' day to tell you my credits. Now, Johnny, tell me the story of Lew Brasil again."

The only reason why Johnny didn't get up right then and there was because of Rizzo. Sinatra's man. The emissary of God.

After the lunch, Jon had to leave. Big meeting, he insisted! Big deal coming up! Oscar-time in Hollywood. Jon shook hands with Johnny Bond, shook hands firmly—mobsters respected a firm handshake. As soon as Jon Emr and his mother were out the door, Johnny Bond turned to Rizzo. "What the fuck? Who is this guy? He looks like a con."

Jilly's eyes opened up a millimeter. He explained that Jon Emr was anything but a con, that, in fact, he was Frank Sinatra's front man. Jilly shook his head quietly. "Look, Johnny. We don't know each other. But, I heard about you and you, I know, have heard about me. So, I ask you, fuck Jon Emr, do you trust me?"

Johnny nodded his head and the two men agreed to meet the next day to sign the contracts.

■ ■ ■

Technically, Gerrie was not a Mob wife. Although Johnny hung out with the Mob and adapted their lingo, he was not a "made" man. Not even close. And though Gerrie made it a point to be friends with the wives of "made men," she herself had been excluded from the inner-inner circle. That had not always been the case. Her first husband was a big-time mobster. But he had had his brains blown out several years earlier and, in her grief, Gerrie turned to Johnny.

The point is that Gerrie was a Mob wife at heart. And Mob wives can be unrelenting. When Johnny came home that day, full of stories of a movie in their future, with tales of Jilly Rizzo and Frank Sinatra . . . and this . . . Jon Emr fellow, she was dumbstruck.

She was standing at the stove of her $1,000-a-month apartment when Johnny opened the door with a big grin on his face. When he was done telling her about the events of the day, he couldn't help but notice that there was no smile on her face, not even a wrinkle. "What's the matter?"

She stopped in mid-stir and turned to her husband. "You just gotta be careful, Johnny. We've been down this road before. You don't even know who you're dealing with."

"But I do! I do! I'm dealin' with Sinatra."

She loved her husband, but he could be a bit of a putz. "Now, Johnny, was Sinatra actually there?"

"This, uh, Jon Emr was! And besides, there's Ralphy!"

A slap to the forehead. "I don't trust that guy neither. He's too, ya know, nice. Sleazy nice."

"Well," he said. "For what it's worth I didn't like this guy Emr. But, fuck, if Sinatra is behind it what the fuck do I care?"

The next day it was peppers, bread, and Italian soup again at Matteo's. Great roasted peppers. Johnny had to admit it. Best that he ever had! He'd have to bring his own "people" here to Matteo's. Sitting next to Johnny was Ruth Charney. He invited her because he needed to have somebody in there with him who knew the business. The bizarre thing was that, there in the corner, up at the bar, was Rizzo. Jilly was making a point of not sitting at the table. It was just Jon Emr at the table.

"We can make millions! Millions!" Emr was screaming. He promised Johnny a major percentage! Twenty percent! Thirty percent! It would be a four-hour miniseries! A major motion picture!

Johnny Bond was chewing away as Jon spoke. Jon's head was bent over, staring right down into the soup, his hands moving faster than the turnstiles in the Times Square subway. None of what Jon said made much sense to Johnny. All he knew was one thing: Johnny Bond would get $40,000 up front! That was 40Gs, baby. Enough to get him and his family on their feet. Even if the movie never got made, 40Gs was worth it.

At some point Ruth decided that she'd had enough. She patted Johnny on the shoulder and told him that she had to call it a night. All the men stood up and Ruth excused herself.

It was then that Jilly ambled over and sat next to Johnny Bond. Johnny looked him over. "What the fuck, how come ya waited until my agent left before you sat down."

Jilly gnawed at his bottom lip with his jagged, yellowing teeth. He explained that it was essential nobody connect Sinatra to this project. Indeed, not even he could sign the contract. They would have to sign his son Willy's name on the contract.

Johnny Bond was loving it. At the very least, the boys back home would love the fact that he, not even a "made man," was being brought into the inner sanctum of Frank Sinatra, the greatest fuckin' goombah entertainer in the history of the whole fuckin' universe.

Jilly asked Johnny if he wanted to read the contract. Then Johnny hit him with the bombshell: "The truth is I can't, uh, ya know, read or write," Johnny said.

Jon Emr leaned forward, doing a little thumb dance. "That so?"

"Got outta school in, what, the third grade?" Johnny explained.

"That so?" Jon Emr said again. "Tell you what, Johnny. Why don't you meet us back here in a couple of hours. Say, five-thirty. We'll sign the papers then. If you have doubts about us, then you can bring your agent."

Johnny Bond laughed. "I don't need no fuckin' agent!"

Johnny Bond could recognize letters. There were even a few words that, if he concentrated real hard, he could nail. But, basically, the English language looked to him like hieroglyphics. Just images. Meaningless images. It was a pain in the ass, really. His wife had to read to him: the newspaper in the morning, the mail that came in, street signs.

So this is what Johnny had in front of him now. Images. All he saw in front of him were typed pages, three or four of them. Once in a while he saw his name within the images. His name was one of the few things he could read. He also noticed that there were blank spaces throughout the document. "What are these blank spaces?" he asked.

"Don't worry about it," Jilly said, as he and Johnny sat at the same table at Matteo's. This time Jon was not there. Johnny just figured that Jon Emr had caught on to the fact that he didn't trust him.

"C'mon, what are these blank spaces?"

Jilly was angry. He told Johnny that this deal could be cut off at any moment, that Sinatra had several projects up his sleeve. Jilly jabbed at a section of the contract. "This here, Johnny, this part right here. This part says that I gotta give you twenty grand in the next couple days. Then, in this section here, I gotta give you two hundred thousand when the movie's set up. If that doesn't sound fair to you, then—"

"Twenty grand? In a couple days?" Johnny's eyes widened with excitement. Then a smile burst across his face. "Awwww, shit, lemme sign. Where do I sign?"

Johnny snatched a pen from Jilly's hand and put his sloppy "Johnny Carbonnara" at the bottom of the second page of the contract. Then he said, "But, I gotta tell ya, I still don't like this Jon Emr guy. I'll tell ya, I think that he's a con artist, a motherfucker!"

Jilly told him not to worry about it.

"Johnny, you're a stupid fuck! What do you mean you didn't get a copy of the contract!"

Johnny didn't want to hear this shit from Gerrie. He picked up the phone and called Ralphy. He wanted him to get his ass over to the apartment! With the contract, goddammit! When? Now!

Ralphy showed up at the apartment a few hours later. He handed over the document, gave a sharp salute, and then said he had to go. He told Johnny he would be by the next morning to take him to a notary public.

Ralphy had left by the time Gerrie finished reading the contract.

"Jesus Christ, Johnny, you really are some kinda stupid fuck!" she said to him, hands-on-hips in classic pissed-off Italian style. "You know what you're getting for these rights?"

She shoved the paper in front of John's face. Johnny smiled at his lass. "Twenty grand! Personal assurance of Mr. Sinatra!"

"Well, then, Sinatra just fucked you big time! Because you just signed the rights to your life story away FOR FRIGGIN' NOTHING. You got taken, JOHNNY."

"Taken. What the fuck are you talking about?"

"There's nothing here. It's blank. You signed a blank contract."

Johnny was dumbfounded. "It don't say nothing about twenty grand?"

"No, Johnny, it doesn't." She became suddenly gentle. "Johnny, honey, you got taken. You're a fool. And this Jon Emr, he's behind it. He thinks that you are a fool too. There's one thing you've preached ever since I known ya. Never sign nothin' till you're sure. Jesus! Mother of Mary! Sinatra this, Sinatra that!" She sat down and shook her head, giggled a bit, too. "The great Johnny Bond signed his life over to this Jon Emr for nothing."

The next day, Johnny Bond grabbed Ralphy by the collar and pushed him up against the wall. "You're all a buncha crooks!" he screamed at little Ralphy.

"What're ya talkin' about, Johnny? Relax, Johnny."

Johnny eased up and Ralphy slid down the wall ever so slightly. "Where's my money!"

"Johnny, it's comin'. I got a meeting all set up for you."

"I want you to remember this, Ralphy. Sinatra aside, if this thing fucks up, then, Ralphy, you had better say your prayers 'cause I'm goin' to kill you." He paused for a moment. "If anything's wrong with this, I don't get my money tomorrow night, a lot of people are going to answer to me fast."

"Okay, Johnny," Ralphy said. If the little twerp was scared, then he wasn't showing it. Maybe this thing was for real, Johnny thought. "You got it, Johnny. We'll go to the notary public, then you meet us at Matteo's around two. Okay. Now, let's go and get this thing notarized."

■ ■ ■

Johnny felt like a damn moron. Here he was at Matteo's and nobody showed up. It was just him and Ralphy.

"I'm tellin' you, Ralphy, Jilly doesn't show up with the money and I'm going to give you the beating of your life."

"Look, Johnny, you're blowing it here."

Johnny's fist came crashing down on the table. The plate with the peppers rattled around. "What the fuck—"

"Truth is, Jilly's talking with Sinatra about you right now. Right now! Here's the thing. You know this group New Kids on the Block? Big-big-big new group! Now, don't tell nobody, but Sinatra wants to make an album with them. And Sinatra wants you involved. They want you to produce it and promote it."

That was good for a few minutes of Johnny's time. Then Johnny came back to "Where the fuck is Jilly?"

"Look, Johnny, the truth is that sometimes Sinatra goes off. Barbara is feedin' him some pills. She's trying to fuck him up bad. She ain't giving him the right medicine. She hates him."

Hmmm. Mob gossip. "Are you shitting me here? Frank and Barbara hate each other?"

"Lemme tell you something," Ralphy began. He leaned forward conspiratorially. "She wanted Frank to adopt her kid. He lives in New York or something like that. But, ya know, the whole family hates her—Nancy, Tina, Frank Jr. Now, this is what Jilly tells me. It's not coming from Barbara. Frank's losing his mind and Barbara, she ain't helping. I think that she's trying to get Sinatra nuts. That's what I think. And, lemme tell you something. She's fuckin' somebody big."

This was as good as Mafia bullshit rumors got. "Barbara's fuckin' somebody? You gotta fuckin' be kidding me. She's fuckin' somebody behind Sinatra's back?"

"That guy, uh, James Bond. Double-O Seven. That Roger Moore guy."

Bango! This was as good as being a made man in the Mob. Johnny was one of the few who were given access to the inner sanctum of Sinatra Sleaze. It didn't matter that both men knew this was all nonsense. "Jesus!" Johnny said. "Frank knows?"

"She-iiit! They're doin' it right in front of Sinatra. Frank just sits around in his pajamas."

After the rumors ended, Ralphy got up to make a call. When he got back to the table he said, "I just talked to Jilly. He said Frank's sick. Jon

Emr ain't here because Jilly said that he would take care of things. Can we do this tomorrow?"

"Ohhhh, suuuuure," Johnny said.

The next day, Johnny walked into Matteo's, Ralphy by his side, and saw that there was no Jilly Rizzo and no Jon Emr there. Johnny grabbed Ralphy by the collar. The restaurant went silent as old Italians plunked down their forks and knives to see what was going to transpire. "I'm goin' to kill ya. I want my fuckin' contract back."

And it was at exactly that moment that old man Rizzo came sauntering through the doors. Jon Emr was not there with him. Good thing, Johnny thought, he didn't want to see that "sorry fuck" in any case.

Jilly and his group sat down at their traditional table. Jilly took out a wad of bills. Hundreds! Johnny's heart lifted slightly. He should never have doubted. One thing he knew from the Mafia corner, when a man such as Jilly said something, he would honor it. He told Johnny that he had four grand on him, but could give up only three.

"Three thousand?" Johnny was flummoxed. "FUCK YOU!" Johnny snatched the bills out of poor old Jilly's hands. *Wooosh!* "You're a miserable little fuck." He stood up. "You owe me sixteen thousand. I want it tomorrow, you sorry motherfucker!" Johnny dropped a twenty-dollar bill on the table. "Lunch is on me." Then he was out the door.

That night, Ralphy phoned Johnny Bond and told him that he was outta line for snatching the money. And so Johnny Bond did the only reasonable thing. He asked Ralphy to meet him for drinks, just the two of them, so that he could make amends in person. They agreed to meet at Chadneys, an old-time Burbank hangout for NBC employees.

There was Ralphy sitting at the bar, sipping some concoction. The television set behind the bartender was tuned into ESPN. Some ballgame. Couldn't be too important. People were actually socializing. It was very loud in the bar. Johnny walked up to Ralphy, who didn't see him coming. He just placed his hand on Ralphy's shoulder and he spun around, like a whirling dervish.

Johnny asked Ralphy to go up to the men's room. It was too loud in the bar. As soon as Ralphy walked into the restroom, Johnny was on him. He gave him a kick and a push and then, all of a sudden, Ralphy's face was buried in a toilet bowl. He'd fucked with Johnny Bond! And now the little faggot was going to drown in a toilet bowl. That would send a message! Goddamn right! Too bad there wasn't any piss or crap in the toilet bowl. That would have been the clincher. Johnny had his foot on Ralphy's back, and the little faggot was waving his ass around trying to get out of there. Here, this would be fun! Johnny flushed the toilet.

Johnny heard some rumbling outside. Maybe this wasn't the best place to kill Ralphy. Maybe he'd get the message back to that Jon Emr. Johnny stepped backward and gave Ralphy a kick, smack in the center of his ass. Johnny left, hoping the cops wouldn't be waiting for him at home.

That night, when he recounted he story to his wife, Johnny could tell that he was regaining some of her respect. She told Johnny that he should give Jon Emr a call and tell him what had happened. Maybe that would put the fear of God into him. It was only then that Johnny Bond realized that sonofabitch Jon Emr had never given him a phone number.

"Johnny, Jon Emr!"

"Jon Emr! You miserable fuck!" Johnny said into the phone receiver the next day.

"C'mon, Johnny. What'd you do to Ralphy last night? I thought that you were interested in making some money!"

"Money! money! You motherfucker, I'm going to kill you! When I'm done with you, motherfucker, you're gonna need an army. Frank Sinatra, my ass! I find out that it was Sinatra that fucked me, I'm goin' to the Mob. Believe it, motherfucker! I'm goin' to get permission to whack Sinatra, you, the whole fuckin' lot of you!" Johnny slammed down the phone.

Ringringringring!

Johnny snatched up the phone, "What!"

It was Renee Emr in her low monotone voice. "Johnny!" Jesus, Johnny thought. A woman! He couldn't argue with a woman. He didn't do that kind of shit.

"Look, Renee, I can't talk to you. Put Jon back on the line." Then he said it. Couldn't believe he said it. Nobody could believe he said it to a woman. "Lemme speak to the cocksucker."

"If you're speaking to me, then you are speaking to Jon."

"Oh-o really? SUCK MY COCK, RENEE!" Damn! That felt good.

Didn't faze Renee though. She stayed calm. She told Johnny she'd have to get a restraining order against him.

"SUCK MY COCK, RENEE!"

Whap! The phone went slamming to the floor. Johnny picked it up and banged it against the wall. "SUCKMYCOCK! SUCKMYCOCK! SUCKMYCOCK . . ."

The next phone call that Johnny got was from a Detective Harking who said that he was with the Burbank Police Department. He said he was calling in reference to a complaint that had been filed by one Jon Emr. Emr, it seemed, had asked that a restraining order be issued.

This Johnny could not believe. What kind of . . . of . . . of faggot would get the state to protect him? Real men, the giants who roamed the earth, settled their differences nose to nose, usually with their fists, sometimes with knives, maybe guns, never with pansy-ass pieces of paper. "Look, motherfucker, you bring that piece of paper here and then I'll leave 'em alone. So fuck you, you asshole!"

"You know what? You deserve your fuckin' mouth cracked!" The man who said he was a cop growled.

"Come on out here and talk to me that way, cocksucker! Come out here!" Johnny slammed the phone down. He pointed to his wife, standing in the corner aghast. "This is war."

The only way to find Jon Emr was to hang out around Matteo's. And so that's what Johnny did on this day. He took the Johnny Tank and circled the block. All the while, he was dragging on his cigarettes like a condemned man. The air freshener, a big Playboy emblem, swung from side to side like a pendulum from the rearview mirror, spritzing the air with the scent of peppermint.

It took maybe half an hour, but there was Jon Emr leaving. The dumbfuck, Johnny thought. Returning to the scene of the crime. Doesn't he know I'm going to beat the ever-living shit outta him? Doesn't he know who Johnny Bond is? Hadn't he told him? Warned him?

Scccrrreeeech! The Johnny Tank stopped dead in the middle of Westwood Boulevard. It was the horns blaring behind old Johnny and his Tank that got Jon Emr to turn around. That's when he saw Johnny and that's when he began to run.

Johnny snapped opened the glove compartment. Had he been a "made man" he would have pulled out a revolver. Instead he had to settle for a hatchet, one that he had sharpened all morning. Johnny got out of the car and began running, running as fast as his spindly sixty-year-old legs would carry him. Jon Emr took a right and disappeared into an alley. And there was Johnny chasing him, waving the hatchet over his head as if he were Jack Nicholson in *The Shining*, screaming "MOTHERFUCKER! I'M GONNA KILL YOU!"

It was certainly inevitable that Jon Emr would outrun his much older foe, which explains why Johnny Bond winged the hatchet so that it went bottom over top, sailing through the air, and just about gave Jon Emr a haircut. The hatchet bounced off the wall of the building, creating a small spark. Then something curious happened. Jon Emr, martial arts expert, who could have faced down Johnny Bond, or so he claimed, just kept running.*

That night Johnny had a call with his geriatric buddy from Philly, Anthony "the Bunny" Costello. Johnny told the Bunny about his problems with Jilly Rizzo and with "this fuckin' " Emr.

Bunny listened quietly and patiently. When Johnny was done, Bunny passed his edict. "I guess we gotta whack these two!"

"And don't forget Sinatra!" Johnny chimed in. "He's fuckin' me too!"

"I guess we can work on that. We'll fly out there soon."

"How you gonna get the guns on the plane?" Johnny was good with the strategizing.

The Bunny thought for a second. "I guess we gotta take the acid route."

"Ooooooh." The acid route. Now this was very serious business indeed. Simply stated, the whacker would splash the whackee's face with acid. In almost every instance, the victim's eyeballs would be the first

---

*Even though Renee was not present, she insists Jon would never run from Johnny Bond.

thing to burn. Then the skin would start to melt, right to the skull. Fuck you up good. And so, Johnny said it again. "Ooooooh."

A week later Johnny picked Bunny up from the airport. Bunny was a small wiry man with the cutest little rabbit eyes you ever did see. As Bunny crawled into the Johnny Tank, Johnny gave him the bad news. "We can't do it, Bunny."

Bunny gripped his little suitcase, the one containing all the chemicals necessary to melt somebody to death. "Why not?"

"I got this fuckin' cop on my case," Johnny said with a groan. He was referring to Detective Harking. "He says that he's gonna help this Jon Emr motherfucker get a restraining order on me. Anything happens to him or to Jilly and they'll know where to go."

Bunny nodded. Sometimes killing didn't come that easy. "So what're we gonna do. You're gonna introduce me to Sinatra."

Johnny laughed. "I'll tell you what! You want to fuck Angie Dickinson? This I can do. I just did her!"

"I'd like to fuck that Jon Emr and that Jilly Rizzo."

Johnny burst into laughter. "Look, the boys told us we could whack them, so we will. We will! Just later. Hey, you wanna hear something real fucking funny?"

"Yeah, Johnny, make me laugh."

"I hear Jon Emr's gonna make a movie about James Dean."

Bunny indeed laughed. "If he lives long enough."

Jilly Rizzo died on May 6, 1992, his seventy-fifth birthday. He was killed when his car exploded after a man later charged with drunk driving broadsided Jilly's white Jaguar.

A Twist in Paradise Valley:
August 29, 1991

All right, let's play twenty questions. If you answer them correctly,
maybe I won't knock your teeth out.
—Mark Stevens to William Bendix in *The Dark Corner*

In early August a young woman walked into Detective Alan Laitsch's office in the Paradise Valley Police Department with an envelope containing a microcassette. The woman told Laitsch that she had taped a conversation with a man whom she believed to be Suggsy.

A year earlier she had left her husband, who had ferociously abused her. She was so frightened that she had obtained a legal name change and moved hundreds of miles away. Recently, she had gotten a phone call from a smooth-talking private eye named Robert Suggs who said he had been hired by her husband to find her.

She, of course, denied that she was married to Suggsy's client. However, after three more phone calls she gave in. All she could do was appeal to Suggsy's humanity. This was a wife beater! A cruel man! If he turned her in, she was not sure that she could survive. She offered to pay his fee if he would let her be.

Laitsch got all of this from the tape recordings that she had made. But then there was something interesting. The woman asked him what she should do the next time she wanted to disappear and never be found.

Suggsy was quite helpful. He went down a list of the basics. Then he hit the one that got Laitsch thinking. "Whatever you do," Suggsy said, "never use your credit cards. That's the easiest way to find somebody. If you want to be sure that you are found, use your credit cards."

And so Laitsch and, later, Hank Davies had to ask themselves, why had Suggsy used his own credit cards during his drive with Benny? And why did he have Benny sign the receipt for one of the purchases?

Could it be that Suggsy *wanted* the cops to "discover" Benny? Maybe he wanted his friend to crack and speak to the police. Could it be that Suggsy had schemed to give Benny disinformation all along?

A few days later, Hank Davies and Steve Yoshida were back out in the desert. Only this time they brought out ten Culver City cops with them and Alan Laitsch. He had come to California to bring the bullets that had been used to kill Art Emr Sr. Hank had asked Alan if he wanted to spend a few hours wandering around the Mojave desert trying to find the remains of Susan Calkins.

Laitsch must have regretted his decision as he searched among the tumbleweeds and cactuses. This is ridiculous, Laitsch thought to himself. Here they were searching for a body without any sense of direction or any clear idea where, in this vast, vast wasteland it might be.

After several hours, Hank Davies began thinking that Benny was simply full of shit. Why, he was probably at home with his homely wife and eight or nine, or however damn many there were, children laughing his ass off about the moron cops who were combing the desert for a body they would never find. Davies gathered all of the cops together and instructed them to wait for his call at a local Denny's restaurant. He was going to pick up Benny yet again and asked Yoshida and Alan Laitsch to come with him.

Davies did not mince words when Benny opened his front door. "LOOK! I'm really tired of all this bullshit. You had better start coming up with the right answers." Yoshida and Laitsch stood silently behind Davies as he reamed Benny.

Benny stepped outside and closed the door. He didn't want his kids to hear any of this. "But, Hank—"

"If you don't level with me I'm going to place you under arrest."

"Hank, really, I don't know anything more than what I told you."

Hank swung Benny around and handcuffed him. He read him his rights and then told him that he was being arrested for a conspiracy to commit murder.

Instantly, Benny began blubbering like a baby. Davies led him to Laitsch's rental car and put him in the backseat. Then he went back to the house and knocked on the door and told Benny's wife, Jennifer, that her husband was being arrested.

Davies did not immediately throw Benny into the slammer when they walked into the Culver City station. Instead he and Laitsch escorted him up to the only free interrogation room.

As Davies grilled Benny, Laitsch stood in the background, not say-ing a word. He was, after all, a guest in this town and in this police sta-tion. In any case, since the interrogation was being tape-recorded it would only confuse the transcriber if there was more than one voice intimidating Benny. Whenever Laitsch had a question he would just signal Davies to step outside the room and tell him what he wanted asked.

After hours of fruitless questioning, Davies finally gave up. He took Benny down to one of the holding cells and gave him a "private room." He figured that Benny would finally come to his senses.

Over the next three days, including the weekend, Benny just kind of mulled his life over. It had been a hell of a year. On top of this very obvious and profound crisis, his wife had accidentally run over his first child, his real pride and joy. And now, this bullshit.

For the first time, Benny felt genuine anger at Suggsy. The last time he was this pissed was years earlier. Suggsy had been staying with Benny and Jennifer and their then five children. Benny had made a point that their mutt, Alex, named after Michael J. Fox's character on the popular sitcom *Family Ties*, was an unbelievable pain in the ass. After months of trying, Benny had still not managed to housebreak him. On top of that, the damn dog was digging up the garden. "I'd just get rid of him if I had the heart," Benny told Suggsy. Later that after-noon, Benny came back from work and found Suggsy on the couch watching television. In the middle of the floor lay the little beast, com-pletely still. "You've gotta bury your dog," Suggsy said.

Now, as he sat in this dank Culver City cell, Benny was truly furious with Suggsy. On occasion, he even balled his hands into a fist and laid into the cement wall. Of course, Benny had to accept some of the re-sponsibility. He knew it. As he sat on the uncomfortable, wooden bench, drinking down the rounds of coffee that Steve Yoshida kindly brought down to him, he figured that he should have talked with Suggsy about God some more. Suggsy was an avowed atheist and claimed that nothing could make him waver from that position. But, then again, Benny was the son of a preacher. If he had only been able to convert Suggsy to the goodness of the Lord things might be much different today.

The way that Benny figured it, Suggsy was either dead or in Aca-pulco or maybe at a neo-Nazi camp somewhere. In any of those sce-narios he was better off than Benny was at this precise moment. Benny, after all, had a wife and a gaggle of children to take care of. What he didn't have now was a job. When Jennifer came by to visit him she told him that he had been fired. That, in effect, had been the turning point. Benny let the guard know that he was ready to speak. Within a few minutes, he had an audience with Hank Davies and Steve Yoshida.

Benny was hesitant at first, mumbling a bit, and so all Davies had to do was once again describe what Benny's jail-bound future would be like. "I'm sorry I lied to you, Hank," Benny said.

"Okay, Benny. Why did you lie?"

"Suggsy's nuts. He's nuts. I didn't know that he wouldn't come back for me. I got seven kids."

"Well, Benny, don't you think that you would be better off if we captured him? Then you'd be completely safe from him. Don't you think?"

"Yeah, I suppose so."

"You should have just explained your fears to me from the start."

"I'm sorry, Hank."

"You want something to eat?"

"I'm not hungry."

"You sure, Benny? Our food here is pretty good. I mean, as good as jail food can get."

"No, I'm not hungry. I just want to get over this." Benny sounded like he meant it.

"All right, Benny. Let's hear it, then."

And so Benny told all.

The next morning Hank Davies went to see the Culver City district attorney. For an hour he went over all he had on Benny. It was pretty damn clear that Benny was a coconspirator. He should fry right there by Suggsy's side.

The district attorney agreed. But there was one complication. "Arizona has a better case against him."

Davies could barely believe what he was hearing. "You're not telling me to release him."

"I'm telling you that Arizona has a better chance at convicting this character."

"So, let him go?"

"That's right," the D.A. said. "Let him go."

When Davies released Benny from his jail cell, he didn't tell him what the district attorney had said. Instead, he used this defeat as a means to gain more of Benny's confidence. "Look, I talked about it with the guys," Davies said, one hand on Benny's right shoulder. "I told them that you were being kind of cooperative. You know, there are a couple of warrants out there on you."

"Yeah? Really."

"Pretty serious stuff. Driving without insurance, something like that. But, look. You've proven to be loyal to our search. We're going to release you—"

"God bless you, Hank." Benny gave Davies a big old hug.

"Okay. But, you'd better be available every day! And we're going to need for you to take a polygraph test. A lie detector. Are you okay with that?"

"Yeah. Can I call my wife?"

"Sure you can." Hank led Benny up to his cubicle and then dialed Benny's number for him. Benny sure was excited when he called his wife. He told her that he was clean off-the-hook. He told her that Sergeant Davies, God bless him, had saved him from spending several years in the big house. They owed Davies. They owed him big. At one point, Benny covered the mouthpiece and turned to Davies, "Would you like to come to dinner tonight?"

Davies shook his head. "Some other time, Benny."

To be honest, there was only one reason why Hank Davies was back out in the desert looking for a body that he damn well knew he would never find.

The reason was The Psychics. Not psychics hired by Culver City. These particular tarot card gurus were paid for courtesy of Kathy Calkins. What was striking about all of the three who had presented their visions to Kathy was that they were all so similar. The common denominators: Susan was dead. She was killed with a blunt blow to the head. She was buried somewhere in the desert, the Mojave probably, and there was water nearby.

Davies didn't want to give Kathy his opinion that all of the psychics were quacks or con artists. There was no purpose in that. Instead, he simply assured Kathy that once again they would comb the desert. In fact, they would do it near the Los Angeles water and power aqueduct.

When they searched the desert this time, it would be different.

Somehow Davies had convinced the FBI to send in their super-secret, ultrasophisticated plane called "Night Stalker." The jet was designed to fly over and pinpoint areas where there was unnatural heat emanating from the ground. It was a real coup for Davies. Use of the Night Stalker was very expensive. Not only that. With the plane came several FBI agents.

Davies and Yoshida met about thirty feds at a grocery store at the junction of Highways 62 and 95. The grocery store owner had never seen so many people in his store at one time. And they were buying up all the cop food in the joint. Cokes and bags of chips were disappearing off the racks.

After the perfunctory introductions, Davies divided the agents into six groups. He felt genuinely exhilarated. Imagine this! Being able to take command of feds. This was every cop's dream.

Each team had a four-wheel-drive. They drove out to various sections of the desert that had been preselected by Davies. Then they waited. Simply waited. After half an hour, they heard the very unsubtle roar of the plane overhead. And that's when all the silly business began.

For four hours, the pilots radioed in to Davies the locations where their machinery sensed intense heat and density. Then Davies would contact the appropriate team and they would go to the area, shovels in hand, and tear up the ground.

In that span of time Susan Lynn Calkins's body was never found. However, there were plenty of dead rabbits and dead coyotes.

Davies and the crew quit fairly late at night. Davies wanted to get home early. The next morning he would board a Southwestern Airlines plane for the fifty-minute ride to Las Vegas. With him he would have the few photos of Suggsy that he had collected. He had Suggsy's credit card receipts and his notes from his talk with Benny and knew what restaurants and hotels and shops to go to. He knew that the trip was futile. But it was procedure and, anyway, it would give Hank a chance to play some blackjack.

BOOK TWO

Robert Suggs, Seattle, and the Hollywood Dream

In a movie, the hero as well as the heroine has to be a virgin. The villain can lay anybody he wants, have as much fun as he wants, cheating and stealing, getting rich and whipping the servants. But you have to shoot him in the end.
—Herman J. Mankiewicz, 1927

A Big Break in Culver City:
July 15, 1991

Was I demoralized? You bet I was. Particularly as the studio thought it would be a good idea if I wore my hair like Elvis Presley and changed my name. I suggested Kurt Affair. After that, there was no more talk of changing names.
—Harrison Ford, 1984

Hank Davies picked up his phone. Pat, the department secretary, told him that the person on the other end was absolutely insistent that he be able to speak with the "detective working the Emr murders."

"Detectives. Sergeant Davies," Hank bellowed into the phone.

"I'm surprised that you haven't contacted me," the cool voice said.

"Who is this?"

"I'm Max Caulfield," the voice said. Caulfield paused, awaiting recognition from Hank. When none came Caulfield went on. "I used to work for Robert up here in Seattle. I now run my own company."

Davies sat up in his seat. *Max Caulfield.* Of course. "Yes, Mr. Caulfield. What can I do for you?"

"I thought that you might have some questions for me."

"I do. I'm wondering if you might have any—"

"Let me just tell you what I know."

Hank resigned himself to the fact that he was on the phone with a typical control freak private eye. He hated gumshoes. There wasn't a private eye on the planet who didn't think that he could outwit, outthink, and outplay the police. "Go ahead," Hank said, pulling out his pen.

"I knew that Rob and this Jon Emr guy had problems. I knew that. At first, Rob would call me and tell me that this was his big break, that this big producer had taken him under his wing, that soon he would be some kind of household name."

"Let me interrupt you. Did he tell you about any projects he was working on?"

"Yeah, I think Rob said that he was going to be producing this movie about James Dean. Anyway, a couple of months later, Rob calls me from California. I could tell that he had been crying. He said that he was sitting in a bare apartment, that he had been kicked out or something like that. It was the last call that he was making from the place."

"Did he say that he and Jon Emr had fought?"

"Yeah, he said it was over. He also told me that he had gotten work in Salt Lake City, with one of Jon Emr's enemies."

"Enemies?"

"That's right. Whenever Rob would call me he would tell me about how Jon had instructed him to get even with his enemies. There was one in particular—"

Hank Davies did not have to think this one through for too long. "Scott Barnes."

"That's right!" Caulfield said with a kind of joy. "Scott Barnes! Man, this Emr was obsessed with destroying Barnes. Anyway, so was Rob. I mean, Rob just hated this motherfucker. I remember he called me once and told me, 'Max, I have finally found my match.' You gotta understand, this is a pretty big deal. Those words didn't come easy to Suggs."

"So who was Jon Emr's enemy in Salt Lake City?"

"I dunno. But, really, that was not the most interesting thing. When Rob called me that last time he said he had two favors to ask me. The first was this. He told me that he had a customer in Arizona who was an American woman married to a Mexican man. Apparently, the man had kidnapped their kids and brought them across the border. Anyway, Rob said that he had gotten this assignment to kidnap these kids. He told me that this was a three-man operation. He had the other guy all set. Somebody who he knew from high school. He asked me to be the third guy."

"Really?" Davies said. "And what did you do?"

There was silence on the other end for a while, as if Max were angered that Hank even had to ask. "Of course I wouldn't do it. That's what I told him. I wasn't going to do anything illegal. Not for him or anybody. So I asked him what his second favor was."

Hank was taking all this down in his notebook, a little upset that he had not had a tape recorder running. "Go on. What was it?"

"I don't know. He just kind of laughed and said that if I would not do the first, then I sure would not do the second."

"So what do you think he wanted you to do?"

"Isn't it obvious?"

Davies was amazed at the arrogance of this guy. "Humor me."

"It's now clear to me that this kidnapping thing was bullshit. He just sort of wanted to ease me into the notion of blowing away Emr and splitting the money."

Money? Did Caulfield say money? "What're you talking about, Max?"

"I'm sure he was hired to kill Jon Emr. You know how many people wanted to see this fucker dead? Anyway, for the record, I would have said 'no,' had he asked me."

"I'm happy to hear that, Max. Do you know where Suggs might have gone? A favorite hangout, a hiding place, something like that?"

"Oh, he's dead. I'm sure he's dead. I'm sure the girl is dead too. Whoever hired him to do this probably blew him and Susan away."

"Hmmm. Dead. Interesting theory. You think there was a conspiracy?"

Max laughed. "Fuck, yeah."

"So, Max, tell me about this guy. What made him tick?"

"Tell you about Suggs? Well, I guess it would be fair to say that he was a motherfucker. A brutal, racist motherfucker. Listen, Sergeant Davies—"

"Hank."

"Hank, I have to go. I'm doing a surveillance. Do you have a home number or something, you know, if I think of anything—"

Davies gave Max Caulfield his beeper number and told him to call him at absolutely any time. It took Max three days and a dozen phone calls (sometimes after midnight) to tell Hank the stories that would fill out the character of one Robert Suggs.

Robert Suggs in Seattle, 1989

You make a star, you make a monster.
—Sam Spiegal on casting Peter O'Toole in *Lawrence of Arabia*

By 1989, Robert Suggs was an established private investigator in the Seattle-Tacoma area of Washington State. All that really meant was that he had placed an ad in the phone book. In fact, it was the biggest ad for a private eye in the book. SUGGS INVESTIGATIONS promised first-rate work on everything from spousal surveillance to the serving of summonses. The ad also bragged that the company utilized vehicle-tracking devices, two-way radios, and night-vision video equipment.

Like most of the jobs that Suggs had held since he left the air force several years earlier, this one was proving to be a bust. During the twelve years since he'd graduated from high school, Suggs had failed at being a bus driver, a gas station attendant, and a repairman. He had become enamored of private investigation after an attorney had given him some work doing minor research and surveillance.

Suggs had even failed when he was a contestant on the game show *The Price Is Right*. After announcer Don Pardo, in his trademark boomingly enthusiastic voice screamed "Robert Suggs! Come on down!" Suggs's Hollywood dreams flashed across his eyes. It's star-time, baby.

The first item up for bids was a beautiful oak lady's table. Suggs was the first to place his bid. He guessed that the price of the item was $450. The last contestant, a woman, looked over at Robert and then asked host Bob Barker, "How much did he bid?" When Barker told her Suggs's bid she smiled and said $451.

Over the next three bidding wars, Suggs was always off. Way off. And each time he would get increasingly angry. By the end of the telecast, Suggs was slamming his hands together and looking at his competitors in disgust.

When he got home, Suggs told nobody about his appearance on the show. He was too ashamed. When the show aired, he made sure that the two people who worked for him were busy and not sitting in front of a television set.

Max Caulfield had already worked in several security jobs across the country, and was now working as a guard at a clothing store near Seattle. He saw the big ad for Suggs Investigations in the phone book and contacted the company with the hope that Suggs might be looking for a bodyguard.

Suggs was not impressed with Caulfield and said he was not looking for extra help. Business was slow. During the recession, the idea of snooping on your husband seemed like a frivolous expense. But Suggs was nonetheless curious about Caulfield. He claimed to have taken a course at the Lethal Weapon Institute. Suggs had also been "trained" there. His instructor was a beefy Arab named Moosad Abab. Suggs had trained in Abab's Los Angeles clinic and Caulfield in a seminar that had been held in New Hampshire. Suggs agreed to meet with Caulfield a few days later at Max's apartment, which he shared with his gorgeous girlfriend, Christine, and his two children from a previous marriage.

Suggs showed up with a couple of beefy guys. Real stereotypical goons, Max thought. One was Mike Hill, an old friend of Suggs, and the other was Michael Casey. He introduced them as his employees. The first thing Suggs noticed was that there were guns and weapons in every corner of Caulfield's apartment. He also noticed a couple of children running around.

As they sat down, Suggs got right down to business. "Look," Suggs told him. "I am going to be checking you out before I even consider hiring you. I want no surprises. If you work for us, then your problems all of a sudden become our problems. If we are going to work together, then we have to know what we are going to be getting into. So, it's like this: I want to know everything, I want to know now, or I'm out of here. It's up to you."

Caulfield immediately hit Suggs with a bombshell. He told the three men that he was in the Federal Witness Protection Program. His name was not really Max Caulfield. If they tried to do a background check on him they would come out empty-handed. He had been a bagman for an Italian mafioso back East. He had never done anything illegal, he said. But he knew enough to testify against his bosses.

The Suggs Thugs, as they liked to call themselves, were entranced. Goddamn it all if this Caulfield character wasn't one of their own. And he could be trusted! After all, he had told them—all three—a secret that could be used to destroy him. Without asking Caulfield for any evidence to back up his story, Robert Suggs hired Max on the spot. "At first you'll be working for free. We have to train you. You can consider yourself an intern."

What Max soon learned was that this was a private investigation firm in name only. It was not infrequent for a client to hire the investigators to do forty hours of surveillance on a spouse. In almost every case, Suggs would deposit the money in the bank and then tell Max that the whole thing was nonsense and they were not going to do any work whatsoever. Rob would often say, "Forget it, let's go home and watch TV."

In fact, Suggs seemed to get severely stressed every time he caught Caulfield working. When Suggs told Caulfield that he was "wasting time" by doing surveillance, Max would say, "That's our job. We get paid to waste our time."

This did not get past too many of the clients. By the time Max had come into the picture, the complaint file on Suggs with the Washington State district attorney's office had become a monster. All the complainants had the same thing to say. They would pay a fee to Suggs Investigations and that is the last time that they would hear from the detective.

But then something odd happened. Max Caulfield began to meet with clients and, through his charm and professional demeanor, increased business by almost 200 percent. In the year that Max was serving as the front man for the company, Suggs Investigations came up with something like a quarter of a million dollars. With the increased fees the pressure was on the detectives to actually deliver.

For weeks, Max Caulfield had been proposing that Suggs hire a woman to work for the company. His philosophy was simple. "I can't send a guy into a ladies' room. There are certain things that only a woman can do in this business and we need a female investigator."

In fact, Max had a very special woman in mind: his girlfriend Christine. Christine was a knockout half Hispanic-half white who supplemented the family income by posing for mercenary magazines in skimpy, camouflage outfits holding machine guns. Max had already been using Christine in various capacities. Of course, she was not being paid. Max simply figured that Suggs would eventually capitulate to allowing a woman into the organization.

Late in 1989 that happened. Rob had been on business down in Los Angeles when Max received a call from him. "Max, I got you a female investigator!" he said.

"What are you talking about, Rob?"

"I got her, man! She's college-educated, blond, beautiful—the All-American Girl! Done! I'm bringing her back there. I'm going to train her to be an investigator. It's going to be great."

Rob explained that he had met the girl while sitting in a hotel lobby lounge in Newport Beach, California. She was a cocktail waitress, but was also well educated. She had graduated from the University of Michigan, where she had a double minor in journalism and philosophy, and a major in communications. She had no family or boyfriend in the Los Angeles area (her parents lived in Michigan and her sister, Kathy, in the San Francisco Bay area) and thus no attachments. She would be perfect.

Max knew what was going on. In his mind, since Christine was easily the best-qualified person for the job, there could be only one reason why Rob wanted to bring this blond up from California. And it had nothing to do with her abilities as a gumshoe. But Rob had even more to say. "We're also going to be hiring my dad."

Now Max was blown away. For months, Rob had been confiding in Max about the abuse he had taken from his father. "You're kidding, right?"

"Look, my old man is all by himself, he doesn't have a job, and he needs something to do."

"Something to do? Look, what does your dad know how to do?"

There was a blank pause. "I don't know, Max. I just don't know."

Another lost case, Max thought. "Well, I guess that he can be our elderly investigator," he said with a gentle sigh.

Max didn't get an opportunity to meet the "new girl" until a week after her arrival in Tacoma with Suggs and his father. Suggs had made a brief appearance at Max's apartment when they first hit town and then disappeared until he told Max that he and the new girl, Susan, would be accompanying him on a surveillance job.

This was a stolen limousine case. The chauffeur had simply driven off with it one day and then went into business for himself. The limo's owner had hired the Suggs Thugs to get his car back and collect evidence that would put the thief away for a long time.

It had taken two weeks for Max and Christine to find the limo. And now, finally, they were ready to do their monitoring. When Max told Rob about it, he became excited. This would be a great opportunity for Sue. She sure could learn a lot from this experience. Max reluctantly agreed.

Suggs showed up with two women. Max could tell right away who Susan was. *Fuckin' bimbo*, Max thought to himself. She had long blond hair, a mess of makeup, and designer clothes. She looked like she had never gotten her hands dirty in her life.

The girl with Susan was her friend Patti, a pretty brunette from Michigan. Both of the girls were giggling and their breath reeked of alcohol. Suggs told Max that the two women would be joining them. They would follow in Suggs's car.

Then something rather remarkable happened: A breach of private dick professionalism even for Robert Suggs. As they were tailing the subject—the limo thief—Rob called Max over the radio. "Yo, Max! We gotta pull over. Susan and Patti want to go to a liquor store and pick up some wine."

Pick up some wine! Had Rob lost his mind? Max could even hear the two girls giggling over the radio. "What kind of shit is this?"

"Just pull it over," Rob said.

At the liquor store, a steaming Max pulled Rob to the side. "You know what we just did? We lost a fucking limousine! A big fuckin' white limo! A big limo with six doors!"

"Max, you're going to have to relax." He pointed to the two women stumbling down the aisle. "She's in training."

"You have gotta be fucking kidding me. Susan is your girlfriend. That's just fine. But don't fucking tell me that this is a female investigator."

"Well, she'll learn. Look, I have an appointment to meet with a client in a couple of hours. Why don't you take it?"

"All right, Rob."

"—and take Susan with you."

"Aw, Jesus!"

But there was no argument beyond that. Susan got into Max's car and they drove off to meet the client in question. Midway through the drive, Max told her what plans he had for her. "I think that we're going to start you off doing some surveillance work."

And then Susan blew him away. "Well, Max, I came up here to make some money."

"Money?"

"Well, I'm not going to be working for twenty dollars an hour forever."

Max was stunned. Max had only been getting about $10 an hour. And he had become the heart and the soul of Suggs Investigation. Not only that, but Max's wife, Christine, had been working for nothing for months and months now. And here was Rob's new girlfriend telling him that she was in this for the cash. "You've gotta be kidding me, Susan," he said.

"No," she said. "I plan to make money. Big money!"

Max weaved the car to the side of the road, brought it to a screeching halt, and then leaped out of the car with his cellular phone in his hands. He pressed the speed dial to Suggs on the other end. "You son of a bitch! This fucking broad's crazy, Rob! I want her out of the car right fuckin' now! I don't want this bitch anywhere near me!"

"C'mon, Max," Rob said. "Chill the fuck out!"

Chill the fuck out? Is that what Rob said? "I've been working hard for you, Rob. Very fucking hard! Now along comes this honey from California without a goddamn bit of experience! This bitch told me that she's going to make more money than me and I'm afraid that she's right! I'll bet this cunt can't even spell surveillance!"

Max turned off the phone and went back in the car. "Let's go."

Suggs, as it turned out, was capable of enormous cruelty, which he would often impose on his beloved German shepherd Joe. The slightest act of disobedience by the dog, like walking too far in front of his master, would result in hellacious punishments. Suggs would laugh like Torquemada in describing them. One of his favorite punishments was lifting the dog up by the collar and hanging him in the air until he defecated. At other times, Suggs would attach a leash to the dog and then twirl him through the air. Suggs called this "the helicopter" and insisted that it was a wonderful training tool for the animal.

The walls inside Suggs's trailer were filled with holes that were created when he had punched them out. To make use of the holes, Suggs would park his myriad weapons in them. Often he would go into the woods and shoot up trees. One day he took a machine gun and, with as fine a precision as anybody who was present at the event had ever seen, used 2,000 rounds to mow down a huge pine tree.

Even after their divorce, Carol Casey, a beautiful attorney who had married Robert when she was "young and silly," had to deal with Suggs's violent outbursts and promises that he would "fuckin' kill" her. There are two restraining orders on file against Robert Suggs in King County in Washington State, ordering him to stay away from his wife.

In the meantime, Suggs's father, Doug, was holed up in the trailer. He was drinking constantly and would often join his son in beating the dog. But the most unpleasant development was the way in which Doug would treat Susan. Suggs would describe them as "two cats in a bag."

Eventually, one of them had to leave. Suggs decided that it was going to be Susan, so he set her up in an apartment in Tacoma. Susan didn't mind that. She needed the additional space. Besides, her sex life with Rob was only mediocre and she suspected that Suggs may have cheated on her a couple of times. But what could she do? She had become 100 percent financially dependent on Rob.

One day, Suggs and Caulfield set up a meeting with a prospective employee. Susan, all gussied up, was at the meeting as well. They asked the young man, Patrick Gulliver, to meet them at a restaurant named Thirteen Coins. This restaurant, located right next to the Seattle-Tacoma Airport, was the primary meeting place of employees of Suggs Investigations.

There were two reasons why offices were never used. First, Suggs could not afford it. Second, as Caulfield would later put it, "We'd have bombs thrown through the doors every other day. We would have to be fucking insane to have offices." Hell, Suggs Investigations did not even have a direct phone line. The number in the phone book belonged to an answering service.

Very few of the questions that Suggs fired off at Patrick correlated to being a private investigator. At one point, for example, Suggs asked him what he thought about blacks. He asked him what his favorite movie was. Eventually, Suggs came around to asking the most relevant question. "Here is a hypothetical situation. You are supposed to go and collect a fee. When you get to the address, a little old lady answers the door. She tells you that she does not have the two hundred dollars that she owes us. She even tells you that she has no food in the fridge. What do you do?"

Patrick was an actor by trade. He had even had a bit part in the Seattle-based Touchstone movie *The Hand That Rocks the Cradle*, in which he played a police officer. Furthermore, he fancied himself as a film director. While in college, he produced and directed a documentary on prostitution. During that time he had formed friendships with members of the vice squad. He knew how to put on a show and he knew exactly what Robert Suggs wanted to hear. "I would grab her color television and then haul her down to the pawnshop and get our money that way."

Suggs and Caulfield looked at each other and smiled. "Very good," said Suggs. "But you left out the part where you bash the old bitch's fucking dentures out! Then you tell her that you're coming back tomorrow and she'd better have the money or she ain't going to eat for a week!"

After a good laugh, Suggs told him more about the business. "We're mercenaries," he told him. "We are soldiers of fortune. Simple as that. We are not here to do charity work. I don't care if a nun has asked you to look for a missing five-year-old. If she has no money, then fuck her."

Suggs explained that, on the subject of money, there were a few rules. The most important of which was that there were absolutely no refunds. The P.I. business, perhaps more than any other, was crammed with dissatisfied customers. Often, the detective would have to tell the suspicious wife that, no, her husband was not banging the baby-sitter. Defiantly, the customer would routinely insist that the detective had obviously not done his work and that she wanted her retainer back. "You just tell them to fuck off!" Suggs said.

On the other hand, Suggs suggested, no money was bad money. If a prospective client had no cash in the bank that was not a problem.

"You take his ass down to the stereo shop and have him buy a two-thousand-dollar television set on credit. He'll make payments and we can either keep it or sell it."

Suggs and Caulfield bragged that their homes were like giant electronic warehouses. Suggs claimed that he had fifteen big-screen televisions and if Patrick played his cards right, he would get one.

"I want you to know something. It's not like we really need to hire anybody. I just want to be less involved. I'm not interested in actually meeting clients anymore," Suggs said. He pulled out a thick envelope that contained Patrick's résumé and a videotape. "I'm talking to you because of this. I get dozens of requests to join the company. But you went the extra step."

Suggs pulled out the videotape. It was the documentary Patrick had done on hookers in Seattle. He smiled wide. "Any guy as fascinated with fuckin' whores as much as you seem to be has gotta be a good guy."

As they walked outside, Suggs gave Patrick a big bear hug and welcomed him into the fraternity of Suggs Thugs. Then he pulled some keys out of his pockets. "You need a new set of wheels." He put the keys into Patrick's palms. "This is for that Grand Am over there. It even has a cellular phone in it. You don't have to pay me now. When you start to make money we'll deduct it from your pay."

What Suggs failed to mention was that the Grand Am was not his to give away and that it actually belonged to his ex-wife, Carol Casey, the attorney.

That same night, Suggs informed Patrick that they would be spending the evening in a lounge called Celebrities. It was a jazz lounge in downtown Tacoma.

As soon as Patrick, Susan, and Rob sat down, Patrick lit up a cigarette. Suggs reached across the table and snatched it out of Patrick's mouth. "That's rule number one."

Patrick was a bit stunned, but he didn't say anything. Susan gently smiled at him. "Welcome to the club," her eyes seemed to be telling him.

Suggs was not only a consummate teetotaler, he considered it ugly and outrageous that anybody would smoke or drink hard booze around him. On several occasions he would make Susan, who had a bad nicotine habit, stand outside the car while she smoked. It didn't matter if it was raining, hailing, or snowing. It was always the same. Susan would be standing outside her car, smoking like a condemned prisoner, and Robert would be glaring at her from inside the car.

Suggs ordered a Diet Coke; Sue had some wine, as did Patrick. That's how it went for the night. Patrick and Sue were knocking back alcohol and Suggs was drinking diet colas and munching on peanuts.

After a little while, Suggs said to Patrick, "Go dance with my girlfriend."

"What do you mean? I don't want to dance with your girl." Patrick was sure that this was some kind of test. That would be just like Rob.

"Go dance with my girlfriend!" he said again. "I don't like to dance. You go and dance with her."

Patrick looked Susan over. She sure was pretty, he thought. She had big blue eyes that never seemed to blink and, here was the best part for Patrick, she was stacked. He thought that he would nickname her Bunny. If Rob wanted him to dance with this beautiful woman, then who was he to be anything but a loyal servant.

From that night on, Susan would always insist that her dancing partner, Patrick, join them when they went to clubs. Indeed, Patrick was not only a good dancer, he was also a great lookout. The few times that Susan could catch a drag on a cigarette was when Rob went to the men's room.

It seemed that Suggs was getting less and less interested in the business. His dreams of being a super spy were being supplanted by his dreams of being a mogul. He often compared himself to Ray Kroc—the head honcho of the McDonald's chain. He expected Caulfield to work hard for the 20 percent of the business he was now getting.

Suggs began to make frequent trips to Las Vegas. He would tell Caulfield that he was leaving for a weekend and then, seven days later, call Max and beg him to send him some money at the local Western

Union. Sometimes Suggs would disappear for days at a time, "on assignment." He had bought a beeper so that none of his employees knew where he was. Whenever he called in, he would say that he was in Los Angeles or Arizona, but his men would recognize the sound of slot machines jangling in the background.

Suggs would spend week after week in Vegas, sometimes bringing Sue Calkins with him and sometimes leaving her behind to fend for herself in Tacoma. Often, when Rob called in to the office, Caulfield would tell him that yet another customer was at their throats and that Suggs needed to get back right away. Each time, Suggs would have the same answer. "Don't worry about it. I'll take care of it. You just get the money, you do the surveillance, and I'll worry about the rest of the shit. And if they sue anybody, they're going to sue me."

Caulfield wasn't buying into any of this. At one time he said, "Look, if you are not going to come back here and you are not going to do the work and you are going to be staying in Las Vegas, then you need to do something! Fuck, why don't you open a business now? Why don't you open up Suggs Investigations South? Then at least you could get something accomplished when you are doing all of this shit!"

When he was not in Las Vegas, Suggs would lock himself into his trailer, deep in the woods of Port Orchard, about thirty miles away from the civilization of Tacoma. Suggs had the sleazy little home wired with an elaborate alarm system. There was even a red laser beam that streaked across the driveway and set off the alarm if anybody came on the property.

Suggs never, at least to anybody's recollection, cleaned the house out. He treated it as if it were a college dorm room. Eventually, the dog hair had become an inch thick on the carpet. Dog shit remained under his bed for over two years. Since he was too lazy to have his trash taken to the local dump, Suggs would pile it in his front yard and set it on fire.

By far, Suggs's favorite hobby was watching television. Only, he never wanted to see what was actually on the tube. He wanted to see what else was on. He claimed that his satellite dish gave him the capability of having over two hundred channels. He would often command his foot soldiers to his home to sit with him as he went through every channel for hours on end. Suggs would sit in his armchair, with a remote control in both hands, firing away at the screen as if it were a video game. He was especially excited that he could watch a film on television twice. Once on East Coast time and then on West Coast time.

The only time that Suggs could watch television without a remote control in his hand was when he was watching his two favorite films on video, *The Getaway* with Steve McQueen and Ali MacGraw, and *Thief* with James Caan and Jim Belushi. Eventually, he saw both films over one hundred times.

It was *Thief* that really got to Suggs. Once, Suggs ordered Caulfield to sit through the movie with him for, maybe, the twentieth time. There was a scene in which the Godfather figure tells Caan, "I'll be your father. Cars, guns, money, whatever you need." The idea was that, in return, Caan would be faithful to the Godfather and do whatever he wanted.

"That's what you are, Rob," Max said to Suggs. "You're our daddy."

Daddy? Suggs smiled. He kind of liked that.

Robert Suggs in Seattle, 1990–1991

The telephone stopped ringing. That's all. I knew what that meant.
—Howard Koch on being blacklisted

One night in late December 1990, Suggs contacted Patrick at his home. It was around midnight. "I'm leaving for Arizona," he said. "Come over to Susan's apartment and help me pack all of this shit up."

Patrick arrived at Susan's apartment building in Tacoma. Outside a large U-Haul was attached to his Buick Regal. Suggs and Susan were loading up clothing and small pieces of furniture into it. Suggs instructed Patrick to go and help clean the place out. He explained that he didn't have time to do it all by himself and he needed the place clean in order to get his deposit back.

"Now hold on a second, Rob," Patrick said. "What are you moving for?"

"There's one reason," he said. "When I walk into a grocery store in Arizona I get a full bag of food for, shit, eighty dollars. It's always sunny down there. There are rich motherfuckers down there and there is a lot of money to be made. You can't fuckin' beat that."

And you can't fuckin' beat the fact that Arizona was much closer to Vegas than Seattle, Patrick thought. "Okay, Rob," he said.

Patrick stepped into the apartment. Within a split second, Joe, the German shepherd, was sniffing around Patrick's legs, whimpering.

Suggs showed up. "Shut up!" he screamed at the dog.

The dog continued to whimper. "Shut the fuck up!"

By now, Susan had entered the room. What she witnessed then was unlike anything she had ever seen from her boyfriend. Gritting his teeth, Suggs slowly pulled off his belt and let the buckle dangle beside him for a short period of time. He cocked his head slightly, like an archer examining a target, and then, with a big overhead swing, let the buckle come crashing down on the dog's head. Instead of running away, the dog fell to the ground, completely in place. Suggs gave the dog another wallop, this one with more intensity. The dog refused to move. Suggs hit him again and again, his face turning crimson, red veins appearing in his eyes, sweat beginning to roll off of his forehead. The buckle came down over and over again. Eventually, Suggs became so furious that the belt was now bearing down on the dog wildly. It would hit him on the head, the back, the tail, the nose, and sometimes would miss him completely. A puddle of urine formed underneath Joe.

When Suggs was done he stared down at the animal. Joe was no longer whimpering. Suggs was out of breath, his shirt soaked with perspiration. He looked up at Patrick and Susan to see if they were nervy enough to question his disciplinary tactics. They didn't say a word. Suggs nodded his head. He gave Joe a friendly pat on the head and then calmly put the belt back on.

He walked over to Patrick and shook his hand. "I want you to go over to the trailer and clean it up," he told his protégé. "Keep what you want."

Patrick found quite a bit. In fact, not only was the trailer still fully furnished, but Suggs had left behind plenty of very personal items: mementos, trophies, certificates, photographs, and so on.

Max Caulfield was awakened by the ringing of the phone. "What?"

It was Patrick, "Jesus, man. Somebody stole the Grand Am."

"Say what?"

"Yeah, somebody stole it."

Max rubbed the sleep out his eyes. "You've gotta be fuckin' kidding me. Man, when Rob hears about this, he's going to go through the fucking roof. The fucking roof! Hold on, there's a call waiting." Max pressed down on the button. "Yeah."

"It's me," said Robert Suggs. "I'm in town."

"Well, good," Max said. He had not heard from Rob in a couple of weeks, but, nevertheless, there was no time for niceties. "I'm glad that you're here. Because your fucking Grand Am got stolen tonight."

"No it didn't." Rob was calm. Too calm for Max's taste.

"What do you mean?"

"I mean, I took it from Patrick."

"You what?"

Now Rob's voice was just kind of sliding from between his lips. "You wanna know something. I'm gonna show you assholes who runs this show. I don't like to be fucked with."

"You don't like to be fucked with?" Max said, completely confused. "What are you talking about?"

"I know what your plans are, fucker! I know your plans. You want to just steal everything. Well, you're not going to get the car."

Max sighed. "I've got Patrick on the other end. We need a sit-down."

"When?"

"When? Right now! Jesus!"

"I'll be there in half an hour. Bring Patrick. I want that fucker there also."

A "sit-down," by tradition, took place at the Thirteen Coins restaurant. A sit-down was a grievance or problem-solving session. The participants agreed to sit down with minimal drinks (water or coffee), no food, and no bathroom breaks until everything was resolved. In the months leading to Suggs's departure to Arizona, "sit-downs" had become a regular event.

Thirteen Coins had been chosen because it was the only twenty-four-hour gourmet restaurant in town. It was pricey, a breakfast entrée cost close to $10 and a dinner entrée twice that amount. Suggs theorized that the high cost would keep out the riffraff. The restaurant's gaudiness was also helpful. The booths had leather-bound benches with backs that reached up nine and a half feet, giving a feeling of privacy unmatched by normal, low-backed booths at other restaurants. The only drawback to the restaurant was that, as a sign in the lobby proclaimed, it was a "smoking restaurant."

This was the only restaurant close to the airport that could not be seen from the street. It was housed on the ground floor of a pair of office towers. In order to enter Thirteen Coins you had to go in through the side of the building. You had to be a knowledgeable resident of Seattle even to have heard of the restaurant.

The folks at Thirteen Coins would let the Suggs Thugs stay as long as they wanted. Over the past year, they had become the restaurant's best customers, sometimes paying checks of several hundred dollars. Suggs paid every bill. He insisted that was what was proper. He, after all, was *daddy*.

This sit-down was going to break the all-time record. The three men sat in the booth for thirteen hours. Over that time, fists were banged on the table, voices were raised in terrible anger, and, at various points, all three of the men cried.

The main issue of the sit-down was whether or not Suggs Investigations was going to keep running in Seattle. Suggs came insisting that it was over. He could not afford to keep an Arizona company and a Seattle company open simultaneously. "Why don't you come down and work with me down in Arizona!"

"Because I live here," said Max. He turned to Patrick. "You want to know why he's leaving? Because there's a complaint file on him here that is one-inch fuckin' thick! There are going to be dozens of people who are going to sue him! Because he doesn't pay his taxes. He's afraid that the bogeyman is around the corner. He wanted to leave town before Butch Cassidy came into town and ripped him up." He turned back to Suggs. "Isn't that so, Rob?"

"Fuck you, Max. You want to know why I moved down there? It was your fucking idea! You told me to open up Suggs Investigations South. So fuck off! Patrick can come down with me and Susan to Arizona. He can be my new Max."

"I'm with Max," Patrick said softly.

"This is all bullshit," Max said. "It makes no sense. Look, Rob, we make all the fucking money. We've had you at a penthouse at the Hilton in Las Vegas for who knows how long. You have not had to do a goddamn thing! Why don't you just let us do what we've been doing? You just keep gambling and fucking whores."

"How is business down there, anyway?" Patrick wanted to know.

"Well, it could be better. I took a half-page ad in the phone book. I'd ordered it some time ago. But there are many half-page ads. There are guys who have been down there for twenty years. It's just tough. I'm not getting too many calls. And I'm all alone down there, man. All I got is Susan. She's learning but she's not a professional."

By lunch time, Caulfield and Patrick simply wore Suggs down.

They had Suggs convinced to give it a go. And not only that. Caulfield would be getting 40 percent of the proceeds. Furthermore, Suggs was going to leave his two associates with a great deal of surveillance equipment: Maxivac radios, Motorola hand radios, video cameras, night-vision devices, and several guns.

In the parking lot, all three men had to adjust to the sunlight. They gave each other bear hugs and acknowledged that, after all was said and done, they were more than a team. They were a family.

A few days later, after Robert Suggs had returned to Arizona, Patrick received a call on his regular phone from Max Caulfield. "GET OVER HERE!"

Patrick didn't need to hear anything else. He climbed into his car and went over to Caulfield's home. That's where he found Max pacing like a very irritated lion, dragging an M-16, cursing to himself. "What's wrong, Max?" he asked with an innocent smile.

Max lifted up his arm, inadvertently pointing the gun at Patrick. "Call me from your car. Use your car phone!"

Patrick went to his car and punched in the number. Then he got a recording telling him that the number was shut down.

When he went back in the house, Patrick stood back and listened to Max as he contacted Robert Suggs. "ROB!!! WHAT THE FUCK IS GOING ON HERE??!!! . . . WHAT ARE YOU DOING??. . . I THOUGHT THAT WE HAD THIS TAKEN CARE OF. . . . Wait a second."

Max went outside and within a half minute reentered with a large piece of monitoring equipment. Then he got back on the phone. "Look, Rob, I've got the Maxitrack here. I've got a hammer. If this phone isn't on in thirty minutes, Patrick and I are going to go into the driveway and beat the Maxitrack into the fuckin' driveway! So you had better call me back on the cellular phone in thirty minutes. If you haven't turned it on, then every half hour after that we are going to break another Maxitrack. After that, we are going to bust your goddamn infrared scope!"

Max slammed the phone down. Now, this was something else. For the first time Max felt like he had some sense of power. It was like the Arabs negotiating with the Israelis, promising to kill a hostage every half-hour until their demands were met.

Twenty minutes later, Rob Suggs called back, begging for another forty-five minutes, "Now, listen to me, Rob," Max said coolly. "These phones better be on in fifteen minutes or I am going to take my fucking Uzi and blow the shit out of your Grand Am until it's a fucking heap on the driveway."

A few minutes later, the cellular phones were reactivated.

What signaled the end of Suggs Investigation was the case of Jenny Wright. Caulfield received a call from Wright in December of 1990. She told Max that she had met Suggs on the Narrows Bridge in Seattle a year earlier. He was riding a motorcycle and she was in a convertible. He had handed her his business card and asked her to have a drink with him. They got together, but nothing really happened.

Now, Jenny said, she was in trouble, and had nobody else to turn to. Her daughter, who was thirteen, had run away. She had gone through her purse and found Suggs's business card. Max told her that Suggs was in Arizona, but that they would be happy to take the case. It would cost her about $2,000. That was fine with Jenny. All she wanted was for her daughter to be found.

Max, Patrick, and Christine were on the case over the weekend. On Monday, the daughter came home. Just like that. Then Max did something that was out of the norm for him. He offered to refund $1,400. This woman, after all, was an old friend of Suggs.

Max contacted Suggs and told him what had happened. "Look, Jenny's daughter has come back."

"Yeah," Suggs said. "So what?"

"Well, we need to give her fourteen hundred dollars back."

"What? You told her that?"

"Yes, I did," Max said. "As a matter of fact, her lawyer called me and I had a conversation with him that was unrelated. He wanted some information from us, because she was going to file papers on the father so that she can't run away over there anymore. Anyway, I mentioned to him that we were going to give the money back."

"Fuck, Max. I ain't giving her nothing."

"Rob, her daughter came home. So, what the hell do you want me to do, disappear her again for a few hours until she owes us more money? Christ! Rob, this woman is a friend of yours. She didn't call from the ad in the yellow pages. She's had your dog-eared card in her purse for three years. Give her the money back! Jesus! Are you out of your mind?"

There was blankness. "Nah, the truth is . . . I don't have it."

"Uh?" Max said. "What do you mean?"

Another pause. "Well, I spent it."

"JESUSJESUSJESUSJESUSJESUS! THIS IS NOT RIGHT, MAN!" Max said. He composed himself. "I told this lady that she was going to get her money back and you are going to make an idiot out of me."

"Well, Max. Tell her to call me. I'll take care of it."

"Okay," he responded. "What is the money situation?"

"I don't have any money, Max."

"LOOK! You don't have the money! Go into your personal account!"

"Well, there's no money there either."

"Rob, we made two hundred thousand last year. Two hundred thousand! Where's the money! Where in the world can it be!"

"I spent it."

"Spent it! On what? Funding for the spotted owl? I hope so, man. Because, you know, we're having some kind of fuckin' problem up here with the spotted owl."

"C'mon, Miracle Max."

"You spent it on gambling. Jesus, you are some kind of sorry motherfucker. Walking around with two-hundred-dollar watches and zillion-dollar shoes."

"Look, Max. It's over. It's just over. The business just can't go on. It's that simple."

"Christ!"

"I'm out of the business, Max." Suggs was crying, actually crying. It made Max almost embarrassed.

"Out of the business? You don't know anything else."

"Max. Now you're gonna laugh at me. I'm gonna be going into the movie business."

"The movie business? What the fuck do you know about the movie business?"

"Well, in the next couple of days, I'll know plenty."

"What do you mean?"

" . . . and, Max, when I make it . . . I won't forget you."

"Great," said Max before he hung up the phone in disgust.

What Rob had failed to tell Max was that the authorities in Arizona were beginning to give him a hard time and that his business had been hampered by the bad word of mouth that had been created when the Consumer Representative of the State of Washington had written a letter to the Arizona Public Safety department.

> Dear Sir or Madam:
>
> As a representative of the Washington State Attorney General's Office, I would like to apprise you of the business practices of Robert M. Suggs, operator of Investigative Group International, aka Suggs Investigations.
>
> Mr. Suggs has incurred many unadjusted consumer complaints in this state, some as recent as May, 1990. . . . At this time our office is conducting a preliminary investigation of Mr. Suggs' business practices. We are writing to alert your office and will keep you informed of our progress in this case. . . .

A few days later, the cellular phones registered to Suggs Investigations were shut off for good. When Robert reached Max that evening he told him that he was for certain going into the movie industry.

Max was floored. "How did you manage that?" he asked.

"I met a guy. He's a producer. His name is Jon Emr. He's making a movie about the life of James Dean. This is it, Max. I can feel it. It's time to be a fucking star. Nothing's going to go wrong."

BOOK THREE

The Trail of the Assassin

*Millions are to be grabbed out here and your only competition is idiots.
Don't let this get around.*
—Herman J. Mankiewicz to Ben Hecht on Hollywood

The James Dean Con:
August 1987

TAYLOR: Money isn't all, you know, Jett.
DEAN: Not when you got it.
—Elizabeth Taylor and James Dean in *Giant*

October 1, 1955, was hardly a slow news day for the *Los Angeles Times*. President Eisenhower, whose reported ill health had jeopardized the possibility of his running for a second term, had been given a resounding medical go-ahead by his doctor. Los Angeles's newly created Air Pollution Control District declared the very first "smog red-alert" day in the history of a city that would have thousands and thousands of such days to come. The French ambassador to the United Nations stormed out of the General Assembly after that body voted to address the issue of France's controversial presence in Algeria. The Los Angeles Dodgers had just beaten the stuffing out of the perennially successful New York Yankees, 8–3, in the third game of the World Series. It was the Dodgers' first victory in the championship series.

Nevertheless, the massive, double-truck banner headline for *that* day had nothing to do with any of these topics. Instead, bathrobed Los Angelenos woke up to the news "FILM STAR JAMES DEAN KILLED IN AUTO CRASH." According to the article, which appeared on the right-hand section of the front page and above the fold, Dean had been involved "in a head-on collision at the rural town of Cholame, about 19 miles west of Paso Robles." The *Times* story went on to report that James Dean had been declared dead on arrival at the Paso Robles War Memorial Hospital. His passenger, a mechanic named Rolph Wuetherich, was badly injured, suffering a fractured jaw and hip as well as several body lacerations. Donald Turnuspeed, the young man who had been driving the other vehicle, suffered only minor injuries.

Over the next few days, the *Times* followed through with several other "related" stories. On October 2, for example, the *Times* came out with the tabloidish revelation that Dean had had a "death premonition" not long before the fatal accident: "Young actor who dies in crash was always trying to outspeed his doom, friends say," the subheadline read. The following day the newspaper reported that just two hours before his death, the actor had received a speeding citation for driving sixty-five miles an hour in a forty-five-mile-an-hour zone.

There was something rather remarkable about the extent and the bombastic nature of the *Times* coverage. For example, the typeface announcing Dean's death was abnormally large for the paper. The editors at the *Times* apparently felt that this "event" warranted the same size headline as the one that had heralded the dropping of the atomic bomb on Nagasaki and, eighteen years later, the assassination of President John F. Kennedy.

In fact, it was rather astonishing that Dean's death should have gotten any attention whatsoever. On the day that Dean crashed that elegant silver Porsche Spyder, only one of his films had even been released. It was called *East of Eden* and had been based on a popular novel by John Steinbeck, the man who had pretty much assumed Ernest Hemingway's mantle as America's Greatest Living Author. The film was directed by Elia Kazan, who one year earlier had won the directing Oscar for his classic *On the Waterfront.*

East of Eden had opened to mixed reviews, certainly not the kind that would earmark it, in typical film critic overkill, as an "instant classic!" Dean himself fared especially poorly, particularly in the eyes of the nation's more distinguished analysts. Bosley Crowther, the legendary film critic for the *New York Times*, had this to say about Dean: "He scuffs his feet, he whirls, he pouts, he sputters, he leans against walls, he rolls his eyes, he swallows his words, he ambles slack-kneed—all like Marlon Brando used to do. Never have we seen a perfomer so clearly follow another's style. Mr. Kazan should be spanked for permitting him to do such a sophomoric thing."

Ultimately, what really mattered was not the wit and wisdom of the critics, but rather what audiences thought and what audiences said at cocktail parties. *East of Eden* took in $5 million at the domestic box office. In the month following the film's release, Dean received over four thousand pieces of fan mail at Warner Bros., where he had signed an exclusive contract (in fact, the richest contract in Hollywood history at that point: $1 million for nine films). His closest competitor was the Milk Dud teen idol Tab Hunter, who collected thirty-nine hundred pieces of mail.

For whatever reason, Dean became, with just that one film, a genuine movie star. After the car accident, Dean's grandparents claimed that on average about thirty visitors a week, usually teenage girls dressed in black, intruded on their home in Fairmount, Indiana.

The Dean phenomenon would only grow with two more of his films, both released after he was interred at the Park Cemetery in Indiana: *Rebel Without a Cause* and *Giant*. This time the critics seemed to join in singing the hosannas with the rest of the world. *Daily Variety* said of Dean's performance in *Rebel*, "The Marlon Brando mannerisms displayed in the initialer are gone and the role here carries much greater audience sympathy and response as a result."

In 1956, the Academy of Motion Picture Arts and Sciences announced the nominees for the annual Academy Awards. The American princess Grace Kelly read off five names: Ernest Borgnine, James Cagney, Frank Sinatra, Spencer Tracy, and . . . James Dean for *East of Eden*. When Dean's name was announced, it prompted a standing ovation from the small audience that had convened for the nominating ceremony.

It was Borgnine who won that year for his performance in the Ugly Duckling love story *Marty*. Nevertheless, the following year Dean was posthumously nominated for *Giant*. Burt Lancaster won that year. Indeed, no posthumous acting Oscar would be handed out until 1976, when Peter Finch's widow accepted the best actor statuette for his panting performance in *Network*.

Dean bequeathed to society more than just this smashing albeit tiny body of work. Dean also left behind a psychological grip. Like Monroe and Presley, Dean came to represent the entire raison d'être of a generation, maybe a few generations, and in death he was able to have a greater impact on society than he ever possibly could have had if he had stayed alive and continued his career. If nothing else, the word "cool," as applied to human demeanor, was born when he died.

The legacy of James Dean is not a phenomenon, nor really even an industry. It has become simply a state of being. Dean merchandising—T-shirts, underwear, posters, mugs, videos, postcards, books, lamps, clothing, the list is seemingly endless—is as much a part of the American landscape as the McDonald's arches or the New York skyline.

But in Hollywood, when the focus of conversation shifts to Dean, as it still so often does, the focus is on something nebulous to the world that exists outside the smoke-drenched booths of the Polo Club. The focus is on the Curse of Jimmy Dean. Even the least superstitious citizens of a town that is inherently, unabashedly, unflinchingly superstitious will make at least this one stipulation: Most of the public figures who had close contact with James Dean, professionally or even privately, were themselves confronted with some diabolical tragedy.

Rock Hudson costarred with Dean in George Stevens's *Giant*. In the film, Hudson played an oil tycoon and Dean a rebellious ranch hand who strikes oil on his property. Thirty years after Dean died, *Variety* reported a shocker about Rock Hudson, one of the great romantic leading men of the fifties. In the paper's July 25, 1985, gossip column it was revealed that the actor had AIDS. Hudson's publicist said, "[Hudson] doesn't have any idea how he contracted AIDS." After a long and bitter struggle with the disease, which included massive doses of an experimental drug called HPA-23, Hudson died on October 2, 1985, exactly thirty years and one day after Dean's death.

Elizabeth Taylor also appeared opposite Dean in *Giant*, playing Hudson's wife. A year after the film opened, she married the producer-showman Mike Todd, who would win an Oscar for *Around the World in 80 Days* a few years later. One day, Todd was flying in a small chartered jet from Los Angeles to New York. It was a weekend trip. Todd was to be honored by the legendary Friars Club as the "Showman of the Year." A bad cold had prevented Taylor from actually being on the plane (which was ironically named the "Lucky Liz"), as she had originally planned and hoped. Somewhere over New Mexico, ice accumulated on the wings of "Lucky Liz" and the plane went down. All the passengers on board were killed, including Todd's biographer, Art Cohn. The crash and fire were so intense that Todd could be identified only by his wedding band.

Natalie Wood, who had begun her career as a child star, appeared with Dean in his most famous movie *Rebel Without a Cause*. In the film, Dean played Jim Stark and Wood played Judy, teenage characters who came to symbolize the alienated youth of the fifties. On the weekend following Thanksgiving in 1981, Wood and her husband, Robert

Wagner, took a boating trip near Catalina Island. Though nobody remembers her falling or diving overboard, Wood, who was forty-three at the time, drowned. The full circumstances surrounding her death still remain a mystery.

Pier Angeli, the beautiful Sardinian actress, dated Dean briefly but intensely. Their romance was stymied and their dreams of marriage decimated by the objections of Pier's mother, who was disturbed that Jimmy was not a Catholic. Pier was married twice, both weddings (to Vic Damone and Armando Trotajoli) taking place after Dean's death. The marriages were failures and Pier blamed James Dean. "I never loved either of my husbands the way I loved Jimmy," she said in an interview with a fan magazine. "I would wake up at night and find I had been dreaming of Jimmy. I would lie awake in the same bed with my husband, think of my love for Jimmy and wish it was Jimmy and not my husband who was next to me." In 1972, she died from an overdose of barbiturates during the same period of time that she was making a "comeback" in a small film called *Octaman*.

Then there was Sal Mineo, who played Dean's sidekick in *Rebel*. He was nominated for the best supporting actor for that role. He would again be nominated for his performance in *Exodus*, a film starring Paul Newman, the actor who most probably inherited the trophy of the Great Screen Antihero from Dean. Mineo was very public about his homosexuality and lived off the area on Santa Monica Boulevard which was nicknamed "Boys' Town." On February 12, 1976, which was little more than a month after his thirty-seventh birthday, Mineo was murdered. He was ferociously stabbed and then mercilessly left to bleed to death on the concrete alley that was adjacent to his apartment garage. It was never determined whether or not the murder was homophobic.

Mark Roesler, the president of the Curtis Management Company, acknowledges that, because his company is based in Indiana, very few people outside the *business* tend to take it very seriously: that business being the handling and licensing of the names and images of public figures, particularly those who are deceased. Traditionally, when death snaps up the super-famous—Monroe famous, Presley famous—part of their legacy is in their likeness, which will ultimately serve as the design for T-shirts, calendars, and so on. Somebody has to get rich from all of that merchandising and, in several cases, it's the job of Mark Roesler and his Curtis Management to see to it that the money gets into the right hands.

Curtis is one of the biggest companies of its kind. The company has a particular lock on baseball greats. They represent, for example, the estates of Babe Ruth and Lou Gehrig. In Roesler's office there are two ancient Louisville Sluggers, one from the Detroit Tigers and the other from the New York Yankees. On one of the walls, next to Roesler's law degree from Indiana University, there is a photo of the Babe with his daughter. Curtis Management had a legal dispute with Universal Pictures over the licensing connected with their film *The Babe*, which starred John Goodman as the onetime home run king. There are plenty of other photos of Roesler with various giants of the diamond. Curtis also has a professional relationship with the families of several football and hockey celebrities. Roesler's proudest artifact sits in the corner of the office. It is the hockey stick that was used by Ron LeBlanc in the 1980 Winter Olympics in Lake Placid.

There also are a number of entertainers in the Curtis stable. Abbott and Costello and many of the singers from the old Polygram Records label are among them. Roesler also has a framed autographed picture from the former *Today Show* host Jane Pauley, but only because she's from Indiana.

Then, of course, there is James Dean. In 1983, Dean's family members—including his father, aunt, and cousin, assigned Roesler and Curtis Management the contract to handle the marketing of their famous relative.

The name and the likeness of James Dean has become the biggest single moneymaker for Curtis Management, with Babe Ruth coming in a distant second. In fact, Dean's severe face can be found on everything from calendars to posters to condoms. He remains the very personification of the word "cool." Dean became a bigger moneymaker in death than he ever was in life.

Roesler's office, though crammed with memorabilia from other Curtis clients, is essentially a shrine to Dean, who grew up not far away in Fairmount, Indiana. There is a mammoth James Dean painting by the modernist Helnwein that is a creative incorporation of neon and oils. There is a bottle of James Dean perfume. There is even a framed check from the Chase National Bank for $10 written to James Dean and signed by James Dean, dated December 23, 1953.

The Dean descendants, or The Family, as they are known in the hallways of Curtis Management, own all the licensing rights to the trademark of James Dean. Warner Bros., which produced and distributed all three major Dean films, sued Curtis Management and The Family in 1992, claiming that an old contract signed by Dean gave Warners these very same exclusive rights. After three days of arguing in a Los Angeles courtroom, Warner Bros. lost its case.

One of Roesler's routine duties has been to deal with the Hollywood honchos who stormed his offices wanting to make a movie about James Dean. Over the years, The Family had been sent about ninety treatments for consideration. For years, they had resisted supporting any of the projects. Their reasons were simple and understandable. First, they claimed a regard for their own privacy. Two, they were "distrustful" of traditional movie people. Third, nobody had ever come up with a script that they felt painted a positive enough portrait of "Jimmy."

Of all the people wanting to make a movie about Dean, the most persistent was Loren "Randy" Pike out of Palm Springs. Over the phone, Pike sounded loud, oafish, and unprofessional. In fact, true to Roesler's initial suspicions, Pike had never made a movie in his life, nor had he even claimed to have been in the industry. He was simply a builder who had been a huge fan of James Dean. He said he had researched Dean's life thoroughly. He had read every book and magazine article available on the iconic actor. He had even gotten Dean's old pal, the counterculture actor Dennis Hopper, to sit for an interview.

Pike's goal was to put the funding together for a movie about the actor's life. Pike was a sharp businessman who thought that he could get countless investors behind the project if he could only secure the cooperation of the Dean family.

After many futile calls to Roesler, Pike eventually went directly to Marcus Winslow. Winslow was Dean's cousin and had lived with the actor as they were growing up. Pike gave Marcus Winslow his absolute assurance that the Dean family would have total control over the script. "Look," Randy told him, "we ain't gonna put in some fuckin' sex scene just to see the box office receipts go up!" What Randy was intimating was that none of *those* allegations that Dean used gay sex to climb to the top would make it into *his* film.

When Marcus Winslow and The Family asked Mark Roesler what he thought of Mr. Randy Pike and his intentions, Roesler grudgingly agreed that Pike should probably be allowed to buy the film rights from them. "There is so much interest in this," Roesler explained. "Every week I get a phone call from some Hollywood type on this very topic. Eventually, a film will be made. It will be either authorized or unauthorized. That's up to you. But I think that we can make some money off of this."

There was another point. Roesler understood that, business in Hollywood being what it was, there was only a one-in-twenty chance, if even that, that this movie would ever get made. As long as The Family had signed with Pike, it was very unlikely that anybody else would bother to make a movie about James Dean.

Mark Roesler informed Pike that The Family would sign with him and his production company, Sun King, which was incorporated in Palm Springs, California. The rights for a one-year option cost Pike $50,000.

On August 1, 1987, Randy Pike officially bought the James Dean rights, though not with his own money. Pike's friend Stan Esecson, who owned a company which made city-information tapes that ran on hotel cable systems, loaned him the $50,000. According to the terms of Randy's contract with Stan Esecson, if the money was not returned to Stan within seven months, then the rights to Dean would be his. In turn, Stan Esecson could do whatever he wanted to protect his rights and his money.

Randy Pike's relationship with Curtis Management and The Family went into the dumper almost immediately. The first problem lay in the different scripts that Randy was sending to The Family. Roesler would often be contacted by Marcus Winslow or David Lohr, the nation's leading expert on Dean and a close friend of The Family. They had complaints of gross inaccuracies in Randy Pike's script. Marcus Winslow was putting a huge amount of time into correcting and proofreading the screenplay and was beginning to wonder if the money he and the rest of The Family had received was actually worth their efforts.

Then there was the bizarre case of Gene Kirkwood, a producer who had won an Oscar for the Sylvester Stallone classic *Rocky* in 1977. One day, Kirkwood inquired about the rights to make a movie about the life of James Dean. When Kirkwood came calling, Roesler was excited.

Maybe if a person with Kirkwood's clout became involved, the project would indeed move forward. He told Kirkwood that the rights were tied up. But, hell, why not go and have a chat with this Randy Pike guy and see if the two of them could perhaps work something out.

Kirkwood never did call Pike. James Dean was a public figure and, as such, his life story was open game to anybody who wanted to make a film about him. Kirkwood apparently decided to have a go at it without the help of The Family. He began making the type of motions that indicated he was very serious about making a movie. He even set up an entire "James Dean: The Movie" booth at the American Film Festival in New York.

Sure enough, Pike was also at the same festival and, sure enough, he got a load of the Kirkwood booth. Steaming, he banged on the side of the booth and demanded of the young girl manning the display that he get to speak to Gene Kirkwood. Since Kirkwood was not there, Randy phoned him.

A few days later, a distraught Kirkwood called Roesler and asked him how he could have sent a "lunatic" like Pike after him. Kirkwood dropped the project altogether.

If the Kirkwood situation was not enough to make Randy's name absolute horse dung with Curtis Management and The Family, then the Audrey Gillette situation would absolutely ensure it.

Audrey Gillette was a Tucson, Arizona–based woman who had come into some inheritance money. Looking to invest some of the cash, Gillette answered an ad in the local paper that read "Money Wanted" and which promised a big return on any investment. Having never seen such an ad before, Gillette decided to make an appointment with a Myra Sabell (fictitious name), the woman who answered the phone after Gillette answered the ad.

When Gillette met Sabell, she was very impressed. Although Sabell was obese, she clearly had money. Her clothes and her car were nice and she even had her own plane, which transported her between Tucson and Palm Springs. Myra also claimed to be a born-again Christian, which greatly comforted Audrey. After a few meetings, Myra told Audrey about a fabulous opportunity. For a few thousand dollars, Audrey could become a Hollywood player. She told Audrey about her boss Randy Pike, and his intentions to make a movie about the life of James Dean. Pike, she intimated, was a creative genius who was on the cusp of becoming the new Steven Spielberg or George Lucas. In all, Myra needed and received $70,000 from Audrey. According to the contract she signed with Myra, Audrey was to be repaid in three months, with 18 percent interest.

Needless to say, the return of the investment never occurred. Myra virtually disappeared. Audrey would call Randy Pike and would, she claimed, get no satisfaction, that her money would come when it damn well came. Audrey also called Mark Roesler, whom she remembers being very curt with her and telling her that, sure enough, she had gotten into bed with a couple of con artists.

Pike says the FBI raided Randy Pike's Palm Springs office complete with a search warrant. No evidence was found to actually incriminate Pike. Indeed, Pike says that he himself was duped by Sabell. He claims that instead of giving him all the investor money that she collected on behalf of him and Sun King Productions, Myra pocketed at least half of it.

Over time, Roessler would hear from a distraught, financially wiped-out Audrey Gillette several times. He was also contacted by several other Arizona-based senior citizens who had seen their investment in the James Dean project go *whoosh* right out the window. Roesler was dismayed. The complaints of little old ladies did not do much to enhance the image of Curtis Management, The Family, or, for that matter, James Dean himself.

THE TRAIL OF THE ASSASSIN: ONE

> *Your eyes are full of hate, Forty-one. That's good.*
> *Hate keeps a man alive. It gives him strength.*
> —Jack Hawkins to Charlton Heston in William Wyler's *Ben-Hur*

Benny sat in the uncomfortable chair attached to the polygraph machine, hooked up like the Frankenstein monster. He seemed oddly relaxed. He had spent so much time evading the truth in his talks with Detective Sergeant Hank Davies that it had felt good to have gotten everything off his chest. Davies sat directly in front of Benny. Hank nodded to the polygraphist, who began the examination.

When it was all over, the conclusion was reached that Benny had fi-nally been truthful in his account of what happened between him and Robert Suggs beginning July 5, 1991.

It was on Route 10, the principal highway that connects Los Ange-les and Arizona, that Suggsy broke down and told Benny the most in-credible story he had ever heard. It came after hours of silence. It was that silence that made Benny realize that some kind of bad shit was coming down. Suggsy wasn't exactly the strong, silent type. He was the obnoxious-overbearing-big-time-pain-in-the-ass type.

For just about an hour, the only sound that Benny heard was a coun-try music station fading-in-and-out-in-and-out on the radio and the clanking of an ineffective air conditioner that had no chance in its war with the uncomfortable sting of the desert sun.

There is perhaps no highway in the whole of the United States where drivers feel so cavalier about posted speed limits. Sixty miles an hour! *Thatssomekindajokeright!* Baby, if you're takin' it less than ninety, you're slowing down the entire world. There are only a few towns— and thus only a few patrol cars—on the way to Phoenix once you get past Palm Springs.

Drivers run out of gas so frequently on this route, thinking always that they'll wait for the next, less expensive gas station, that the state police have a problem with pirates who patrol the streets, ripping off cars left on the side of the road as drivers go hitchhiking for fuel.

It was about an hour before Blythe that Suggsy wanted to start talk-ing. He turned to Benny, who was doing a bob-and-weave with his head, half asleep now, one arm hanging precariously out the window. Suggsy tapped Benny, who got up, bolted up actually, with a funny, startled look on his face.

Suggsy sighed. "I love that girl."

"Susan?"

"Yeah."

"Yeah. Where is she anyway, man?"

Suggsy dropped his bombshell. "The truth is, we broke up."

"Broke up? You and Susan?" This was it, man. This-was-fuckin'-it! The goddamn apocalypse! People like Suggsy and Susan did not just break up! Their relationship was a force of nature. Susan was as much a part of Suggsy as was his blond hair.

"Yeah. She and I went on a last fling. She gave me that." He was speaking slowly now, somber. Benny was not sure what to think, but instincts told him to be scared. "Well, what happened?"

"You mean why did we break up?" Suggsy stared straight ahead. "Truth is, she dumped me, man. That fuckin' Jon Emr. He scared her off." He slammed a fist into his open hand. The car swerved slightly to the right before Suggsy regained control of the wheel. "That motherfucker. Motherfucker!" He paused. "She told me she could not take it anymore. I couldn't blame her because, dammit, I couldn't take it anymore either."

"Yeah. I know what you mean. Susan was talking to Jennifer. She told Jennifer 'bout all the shit."

"So, man, I asked her, you know, if she'd go with me for one more weekend. One last, real, romantic fling."

"And she said yes?" This sounded preposterous to Benny. Every time a girl had dumped *him*, there was no chance of her agreeing to one last lay for old times' sake.

But, with Suggsy, the king of suave, most anything was possible. Suggsy nodded his head. "Yeah. Can you beat that? I picked her up and she wants Joe to come with us." Joe was Suggsy's German shepherd. "That meant that we couldn't stay in a classy hotel. We had to stay in a motel. Can you figure that shit out?"

To Benny, this was a considerable enigma. "Bummer," he pondered.

"So, we get to the motel. It was in Westminster. And I'm hot for her, man. Really want her. So I took the dog and I put him in the bathroom. If Joe saw me fuckin' Susan, then he might think that I was attacking her and he might go for me. He might chew off my fuckin' balls. So Susan knew exactly what I wanted. And she just smiled. She was hot for me too. So before you know it we're both naked. We're on the bed and we're making it. It's like the best ever. We're really going at it."

"Yeah?"

"Yeah." Suggsy said. "We are so into it that we roll right off the fuckin' bed. The dog must have been going crazy because we were making so much noise. He was barking like a motherfucker. I'm surprised that the motel Gestapo didn't break the door down."

"That's funny."

"Funny. Yeah. Well, right in the middle of things I pull out these plastic handcuffs. I've never done this before and she's like shocked. Shocked, man. But she's got this big grin on her face. Like she's saying to me, 'If I'd only known.'"

"Yeah?"

"We've never had any kind of rough sex before because she was once in this real abusive relationship. So I had always been careful to be real gentle with her."

"That's what she told my wife. You're gentle."

"She told that to Jenny?" Suggsy smiled and shook his head. "You know what? Women talk, man. They talk more shit than we do."

"Yeah?"

"Yeah. And so I handcuff her hands. I'm really going at it now. She's loving it. Loving it!"

"Yeah? And then what? And then what?"

"And then what? Well, I decided to really make it interesting. I had this rope under the bed. I left it there just for this moment."

"Jesus, man."

Suggsy paused for a moment, stared straight ahead and then lowered his voice into a hush. "So I take the rope and I put it around her neck. She had this look on her face like, you know, this doesn't seem right to me but I'm not going to say anything in case it is right."

"Yeah?" Benny said very slowly this time. "Then what?"

"I tightened the rope. I pulled it tighter and tighter. She started going absolutely pale, and she's making this spurting little sound, and her eyes were getting watery." He paused. "You ever seen a person dying?"

"No." Benny said. Then his voice and his smile turned sour. "Suggsy, man, you strangled her? While you're fuckin' her?"

"Yeah."

"That's dangerous, ain't it?"

Suggsy laughed. "Not as dangerous as what she did to me. She grabs my nuts and squeezes the shit out of them. I think that they started to turn blue and shit."

Benny laughed. "I'll bet that got your attention."

Suggsy giggled along. "You bet. So, I just pulled the rope tighter. In fact, I had this hammer, it was also under the bed. So, I used that to cinch the rope around her neck. When she died her grip loosened."

"Jesus."

"I was going to kill her bitch of a sister. But it was too much of a hassle. I didn't have time."

"Christ!" Benny grabbed his head. "You killed Susan!"

"I've taken care of things. I put Susan in this trash bag and brought her into a U-Haul that I had rented. I got Joe out of the bathroom and I put him in the car with me."

"What did you do then?"

"I drove, man. Drove and thought," he said. "I was driving out toward Phoenix." Then Suggsy pointed in the direction of Highway 62. "I buried her about a hundred fifty miles away from here. In the desert. I got off the highway. I took this little road until the sand began to get soft. I made a U-turn and went back to where the sand was still hard. I didn't want to get stuck. So, I took her body from the trailer. It was fucking weird, man."

"What was weird?"

"Well, she was stuck in this folded position. Like she was frozen or something. And so I dragged her to where the sand was soft. I got this shovel outta the car and I dug a shallow grave. So, I kind of dropped Susan into the grave." Now—what was this—Suggsy was actually crying. "Joe had been running around, just being a dog. I love that dog."

"He's a good dog."

"I called Joe over and I had him lay next to Susan. Then I shot him."

"You shot Joe?"

"Blew his head clean off."

"Jesus." Benny was at a loss. It didn't seem fair to kill old Joe. At least, Susan had grabbed Suggsy's balls. But what had Joe ever done to him? It wasn't right. And then Benny had a troubling thought. What was to stop him from killing good old Benny? Time for some quick thinking. "You gotta lay low, Suggsy," thinking that serving as a counsel would make Suggsy think twice before knocking him off.

Suggsy laughed. "Lay low? Lay low? Benny, this has just begun. I'm going to do those boys."

"What boys?"

"The Emr boys: Bobby and Roger. That'll be worse to Jon than killing him." Suggsy blinked for second. "You in?"

"No. Christ, no. Keep me out of this."

"I just need you to be with me. You don't have to do anything."

"I won't, I mean, I can't."

"Okay. Okay. Well, you're with me now." Suggsy quieted down for a while to allow Benny to ingest the moment. "Look, you just stay in the motel. That way you won't be involved."

He would reason with him later. "That's fine, Suggsy."

Then Suggsy became excited again. "I gotta idea."

"What's that?"

"Fuck Phoenix for now." And Suggsy took the turn that would get him on Highway 177 to Laughlin, Nevada. Then Suggsy blew a kiss in the direction of Route 62. "I'll be there soon, baby."

The James Dean Con:
August 1988

If you want to give me a present, give me a good life.
That's something I can value.
—Raymond Massey to James Dean in *East of Eden*

O ne day in July of 1988 two well-dressed men walked into GMT Studios in Culver City, representing that they worked for Randy Pike out of Palm Springs, who was "putting together a major motion picture." One of the men was Michael Britton, the writer whom Randy Pike had hired to pen the James Dean screenplay, and the other was Kyle Eidson, who had been commissioned to write the film's score. They had scheduled an appointment to meet with the president of GMT Studios, Alan Hauge. After an introductory handshake, the trio got down to business.

"We'd like to know if you'd be interested in distributing a motion picture," they asked Hauge.

As far as Hauge was concerned, the conversation did not really need to go much beyond that. "To be honest, we're only interested in distributing our own product."

The men frowned. Pike had told them that Hauge was an elephant that absolutely, categorically needed to be bagged. A "major" investor named Brian Anderson had agreed to finance a good portion of the film if—*and only if*—GMT Studios would act as their distributor. Anderson had become friendly with Hauge months earlier and enjoyed Hauge's company as well as his philosophy on film and film distribution. Anderson was representing Codepa, which claimed to be a lumber company. Codepa had promised Pike that they would invest millions of dollars in the James Dean project if Alan Hauge took the reins of the distribution. Anderson would not explain why he had so much confidence in Hauge. That made Pike very curious. After all, GMT and Hauge were not exactly heavyweights in the film distribution world. But, hell, Codepa was talking in terms of millions and millions of dollars, more than enough to get the cameras rolling. Who the hell was he to deny the investor the distributor of his choice?

Britton pushed the issue with Hauge. "It's a great topic."

"What's that?" Hauge asked.

"It's the life story of James Dean. We own the rights."

Hauge felt the tiniest twitch in his ass. When Hauge was thirteen years old he had seen *Giant*. It was a movie that profoundly affected him. He was, he recalls, simply stunned by Dean's method acting. For years, in fact, he did not know that was even James Dean up there on screen. All he saw or knew was the character Jett Rink. It was the one motion picture that most influenced his decision to get involved in cinema as a profession.

"You guys are right," Hauge said. "That *is* interesting. But it has to be a great story. And it has to deal with more than just James Dean the movie actor. We need to know about him as a person and what makes him tick. I don't care about all the books and all the crap that's out there." He paused to consider the possibilities of getting involved with this project. "You guys say that you have the rights? You have all the paperwork, all that stuff?"

"Oh yeah."

"I might be interested in distributing this film. It depends on the screenplay."

"Well, that's not ready yet."

Before the meeting ended, Hauge agreed to meet with Randy Pike at his Sun King offices in Palm Springs.

In the early summer, Hauge showed up at Sun King Productions, which was situated in a building very close to the Palm Springs airport. At the moment that Hauge arrived, Pike was in the throes of running a meeting. It took place in a large room with thirty to forty people surrounding a mammoth conference table.

With his fist crashing down on the table over and over again, Randy was demanding that there be no more "bickering" in the group. Hauge figured that Pike had been experiencing some kind of chaos in his office. The friction was intense. At one point, Randy stormed out of the room. Hauge stood in stunned silence as he listened to everybody whisper their moans and groans about their wacky boss. Hauge kind of felt sorry for Pike. Here was a guy who was trying to run a business, one in which he was clearly an alien, who couldn't get even an ounce of respect.

After the meeting was all over, Randy walked Hauge to the parking lot. "Well, what do you think?" he asked Hauge.

"Randy, this is our first meeting and it will probably also be our last. I'm going to tell you what I think." He considered his next words carefully. "You probably are not ready to do a motion picture. You just don't have a team in there. What you need to do is close your office, fire everybody, get your screenplay together and package it properly. I looked over your records and I see that you have paid somebody twelve thousand dollars to do a storyboard for a script that is incomplete. It's silly. That's what I think."

Randy nodded his head. "Thanks for at least being honest." Hauge smiled, got in his car, and drove off.

A few days later, Pike called Hauge with the news that he had followed his advice. Immediately after Pike had left Hauge in the parking lot, he had walked back to the conference room and fired his entire staff, the whole sorry lot of them, and immediately closed down his offices. Hauge was mildly blown away. In one throwaway piece of advice, Alan Hauge had managed to derail a major motion picture and alter the employment situation of a few dozen people.

Around Christmas, Randy offered Alan Hauge the "distribution rights" to the James Dean film for a mere $25,000. Hauge was a bit taken aback. He had never considered the possibility that he would have to put his own money into the project. Nevertheless, when Hauge contemplated the potential windfall from a film about one of the great icons of all time, he somehow managed to come up with the needed cash, most of it from the coffers of GMT Studios itself.

The exchange of money took place in a small conference room on the second floor of GMT Studios. In attendance were Hauge, Pike, and a young actor named Damian Chapa, who was Pike's "discovery" to play James Dean. According to the terms of their agreement, Pike himself got a cashier's check for $20,000 and $5,000 in cash. Randy immediately turned over the cash to Damian Chapa.*

On January 16, 1989, Alan Hauge's father died. Because the illness was especially painful and enduring, Hauge found himself by his father's deathbed for sixteen days, day in and day out, not once thinking about the James Dean film.

Hauge was out of the loop for a while. But in late February, he began negotiations with various theater chains about gaining commitments to putting the Dean film on screens. By April he had convinced the United Artists theater chain to distribute the James Dean film on fifteen hundred screens. It was a monumental tribute to Dean that UA made this level of commitment without having been given a script to read. Of course, no script had been completed. The fact was that the script had been written up to page 88 when Hauge first met Randy Pike and it was at page 88 now.

After getting the United Artists deal, Hauge decided that he was going to take his family, including his mother who had been widowed after sixty-two years of marriage, on a cruise. With him, Hauge took a biography of James Dean, which he found engrossing and captivating. Hauge reread the book several times. By the time he was done, he had completely marked it up with comments and underlinings and had dog-eared it. Alan Hauge suddenly felt driven by what he felt was an amazing story.

Midway through the cruise, from a port in Mazatlán, Mexico, Hauge called one of his partners at GMT to see how things were going back home. It was then that Hauge was hit with the news that Randy Pike had called to say that he was firing Alan. "He says that you're out of the project," his partner dourly told him.

Alan could not believe what he had just heard. Back on the ship, he told his wife, Lanette, what had happened. What the hell was this all

---

*Chapa has had some strong roles since. He had a supporting role in the Steven Seagal action film *Under Siege* and the lead in Taylor Hackford's *Blood In, Blood Out.* He also played one of the Menendez brothers in the television film on the famous case of patricide. In an interview with me, Chapa insisted he had received no money at all. Pike says he gave Chapa "a couple of hundred bucks."

about? He hadn't done anything wrong. In fact, he had forked over $25,000. If anybody had not met their end, it was Randy who had failed to deliver a screenplay. Was it possible, Hauge thought, that he had actually been conned?

Remarkably, by the time Hauge arrived back at work in Culver City, Randy Pike had just upped and changed his mind. Apparently, Pike had been in conversation with the production company of George Lucas, the creator and director of the enormously popular *Star Wars* series. They were interested in the Dean project, or at least that was the impression that Pike walked away with. If that was the case, Hauge and GMT would certainly have to be out. In any case, to the surprise of nobody, that potential deal dissolved and Hauge was back in.

Hauge told Pike that while he was on the cruise he had made a decision. Michael Britton seemed to be going nowhere with his script, so he, Alan, was going to take a crack at it. He was so stoked about the whole Dean concept that maybe his adrenaline and enthusiasm could produce a high-powered piece of work. Pike was resistant to the idea. But Hauge argued that since his distribution contract with Pike did not permit him to work on any other film while working on the Dean project, he simply needed to do this. He *needed* to write. He *needed* to have a script to deliver to United Artists, who were starting to get antsy about their commitment.

Hauge wrote a rough draft in fourteen days. He knocked out about twelve pages a day, doing nothing else but researching and typing, working for eighteen hours at a pop, typically adorned in sweatpants and a T-shirt.

One day, Pike called him from the home of his own writer, Michael Britton, to whom Randy had already paid $40,000. "What're you doing?" Randy asked Hauge.

"I'm working on the screenplay."

"I don't have a contract with you to write the screenplay."

"I know you don't."

"Then stop writing."

"You can't tell me to stop writing a screenplay! I don't have a contract with you about any screenplay."

"Well, what page are you on?"

"I'm on page ninety-six."

Then Hauge heard Randy yelling to his writer, *"He's on page ninety-*

six." Britton yelled back, "*Cancel his contract.*" Randy, acting as if Hauge were not even there, shouted back, "*I don't have a contract with him. How can I cancel it?*" The writer came back with, "*Don't pay him any more money.*" Randy responded, "*I'm not paying him anything.*"

When Hauge's script was done, Pike wanted to see a copy of it. Reluctantly, Hauge mailed one to him. To Alan's surprise, Pike phoned him and told him that he was very impressed. In addition, the brass at United Artists were also satisfied, especially considering that what Hauge turned in was a rough draft. However, the real hosannas came a few weeks later when Hauge tightened it up and collapsed the script down to 120 pages.

One day, Randy asked Hauge to meet him at a Red Lion Inn restaurant in Ontario, California, which is located about halfway between Los Angeles and Palm Springs. Hauge was actually happy that he was going to have a sit-down with Pike. He had become so psyched by having written the screenplay that he was going to ask Randy for something that at one time seemed unthinkable. He wanted to direct the film. He simply figured that there was no harm in asking.

When Hauge arrived at the restaurant, he walked over to the table where Randy and another gentleman were sitting. The stranger was about six feet with a thin build, a mustache, and jet-black hair. Throughout the meal, the stranger, who was introduced to Alan only as Stan, was quiet. As soon as Alan brought up the topic of directing, Randy started spitting out vindictive, telling Alan that he was in no way qualified to do the job. "You're just a distributor," he said with a condescending sneer.

"That's what people told Spielberg and Lucas," Hauge retorted. "That is what people told Attenborough before his first film. Besides, I have a lot of experience in editing and production."

Randy was nonetheless dogmatic about not allowing Alan to direct. Eventually, Hauge began to talk about an investor on Wilshire Boulevard in Los Angeles that he had been meeting with personally. Alan told Randy that the film was too slow in getting financed. Alan said that he had taken the liberty of trying to locate investors on his own.

■ ■ ■

The next day Alan learned that this fellow Stan, the man who had been at the meeting at the Red Lion Inn, had actually contacted the very same investor whom he had mentioned during the get-together. That was the old Hollywood shuffle, Alan thought. But, hell, he wasn't going to have any of it. Alan arranged a conference call with Stan and Randy.

"Hey, this is my investor on Wilshire," Hauge said from his end. "Christ, Stan, I meet you, we have a nice lunch, and all of a sudden you're talking to one of my investors. What the hell are you doing?"

Then Stan gave old Alan the shock of his professional life. Very softly, with just a hint of surprise, Stan said, "Well, I own the project."

Pike blasted in. "Hey, this is my project too! I got this project started."

Esecson then gave Hauge the facts. He had loaned Randy the money to buy the rights. The cash had never been returned. According to the contract between him and Randy, the project had reverted to him months and months ago, long before Alan Hauge had even met Randy. "I am stepping in to protect my investment," he said. "I'm taking control of the project."

Alan's mind flashed back to the time when Randy demanded $25,000 from him for the "right" to distribute the James Dean film. That was done at a time when Randy apparently no longer controlled the rights to the film. I've been conned, Alan thought to himself.

"You and I have gotta talk," Alan said to Stan. "I think we need to talk without Randy."

Stan and Hauge met in Orange County, close to the airport. Neither man liked the other. They both thought that the other was "one of those weird friends of Randy Pike."

Over the course of the afternoon, the two men compared notes. Stan showed Alan the paperwork to prove beyond a shadow of a doubt that he in fact owned the rights. Randy, for all intents and purposes, was out of the business of owning the Dean rights. Hauge felt stupid and duped that he had ever given Randy $25,000. Stan felt for Hauge and assured Alan that he would let him stay on as the distributor. By the end of their meeting, each felt a kinship with the other. Alan figured that he was done dealing with Randy and would start to work solely with Stan.

THE TRAIL OF THE ASSASSIN: TWO

The first thing that Benny thought to himself as he walked into the Flamingo Hilton in Laughlin, Nevada, was that, goddamn if this place wasn't a REAL-LIFE honest-to-goodness casino town. He hadn't believed it when Suggsy promised him that this town was Vegas redux, but complete with waterworks, a big river that ran smack down the middle of the town. Laughlin was even lit up like Vegas, only not quite as crass.

It had been a long day. Suggsy's revelation about Susan was enough to knock the wind out of anybody. Then, to heighten the anxiety, they had stopped in the small town of Parker. They got some gas—goddamn expensive gas, but what the hell else could you expect in the middle of the desert—and they visted the decaying, weed-ridden cemetery where Suggsy's grandfather was buried. They stood in front of the tombstone and neither man said a word until Suggsy just kind of smirked and said, "Okay, Benny, let's get a move on."

They arrived in Laughlin late at night, maybe around ten. Benny had his nose and the palms of his hands pressed up against the window. Everything was so exciting. Suggsy pulled up to the parking lot of the Ramada Express, one of the handful of casinos in the town. "Let's get something to eat," he said to Benny, who had not put food in his stomach since that morning.

They ate dinner at the casino. Casino food was always cheaper than dirt. Nonetheless, Benny was grateful that Suggsy was willing to pay for the meal. When they finished eating, Suggsy gave the waiter a big fat tip. Ten bucks on an eight-dollar meal.

"Jesus, Suggsy. What're ya throwin' money like that around for?"

"Benny, there's not going to be any need for money soon. Besides, there's lot's more where that came from."

"Yeah?"

"Oh, yeah."

■ ■ ■

There were no rooms available at the Ramada Express. In fact, the clerk at the front desk looked at the men with slight antipathy when they asked for a suite. This was the height of arrogance. Asking for a room—and not just any room: they wanted a suite!—at damn near midnight.

Benny and Suggsy realized that in order to get a room in this . . . this . . . pipsqueak town they'd have to do some casino-hopping. Benny wasn't up to it. There probably was not one room available and, anyway, Suggsy would get distracted at the craps table, or he'd see some cocktail waitress with a perfect ass, or he'd just get the sense that a roulette wheel was going to drop the ball his way, or . . . Anyway, it just wouldn't be worth it.

So they elected to go to a campground nearby, took showers, and then they slept in the car.

The next morning Benny heard a *tap-tap-tap* on the passenger-side window. He swung up like a jack-in-the-box. "JESUS CHRIST!"

A cop with reflective sunglasses was trying to wake him up.

"You guys okay?" he asked.

Benny was shaking off his panic. He looked over at Suggsy, who was beginning to do a bit of a growl, which he recognized as his wake-up growl. Benny didn't want Suggsy to see the cop because, who knows, he might panic.

Benny nodded. "Yeah, sir. We're fine."

The cop pointed at Suggsy. "That guy okay?"

"Yeah," Benny said, hoping the cop would leave soon.

The cop paused and took time to look around the inside of the car. "You guys been drinking?"

"No sir."

"Well, you can't stay here. You'd better get on outta here."

Then the cop climbed back into his car and left.

"What the fuck did he want?" Suggsy, now awake, said.

"He was just checkin' on us."

"Faggot. Can you imagine being a cop in this dipshit little town."

"Let's go."

"Okay." He smirked the Suggsy smirk. "Let's go party."

The men took showers again and then headed to the Colorado Belle—the oldest and the least expensive casino in all of Laughlin. They were turned away because the hotel was booked. That's when they decided to go to the Flamingo Hilton, which, oddly enough, was as expensive as hotels in these parts got.

"Any bordellos 'round here?" Suggsy said jokingly to a hotel employee.

"Uh, no. That's illegal." Then, with the smirk of a conspirator, "You call down to the bell desk later and they can help you out."

"Really?"

"There's some girls that work around here. But the bellman won't speak to you on the phone. They'll come up and give you a number. It's illegal, ya know."

Suggsy turned to Benny, who clearly wasn't comfortable with the conversation. "We're goin' to have to win tonight," Suggsy said, slapping Benny on the back. "That's what we're goin' to have to do. Then we have to get some pussy."

Pussy was not on Benny's mind. Benny had a goddamn wife and goddamn seven kids and he was only thiry-one. Thirty-one-year-old men with seven kids rarely think about pussy. Pussy is what got them in trouble in the first place. Besides, Benny was tired as all hell.

Suggsy took out his credit card and sort of flung it at the hotel employee.

Before going up to the room, Suggsy paid a visit to one of the many ATMs that were scattered ominously throughout the casino floor. Suggsy wanted to get $500, but the ATM was only authorized to spit out $300: for the protection of the player.

As they were heading up to their room, Benny chided Suggsy. "You gotta be careful, man. You ain't being careful."

"What are you talking about?"

"You used a credit card, man. They can trace that."

Suggsy laughed as the elevator climbed fifteen stories. Imagine, Benny telling him about covert action. "I have a zillion different credit cards with a zillion different names to go with a zillion different driver's licenses."

Benny let loose with a smile of relief. Suggsy sure thought of everything.

The James Dean Con:
December 1989

If I live to be 90, I'm never going to be able to figure you out.
—Rock Hudson in *Giant*

In December of 1989, Stan Esecson signed an extension with Curtis Management that allowed him to maintain control of the Dean rights. It cost him $100,000 for a period of six months. One of the provisions of the contract was that Randy Pike could *absolutely* and *categorically* not be a part of the project. Mark Roesler, The Family attorney, and Marcus Winslow, James Dean's cousin, had come to despise the volatile Randy Pike. They had also come to the personal and distasteful conclusion that Pike had been bilking "little old ladies" and using the memory of James Dean as the bait.

In that same period of time, Hauge flew to Indiana to meet with Roesler and the Dean family. He would now be able to research Dean's life from the inside out and that greatly excited him.

Mark Roesler liked Hauge the minute that he met him. What really clinched it for Hauge was the script. Without exception, everybody in The Family loved it. It was a real tribute to "Jimmy." They saw a few changes that they wanted made, and Hauge readily agreed.

On his several trips to Indiana, Hauge sat with Marcus Winslow in a dining room, tape recorder on the table, and took notes. Even David Lohr from the James Dean gallery agreed to do research for Hauge. Winslow was especially concerned that Dean not be shown as a homosexual and that there were no shots of Dean flailing around during his horrific car accident. Even more important to Winslow was his demand that the script not portray James Dean as hating his father, which was widely reported in the press and in several "unauthorized" biographies of Dean.

One day, after about six months, Marcus Winslow told Alan that he was going to trust him with something. "I'm going to give you twenty-two letters that Jimmy wrote home," he said. "I don't want to see them in the *National Enquirer.* I don't want you to spread them all over Hollywood. I just want to give you more insight into Jimmy."

Hauge put the letters in a special file at home that not even his wife could get into. The letters were from New York, Hollywood, and Toronto and, indeed, they did give Hauge an extra appreciation for the actor. The letters included frustrations that Dean had with the film industry and how he missed home. To Hauge, the letters signified more than just having an addition to his Dean bibliography. It meant that he was finally in The Family's inner circle.

In fact, Alan had even made a theatrical trailer for his proposed film. Of course, it is not standard operating procedure in Hollywood to create a trailer for a movie that has not even had a millisecond of it filmed yet. Nevertheless, both Hauge and Pike had decided that they needed some product to display the talents of their star, Damian Chapa, an actor who bore an eerie resemblance to Jimmy. Hauge paid for the full day of filming. The trailer was used for market-testing in Arizona, Florida, Nevada, and several times in Los Angeles. According to the research cards that Hauge received after each screening, the response was extraordinary. The average rating, based on a scale of one to ten, was nine and a quarter. For Hauge, it was not just a vindication that he and his team were right all along about the interest level in James Dean, it was also a vindication of him as a director.

Roesler and The Family loved the trailer. They thought it looked very professional and buttressed their feelings that they were finally in the hands of a competent director. Roesler and The Family had grown personally fond of Hauge. Even though he owned a studio, he seemed to go to great lengths to separate himself from the Hollywood community. At their first meeting, Hauge was dressed in blue jeans, a slightly open shirt, and cowboy boots. He was just like a kid who had grown up on a farm in Montana, Roesler thought. Most important, Hauge viewed James Dean as a kind of acting legend. That's the way The Family liked it.

And then Alan Hauge brought Jon Emr to Indiana.

THE TRAIL OF THE ASSASSIN: THREE

When Benny woke up that afternoon, Suggsy was sitting on the edge of his bed with his back turned toward him, bent over, and the water from the shower was still dripping off him. He was on the phone. "Hey, Mom . . . Look, I ain't got a lot of time. I don't . . . I just want to say that I love you, Mom . . . Yeah, me too . . . Look, Mom, I'm going away . . . I can't tell you where . . . As a matter of fact, Mom, I don't think I'll be seeing you." His voice was choking up now. "No, Ma . . . Mom, please, don't be crying . . . I'm going to be fine . . . Mom, you're going to be hearing many things about me. Some of them might be true . . . most will not be . . . Look, I gotta go . . . I love you, Mom."

Suggsy hung up the phone and stared straight ahead, motionless.

"Hey," Benny said meekly.

"Hey." Suggsy was still not turning around.

"Whatcha doin'?"

"I've been thinking about doing those boys," Suggsy said. This made Benny happy. At least he was thinking. If he was thinking he might come to his senses and abandon this absurd vendetta. No such luck. "I was thinking that I should also do Nicholas Karino."

"Who?"

"Somebody else that fucked me." Suggsy growled. "If I am going to get fried for doing one of them, may as well do the whole fucking lot!"

Benny sat up in his bed. He had heard the name Nicholas Karino (fictitious name) before, probably from Suggsy, but he could not quite attach it to anything. "What did he do?"

"He promised me a job. He told me to leave Emr and to join up with him. He didn't follow through."

"Suggsy, you can't just kill him."

Suggsy turned around. "Oh, but I can." Then he smiled. "C'mon, let's go gamble. I cashed some checks."

"Under a different name?"

"Fuck, those checks will be bouncing like a ball at the Felt Forum!"

Sounded like a good plan to Benny. "Suggsy, I heard you talkin' to your mom."

"Yeah."

"You told her you wouldn't see her again."

"I don't want to stress you, Benny," he said seriously. "But after all this is done I'm gonna be with Susan."

"What do you mean, Suggsy? What do you mean?"

Suggsy smiled and moved over to Benny. He patted him on the back. "Get dressed. Let's go gamble."

And so they went down into the bowels of the casino. Casinos were Suggsy's arena. He had made minor fortunes in casinos and had also lost major ones. But today, as he sat at the blackjack table, flirting with the various lady dealers that came his way, he racked up almost $700. After a few hours, he turned to Benny, who was standing directly behind him. "See her?" He was pointing at two plain-looking women a few yards away.

"Uh-huh."

"They keep looking at you. Let's go talk to them."

There was no use in arguing with Suggsy. It didn't matter that this would fall into the category of cheating on his wife; once Suggsy got the notion to nab a lady, all bets were off.

The men walked over to the ladies and Suggsy began making the smooth talk that Benny had for so long admired. Eventually, Suggsy made a date to meet the two women the next day at the world-famous Laughlin, Nevada, beach.

Suggsy and Benny never did meet the girls on the beach the next day. That was fine with Benny. He was a good Catholic. They spent the rest of the day wandering around the few city streets in Laughlin, cashing a few more bad checks, laughing like a couple of mailbox-bashing teenagers each time they did, and playing a hand here and there of blackjack.

By the end of the evening, while Suggsy was having a pretty good run at cards—there were chips up to his chin—Benny decided that he was going to make a call to his wife, Jenny, who was sitting at home with her seven hysterical children.

"Something ain't right," he told Jenny. He was whispering. What if Suggsy popped up right behind him?

"What're you talking about?" Jenny wondered.

"I dunno. It just ain't right. I gotta come home."

"So take a bus."

"Okay."

"Okay?"

"Yeah."

Benny called the bus station and was told by the dispatcher that he would have to shell out $50 for the ride back to Orange County. He walked over to Suggsy, who was busy contemplating whether or not he should take a hit on fourteen if the dealer was showing a nine. "Hey. How you doing?"

Suggsy looked over his chips. "I'm up."

"Can I have fifty dollars?"

Suggsy asked no questions. He just handed Benny the appropriate number of chips. Benny exchanged the chips for cash at the cage on the far end of the casino, took the elevator up to the room, got his bag, and walked out of the casino and to the Riverside bus station.

Benny just stood there for hours waiting for the bus that said "Los Angeles" on it. What he didn't know was that he had to catch the "Vegas" bus, which would make a stop in Las Vegas and then would mosey on over to L.A. And so Benny stood there for hours watching bus after bus leave, none of them with L.A. on a brightly lit sign in front.

Benny returned to the Hilton, walking down the hallway like a re-treating soldier. Suggsy was standing by the doorway looking at his watch. It was a bit after midnight. Suggsy had Benny's letter in his hand. As Benny entered the room he saw the bellboy collecting some luggage.

"What are you doing?" Benny asked.

"I was gonna check out. I thought you had left."

Benny shook his head. "I couldn't get a bus." He paused for a moment. "Suggsy, man, we gotta talk."

"Okay." Suggsy gave the bellboy a whole dollar and told him that they would be staying awhile longer. The bellboy left and Suggsy sat down next to his pal. "Okay. What's up? What's on your mind?"

"Suggsy, man, I don't like what's going on here. I just can't, you know, be a part of it. That's why I tried to leave."

Suggsy thought for a second. "Okay. Here's what we are going to do in that case. We're going to go straight to Arizona and we are going to take care of those Emr boys—"

"Suggsy, this is what I'm talking about. I can't—"

"Hold on. I'll take care of the boys. You just stay in the hotel room. That way you're not a part of it. Then I'll take you back home."

Boy, Benny thought, Suggsy really looks out for me, doesn't he? "Okay. Suggsy," he said, "I'm gonna get some sleep."

As Benny was falling asleep he considered how damn curious it was that Suggsy had not even asked him if he was planning to go to the police.

Trust is a beautiful thing, Benny thought to himself. A beautiful goddamn thing.

In the dream it was an earthquake. But it was only Suggsy, shaking the shit outta Benny. "C'mon, man, wake up."

Benny sat up. "What's up?"

"Get dressed."

"What time is it?"

"I dunno. Get dressed. I want to go to Vegas."

"Vegas?"

"There's something there that I want to do."

"What?"

"You'll see," he said with a smile. "Just something."

"And we go home after Vegas?"

"After Vegas we go to Arizona."

"I thought—"

Suggs put his hands on Benny's shoulders and stared down at him. "All you have to do is ride with me, pal. That is all."

The James Dean Con:
July 1990

Man has a choice. You used to say that was where we differed from an animal.
See, I remember, "Man has a choice, and it's—the, the choice is what makes
him a man," see? You see, I do remember.
—James Dean in *East of Eden*

On July 1, 1990, Stan Esecson was required by his contract with Curtis Management to come up with $100,000 if he wanted to retain the rights to the James Dean project. Unfortunately, there had been absolutely no progress toward getting investors to finance the film. The "producers" could not raise a dime, let alone one hundred grand to pay off The Family. Roesler sent Esecson a default letter, telling him that he had fifteen days to clear the debt.

Sometime in July, during a meeting between Roesler, Esecson, and Hauge, Roesler announced that Curtis Management would have to start legal proceedings against Alan Hauge and Stan Esecson. The Family wanted the second half of the option money that was contractually owned to them. It was nothing personal, Roesler explained. Just business.

Hauge was dumbfounded. "Look, Mark, you can sue him all you want," he said pointing at Esecson. "But if you sue me I'm going to own your company. Okay? I don't have a written agreement with Stan and I don't have one with you. I can't get *anybody* to give me a contract! And, Jesus, this is my script and I put together the trailer to promote this movie."

Everybody laughed. Then Hauge asked Roesler a question. "What would happen if I came back here and wanted to buy the rights. For myself? Then what? Are you going to hold all of this against me? Am I going to pay for what Randy Pike has done in the past?"

Esecson was shocked by Hauge's outburst. But what could he do? His failure to sign his partner under contract had inadvertently made Hauge an absolutely free agent.

"Alan, if you want to buy these rights, I would certainly talk to you about it," Roesler said quietly.

Alan turned to Esecson. "Stan, you're about to blow this away. I want to see this project done. I'm not interested in cutting you or anybody else out. But I'm not going to allow Warner Bros. or Paramount to come in and do it. I have a relationship with The Family. Why lose all of that stuff?"

All Stan could do was nod.

Hauge considered driving up to see his good friend Marcus Winslow and begging him to let him have the rights to the James Dean story gratis. Wasn't the goal, after all, to get a decent version of Dean's life on screen? Hadn't he demonstrated, time and time again, that he was the one to do that? Wasn't he the one with the heterosexual, father-loving version of Dean? Anyway, hadn't Marcus and The Family received enough money already?

Hauge was sure that Marcus would go for it. Marcus was an unconditionally decent man, Hauge thought. But he was equally certain that making any side deal with the Dean family would only serve to alienate Mark Roesler, and who, after all, needed that to happen?

A few days after the meeting in Indiana, Mark Roesler filed for arbitration against Stan Esecson, who had resigned himself to the fact that he was very much out of the business of creating a "tribute" to Jimmy.

In October of 1990, Randy Pike contacted Alan Hauge and told them that *their* problems were solved. Even though Pike was contractually out of the picture, he still considered himself integrally involved. As far as he was concerned, he had started things and, damn it all, he was going to be there when it was finished.

Pike told Hauge that he had run into a man named Jilly Rizzo at his country club in Palm Springs. Hauge recognized the name immediately. Rizzo was the former road manager and current best friend to Frank Sinatra. Some people referred to Jilly as the "Man behind the Man." Anyway, Pike had laid it all out for Jilly Rizzo. He told Jilly how he, Stan, and Alan had devoted their lives to this James Dean picture, that they had poured much of their own cash and that of their friends into buying up the rights, and how they were just flat broke. He told him that there were investors banging on his door wondering where the hell their money had gone. What he desperately needed was some kind of white knight.

The great news was that Jilly indeed had a "guy." When men like Jilly have "guys," those people should be taken seriously. That was Randy Pike's feeling. Hauge sighed to himself. He was loath to allow yet another player into the picture. But at this point he would do anything to help keep this dream alive.

He agreed to meet with Jilly's "guy"—a man named Jon Emr—at the "guy's" favorite hangout. It was an Italian restaurant on Westwood and Santa Monica called Matteo's.

When Alan Hauge arrived at the restaurant, he saw Randy sitting with a plump, grandmotherly lady. A few tables away, another man, one who bore a remarkable resemblance to Clark Gable but with a slick, greasy face and much heavier, was involved in a loud and hysterical meeting. The Gable look-alike was waving his arms frantically, a cigar wedged in between his teeth, heavy clouds of smoke puffing out of his mouth every time he made some sort of exclamatory remark.

When Alan sat down, Randy pointed over to the cigar-smoking greaseball. "That's Emr. Motherfucker," he sneered. Nobody—*nobody*—kept him waiting. He slammed his fist on the table, his many brass rings rattling the glasses of water that had been left there by the waiter. Randy excused himself and barged into Jon's meeting. Jon told him he'd be a minute. Randy returned to the table. But, after a few minutes, he was fed up again. He walked over to the table where Jon was sitting and actually sat down and gave Jon a piece of his mind. A few minutes later, Randy came back like a wounded puppy dog.

In the meantime, Alan Hauge was asking the old lady at the table, Renee Emr, Jon's mother, what projects she and her son had produced. She told Alan about a movie called "The Bobby Garwood Story." Renee claimed that she and her son Jon had just produced a project for ABC Television called "The Bobby Garwood Movie." She told him the full story. She also told him about her vast experience writing the story and about her and Jon's relationship with the actors Ralph

Macchio and Martin Sheen. Alan nodded his head in faint recognition as Renee talked. "You're familiar with Bobby Garwood? Do you know him? Some people refer to this as a 'spook' story," Renee said.

"What do you mean by that?"

"A spook is a CIA operative."

"I was involved with an operative once. It cost me a lot of money."

"Yes," she responded with a sigh. "That can happen."

Alan shook his head. "His name was Scott Barnes. The worst thing that ever happened to me."

Renee turned white. Hauge thought she was going to literally die right then and there. "Did you say Scott Barnes?"

"Yes. Do you know him?"

Renee laughed nervously. *"Do I know him?* We bought his rights. We bought a book he wrote called *Bohica.*"

Alan laughed. "You may *think* you own the rights to *Bohica.* I bought the rights in 1981. He sued me in court to get the rights back and he lost, so I still own the rights." Alan smirked. "He just conned you, Renee. He doesn't own those rights. I must say, this is a real million-to-one shot. I mean, you and I meeting like this."

At this point, Jon Emr came storming back to the table. He sat down and then lunged his body across the table, sticking his index finger into Randy Pike's face. "Nobody ever interrupts my meetings. You understand? Nobody ever does that." His voice had enough acid to melt steel.

There's no money here, Hauge thought to himself. Even if there had been an opportunity, it appeared Randy had blown it. Before he could actually leave, the seventy-dollar check was presented to Hauge, who had had nothing to eat or drink. Emr and Randy smiled and acknowledged their gratitude to Hauge. "Hey, I'm outta here," Hauge said. He put his hands on the edge of the table and pushed his chair back.

The next day Alan Hauge was contacted by Renee Emr. According to Hauge, she told him that on the way home, Jon said that he did not want to have anything to do with Randy. But the fact that Alan had had an experience with Scott Barnes intrigued the Emrs.

Alan promised Renee he would meet with her and her son and

would tell them the story of his rather remarkable encounters with Mr. Barnes.

When they met at a Manhattan Beach restaurant called Salsalito South, Hauge explained to Jon that he had met Scott Barnes about nine years earlier. He was introduced to him by his minister and best friend, Ralph Moore. Hauge was a born-again Christian and GMT Studios, which he owned, was named after the phrase "Great and Mighty Things" in the Bible.

"I was introduced to Scott and he had a great life story. I paid a lot of money for it. I went out to research it, I worked with the *Los Angeles Times*, Ted Koppel, Bob Woodward of the *Washington Post*, Ben Bradlee Jr. of the *Boston Globe*."

"Christ," Jon said. "You got to some big people."

"Well, the main guy was Mark Gladstone and I cannot think of the other guy's name at the *L.A. Times*. They traveled all over the world to validate Scott's story. They came back after thirty-five thousand miles and said, 'Hey, this guy lied to you. It's a totally bogus story. You've wasted your money.'"

Jon could not help but guffaw. "I could have told you that!"

"Well, anyway, I got ahold of Scott. I said to him, 'Hey, you ripped me off!' Later I met with Ted Koppel regarding the story. He flew to L.A. and he confronted Scott and told him that he wasn't going to run the story. So I told Scott, 'I don't want to have anything to do with you.' Well, he wanted all of his stuff back. All his material on his MIA/POW stuff because I had it."

"So what did Scott do? I'll bet he just fuckin' freaked out."

"What did he do? He did what Scott always does. He sued me to get the rights back. Anyway, the trial eventually came up. And two days before the trial he calls me up and said, 'You know, I've decided not to sue you. It's really a mistake. And I should have listened to you, and I'm sorry that I lied to you. I'm canceling the court case.'"

"Shee-iiiitttt! I hope you didn't fall for that line of bullshit," Jon said.

"Wait, wait. This gets very good," Hauge said. "So, I said to him, 'Well, would you send me a letter to that effect?' He said yeah. So, he sent me a letter that was going to cancel the court case. I showed it to my attorney who told me, 'You'd still better check on this guy because he sounds like a weasel. Call this guy on the morning of the trial.'"

"Because Scott lives in Kernville. That's a hundred fifty miles away from L.A."

"Exactly, Jon! I called his house at seven-thirty in the morning, and his wife answered. She said that he had an appointment at eight-thirty A.M. in Los Angeles and he'd left at five-thirty A.M. that morning."

Jon was laughing. "I fuckin' knew it. Knew it!"

"So, I went down to the courthouse. I had nothing with me. You can imagine how I felt. All I had was my attaché case. Well, there was Scott with his whole case just laid out in front of him. He did not have a lawyer with him. He was going to do the case by himself."

"Doesn't surprise me. So the judge must have thrown Scott out on his ass."

"Well, I handed him Scott's letter. The judge read it and looked at me and said, 'He lied to you. The trial starts in five minutes.'"

"MOTHERFUCKER!"

"I had nothing, Jon. I mean, I didn't have a scrap of paper. So, the trial lasted about three hours, and this judge would not let me talk. He kept cutting me off and he kept allowing Scott to accuse me of all these things . . . All this garbage."

"So, what? You mean to say that you lost the trial?"

Alan allowed the first smile of the meeting. "Scott lost. Scott even had to pay my court costs. Hell, not only did he not get his rights back, I could have sued him and taken everything that he had. But he didn't have anything, absolutely nothing, zero."

When Hauge was done telling his story, Jon Emr said, "Yeah, he really is some kind of motherfucker. Some kind of motherfucker!"

"What's your story?" Alan wanted to know.

Jon laughed. "That would take a fucking book. But I'll tell you this. We are involved in a major, major lawsuit with Barnes. It would be helpful if we owned the rights without any complication. How would you like just to hand over your rights to the Barnes story to us?"

"Jon, that's fine. I don't want anything to do with him. At all. I don't want to talk about Scott and I don't want to hear his name. All that I'd ask is that if you make this film or beat him in the lawsuit, I get something for it."

Jon lit up a cigar. "That's fine."

Emr and Hauge signed an agreement in which Hauge assigned his rights to Emr. According to the deal, if *Bohica* ever got made, Alan would receive $50,000.

A few days later, Jon contacted Alan and told him that he wanted to meet with him at the Holiday Inn restaurant in Torrance. He said that he wanted to discuss the possibility of his coming aboard the James Dean film.

At the meeting, Jon claimed that he was so enamored of the project that he would be willing to put on the back burner a $15 million project that he was "putting together" for Tom Selleck, the star of the CBS television series *Magnum, P.I.* His coproducer on that particular project was Cecil B. DeMille's grandson.

Jon told Hauge that he was tremendously well connected with the Douglas family. He had personally worked with Michael Douglas. Connections didn't come better than that, he insisted. Jon said that it would not be a problem to raise the money for either the rights or the funding of the James Dean project.

"Here's the thing, Jon. I like what you're saying. But I've been screwed and screwed. I'm not going to give you anything at all if you don't raise the cash. You know, if I raise the cash or something like that, you're out."

Jon nodded. "Yeah, yeah. But I know I can do it. Let me raise some increment capital so that we can buy the rights."

"It's real simple, Jon. You are either going to come up with it or you're not."

Jon pulled out a contract that he had prepared. Alan looked at it and flashed back to a conversation he had once had with Randy Pike. Pike had begged him not to sign anything with Emr. "He's a fucking con" is the way Randy had put it. At the time, Alan smiled and said, "Randy, you should talk."

Alan read and reread the contract. Then he squinted up at Jon. "Let me give it some thought."

The next day, Alan had a hastily slapped together meeting with a man who said he represented yet another major investor who might be interested in the James Dean project. Not long into the conversation, the man started to talk about his relationship with, wouldn't you know it, Joel and Michael Douglas. Hauge smiled politely. What a fluke. In his mind, he thought that this might be a great way to do a due diligence on Jon.

"You know," Alan said to the investor. "I have another guy making an approach to me on this film. He wants to be an executive producer. He says that he knows the Douglas family. Could you do me a favor and contact Joel Douglas and see if he actually knows this guy Jon Emr?"

A few days went by and Hauge again found himself in conversation with the potential investor. "Yeah, I made a call to France," the investor said. "I talked to Joel and he said that Jon's a great guy."

And there it was, the independent verification. Jon Emr was in.

Randy Pike walked up the stairs in the lobby of GMT Studios, past a crew of receptionists and rooms that were sparse save for the occasional movie poster for films that had been made on the property. One of the posters was for a movie called *Over the Top*, which was a failed Sylvester Stallone film, one of those overwrought, overproduced pictures that had brought down Canon Pictures a year back.

Randy enjoyed walking into the studio unannounced. It kept people off guard. That's when employees were at their most honest. Anyway, as far as Randy was concerned, he didn't need a goddamn invitation. Although his name was not emblazoned on the GMT prospectus as a partner, he felt that it was he and he alone who would be keeping the studio afloat. The James Dean movie was going to be bigger than anyone could even have dreamed of and he was the man responsible.

Randy was here to talk with Alan about business, though nothing terribly serious. But when he walked into Alan's office he had a surprise waiting for him. There was no Alan there. Just . . . Jon Emr. Emr was dressed like a pimp, Randy thought: a floral shirt, gold chains, and a howitzer cigar balanced between his teeth as he spoke on the phone. Sitting in the chair next to the table was Renee, her hands folded politely on her lap.

"Hey!" Jon yelped as he put down the phone.

"What the hell are you doing here?" Randy demanded of Jon.

Randy felt a tap on his shoulder and he spun around. It was Alan Hauge. "Let's go and talk, Randy."

They took the stairs down to the parking lot. As they were walking, Randy was muttering obscenities, clearly outraged by all of this.

"Randy, it's like this," Alan said to Randy once they were outside. "I have signed a contract with Jon."

Alan explained his rationale to Randy. After their failed meeting at Matteo's, Jon and Alan had spoken often. Jon had been able to convince him that he was not only an able producer, but a master financier. Jon's job would be to raise $40 million to make this movie. Alan was confident Jon could do the trick. Alan had seen his portfolio. "Do you know that he was once in a partnership with the Douglas family?" Hauge asked Randy.

"I can't fucking believe this!" Randy said. "I just can't. This guy is bad fucking news. Why didn't you consult with me?"

"Well, Randy, you know, your name is not on the contract with Curtis and the Dean family. It just isn't your choice." Hauge's eyes lit up. "This guy says he can come up with the option money in a snap."

"I can't believe this."

"You know, Randy, you're the guy who brought Jon Emr in. I'm ready to bail on this project. In fact, if this guy cannot finance the picture, then I'm out. I am tired of the aggravation and I'm tired of all the headaches."

"You guys are all stupid fuckers." Randy said before he stormed off.

Emr literally moved right into Alan Hauge's office. Alan wasn't terribly bothered by that. He was mostly working at home now anyway. In any case, Jon insisted that he would lease Alan's office space for $1,000 a month. He would pay him in full once he got the movie financed.

On December 27, 1990, and January 9, 1991, Stan Esecson and Randy Pike officially signed over what rights they may or may not have had in the Dean project to Jon Emr. After all, Esecson and Pike knew that once the arbitration went through they would have nothing. This way, if Jon Emr could come up with the cash, they would be part of something rather than nothing. Emr had agreed to let both men be players in the project and assured them that they would get some sort of screen credit.

At about the same time that Emr became a fixture at GMT Studios, Alan Hauge was contacted by his friend Brian Anderson, the man from Codepa who had gotten him on the Dean project in the first place. Anderson had been talking on and off with Hauge about his Codepa company investing in the Dean film. All that Hauge knew about Codepa was that it was a hardwood lumber company that did business in South America. Hauge was told that Raul Lopez, the man who claimed to be the president of Codepa, had spent much of his adult life as a CIA operative.

Hauge, in fact, made a quick trip to Miami to meet with Lopez. The meeting took place in an apartment, not an office. Lopez did not even have a business card. When Hauge challenged him about where the money for the Dean investment was coming from, Lopez mentioned something about the selling of gold certificates to Peru. "He was not a guy that I really trusted," Hauge would later say. Nevertheless, the one thing Hauge knew was that Lopez was floating around some mighty lofty figures at him.

"Listen, our financing has come in," Anderson told Hauge when he phoned him in December. "Who owns the rights to the film right now?"

Hauge didn't bullshit around. "It's up in the air right now; there may be an arbitration."

"Well, we want to fund it."

"How are you going to do that?"

"The details are not important. Let's just do it."*

Of course, Hauge could have cut the deal with Codepa all by himself. If that were the case, then he would not have had to pay Jon Emr any fee at all. But, at this point, Hauge was still toiling with the script and was studying the concept of "method acting," an art form popularized by actors like Marlon Brando and James Dean and, later, their protégés Robert De Niro and Sean Penn. Hauge felt he didn't have the time or the energy to deal with investors on his own, even if it meant that he could save $1 million. Hauge told Jon to take care of Codepa and, for God's sake, make sure that this was a legitimate company. He had had about all the heartache he could endure.

Brian Anderson despised Jon Emr. He found him cocky, foulmouthed, and dishonest. On more than one occasion he would overhear Jon telling potential investors that Codepa had already placed an

*In a letter written in December to Hauge, Codepa president Raul Lopez explained that his company had signed a contract to supply Bolivian hardwood and other products to a West German company for $127 million.

initial payment into American Icon, the film's corporate entity. On the one occasion when Anderson confronted him about his lying, Jon angrily told him to "not worry about it," that he knew "exactly what the fuck" he was doing. Brian was also stressed that Jon was insisting that Codepa money be deposited into his very own special account. He once even suggested that they all go down to the bank, open an account, and simply deposit $25 million. Emr even went as far as opening a bank account in Panama so that Codepa would have an "easier time" depositing funds. Instead of placing the account under his own name, Emr used the name Dionysus, the Greek god of wine.

Despite all of the suspicions, Codepa remained interested. James Dean, after all, was James Dean.

LETTER OF COMMITMENT FROM CODEPA TO JON EMR

Dear Jon,

Having signed the investor-producer contract today for the James Dean film . . . we will commence the funding of twenty-five million dollars ($25,000,000) on or before January 28, 1991. . . .

[Y]ou agreed to pay off the cash remuneration to the Dean foundation and other items on the pre-production budget which shall include full payment for rights to the screenplay and transfer same into the new corporation. . . .

Jon, I have to be real honest with you, we are very excited—GO FOR IT!

XXXXXX
secretary
CODEPA

When Jon showed the letter he had "negotiated" out of Codepa to Alan Hauge, Alan became quite excited. The letter was like a piece of celluloid gold. Not only would it show Curtis Management that the movie "James Dean: The Legend" now had the financial status to forge ahead, but it would encourage other investors to jump on the bandwagon.

What Hauge did not notice at the time was that the letterhead for this Codepa company was almost laughingly unprofessional. It was simply a sheet of paper with a company logo atop it and without a phone number. At the bottom was an address in Miami, Florida. Had anybody bothered to check on the matter, as the police and FBI later did, they would have discovered that the address was a fake. In fact, there was no company anywhere in the United States known or incorporated as Codepa.

Jon Emr simply couldn't have cared less about the ambiguities of Codepa. As far as he was concerned, the commitment letter was like a siren to a navy of potential investors. He gave the Codepa correspondence and the Dean correspondence to several of his friends. He also gave them a letter from the man who would be in charge of the film's "merchandising" which stated that the revenue from "James Dean: The Legend" projects could net over $1 billion. Emr told his friends to go to their families, neighbors, anybody at all, and start pitching them as investors.

Jon Emr told Alan Hauge that he wanted them to fly up to Las Vegas on January 19, 1991, where they were going to meet an investor. When they got there, Jon had arranged rooms at Bally's where Willy Rizzo, Jilly's son, worked as a pit boss. While there they went to see the Oak Ridge Boys.

Emr introduced Alan to two men. One was a "friend" of his called Robert Allen who had a blond with him named Lynn. The other was a man from Nashville named Rod Buckle. Nothing ever came of the meeting in terms of business. Nevertheless, Hauge became intrigued by Rob Allen, whom he found charismatic and charming. Alan even went downtown with Rob to go gambling, which is not something he normally enjoyed doing. They played a game called Red Dog. In it, the dealer turns over two cards. The player bets whether or not the dealer is going to get a card that will be in between the ones that he has rolled. Alan won $300 that night. Oddly, through the entire night, Alan never asked Rob what he did for a living or what his connection to Emr was.

In mid-January, Jon received amazing news from his good friend Kirk Heinlen, one of the people whom Jon had asked to find investors. Heinlen, amazingly, had gotten his own family to invest over

$600,000 in the project—they had been so damn amazed by the Codepa letters and the promise of over a billon dollars in merchandising revenue.

THE TRAIL OF THE ASSASSIN: FOUR

Benny went to get the car while Suggsy paid for the rooms. And then they were off, making the ninety-mile trip to Las Vegas. Along the way Suggsy drove the car far into the desert itself, too far for Benny's taste. After he slammed down on the brakes, Suggsy gave Benny a glare and then grinned at him. "Target practice!" Suggsy said.

When they both got out of the car, Suggsy opened up the back door, pulled out one brown bag, and unzipped it. Benny was flabbergasted. From his vantage point he got a glimpse of what was in the bag. He saw an array of guns. And so Benny was stumped. Why the hell did they need to travel all the way to an Arizona pawnshop in order to get a gun he had hocked? So Benny, in all of his wisdom, figured that he had been duped. Duped by a master. Duped all along.

"You ever seen a H&K 91 fired off?" Suggsy asked Benny, picking up one of the weapons. "It's a motherfucker."

This is it, baby. I'm going to buy it right here in the desert. Maybe this is where Susan is buried. Oh, God. I shouldn't have tried to leave. That pissed him off. I should have just stayed. "No, Suggsy." Benny's throat had completely dried up.

Suggsy slowly lifted the gun so that the barrel was just grazing Benny's temple.

BOOM!

The gun went off a split second after Suggsy moved it away from Benny's head. A nearby cactus was blown in half—right down the middle. "It's a beauty!" Suggsy said.

"Yeah."

"Here, try it," he said, handing the gun to Benny. Benny hated guns. Guns were the forte of Suggsy's other pal, Robert, an Orange County cop. Suggsy and Robert used to come out to this very same desert to go coyote hunting. The government was rewarding hunters for every beast they could blow to smithereens. They made small fortunes during those happy times.

After a few minutes, the men got back into their vehicle. They didn't talk for the rest of their trip into Las Vegas. Suggsy had made his point quite clearly.

Suggsy and Benny were in their room in the Flamingo Hilton hotel in Vegas only because the Aladdin, about a half mile up the Las Vegas Strip, was all booked up. Funny thing was that Benny and Suggsy did not have to wait in line at the registration desk at the Hilton. Lines were for mere mortals. Suggsy went directly to the VIP line, pulled out a fake ID and a special Hilton card. It took them less than ten minutes to get up to their room.

Their room was nice and clean, with two beds and large desk. But the first thing that Suggsy noticed was the view. It looked directly into the street. Directly down on the Strip.

"God-fuckin'-dammit," Suggsy said.

"What's the matter?"

"The neon is going to be blinking like a motherfucker in here all night."

"We'll just close the drapes," Benny the wise one said.

There was a knock on the door. The bellman, sweating and grabbing hold of Suggsy's bags, came in followed by a lanky security guard who had a corporal's epaulets on his shoulder. He had a black badge with white letters that read "Daubert."

Corporal Daubert was holding one of Suggsy's bags. He held it high up in the air. "Does this bag belong to anybody?" he asked.

"It's mine. What's the problem?" Suggsy said without a hint of anger.

"We had a small accident downstairs. The bag came open. We just want to tell you that we know you have guns in there." He unzipped the bag and showed the contents to Suggsy, demonstrating that he wasn't crazy for bringing the issue up.

"Yeah, yeah. No problem." He gestured to lanky Corporal Daubert to hand over the bag.

"It may be a problem, sir."

"Listen, it doesn't matter. I'm not wearing the guns."

"Are these weapons registered to you, sir?"

Suggsy sighed. Damn rent-a-cops. Suggsy pulled out his wallet and let it flop open so that his identification was apparent. "Daubert, I'm an investigator."

Daubert, who had no idea what he was looking at, nodded his head. "Okay, sir. I just wanted you to know that we were aware of the weapons."

"Very good." He pulled out a few bills and stuffed some into the hands of the bellhop and then offered some cash to Daubert, who shook his head gently.

"Bye, sir. Good luck at the tables," said Daubert.

Luck has nothing to do with it, Suggsy thought to himself as the lanky Corporal Daubert left. Nothing whatsoever.

"Here it is," Suggsy said as they pulled into the Wendy's restaurant parking lot. "What do you think?"

Benny was confused. Suggsy had dragged him out of bed and told him that the two of them were going to do a "job" together. It was unusual for Suggsy to spend this many hours in Las Vegas and not make even one bet. Not even for a quick spin on the roulette wheel. But perhaps there were more important things on his mind. "We're going to eat lunch here?" Benny asked.

Suggsy smiled and shook his head. Benny's stupidity sure had an endearing quality to it. He pointed across the street to the small art deco building, one of the many Las Vegas branches of the Valley National Bank. "We're going to take it. We're gonna make a little bit of money. You'd like that. Some extra money, I mean. Your gun is in the glove compartment."

"Huh?"

"You don't really have to do anything."

It was Suggsy's use of the word "really" that seemed to stick with Benny.

"I don't understand," Benny said. Suggsy believed him.

"I'm going to go in there and rob the place. You just be the lookout. When I get out of the car, you move into the driver's seat. It's just like in the movies, man. I come out, get in the car, and you bolt like a bat outta fuckin' hell."

"No, Suggsy, man. I can't get caught."

"Almost nobody ever gets caught robbing a bank." Suggsy was wrong, actually. Ever since videotape recorders were introduced into bank security systems, robbers were being snatched up at an astonishing 85 percent rate.

"No, Suggsy," he said. "I can't, man."

Then Suggsy got angry. "Don't cross me, Benny. You need to be a part of this." He laid his neck on the headrest and blew out a stream of air. "If I go out in a blaze of glory, this is exactly how I want to do it. If I get shot, I get shot."

Benny was almost in tears. "But, Suggsy, why do I have to be part of it. I didn't ask for any of this shit."

"Because we're best friends."

"But, I don't want to go out THAT way!" he said with a whimper.

Benny battled with Suggsy for two hours. He had a wife. Seven kids. He didn't want his girls to have a daddy who was either dead or a jailbird just because he tried to rob a bank with their uncle Rob. He was a good Catholic. He could not violate any of the Ten Commandments. Or at least not any more of the Ten Commandments. He was sick about this whole thing. Sick about being in Vegas with a fugitive who had just killed his woman and his dog. Benny would panic. He was sure of it, fuck it up. Get both their asses thrown in jail. Please, please, let's go home.

They sat in the Wendy's parking lot for close to three hours. Eventually, Suggsy gave up. He stared blankly ahead. "Tomorrow, we go to Arizona. Tomorrow, we do the boys."

All that Benny heard was the word "we."

The James Dean Con:
January 1991

Jim, do you think the end of the world will come at nighttime?
—Sal Mineo to James Dean in *Rebel Without a Cause*

A lan Hauge gave Mark Roesler only a few days' notice that he was flying out to Indiana to mend their business relationship and that he now had the funds to buy up the rights. He told him that Stan Esecson had simply dropped out of the picture and that he had a new partner. His name was Jon Emr. Emr, he explained to Roesler, was a very successful producer. He had been involved in the making of those wonderful Michael Douglas–Kathleen Turner comedy-adventure films, *Romancing the Stone* and *Jewel of the Nile*.

Roesler was impressed, but careful not to get excited. He also made it clear to Hauge that it would take quite a bit to "mend" their problems. First of all, Roesler wanted the $100,000 in option money that The Family was owned. In addition, he wanted another $13,000 to take care of both the interest and the attorney fees that Curtis Management had accumulated during the arbitration process. Then Roesler made it clear that the rights to the Dean story were going to get even more expensive. He wanted to make damn sure that Hauge and this Emr fellow had the cash available to get into serious preproduction on the film. Hauge and Roesler talked price over the phone. Roesler began by asking for $500,000 and then settled for $150,000—up front—paid in full.

Before going to Indiana, Jon Emr spoke with Mark Roesler. He assured Roesler that he had already lined up guaranteed financing for the film—that is, from Codepa. He had the correspondence to prove it.

In a little over a week, Roesler received an overnight package that included two checks: one for $100,000 and another for $13,000.

■ ■ ■

The air was biting with subzero anger when Hauge and Emr arrived in the snow-covered Indianapolis airport. But that did not stop Jon Emr from dressing as if he were still in Southern California. When he showed up at the offices of Curtis Management, Jon was adorned in his customary floral shirt, which was unbuttoned to the navel, and gold chains, which were draped around his neck. By contrast, Alan Hauge and a lawyer named Doug Smithers, who Jon insisted be hired as the "project attorney," were wearing well-tailored suits, which Mark Roesler found more appropriate for the occasion.

Roesler decided to hold the meeting in the large Curtis conference room. In the back of the room there was a blackboard which, as a matter of habit, Roesler enjoyed using. Before the actual negotiations began, Jon began rambling about his kids, his boys: Bobby and Roger. Roesler smiled and responded by talking about his newborn. Then Jon reeled off his impressive credentials. He explained that he had produced three hundred movies and programs, both theatrical and for television. He was good friends with some of the most important people in the film industry, including the "most powerful family in Hollywood"—the Douglases. He showed Roesler his Emr-Douglas Productions business card. Roesler noticed that the card was a bit frayed and didn't understand why Jon did not have fresh ones.

"Look at whose name is first," Jon said, slapping the edge of the card against the table. "There's a fuckin' good reason for that! Joel's just a figurehead. I'm the one that makes things happen. I'm not like all those other fucking producers in Hollywood." Then he smiled a beautiful smile. "I'm honest."

In fact, throughout the conversation, Jon kept reinvoking the idea that he was a man of integrity. "Honest Jon," you could call him. "I'm a man of my word," Jon said. "Call up any of the Douglases! Call up Kirk or Michael or Joel!"

Roesler had made a deal with himself years before. He swore never to trust a man who told you how honest, religious, or rich he was. But Roesler had already received Jon's checks to make up for the option money that Hauge owed Curtis. Furthermore, in Jon's briefcase were two certified checks for $75,000 apiece. That would pay for the new option.

Eventually, the negotiations began. And when they did, Jon turned into a different person, completely disinterested in what was going on. Jon slumped in his seat, doodled, got up, meandered aimlessly, and often, rather inexplicably, started giggling. Once he went to the blackboard and drew a hanged man, with the figure choking hysterically at the end of the noose. He laughed as he wrote the name Randy Pike over the victim. When Jon sat down, he pounded his fist on the table. "That's one motherfucker who'll never mess with me. One time that sorry sack of shit talked back to me. I said to him, 'Don't you EVER talk back to me,' and he backed right down. Just like a fucking woman. HAHAHAHAHAHAHAHAHAHAHAHA!"

Once in a while, seemingly out of nowhere, Jon would object to something. "No!" he would yell, as if to demonstrate his involvement. Sometimes he would scream, "No!" even when he was not aware of what was being discussed.

Mark Roesler and Jon would get into loud shouting matches. Roesler was getting stressed over the time being wasted by Jon's frivolous objections. In every case, the same thing happened: the gentle giant attorney Doug Smithers would intervene and settle things calmly.

As the negotiations were coming to a close, Roesler decided that he would try to get a few extra bucks. "You know," Roesler said in his folksy way. "The Family was once going to get five hundred thousand. I mean, that is how much we first asked for. Now, all they are getting is a hundred fifty thousand. I'm not sure that I like that. Not sure at all. I think that maybe we're getting screwed here."

Jon heard a money figure and came to life as if he had been jabbed by a cattle prod. "What do you want? What do you want?" Jon was on his feet, waving his arms in all different directions.

"Why," Roesler said, smoothing out his tie. "More money for The Family."

"How much?"

Roesler decided to high-ball it. "Say, another two hundred thousand."

Smithers opened up his mouth to make an objection. Two hundred thousand? Clearly Roesler had lost his mind. The price that was to be paid for the James Dean rights was essentially set in stone. Smithers was not going to allow this "barracuda" Mark Roesler to get a single extra dime out of his clients. But before Smithers could get a word out, a generous Jon said, "Okay. Put it in the contract," pointing at the papers that were on the table. "We will give you another two hundred thousand." Then he lifted his index finger. "But only once the filming begins."

Mark Roesler smiled. Once again, his negotiating techniques had paid off a big dividend. Big! Smithers looked over at Hauge, who looked over at Emr. The big smug son of a bitch actually had a smile on his face as well.

At the end of the meeting, the contract was ready for signatures and was passed around the room. There were no major surprises from a financial point of view. However, there was one tiny problem as far as Alan Hauge was concerned. Jon Emr had apparently had the balls to take Alan's name clean out of the contract. As it read now, Jon was in absolute control of the rights.

Alan, who viewed himself as a strong Christian, thought better than to reach across the table, rip Jon's eyes out, and piss on his brain. It was the first time that he was bringing Jon to meet Mark Roesler and The Family and he didn't want it to appear as though there was any kind of division in the ranks.

Hauge asked if they could take a break and then requested that Jon step outside. They needed to have a little talk. Hauge and Jon stood outside in about a foot of snow.

Hauge jabbed Jon with his index finger. "Hey, what the hell is this! My name has been taken out of this whole deal."

Jon pulled a cigar out of his shirt pocket and slipped it in his mouth. His smile was wide and irritating to Hauge. "Hey, old buddy. You already signed a contract with me that says that you get to direct the film, that you get control over the cast and crew. That's already set."

"Let me tell you something, Jon. I don't like the idea that I'm not in that contract."

"I'll tell you what we'll do. We'll put GMT International in there to make sure that you're real happy. We'll make sure that you're the distributor. But on all those other things you're already covered."

Hauge was willing to buy Emr's line. After all, he *did* have a contract with him. Jon *had* come up with the money for the rights. He *had* managed to get Codepa lined up. Hauge figured that if he and his company had control over the film's distribution, then Jon would not be able to go anywhere without him anyway. Most important, Hauge did not want to go back into the conference room and have a free-for-all with Jon. That would have really blown the deal.

The way that the contract was now set up, any investors that decided that they wanted to put cash into "James Dean: The Legend" would have to wire the funds into a bank account that was controlled by Jon Emr.

That afternoon, Hauge dropped Jon Emr and Doug Smithers off at the airport so that they could take their USAir flight home. Hauge then drove to meet with Marcus Winslow and the rest of the Dean family at their home in Marion.

Hauge had the checks with him and a copy of the contract, which Marcus needed to sign. As usual, their meeting was convivial. Over the past couple of years Hauge had almost become family to them. As they were talking, a special report on the television caught their attention. A jet had crashed on approach into Los Angeles International airport.

Hauge went pale. Was that the flight that Jon and Doug were on? He called home to see what kind of information he could get.

Doug Smithers and Jon Emr flew home that night, while Alan Hauge remained to talk with the Dean family at their home on the Fairmont estate. The two men sat in the first-class section of the plane, paid for courtesy of a pair of investors that Jon had managed to scrape up.

Jon Emr was drinking Bloody Marys throughout the entire flight. As he and Smithers sat in their first-class seat, Emr would scream for the stewardess. "HEY, SWEETHEART!" he'd say, snapping his thick fingers. When the stewardess came over, Jon would request another drink. "C'MON, SWEETIE! I'M CELEBRATING!"

"Yes sir."

"Do you know what I'm celebratin' about?"

"No sir."

Emr laughed loudly, banging the chair in front of him, rocking and rolling the hell out of the businessman sitting ahead of him. JAMES fuckin' DEAN!" He pointed at the embarrassed Smithers, who was sitting by the window. "THIS MAN RIGHT HERE JUST GOT ME

THE RIGHTS TO JAMES DEAN!" Then he slapped Doug on the back. "JAMES fuckin' DEAN!"

And so it would go for the entire flight. Jon drinking and yelling and being the type of nightmare that all first-class stewardesses hated.

As their Delta flight descended into LAX, Jon and Doug Smithers looked out the window. Below them they saw a bright orange mass. As the plane got lower, the fire beneath them became grisly clear. And then the disaster became a certainty. A plane, a USAir jet, was on the ground, snapped in two, engulfed in flames.

"Would you look at that?" Jon said in a drunken hush. "Hmmm. Hope it's not somekinda omen. HAHAHAHAHAHAHAHA!"

THE TRAIL OF THE ASSASSIN: FIVE

Benny thought it odd that Suggsy would pay cash for the hotel room and later insist on using a credit card when they stopped for gas on their way to Arizona. But who was he to ask questions? Anytime he would ask a question, it would draw him in further into the muck and the mire of Suggsy's exploits. Unfortunately, as they sped along, Suggsy sucked him in anyway. Deep.

"I got a plan," Suggsy said at one point.

"What?"

"I've got it figured out how I'm going to do those boys."

"Uh-huh."

"First thing that I am going to do is check the outside perimeter of the house. That's something that you always, always gotta do."

"Yeah?"

"Yeah. I'm talking about Arthur Emr's house. I probably will have to shut off the power. Then, when the boys come out I'm gonna kill them. One at a time." He made a gun from his fingers. "Pop!" he said, thrusting his fingers backward from the imaginary recoil. "Pop!"

"I don't wanna have nothing to do with it."

Suggsy smiled. "Yeah, yeah. Don't you worry, Benny. Don't worry. You'll be in the motel. After I've done the boys, I'm gonna collect me whatever money I can from the old man. And whatever I get," he turned and put on a huge smile. "I'll give all to you. All of it, Benny!"

All of a sudden, Benny was very touched. "Why thank you, Suggsy. That's mighty fine of you. I could use the money."

In mid-desert, Suggsy screeched the car to a halt. "I wanna try something," he said. "Get outta the car."

Suggsy opened the trunk and pulled out a .22. Then he attached a silencer to it. "Let's see how this sounds. Walk into the desert a bit there, Benny."

I'm gonna trust him, Benny said to himself. I'm gonna trust him. As Benny walked forward, Suggsy just stood behind him, finessing the silencer on the gun. Benny began to feel like he was walking a plank. If Suggsy popped him he wondered if Suggsy would have the good grace to take care of his wife and kids.

PIF! PIF! PIF!

Benny spun around. Suggsy was shooting in the opposite direction. "Could you hear that!"

"Yeah," Benny said, walking back. Why had Suggsy made him trot those few paces into the desert? Was it some kind of cruel hoax? "But it wasn't loud enough that it would like, wake me from a sleep or anything."

As he came close to him, Suggsy held out the gun. "You wanna try to fire this thing?"

"No, man."

"It's gonna become the most famous gun in the country."

"C'mon, Suggsy, let's go. Let's just go."

CHAPTER 6

The James Dean Con:
February 1991

You know, all that fine riding you used to do and all that fancy roping and all that glamour stuff you did to dazzle me—oh, it was impressive, but none of it made you quite as big a man to me as you were on the floor of Sarge's Hamburger joint. When you tumbled rearward and landed crashing into that pile of dirty dishes, you were at last my hero.
—Elizabeth Taylor to Rock Hudson in *Giant*

Jon Emr's purpose in setting up American Icon, the corporate entity for "James Dean: The Legend," was to establish a bank account into which investors could deposit their money. In order to demonstrate his integrity to Alan Hauge, Jon Emr agreed to have him added as a signatory. Of course, Jon would still have the right to withdraw money at will.

At one point, a total of $450,000 had been raised by Jon Emr. Make that $450,100. The extra C-note came from Hauge himself, who deposited the money so that the account could be opened. One day, Hauge happened to open the bank statement. It said that there was only $5.00 in the account.

According to Jon, all the money went to Curtis Management. But simple arithmetic shows that only half of the cash was used for those purposes. Where did the rest of it go? Nobody was willing to point an accusing finger at Jon. However, all of a sudden his son Roger had a new truck, Jon suddenly started waving hundred-dollar bills around at Matteo's, was promising two women that he was going to marry them, set himself up for a major cardiological operation, and was telling people how much cocaine relaxed him.

There was also the fact that Jon suddenly came up with money to rent a cabin in Big Bear from December 15, 1990, to January 3, 1991.

His boys joined him from Arizona. On New Year's weekend he invited Alan Hauge and his wife, Lanette, to spend some time in the mountains.

When Alan walked into the house he noticed that there was a shotgun in the corner and a .357 Magnum on the coffee table. "What are you doing with all the guns?" Alan asked half in jest.

"Hey, man, you can never be too careful. Know what I mean?"

Alan laughed. "What? Is somebody after you?"

When Lanette got her husband alone, she said to him, "We're outta here tomorrow. I don't like this."

The next morning they were gone.

Of course, money never lasts. That's what Mark Roesler was to find out.

A few weeks after his initial meeting with Jon Emr, the one in which he convinced Emr to give him an extra two hundred grand for the rights to the James Dean life story, Mark Roesler flew to Los Angeles on business. He gave Jon Emr a call and mentioned that he'd love to drop in.

Jon was excited. "Su-uuure!" he said over the phone. "I'll give you a tour of the studio and then we'll get some dinner."

Roesler was happy to hear this. For the past few weeks he had been making calls to various members of the Hollywood community. Not a single person had even heard of Jon Emr. Roesler was not concerned about the money. Most of it was already in his pocket. What he was concerned about was his credibility with the Dean family. They had been nervous about all the frauds who had approached them over the years. Finally, they had found somebody that both they and Roesler thought was for real. It would be catastrophic to Roesler's relationship with The Family if this all turned out to be a sham.

During their trip to the studio, Jon Emr put Mark Roesler and his wife, and Jon's mother, Renee, into a room where they watched a videotape of "The Bobby Garwood Story." Roesler was not qualitatively impressed with the picture. But it was, after all, an honest-to-goodness film and it had actors of some merit, like Ralph Macchio and Martin Sheen, in it.

Later, Jon invited everybody to dinner at his favorite restaurant, Matteo's on Westwood Boulevard. The best little Italian place east of

Milan, Jon insisted. The best roasted bell peppers God ever created! Jon wanted everybody—Roesler and Alan Hauge and their wives—to join him and his mother for one of the best meals of their lives.

Jon had not even gotten to the famous bell peppers by the time he had reached his eighth Scotch. Every now and then somebody else would stop by, slap Jon on the back, and ask him how he was doing. This was clearly Jon's hangout. Every person that came by sat down and had a drink or two. Even Jilly Rizzo, Frank Sinatra's best friend, dropped in for a twenty-minute visit. Through it all, Jon just kept on drinking.

Roesler was beginning to get mighty stressed. His wife, Alice, who was the president of her local chapter of MADD—Mothers Against Drunk Driving—leaned over to her husband and wanted to ensure that her husband was not intending to allow Jon to drive them home. "Certainly not," Roesler whispered back to her.

Roesler then leaned over to Jon and expressed his concern. Jon just waved him off. Then, in a bit of a huff, he got up and went to the bar, slowly disappearing into the crowd that had gathered there.

Within a few minutes, the waitress arrived at the table and dropped the bill in front of Roesler. The costs of the dinner and the drinks had come to over $400. Hmmm. Hadn't *Jon* invited them to dinner at *his* favorite restaurant?

Roesler waited a while for Jon to return to pick up the check. The waitress prowled the table every few minutes. Eventually, Roesler pulled out his credit card, hoping now that somebody would be willing to share in the expenses. But nobody—least of all an Emr—offered to pay the cost of the meal.

Yes, Roesler said to himself, as he signed the credit card receipt, this *son of a bitch* better be for real.

For some reason, Rob Allen, Jon Emr's associate whom Alan Hauge had met in Las Vegas, began to show up more and more at GMT Studios. Eventually, Jon Emr told Alan Hauge that he was going to hire Allen to be in charge of security.

"Security? What do we need security for? That doesn't make any sense," Alan responded.

"Look, you can never be too careful."

"Jon, what are you talking about? Are you afraid that somebody is going to come and get you?"

"I'll say it again. You can never be too careful."

"Jon, I'm telling you this. I'm not paying for this. If you want to pay for this out of your executive producer fee, that's fine. But I am not paying this guy out of the budget for the film."

"Old buddy, don't worry about it."

"I like Rob, he's a real nice guy, a great guy. He's always treated me and my wife with respect. Lanette really likes him. But, Jesus, I don't even know anything about him or how you met him."

"Old buddy," Jon said one last time," don't worry."

Jon Emr had met Robert Allen on April 6, 1990, at a charity event meant to raise money for a little girl who had leukemia. It took place on the Scottsdale Polo Grounds, where country singer Glen Campbell was giving a concert. Jon had convinced the fund-raising committee that he be waived the $200 entry fee. He explained that he was interested in making a documentary about the disease. In fact, he would even bring along his own bodyguards to help protect Glen Campbell and Glen's daughter from overeager fans.

About a half hour after Campbell finished his mini-concert and left, John Emr was in the VIP tent with a blond woman named Randa Jensen. Randa was Jon's "Arizona girlfriend." He was sitting at one of the small tables, eating some ribs from the buffet, when Brian, a young man who worked for him, showed up. Next to him was a tall, heavyset man with a thick mustache. He had a beautiful blond girl by his side.

"This is Robert," Brian said. "He'd like to meet you."

They shook hands and then Robert Allen and his girlfriend, Lynn, sat down. He explained that he was a bodyguard with some investigative experience. He had heard about Jon and knew that he was a major player in Hollywood. His bottom line was that he wanted a job in the entertainment industry.

Jon nodded attentively as Allen laid out his credentials. Jon was especially impressed when Allen told him that he knew martial arts. Jon explained that he himself was a black belt in karate and had even trained with Chuck Norris in the years before he had become an action-adventure movie star.

Jon liked the fact that Rob Allen had a pretty blond by his side. Jon appreciated a man who had good taste in women. After a while, Jon started talking about his projects. He told him about "A Chance to Live." Eventually, he got around to talking about a movie that he was going to make about the life of Bobby Garwood. Allen knew exactly who that was. Rob said that he was too young to have served in Vietnam, but he had been a student of the war.

During their conversation, Allen told Emr that he knew quite a few people who might be very interested in investing in Emr films. Jon told him that would be great and if he in fact could raise cash, he would receive a broker's fee.

After about an hour, Jon told Allen that he might be able to find some work for him. His involvement in the POW/MIA issue had earned him some powerful and dangerous enemies. He might be in need of some security. First, he wanted to test Rob Allen. He wrote down a name on a piece of paper. "Kimo Mata." He pushed it over to Allen. "Here's a test. I want you to find this person."

Allen looked at the name. "This is all the information that you have? Just the name?"

Jon smiled. "It's all the information that I'm going to give you."

Before they parted. Jon told Allen that he wanted him and his pretty girlfriend to have dinner the following night with Randa Jensen and a bodyguard of his named Brian. Allen agreed.

Robert Allen and Lynn met with Randa Jensen and Brian the next evening at a restaurant called the American Grill. Oddly enough, Randa knew Allen. By coincidence, he had moved into the apartment complex next to her home. By an even stranger coincidence, Lynn had applied for a job in Randa's interior design firm, even though she had absolutely no experience in that field.

Allen spent most of the evening talking about his background. He told the group that he had spent some time in the air force, but that his true love was surveillance. He ran down the list of the state-of-the-art equipment that he had at his disposal. It was interesting to Brian that Allen asked no questions about Jon Emr or his work.

Brian told Allen a little bit about the problems that Jon Emr had been having. In a few minutes he gave Jon's side of the story in regard to the Texans and Scott Barnes. Brian explained that these people were not only suing Jon, but terrorizing him as well. If Rob Allen were to be hired for anything, it would be to deal with these no-good bastards.

As the conversation wore on, Brian became more and more impressed with Rob Allen. Allen certainly knew his field. Brian was well aware that Jon Emr was looking for somebody to handle security for him on the set of the Bobby Garwood project. The problem was that Brian himself lived up north and was not willing to make the move down to Los Angeles. As they were eating dessert, Brian said to Allen, "I'll put a bug in Jon's ear and see what I can do about getting you some work."

At the end of the evening, as Allen was paying for the meal, he pulled out a piece of computer paper and handed it to Jon. "Give this to your boss."

Brian looked it over. "What is this?"

"It's everything you ever wanted to know about one Kimo Mata." He grinned widely. "The man who wrote a song for one of Jon's movies a few years ago."

Brian folded the paper and placed it in his jacket pocket. He smiled and nodded his head knowingly. "My guess is that you'll be joining the stable very soon."

Allen certainly hoped that would be the case. At the moment, he and his girlfriend, Lynn, did not have so much as a dime between them. For months now he had been paying for absolutely everything—including his monthly rent of $1,000 a month—via Lynn's credit cards.

For the next few months, Jon Emr and Robert Allen spent time together. Whenever Jon Emr came into Scottsdale to visit with his father and his children, he would make it a point to spend time also with Rob. Jon would not allow Rob to come to the house. He claimed it was for security concerns. "All the more reason to hire me," Rob Allen would laugh. When Jon and Rob were not talking about security, they would talk about movies. Rob made it very clear that "the Industry" was where he envisioned himself.

What made this relationship an odd one was that Jon Emr, who was habitually paranoid anyway, did not trust Rob Allen at all. For one thing, Rob always wore jackets, even in the sweltering heat of Arizona in May and June. Jon figured that Rob was wearing a wire. Second, Jon would tell friends that on one trip to the gym with Rob, he found a tape recorder secreted in Rob's towel. Finally, there was the time that Jon and his girlfriend, Randa, went to see Rob at his apartment. When they got there, Rob was in the shower. Jon and Randa took the time to snoop around. According to Randa, they found the business card of Earl Rutledge, the attorney who was representing the Texans.*

Jon was absolutely sure that Rob Allen had been planted in his life. After all, Jon knew better than anybody else that he was no real producer, that nobody would ever have heard of him. So how did Rob Allen know to approach him at the Polo Grounds? How could he afford this expensive apartment? How was it that he had moved next door to Jon's girlfriend, Randa? What about the tape recorder? The business card.

Then there was another whopper. Brian had called Jon with some big news on Robert Allen. Brian said that most of Rob Allen's résumé was phony, that he had exaggerated or lied almost throughout. His name wasn't even Rob Allen. It had only very recently been changed to that. His birth name was Robert Suggs.

Most people who discover that they are being investigated by a man posing as their friend would tend to dump that person. But not Jon Emr. He believed in the dictum of "keeping your friends close and your enemies even closer," a line he'd heard in Francis Ford Coppola's *The Godfather*. That meant he was going to hire Rob Suggs. That, way he could keep an eye on him. Hell, maybe he could even convert him. If, indeed, he had been hired by one of Jon's enemies, all they were giving him was money. Jon Emr could offer Rob Suggs much more. He could offer him the damn Hollywood dream.

In midsummer, Suggs received a phone call from Jon Emr. He told Suggs that he was pretty impressed with his ability to find Kimo Mata. "Hell, I can't even find him and he's my good friend!" Jon laughed.

"Anybody can be found," Suggs said.

"Well, I need you to find somebody, all right," John said. "Truth is

---

*Even though Randa continually assured me that she and Jon did find the Rutledge business card, she refused to take a polygraph test.

I've been terrorized and my mom has had her life threatened by this one man. I need him stopped and I don't want my fingerprints on it. I want you to move to Los Angeles to handle it."

Jon explained that he would not finance Suggs's move. Right now he did not have the production funds to even pay Suggs a legitimate fee. It would nonetheless be worth it, Emr insisted. He could and would make Suggs a star, either behind or, better yet, in front of the camera.

Suggs was blown-away excited. Move to Hollywood! To the film industry. He could barely contain himself. Wait till he told all the doubters who had ever questioned his dreams. "Sure, Jon," Rob said. "Who is this guy?"

"His name is Scott Barnes. I'll fill you in when you get up here. Right now, were're filming 'The Bobby Garwood Story' for ABC. Scott has been starting problems. I'm going to need you to drive my mother to the set for her protection. How does that sound to you?"

"Great. Out of curiosity, Jon, why don't you just have Brian handle Scott Barnes?"

"You see, Rob," Jon said. "That's the fuckin' beauty of all of this. Brian is Scott's brother."

In early March, Jon Emr decided that he needed to finally meet Damian Chapa, the young actor whom Randy Pike had "discovered" to play the role of James Dean. Alan Hauge and Jon Emr had essentially inherited Damian Chapa from Randy. Hauge felt that Chapa indeed had an incredible talent, one which was only magnified after Chapa spent time with the revered acting coach Robert Easton.

Once, when Hauge asked Easton how Damian's lessons were coming, Easton made the stunning proclamation that Chapa was perhaps the best young actor in Hollywood. Easton had never seen such incredible memory and level of concentration. Back in 1987, Easton trained both Tom Cruise and Damian Chapa, Cruise in the morning for the Barry Levinson film *Rain Man* (which would go on to win the Academy Award for Best Picture) and Chapa for "James Dean: The Legend" in the afternoon. Easton said that what he taught Cruise on a Friday he would forget by Monday. Damian remembered everything 100 percent.

It was during the meeting that Jon Emr called for with Damian and his agent that everything collapsed, as Alan Hauge remembers it. Damian Chapa's agent declared that all the deal points made during the Pike-Esecson regime were now being thrown out the window. Damian was essentially asking for a half-million dollars, first-class air fare everywhere he went, and the basic perks that went with being a major movie star. The negotiations between Emr, certainly one of the world's great control freaks, and the agent were heated, with fists slamming on the conference table, veins near bursting, and curses being thrown around like Wiffle balls. None of this, of course, was unusual. This was Hollywood.

But then it happened. After an hour of bickering, the agent said, "You know, we don't need this picture anyway. I have a deal with Disney for Damian for five pictures."

Damian turned to his agent and said, "What five pictures?"

Jon stared at the agent and pointed at the door. "Why don't you get the hell outta here?" he growled, saliva dripping over his lips. "And take Damian with you."

That night, a relaxed Hauge had a heart-to-heart phone conversation with Damian, who was in a state of quiet shock. "Look, I have nothing against you. But the one thing that I have always said is that when an agent starts to play games, that's it. It has nothing to do with you. But if that is going to be your agent, then I'll have to find somebody else."*

The next phone call Alan made was to a young actor named Rob Keith, whom Alan had met when they had a huge publicity-seeking two-thousand-person casting call on stage four of GMT. *Entertainment Tonight* and a slew of other media were there to capture what was described as an "old-fashioned cattle call," looking for the perfect young man to play James Dean. Hauge noticed young Rob Keith right away. Hauge was blown away with his resemblance to Dean, in both appearance and attitude. Even though they had Damian Chapa locked up at the time, Hauge decided that Rob Keith would be the backup. Now, after the flare-up with Damian's agent, Alan told Rob Keith that he was bringing him on board.

Jon answered the phone as he sat in Alan Hauge's office. The voice on the other end asked for Alan Hauge.

---

*In my interview with him, Damian says he does not recall his agent engaging in such tactics. He does recall his payment demand being $250,000.

"Who is this?"

The person on the other end of the line announced that he was an attorney doing an investigation on a man named Jon Emr. He had been hired by the Randolph Hearst Foundation, which had been hit up for money for the Dean project.

"Hold on just a second," Jon said. He put his hand over the mouthpiece. "Hey, listen, Alan, would you mind stepping outta the office. I have a confidential call coming in here."

Alan nodded his head. "Fine. I have to leave anyway." Alan was quite eager to get someplace where he could work on his James Dean script without interruptions.

When Alan was out of the room Jon returned to the phone call. "Okay, this is Alan Hauge. What's up?"

"We've been doing a due diligence on your studio and on Jon Emr. Listen, we have found out some very, very ugly things about this Jon Emr."

"Great, tell me what it is."

"There are many things. Firstly, he has been telling investors that he actually owns GMT Studios. That was an easy check. It's simply not true."

"I know that. I own GMT. Go on."

And the lawyer did go on. And on and on. He went down through a litany of cons that Jon had allegedly pulled off in Houston, Dallas, Los Angeles, Calgary, Atlanta, New Orleans, and Cannes.

Jon was steaming. "Where did you get your information?"

"The FBI and some other reliable sources."

"RELIABLE SOURCES!" Jon screamed. "Like hell! I've checked out Jon myself. This is a man of honor! What the *fuck* do *you* know? Tell whatever investor you're doing this for to go and fuck himself. I stand by Jon Emr!"

Jon Emr hung up the phone and had a good chuckle. His "personal" call was over.

Jon Emr was very impressed. Robert Suggs, only a few days on the job, had made dramatic progression into slicing the heart out of Scott Barnes's life.

The coup de grâce was a fax that Suggs sent from GMT Studios to several of Barnes's friends, associates, and, most significant, Barnes's current employer, Children's Protective Services in Spokane:

To whom it May Concern:

I feel very sad that I have to make this letter available to you. However, I feel it is very important that you are aware of an individual named Scott Barnes. Scott Barnes has moved to Northeast Washington State in order to be closer to Haydon Lake, Idaho. Scott told me that he wanted to be closer to the Aryan nations compound to show his loyalty to Richard Butler and the neo-Nazi Party. Scott has boasted of having attended "coon hunts" where blacks are used as live prey. Once they are shot, they are then castrated and buried.

I urge you to be extremely cautious about any "freedom" you give him as he will use any and all opportunities to use government computers and records to further his cause; this would especially include recruitment of any young influential minds. His former wife (the first one, not the last one who bore his child) divorced him because of his obsession with the Neo-Nazi party.

Please understand that Scott will deny vehemently any knowledge or involvement with any of these groups. He will also deny having more than one ex-wife. This is because she hates him and will expose him if asked about the truth. I hope I am able to stop Scott from spreading his racist garbage any further. I beg of you to send a copy of this letter to the nearest police, sheriff and F.B.I. office. God Bless you.

A concerned Non-racist.

Jon was absolutely delighted with Suggs's smear handiwork. "I guess you have to fight fire with fire."

Suggs and Jon tabbed the letter they had faxed out as a "Scud missile," named after the weaponry used by the Iraqis during the Persian Gulf War. Jon and Rob agreed to send out many such "Scud missiles." Ironically, neither Jon nor Rob took into account the fact that the Scud was a failed weapon that had no strategic offensive capabilities whatsoever.

Alan Hauge was working late at the studio when his wife, Lanette, gave him a buzz. She had received a phone call in the house. A voice from the past, she said. It was Scott Barnes.

Alan called the Washington State phone number that had been left for him. Scott picked up the phone after a couple of rings and, with a chipper voice, asked Hauge how long it had been, what, ten years since they last spoke?

Actually it was just six years. Six years that had not gone by fast enough. In fact, the only reason he returned the call was that he knew that Scott would otherwise hound him into submission.

"What do you want?" Hauge asked.

Scott asked Hauge if he knew anything about a Mr. Jon Emr.

Alan was taken aback. "He's a client," Hauge answered. He knew that he had to be circumspect while still giving off the air of being respectful and accommodating to Scott Barnes. "He's a client of the studio and he rents office space. That's about all that I can tell you."

Scott told him that he and his boss at Children's Protective Services up in Spokane, Washington, had been receiving harassing faxes which had come from GMT Studios. They had clearly come courtesy of Jon Emr. Why, the rascal had even signed his name to them! And they were doozies, claiming that Scott was a member of the Ku Klux Klan! It had to stop. And that's all there was to it. Scott told Alan he could do his part by not allowing Jon Emr to use the studio fax machine to send out these horrible and, let's not forget, libelous messages. In fact, he said, it would be best if Emr was not even allowed on the premises.

"I don't believe that's the case, Scott," Hauge told him. "We have hundreds of faxes sent back and forth on our fax machine weekly by nearly one hundred or so clients who rent office and studio space here. Anyway, it's not my business to read the private business affairs transmitted by one of our clients."

"Okay," Scott said. "Never mind." If Hauge didn't mind that kind of "literature" going through the studio, then who was he to tell him otherwise. There was, Scott wanted to make clear, a more honorable reason for his phone call. He wanted to warn his old parish member Alan Hauge about this Jon Emr fellow. About what Alan was getting himself into.

Alan Hauge listened with amazement as Scott lectured him about his newest business associate. Scott told him that it was the modus operandi of Emr to prey on small production companies and take their money at the first available moment. "Just wait! It will happen to you!" Scott told Alan Hauge about Joel Douglas. He told him about Aubrey

Brothers and Bob Franks. He told him about Tim Johnson and his lovely mother, Jean, and how Jon almost destroyed their little nest egg at CSI Studios.

As Scott was speaking, Hauge was taking it all in. If anybody but Scott Barnes had given him this information, he might have been quite concerned by now, locked up the hatchets, called up the National Guard, instituted a code red! Alan certainly had his doubts about Jon Emr, though he never expressed them except to his wife. But because Scott was Scott and boy did he know Scott, Jon Emr's credibility had now, wasn't this ever an irony, emerged that much stronger.

Scott recommended to Hauge that he remove Jon Emr from the premises. He told him that Jon had an arrest record in Las Vegas for weapons possession and was considered dangerous.

Then came the whopper. Jon, Scott insisted, was involved in the production of porno films. And not just any porno films—gay porno films. Boys with boys, girls with girls! In fact, Scott said, Emr used his girlfriend Sue Fellows in the films. The films, by the way, were being made at GMT Studios.

"That's impossible," the born-again Hauge said. "I know for a fact that Jon has rented only office space and not studio space."

When they ended their conversation, Alan told Scott that he had no reason to remove Jon from GMT as long as he paid his rent.

Before Scott said his good-byes, he left Hauge with the names and the numbers of a few "witnesses" who could tell him about the real Jon.

The next evening, the GMT fax machine was flooded with newspaper articles about Jon Emr. A few days later, Hauge's pastor received a call in his church from an "unidentified FBI agent." The caller told the clergyman that Alan Hauge was involved in the production of porno films.

Hauge now knew that Scott Barnes, who had thankfully been out of his life for so many years, was back. In a letter to Jon Emr about the incident, Hauge wrote:

> . . . I am in hopes there is something that can be done by the court system to restrain this type of ruthless activity. It is damaging to my own reputation and my family. . . .

Jon assured Alan that Scott Barnes would in no way interfere with the making of the James Dean film. On the phone, Jon said, "Don't worry about Scott. Rob and I are going to deal with this fucker Barnes."

"Listen, I want to have nothing to do with this guy. I don't want to argue with him and I don't want to fight with him. I don't want him in my life. I don't want this guy ruining my organization."

"It's like I said, Alan. Rob and I are going to take very good care of Mr. Barnes."

A few weeks into his employment, Robert Suggs began to question Jon Emr about his payment. In all, Suggs's deal with Emr called for him to be paid $30,000, which had always been defined by the two men as "Get-By" money. That meant that Rob would accept the pittance of a fee until the James Dean film actually got under way. Then he would get the riches due him. In fact, Jon privately told Suggs that he would see to it that he became the film's associate producer.

This was a deal that Suggs was ready to live with. It was true that he had essentially run out of money. It was true that he and his girlfriend, Susan Lynn Calkins, were now living off her salary and tips as a cocktail waitress. It was true that almost all the money he did spend was through Susan's credit cards. It was true that Jon seemed to be more interested in playing cloak and dagger with Scott Barnes than he did with raising money for the movie. It was true that Jon had never let him come to his home. It was true that Jon could not really substantiate his claim to have produced hundreds and hundreds of television and theatrical movies. It was true that all of his friends were telling him that Jon Emr was a con artist. It was true that whenever Jon needed an errand run, Suggs would do it and then hardly ever be reimbursed.

All of this was true. But it didn't matter a damn. After all, didn't all movie moguls have to suffer when they were beginning their careers?

In late February, Jon Emr contacted Debbie Gasperini of Levi Strauss in San Francisco. His aim was to get from Levi's a letter of commitment to having a promotional tie-in to the film. Of course, the benefit of such a letter was prima facie. An endorsement from one of the world's biggest clothing companies could certainly be used as bait for investors. Companies like McDonald's and Coca-Cola had significant and financially successful associations with major films.

The only problem was that Jon Emr's contract with the Dean family did not give him the authority to negotiate with Levi Strauss or any other clothing firm for merchandising James Dean. In addition, Emr out and out lied in a subsequent communication he had with Levi Strauss on March 8:

> ... We are making a movie about making the movie ... which is designed for a cable release on HBO and scheduled to air the same week as the film. ...

Emr's back-and-forth communications (many of them through Federal Express, paid for by Robert Suggs) with Levi Strauss never netted him a contract with the company. What he did have was, as far as he was concerned, just as exciting—correspondence, tons of it, and all on Levi Strauss stationery.

Jon Emr was now at least able to demonstrate his relationship with Levi Strauss. He was able to convince at least one person. In a letter dated March 11, 1991, a company called Ramsa (which claimed to do a lot of business in Europe and South America) threw themselves right into the James Dean jeans fray:

> ... we are interested in purchasing through GMT international, jeans and jeans jackets that carry the name and likeness of James Dean. ... The manufacture must be reputable like Levi's or Lee and display their registered trademark as well. ...
>
> With the production of the motion picture several months away, we are still very much interested in purchasing ten million pair of jeans and approximately two million jeans jackets or more for Europe alone. ...

While Jon was in the business of tracking down "letters of commitment" that he could show to investors, he allowed Robert Suggs the dirty work of nailing "that sorry motherfucker" Scott Barnes. The one thing that neither Suggs not Emr expected, as they should have, was that Barnes would start to fight back.

On March 24, for example, an incorporated company called WE TIP, an organization that took calls from snitches who didn't want to call the police, received an "anonymous" call. The tipster wanted to turn in the team of Robert Suggs and Jon Emr. Here is how part of the report read:

> Robert Suggs, ex-husband of Carol Casey, and Roland Jon Emr are planning to kill Carol Casey sometime before April 8, 1991. Victim is a defense lawyer in the state of Washington. . . . Motive of the possible homicide is divorce wars. Robert and Roland plan to blow up Carol in her car. . . . Suspects are involved in credit card fraud and embezzlement. Robert Suggs is ex-military. He was a hit man for the Air Force.

On March 24, 1991, Scott Barnes arrived at his home in Spokane, Washington. He turned on his machine and found two messages. They were both from Robert Suggs, with whom he had never spoken. In both cases, Suggs was telling Scott that he was calling in order to discuss Jon Emr. He had gotten Scott's number from a page he had received that morning.

At 6:10 that same evening, the phone in Barnes's home rang. Scott smiled. He knew who it would be. "Hello."

"Hi, Scott," Robert Suggs said.

"Hello."

"You know who this is?"

"Who?"

"I thought that I'd give you a call and chat a little bit."

"Who is this?"

"You're pretty good. I like that. I have a lot of respect for you. How did you get my pager number?"

"Well, who's this?"

"This is Rob. You now who it is."

Scott laughed. "Oh, Rob Suggs."

"Yeah, you know who it is. You're an interesting character. How did you get my pager number?"

Scott knew that Robert was masking his stress with curiosity. "Well, when I was up at your house in Pinetop the other day, somebody there gave it to me."

Robert made the decision not to tell Scott that he had no goddamn idea where Pinetop was, had never been there, and certainly owned no land there.

"You really think Jon Emr is a producer, huh?" Scott asked his adversary.

"At first I really wasn't sure," he admitted. "I have to tell you, I was kind of hoping that he was for real because that would be a good deal. Now, with the things that are going on, that seems to be the case."

"You obviously don't know much about him, do you? Have you read any stories about him?"

"Yeah. Some newspaper articles and stuff like that."

Scott then bluffed Robert, telling him that NBC was planning to do a special report on Jon Emr and that many of Rob's family and friends had been interviewed for it. Rob wasn't sufficiently impressed, so Scott moved on to another topic. "The little alien nation fax that you tried to fax to people really backfired. Big time."

"I, I don't understand."

"That little alien nation fax you tried to fax to a few people. Everybody got a kick out of what a big mistake you made."

"You know what? I really don't know anything about that, I know about some sort of document. I don't know if it was faxed or not."

Scott cut off the topic for the moment. As the conversation lumbered on, Scott told Suggs more about Allen's life. Suggs tried to keep in check the surprise he felt when he realized what an extensive job Barnes had done in researching him. "Well, a lot of your information is good," he conceded to Barnes. "Some of it's very accurate. I have to say I'm impressed. Very impressed." There was a pause. "What is it you think I should do? Just disappear from this whole thing?"

Barnes laughed. "I don't care what you do. All I know is I received a stack of paperwork that was sent to me by the authorities in Washington, Arizona, and California. The stack is getting thicker and thicker and thicker. All I can say is that hate-crime fax you and Jon sent is very serious. You will eventually find that out."

The two men talked for a while about the book *Bohica* and its veracity. Rob told Scott that he found it to be a quality book. But Scott wanted to get back on the topic of Jon Emr. "Just tell me something. Jon has promised you a major part in probably one of his major movies?"

"Uh-huh."

"And you know how many people he has done that to? He did that to my brother. He did that to my brother Brian. Now the FBI wants Brian to work undercover to continue to get stuff on Jon and you."

Brian works for me, Rob thought. I know Brian. There was no way he was working undercover for the feds. "I think you know this about me already. I haven't intentionally tried to hurt anybody."

"That's not what I was told. Seriously, Rob." Scott's voice was now consoling. "I'm telling you without judging you."

"By who, though? Who told you I was out to hurt anybody?"

"I've got a list of people here, mostly female, that you have threatened, harassed, that you have gotten into their credit files without authorization."

"Can you give me an example? Because I don't know of any."

Scott's answer was predictable. "I can, but I'm not going to."

Scott then returned to the subject of the KKK letter. "We made sure that we gave a copy to the FBI. I've given one to the sheriff. We've given one to the police. As a matter of fact, the police were just asking me the other day if I knew your driver's license number. I said, 'Well, I've got his last known California driver's license number. They're checking that out. Who knows?'"

Rob smiled to himself. He did not have a California driver's license. "Look, I don't know, man. I don't know. What about Alan Hauge?"

Scott snickered. "You never see Alan's name in Hollywood or major movies or even any minor movies."

"Do you think Alan knows anything about Jon, these things that you are telling me?"

"He must know a lot because he called me two weeks ago and asked me a bunch of stuff on Jon. It's just too bad."

"Yeah."

"Jon has a lot of charisma. He's a charmer. But if you look at his whole background you'll see that he hasn't worked a day in his life."

"Well, he seems to know a lot about production work."

Scott had a ready answer. "He got it from his brother."

"It's been interesting," Suggs said, apparently ready to terminate the conversation. "I have to reinforce what I said. I think that you are a pretty sharp character. I can't say that I know what my next move is going to be."

"Well, Rob, don't take this as a personal slap in the face. I feel sorry for you that you would get involved with Jon without thoroughly checking him out. I have spoken with your father. He feels sorry for you. By the way, my man is going to start tracking down all members of your family and former high school friends and people that may have known you from Spokane. I mean, there's a major investigation on you."

Rob was unfazed. "Well, as I said, I'm sure they can investigate all they want to. But most of it is just a witch hunt. I have not done anything illegal."

"Hmmm." Rob could hear Scott ruffling through some papers. "Do the Hermosa Beach police have a beef with you?"

"Not that I know of."

"I'm just curious. They just did some inquiries on you and I just wondered if they have a beef with you."

Then Scott, yet again, reverted to the KKK letter. "The real KKK has asked questions about you. Your name, address, and phone number has been given to the KKK. They want to know who these guys Suggs and Emr are, passing around this bogus letter. They were very upset. They think that it is sad and sick."

"You know, if Jon has been this way for a long time, how come nothing has happened to him criminally?"

Scott dropped a bombshell. "He's been arrested."

"For what? Possession of a weapon?"

"No, no. He has other arrests for fraud, embezzlement, theft. He was arrested under a pseudonym."

"No convictions?"

"I don't know. Look, some of the stuff that he does is on the borderline of criminality."

"So what's going to happen with this [James Dean project]? Is Jon just going to take off with some money?"

"He has in the past."

Then Scott came back to the Klan letter. "I know that this KKK letter has gotten the attention of several agencies and they don't take it lightly and of course, nor do I."

"Sure. Oh, yeah. I don't blame you."

"And nor does the KKK."

"Right. Don't blame you."

"I think that they are probably more upset with Jon than anybody. They asked who you were and I said I'd never even spoken to the guy. But I offered them your picture and address and number. But they had all that." There was a lull in the conversation. "Does Jon know that you are speaking to me?"

"Not at this minute. No."

"It's too bad he can't settle down and do something because he has the potential of making some positive changes."

"You know, it's ironic that you say that because he says the same thing about you. Not to score any points for him, but deep down he respects you."

"Well, I help people. I have been all around the world a half a dozen times after I got out of the military. I have been written about in several books."

"Right. Well. It's been very enlightening, Scott. I'm not quite sure what to even say to you. I am sure that someday our paths will cross."

"You can count on it. Tell Jon I said hi."

"Oh I will."

"Tell him not to send any more faxes."

"I don't blame you, man. I don't blame you. I appreciate your candor."

"Good luck in Jon's big movie."

"Okay."

"And if Jon wants to make a movie on my book, tell him to give me a call."

A half day later, the phone rang in Scott Barnes's home.

"Well—you've reached me, but I'm not in. Please leave your name and number and as soon as I get in, I'll give you a call right back. Thank you very much and you have a nice day. Thank you."

The customary beep and then the message left by Robert Suggs. "Hi, Scott. You know who this is. You're just not as clever as I thought. You know, in less than twelve hours, I found out how you got all your information. Most of it, unfortunately, was from [my ex-wife] Carol and family. Uh, not much work on your part to get that information and combined with a few other simple little private-eye moves. I'm sorry, Scott, but you're a psychopath, buddy. You're a pathological liar and, uh, it's the beginning of the end for you, bud. Your reign of terror is coming back on you and it's not going to be long before it's all over. I'm really disappointed in you, man, that you. . . . I thought you really pulled something off here, but it wasn't anything at all. Your time is limited, pal. You better quit while you are very far behind before you get any deeper because, believe me, there's things coming at you that you have no idea how to deal with them. You've met your match this time, buddy. Take it easy."

A little while later, Scott picked up his line and there was Robert Suggs, who began speaking right away. "What I said about you is true," Suggs confessed. "You are pretty sharp. Unfortunately, we're in a pretty adversarial position, which kind of puts me in a spot here. This is kind of like Spy Versus Spy in *Mad* magazine. Unfortunately for you, I know your M.O. I know your psychological welfare. . . . I'm going to make sure that I work hard so that in the end, you get what you deserve. I don't know what happened to you when you were a child, but you really went over the deep end somewhere."

Scott began to giggle, "Hee-hee-hee."

"You can laugh. I'm laughing too. I think this whole thing is very amusing. Man, you let your mouth run before your brain can catch up. I am asking you not to persist because then I will be forced into a position where I must follow through on things. Believe me, neither of us wants that. You have my résumé. You see my background."

"Most of it's phony. Hee-hee-hee."

"No, it's not."

"Okay. Hee-hee-hee."

"I got your number, pal. I can do anything I want."

"Well, tough guy, why don't you?"

"No, no, no, no. I'm not trying to be a tough guy, Scott."

This was the first venom coming from Scott. "You are just as much of a puss as Jon is."

"Oh. Is that right?"

"Yeah. That's right."

"It's funny that you should say that, because you now what, Scott? You know what? What you are saying only reinforces what I believe. I've got your number. Jon already told me that you would start to rage like this, like a little baby, and start calling me names and things like that. Everything that Jon said about you is exactly true and that's—"

"I'm glad you work for him."

"You know, last year, I was up on the set protecting Renee."

"Protecting?"

"Wondering if you were going to show up or not," Suggs said. "Look, we're adversaries but we can still talk like human beings. It's like MacArthur talking to one of the Japanese generals. Any time you need to talk to me, feel free to give me a page."

"Okay."

"Remember, remember, Scott. One thing. This is not a threat because I do not threaten people. Please cease from what you are doing because if you continue you'll be forcing me to do things I don't want to do and then I will have to live with myself."

"I would very much like you to deal with me."

"Oh, I will. I will. The problem is that I know how I am going to and you do not. That doesn't mean that I am going to cut your tongue out, although there is a lot of people that would like to."

"You don't scare me at all."

"For every stone that you throw I am going to throw five your way."

"I've been waiting for this for some time."

"Your psychological warfare is getting old. If you use the same war plan time after time, eventually it's going to come back."

"Okay."

"I'll see you in the darkness."

The next day, Suggs delivered a tape recording of his conversations with Scott to Jon Emr, who had them transcribed. He delivered a copy of the transcription to Hauge. Alan could not understand just what the hell Jon was doing. On the one hand, Jon had been promised a huge sum of money to get "James Dean: The Legend" financed. On the other, he was spending a great deal of energy on trying to bring down Scott Barnes.

THE TRAIL OF THE ASSASSIN: SIX

Suggsy and Benny arrived in Phoenix at about 3:30 in the afternoon. For the entire ride, Suggsy had tried to justify what he saw as an absolutely righteous homicide. As far as he was concerned, Jon Emr had destroyed him. Jon had promised him a career in the film industry and could not deliver. Worse yet, Emr damn well knew that he would never deliver, knew that it was all a charade, knew that the only one who would be smiling at the end was Jon Emr himself.

If there was one thing that Suggsy hated, it was to be conned himself. How could he have been so stupid? By now, he had read several articles and an NBC News transcript which outlined the fact that Jon had nailed several people before him. Of course, most of them had been richer and had lost more cash. What had he lost? At least $800 of his own cash and then there was the $30,000 that Emr had promised him once the production on the James Dean film actually began.

Yes, Suggsy said, Jon Emr had it coming to him. Suggsy was not only going to do this for himself, it was for every chump that had lost it all gambling on the roulette table that was Hollywood.

When they actually entered the city limits, nervousness seemed to start flowing through Suggsy. They simply drove around for a while. At one point, Suggsy pointed to a house and said that Jon Emr had promised to buy it for him once the James Dean film became fully funded. Later, they stopped at a record shop so that Suggsy could pick up a tape of a song that he said reminded him of Susan.

At about dusk, Suggsy drove the car to the Fanfol Estates in Paradise Valley. Suggsy took a right on a side street and parked the car in front of the house that was at the end of the cul-de-sac. Suggsy took off his sunglasses. "This is it, Benny. This is the old man's house."

"Jesus, Suggsy. You told me I could wait at the motel."

Suggsy gently put his hands on Benny's left knee. "I want you to relax. It's going to be fine."

What could Benny say? He nodded his head and watched Suggsy as he climbed out of the car and walked up the pathway and knocked on the front door. As Benny saw the door opening, he had to wonder whether or not Suggsy was going to blow the old man away right then and there, right in front of him. One thing Benny knew was that Suggsy had not yet done his search of the perimeter, nor had he cut the power and telephone lines.

After a few seconds, the door closed. Suggsy came back to the car. As he buckled himself in, Benny asked him what had happened.

"The old man says that the boys are in California."

"What does that mean?"

"I guess it means that we have to go back to Los Angeles."

Suggsy and Benny did not go back to Los Angeles that night. Instead they went to get a quick bite to eat and then returned to Arthur Emr's house. Actually, Suggsy pulled the car over about twenty yards from the home and told Benny to wait in the car. "I'm going to go and check the perimeter," he announced.

It was dark, but Benny could make out Suggsy's figure as he trotted in a circle around the home and property. When he returned he told Benny that everything looked fine. "The electrical box looked pretty simple," he said to Benny, who he knew had some experience as a handyman. "If I have any problems with it, I suppose that I can just ask you."

"Sure, Suggsy."

"Let's go to the movies."

After Benny and Suggsy walked out of Arnold Schwarzenegger's *Terminator 2*, they drove to a Motel Six that was near the corner of Camelback and Scottsdale, the two main streets in town. It was all that he could afford, having lost most of his money in Vegas and Laughlin. They took one of the rooms with the double beds. It had a Gideon Bible and an enclosed shower and little, teeny paper-wrapped soaps. The bedcovers had an ugly floral design. Even though it was dark, they could tell that the pool was filled with algae. On the door you were warned to dead-bolt the door "For Your Protection." It was only two miles away from Emr and, just as important, a few blocks away from the theater.

They prepaid for one night.

After they were settled, Suggsy announced that he was going out to get a newspaper.

This is it, Benny thought to himself. In a way he was relieved. Suggsy had finally gotten around to doing what he had set out for. He was going to do the old man. The good part was that Suggsy was keeping his word. He was keeping Benny the hell out of it.

Ten minutes after he left to get his newspaper, Suggsy returned to the room. He sat on the bed and opened the paper to the comics. As he read them he quietly said, "Tomorrow I'm going to kill Arthur Emr." He lifted his head and cocked it toward Benny. He smiled and said softly, "You won't be a part of it."

When Benny woke up the next morning, Suggsy was already showered and dressed and on the phone. From what Benny could make out he was trying to obtain the California address of Jon Emr. At first Benny found it curious that after all this time Suggsy had no idea where his former boss lived. Then he remembered that Jon liked to keep his living quarters hush-hush for security reasons.

After leaving the motel, the two men drove to a local Firestone Tire dealer. After a few minutes examining the car, the serviceman told Suggsy that he needed new brakes and rotors. Suggsy and Benny ate at a coffee shop across the street while the car was being repaired.

When they were ready to leave, Suggsy told Benny that he wanted him to drive. Without saying a word, Benny got behind the wheel. As they drove off, Benny looked over at the passenger side and saw that his friend had a folded newspaper in his lap. He could make out the .22 Ruger with silencer attachment inside the fold.

Benny knew exactly what was going to happen. "Look, Suggsy, let's go to the motel. Just drop me there."

Suggsy stared blankly ahead, his voice flat. "No, you won't be a part of it. Just drive me to the old man's house."

Benny wanted to cry. "Rob, I—"

"Just drive me halfway down their street."

As he drove him to the street where Art Emr lived, Benny was blubbering. "Jesus, Jesus, Jesus, Jesus, Jesus, Jesus."

Suggsy didn't say a word, but he was starting to clench the Ruger tighter. When they got to the street, Suggsy told Benny to take off and return in fifteen minutes.

Benny drove down to a nearby strip mall and then turned the car around. He got back in twelve minutes. As he drove down the street, Suggsy was walking toward him. He saw neither the newspaper nor the gun. Benny figured that Suggsy had shoved the gun in his waistband at the small of his back.

Suggsy walked up to Benny's window, which was rolled down. "I'll drive."

Benny was not one to argue. He jumped out of the car and ran to the passenger side, just about ripped the door open, and then jumped in. He looked Suggsy over. Suggsy was sweating and clearly nervous. One thing that Benny found interesting was that there was no blood on him. "Here is what we are going to do," Suggsy said. "We're going back to the motel. I'm going to take another shower. Then we go back to California."

Benny put his head back on the headrest. "That's fine by me."

Neither man said a word as they drove to the Motel Six. When they got to their room, Suggsy instructed Benny to get all their bags into the car while he cleaned off.

When Suggsy came down after fifteen minutes he was wearing light-colored jeans, a light shirt, and tennis shoes. He left the key at the front desk without actually going through the motions of checking out.

Before actually hitting the freeway, Suggsy took Benny by the apartment where he had stayed with Susan. Then he gave Benny a tour of the area "where the rich motherfuckers" lived.

And then they headed home.

After just a few minutes of doing eighty miles an hour on Route 10, a few agonizing minutes in which Suggsy's silence was interrupted only by a cough, Benny simply could stand it no longer. "What happened in there, man?"

Suggsy told the story simply and softly, as if he were describing what he'd had for dinner the night before. He never turned his head even once to face his best friend, his accomplice. "I knocked on the door and the old man answered. I asked him if I could have Jon's address in California because I wanted to go and visit the boys. He said sure. No problem. I walked in and closed the door behind me. We went into the bedroom. He wrote down the address and gave it to me. Then I grabbed him and I threw him into the closet. I actually kind of shoved him. Well, actually, I told him to walk into the closet backwards. That's what he did. When he got into the closet I shot him in the head."

Benny stared out the window, his thumb and index finger cradling his chin. "You actually did this."

Suggsy let out a small giggle. "You know, I don't even know how many times I shot him. But it was a lot. I shot him a fucking lot. Even when he was dead, I shot him some more. I had to make sure."

"Jesus Christ, Rob."

"The old man didn't put up any resistance." Then Suggsy let out a loud whoop and pumped his arm. "Fuck with me, uh?"

"What are you going to do now?"

"I'm going to go find those boys. I'll drop you off at home. But after I do those little faggots, I'll fill you in."

"Okay," Benny said quietly. He hoped that Suggsy was being

straight with him, that this was the end of his involvement in the crime spree.

"Now, listen. The police are going to come to you. You just keep your mouth shut. If you want to talk to a lawyer, that's fine."

Now, all of a sudden, Benny was insulted. "I'm your best friend, man!"

"That doesn't matter. The cops are good. That's why I didn't tell you exactly where Susan was buried. If they find her and take her away, then we'll be separated forever. Do you understand?"

"Sure."

"Now I need to stop somewhere and get a military crew cut."

Late that afternoon, Suggsy dropped Benny at home. He let him out a few blocks away because he didn't want Jenny to see him.

Before he left Suggsy, Benny went over to the passenger-side window and poked his head in so that he and Suggsy were just about nose to nose. "God bless you, man."

The James Dean Con:
April–May 1991

Dad, I said it was a matter of honor, remember? They called me chicken. You know, chicken? I had to go because if I didn't I'd never be able to face those kids again. I got in one of those cars, and Buzz, that—Buzz, one of those kids—he got in the other car, and we had to drive fast and then jump, see, before the car came to the end of the bluff, and I got out okay, but Buzz didn't and got killed.
—James Dean in *Rebel Without a Cause*

One day, Jon Emr was approached by a friend of his named Bill Schwartz with the news that a business acquaintance of his, a Santa Monica–based businessman named Nicholas Karino, was interested in putting some money into the Dean film.

Jon Emr and Alan Hauge met Nicholas Karino at GMT Studios in late March. Nicholas brought with him a respected entertainment attorney. Karino had a very nonthreatening presence. He was slight, with gray hair and a red-flushed face. As far as Alan could tell, he was fifty-something years old. Alan and Jon found Karino to be flamboyant. They were a little suspect of his cash. Jon told Alan that he was suspicious, from the way that Karino carried himself, that he might be connected to the Mafia.

Karino claimed to own an alcoholic-beverage company that imported liquors that were then supplied to some of the posh restaurants in Beverly Hills. Indeed, Karino often boasted about his connections to the Hollywood elite.

Karino said that he was not going to put his own money into the project. He was, after all, a businessman who understood the necessity of employing OPM, Other People's Money. Karino claimed that he had a "guy" at Metro-Goldwyn-Mayer who would put up the money for the video rights to "James Dean: the Legend." That would be enough to fund the entire production. Nicholas claimed his "guy" was his neighbor at his beach house in Malibu and that they had often talked about putting together a movie deal.

On April 3, 1991, Nicholas Karino and Bill Schwartz went to GMT Studios to meet with Jon and Renee Emr and Alan Hauge. Though they had now met a few times, it would be this meeting that would set the tone for the rest of their relationship. Indeed, a version of what happened at that meeting and the events that followed it was put into memo form and presented to the Culver City police some two months later by Alan Hauge, Renee Emr, and Jon.

During this meeting, according to the memo, Karino asked if he could view a videotape of the television film about Bobby Garwood that Jon Emr claimed to have made. Jon wouldn't screen it, explaining that the film had not yet aired. However, Jon did agree to play a snippet of the film: a scene in which Martin Sheen, Ralph Macchio, and an actor named Noah Black (playing a prisoner) make a pact to tell the American people about the horror of their captivity.

At this point, again according to the memo, Karino begged to see the rest of the film and even offered to take it home and return it immediately. Jon claimed that that would be a violation of his agreement with ABC.

Jon then pulled the tape out of the machine and innocently set it on the conference table. Also on the table were several other documents and another tape, this one of an open casting call that Alan Hauge held to find a Dean look-alike.

At one point, Jon Emr left the room to take a phone call. Sometime after the meeting was over, Renee, it is claimed in the memo, returned to the conference room to retrieve the tape of the Garwood film. She only found one videotape—that of the James Dean cattle calls. At that point, Renee phoned Karino, leaving a message on his machine to get back to her immediately.

The following day Karino indeed did call. He apologized for having taken the wrong tape. He had apparently intended to borrow the audition tape. He assured Renee that he had not watched the program and would not. He also agreed to return the tape.

If the contents of the memo are to be believed, Karino never returned the tape. Each time he met with the Emrs, Karino apologized for forgetting to bring it with him.

It was because of this event, the memo would have us believe, that both the Emrs and Hauge concluded they could not enter into a business relationship with Karino. Bill Schwartz, Emr's friend who had introduced Jon to Karino, felt that it was his responsibility to mend the badly strained relationship that had developed here. He phoned Alan Hauge, whom he respected and found both reasonable and rational. He told Hauge that Nicholas Karino would soon be going back to Ohio for a trip to visit family and he wanted to stop off in Indiana and meet with Mark Roesler and Marcus Winslow. "He would like to have you travel with him," Bill told Alan.

Hauge was stunned. "Schwartz, why would I want to do that? Anytime that I introduce somebody to The Family they try and steal the rights from me. They want to buy me out. There is always some sort of crap. Why do I want to leave myself open to that. The answer is no."

"Come on, Alan, we'll fly you first class, put you in a great hotel, pay all your expenses."

"I'm just not interested, Bill."

After the conversation, Hauge told Jon Emr that Nicholas Karino wanted him to go to Indiana to meet the Dean family.

"What did you tell 'em?" Jon asked.

"I told them I wouldn't."

That night, Bill Schwartz called Alan on his private line at home. He wanted to know if they could meet. Alan agreed.

The first meeting took place at the new Loews Hotel in Santa Monica. Schwartz and Karino were already sitting on the pool patio when Alan arrived. Schwartz told Hauge that they wanted to buy Jon Emr out of the project. "What do you think Jon's price would be? We want to fund the film but we don't want him in it."

"Why not?"

"We've done our investigating on Jon. We checked him out."

"What did you find out?"

"I'd rather not say. But we know a lot of stuff. We don't want to proceed unless we can buy him out."

"What are you talking to me for?"

"We want you in the project."

"Well, I think that you should discuss this with Jon."

The next day, Hauge had another meeting, this time just with Schwartz. It took place at the Rose Café in Santa Monica. Hauge approached the get-together with cynicism. At this point, he simply trusted nobody. As far as he was concerned, there was just rancid garbage going on everywhere.

Again, the question of the moment was, How much would it take to kick Jon off the project?

And again, Alan wanted to know why they did not speak directly with Jon.

"Because he's unreasonable," Schwartz said.

"So you want me to go to him and negotiate your deal?"

"Right."

"I see. So, you kick Jon out. Now you have what Jon has. What are you going to do with me?" Alan knew that if MGM was involved they would not want him in on the project. They'd want to bring in their own director. "When I was a kid, I remember listening to John F. Kennedy. He said, those who foolishly seek power by riding on the back of the tiger shall someday end up riding inside. I could align myself with you, Bill. But when are you going to cut me off?"

Schwartz smiled. "Just think about it, Alan."

Hauge got up to leave. "You deal with Jon."

Hauge told Jon that Nicholas Karino and Bill Schwartz wanted to buy him out. He said that they were throwing around some impressive figures and that he just might want to consider it. Hauge figured that Jon might be able to get as much as a million dollars. But, instead of leaping for joy, Jon went berserk, screaming at the top of his lungs and throwing paper across the room. He promised Alan that nothing— nothing at all—was going to drive him away from the film.

Jon called Nicholas Karino and demanded a meeting to clear the air of all the bullshit. Jon asked that the meeting be held at Karino's hangout, Vito's, probably so that Karino would be obligated to pick up the tab. Emr told Suggs that he wanted him to come along. What follows is a statement from Robert Suggs, written two days later, of exactly what he says happened:

STATEMENT OF ROBERT SUGGS

On May 20, 1991, I was requested by Jon Emr to attend a meeting at Vito's on Ocean Park Drive in Santa Monica. Jon asked that I remain anonymous at the bar. I was to be present at the restaurant in a "bodyguard" capacity. Jon Emr advised me the meeting was to begin at 7:00

P.M. When I arrived, Jon Emr was already standing at the bar with 3 or 4 men that I learned later were employees of the restaurant. After approximately 20 minutes, they went into another room in the back. I sat at the bar and drank one Perrier water and two Cokes. I spoke to the bartender for about 45 minutes when I was approached by Jon Emr and requested to join him in the back.

At this time, my cover was still maintained as Jon asked me to "notarize" a document that was signed by the people who were present, Jon Emr and Nicholas Karino. I jokingly said, "I'll have to see both of your driver's licenses so I know that both of you are who you say you are." I made a joke about them buying me dinner and then walked back to the bar.

Approximately fifty minutes later, Jon came out to the bar and called out my name. I turned around to see him motioning me back. Jon then introduced me to Nicholas Karino. I continued to maintain my cover, but Jon said, "It's okay. It's okay." Jon asked me to return to the bar and said he would be done in five minutes.

I returned to the bar for about five minutes when I heard Jon Emr yelling something like, "You're not going to get anything from me with threats." Jon then came storming towards the front door with Nicholas Karino following him. Nicholas was very obviously trying to calm Jon down and get back to business.

I followed Jon and Nicholas out of the restaurant onto the sidewalk. Jon continued to scream and yell at a calm and cool Nicholas Karino, who was still trying to calm Jon down. Nicholas was apparently ready to grab Jon's arm in an attempt to keep him from leaving. Although at the time I started to get between them, I did not take the gesture as a threat to Jon. At the same time I got between them, Jon summoned me to intervene. As Jon left, I apologized to Nicholas and told him that Jon has a bad temper.

Nicholas and I talked for about two minutes when Jon pulled his car around to the front of the restaurant. Jon got out of the car with unpredictable and unreadable intentions. At this time, I really wasn't sure whom I would have to protect from whom. As Jon walked up, he smiled and stuck his hand out as a gesture of peace. The two shook hands and we all walked back into the restaurant.

I sat at a different table about ten feet from them. They spoke for about one minute when I began to feel the tension in the air. I started interjecting words into the conversation in an effort to mediate. I then moved to their table and it became a three-way conversation. The conversation went for another couple of hours. At times, it was very heated on Jon's part. On a couple of occasions, I had to take both of them away from the other. Most of the conversations were instructions to Nicholas on how to "handle" Jon without making him explode in rage. My talks with Jon were why we needed Nicholas to make this movie.

After much tensional conversation, it was very obvious Nicholas wanted to invest in the James Dean film but he felt Jon had mishandled the film to this point. Nicholas wanted to take control of the project in a manner that he felt his investment would be safe. He told Jon that he did not care about credits and that Jon could have full credits for the production.

Nicholas only wanted to protect his investment. Jon seemed to take this as a complete takeover of the project. Jon seemed to be waiting for an opportunity to jump down Nicholas's throat. At one point, it was mutually agreed that since Jon would be out of town on personal business, I would meet with Nicholas and pick up a check for $200,000 on May 23, 1991. These funds would be an initial payment in order to continue production.

Nicholas was aware that Jon had ABSOLUTELY NO MONEY! He said, "Jon doesn't have enough money to pay for this dinner, does he?" I shook my head in a "that's right" sort of manner with shame on my face.

Nicholas told me that he knows Jon has the best of intentions, but that Jon is buried in half-truths and lies to everyone associated with the "Dean" project. He knows Jon has screwed it up so bad that Jon needs Nicholas's financial help to make it work. He feels that by the slim chance that Jon is able to finance the film, he will be too broke to make it that far; I agreed with him.

Nicholas also says he feels that because Jon and Alan Hauge are essentially nobodies in the film industry they have very little clout. They also cannot convince potential investors that their millions of dollars are safe with only Jon Emr running the show.

At the end of the evening around 11:00 P.M. it seemed as though everything was going to go well. I felt I had convinced Jon that even though he had to "bend" a little for Nicholas, it was still the wise choice since we were all broke.

As we were leaving, Jon was happy and smiling. We were literally starting to walk out the door. Nicholas said in a joking manner, but still somewhat serious, that he would like to pick who plays the part of "Christy" in the "Dean" film. At this moment, Jon went into a rage that I have never seen in a restaurant in my life. He started screaming and yelling at Nicholas, saying things that were not relevant to this discussion. Jon was completely unraveling the entire deal. I stepped in front of

Jon in an effort to calm him down. He started screaming at me saying, "You work for me, get out of the way."

I backed off and continued to listen for what seemed to be several minutes to Jon scream like an idiot and ruin the deal with Nicholas . . . at least for the time being.

I swear that the above statement is true and correct to the best of my knowledge.

As Jon was driving home that night after the brouhaha, he decided to go back to Vito's and confront Nicholas Karino one last time. Jon turned the car around. But as he drove past the restaurant, he saw Nicholas Karino at a table, conferring with Jon's own bodyguard, Robert Suggs. Steaming, Jon turned his Lincoln around one more time and headed for his home, a seedy little apartment in Torrance.

The next morning, Robert Suggs demanded a meeting with Renee Emr. The old lady and the bodyguard got together in the conference room at GMT Studios.

Rob explained his situation to her. He was flat broke and Jon owed him money. He was about to be evicted from his apartment and his relationship with his girl, Susan, was at its end. It seemed that Jon, who had been going nowhere with funding the Dean project, had made a terrible, terrible business decision that would affect them all.

Suggs admitted that he had spent nearly two hours with Nicholas Karino after the meeting with Jon had ended. He said that he was not working for Karino, but that he had promised to try to make the Emrs see the light. All the while, Renee shook her head and stood by her son.

At one point, Suggs became so loud and heated that Jon came into the conference room. Suggs looked him up and down, shook his head, and then gave Renee a kiss on the forehead. "I'm sorry, Granny," he said. Then he left the room and the studios.

It was time for Robert Suggs to move out of his apartment.

Why was Jon Emr so dismissive of Nicholas Karino? At first, it makes very little sense. It would certainly be part of the Emr modus operandi to take Karino's money and run, again having made money off doing no creative work at all. The reason? The theories abound. One, Jon's ego was so ferocious that he could not stand somebody bullying his way through his turf. Two, he wanted, finally, to be a legitimate player in Hollywood and this represented his big break. He was not going to give up control of the Dean project. Three, he was holding out for more money.

However, none of these is actually reasonable. In fact, the real reason that Jon turned down Nicholas Karino and seemingly acquired the wrath of Robert Suggs was very simple: he knew a con artist when he saw one. He knew that Nicholas Karino did not have the cash that he was offering. He had no idea what Nicholas Karino's real motives were and he did not care. The guy was a fraud and there was not even a dime to be made off him.

There was one other thing. It seemed that Jon was nurturing a brand-new investor—a real deal this time, a man who was ready to deposit $1.2 million into the American Icon Corporation. Sure, that was just a tiny fraction of what the film would cost but, hell, this was $1 million that would go directly to Jon. Jon had never told Robert Suggs about this investor. In fact, it seemed he was trying to keep this elephant as quiet as possible.

LETTER FROM ROBERT SUGGS TO JON EMR
JUNE 1, 1991

Due to the reasons outlined in this letter, I am permanently and completely severing all ties with you. I have stuck with you throughout this "roller-coaster" event up to, and including my complete financial downfall. When we were in your office at the end of January, you promised me "get by" money in the amount of $30,000. To date, I have received $10,000 of it. I have invested several thousand dollars of that in my "costs" alone in conducting various "deeds" for you. Not to mention the hundreds of hours put in on top of that.

I have put myself on the line for you and gave my word to various people that they would be paid for their services to help you. One of these "favors" was the printing of over $1500.00 worth of screenplays and financial packages to bail you out because you were broke long ago.

My family and I have been terrorized by YOUR enemy Scott Barnes. How many people do YOU know that would handle that and keep on going??? Not many I would venture to say. When I gave you my Federal Express account number, it was NOT a "carte blanche" to run up an $800.00 bill over a six week period!

[It is] very apparent that you are convinced that someone out there is simply going to drop $40,000,000 in the mail to you because you're JON EMR. It doesn't appear this is going to occur. . . . I will not go as far as to say that all of your enemies are correct in their accusations towards you. . . . You have little chance of succeeding with this project without lawsuits flying everywhere.

If you would have stopped yelling at Nicholas Karino long enough for him to finish a sentence, you would have found out the following:

When he told you that you're not going to make the film without him, you were reacting like a five year old before he had a chance to defend himself. The reason he said this is because you were too broke to even pay for dinner. . . . The so-called threats you heard were no more than mere observations on Nicholas's part. [By speaking with Hauge] he was the only one smart enough to ask questions of somebody else but you. But you did not like this did you? Noooo!!!! When he found out how you were handling this project, he knew he had to have more control over HIS money.

My association with you has caused us more grief than you would ever accept in your adolescent mind.

You see, I do understand that Alan and Lanette Hauge have not been privy to our conversations. Therefore, they are unaware of certain conversations and "activities" that have occurred without their knowledge. If all the people concerned were aware of everything they should be aware of, then this project would have crumbled long ago. I feel it will STILL crumble. I do not see how it cannot. You are broke! Your relatives, I am sure, are running out of money to give you.

Unfortunately for the memory of James Dean and everyone interested, this masterpiece film may never get its due. Please put your colossal ego and your childish temper in your pocket. After you are able to do this, turn the project over to someone else.

The next day, Renee faxed a "cease and desist" letter to Suggs. She forbade him to communicate with anybody regarding the Dean project other than her and the attorney Doug Smithers. In the letter she claimed she was taking this hostile approach because of what she perceived as Suggs' relationship with Nicholas Karino, a man who she claimed had threatened Jon.

On Sunday, June 2, 1991, all through the day and night, Jon Emr got calls in his home from men and women asking about a "gay porno" flick that they heard Jon was casting. When he arrived at the studio the next day, the fax machine was flooded with shots of both clothed and naked men and women and letters requesting a shot at the new Jon Emr X-rated movie. Down in the lobby, various effeminate men and drag queens had been waiting to audition for Jon.

What had happened? Something bizarre was going on and Alan Hauge and his partners at GMT Studios were beside themselves with anxiety.

In simple terms, Robert Suggs was now at war with Jon Emr and had fired the first shot. Suggs had taken out an ad in newspapers in Los Angeles and San Francisco looking for performers in a gay film by executive producer Jon Emr.

Jon Emr changed his home number on June 3. He again had to change his number on June 24 when a similar ad appeared in a Thursday edition of the *Los Angeles Times*. Three days later, the *Times* carried the ad yet again, only this time it was with his aunt Genie's number.

When Alan Hauge demanded of Jon an explanation of just exactly what the hell was going on in the studio, Emr was less than honest when he told Alan Hauge that he had fired Suggs. He claimed that he had caught Suggs listening at the door of the conference room while a meeting was going on. Jon never mentioned a word about Nicholas Karino.

A few days after the "gay" ad made its first appearance in the newspapers, Nicholas Karino and Mark Roesler had a meeting in Indianapolis. They sat in the patio section of Thank God It's Friday restaurant, not far from the offices of Curtis Management. Having had no apparent luck whatsoever convincing Jon Emr or Alan Hauge to let him assume control of the James Dean film, Karino told Roesler, he had flown here to try to make his own headway with The Family.

Over a couple of burgers, Karino cut to the chase. He was interested in the James Dean rights, he had the money to make financing the film a reality, and, by the way, this Jon Emr was a fraud.

"What do you mean, fraud?" Roesler asked. Roesler had obviously suspected from the start that Emr was less than reputable and was happy that, finally, there was a person who might be able to confirm his suspicions.

Karino pulled out a prospectus that Jon Emr had put together in order to lure investors into the Dean project. Karino directed Roesler's attention to one section in particular. Roesler was shocked. Emr was assuring investors that the Dean film and its ancillary profits would top $1 billion.

$1 billion!

No film in history had made that kind of money. The most successful film in history at that point—*E.T. The Extra-Terrestrial*—was not even close. Not even the three *Star Wars* movies combined—action figures and all—approached that kind of figure.

The bottom line was that Nicholas Karino could not buy the rights because they were no longer for sale. The pleasant meeting was to be Nicholas Karino's last involvement with the James Dean project. But, that afternoon, Roesler phoned Jon Emr. He was absolutely fuming. For the first time he found himself cursing Jon out and calling him a fraud. How dare Jon, how dare he tell investors that the picture would net over $1 billion!

Jon was defensive and unapologetic. What he wanted to know was how dare Mark Roesler even meet with Nicholas Karino! Then he assured Roesler that he was going to personally take this controversial issue up with Marcus Winslow of the James Dean family.

On June 6, Marcus Winslow received a lengthy telegram from Jon Emr. In the diatribe, Jon accused Mark Roesler of having violated the rights agreement over the Dean film by having met with Nicholas Karino. Emr described Karino as a man "who wanted to buy us out." He even went as far as to say that Karino offered $10 million for the rights. He ended the letter by accusing Roesler of being very "destructive" regarding the film project. "This is a very serious matter," he wrote.

The following day, Jon Emr received a faxed message from Mark Roesler:

> Dear Jon: Marcus got your telegram. Ironically he also got the enclosed article. He was quite impressed with his mail from yesterday. See you soon—Mark. P.S. He didn't know how he looked until he saw your picture.

The next few fax pages were Randy Collier's *Arizona Republic* article. As he stood at the fax machine, Jon Emr's eyes widened. That *fucking* Scott Barnes had struck again. Jon let out a wail of anger and anguish and then returned to business.

On June 10, 1991, Emr wrote to both Roessler and Winslow:

> . . . Anyone can put a false article in a newspaper . . . The FBI verified that we were not under a probe by them . . . [Nicholas Karino] has threatened that he will destroy the project and has threatened my life if I didn't let him buy me out. . . . Robert Suggs worked for us as production security, but was hired by Karino. . . . If you really want egg on your face at the end of the day, keep following the path that Nicholas Karino is leading you down.

That night, when Alan Hauge came home from work, his wife played a message that had been left on their machine by Robert Suggs. "I just wanted to warn you about Jon Emr, about his past. You really don't realize the things he was into. I just wanted to tell you this because you are nice people. He has already hurt me financially and I just wanted to make sure you get away from him before you get hurt."

THE TRAIL OF THE ASSASSIN: SEVEN

FROM THE INTERROGATION OF BENNY
AUGUST 29, 1991

DETECTIVE SERGEANT HANK DAVIES: Rob dropped you off at home [after killing Arthur Emr] on a Wednesday. Then what?

BENNY: Thursday, I took the kids to Disneyland cause I figured he wasn't going to do it. Friday we were sitting and watching a movie called *Thief* and we watched how this guy totally destroyed everything in his life. And we thought that's what Rob is doing.

Did Rob ever say anything about that movie?

He likes the movie, he liked it enough to have it.

Did he ever tell you to watch it?

No, no. I was sitting there and I was thinking, you know, Jenny doesn't really know what's going on and I didn't know how to react when we were watching the movie. Because, I kind of felt that I was watching Rob, kinda, on TV. I thought, well, I told Jenny I'm going to call Rob and see how he's doing. I called his Sky[pager] and asked him how he was doing and give me a call. And that was the message I left. He didn't call back until Saturday. And when he called Saturday, he asked me to pick him up.

What time was this?

Around five in the afternoon.

Five in the afternoon? Where did you pick him up?

At Jim's Burgers right around the corner. When he called, he said, come pick me up, I'm at Jim's. And I hesitated. I said, okay, good-bye. And then I hesitated, and I thought should I pick him up or is this the last trip. 'Cause I knew he was going to commit suicide. He told me he would.

He had already told you he was going to commit suicide?

He had already told me he was going to commit suicide.

Did, at this time on Saturday, did you know that Jon Emr had been murdered?

Not until I picked Rob up. When I picked him up he said let's go to a hamburger joint. I said Jim's and he said, No. He said let's go to another one. And I said, well there's one right up the road. So we went to the one right up the road. He ordered a burger, I ordered a cup of coffee. He began to tell me, in detail, what he did to Jon Emr. How he got Susan's car from her job.

Okay, did he say when he did this? Was it the night he dropped you off or the next?

He said he did it on the eleventh, the day, the eleventh. He didn't tell me a time. He just said the date of the eleventh. He did it in broad daylight to make it look like a mob hit.

Did he say when he picked up Susan's car?

No, he didn't, he didn't tell me that. He didn't tell me where he left the car. He just said he picked up Susan's car at her work, took it and washed it, and then from there he followed Jon Emr. From Jon's house to his, his place of work. And then, he waited at his job until they come walking out, I guess it was quitting time.

Did he tell you who was in the car with Jon?

Jon, and his son, and two ladies.

Did he know the ladies?

He said one was Monkey-Face—

The girlfriend?

The girlfriend. And then the mother. I think Jon Emr's mother is who it was. He said he waited until they stopped at a light, right in broad daylight, right when the light was red. He went over and lined up the gun on his arm and just put like eight rounds in Jon Emr and the last of the rounds in his son. And during this time, he said, he graphically said, Jon was yelling, "No!" His tongue hung out a little, and he had little pieces of blood all over his face, cause he was riddled with bullets. And then he said the son started to holler out, "No," just as Jon had, and he blew away his face. Rob said that he should have done it to the two in the back too, but he didn't.

Did he say why he didn't?

Just not enough time, I suppose. Then he said from there, he took off, went around, and drove the car up on the bridge. I guess it was a nearby bridge. He watched the Emr car roll down to a stop sign and then people just kinda looked around it. And he said he laughed, thought it was funny, and took off.

Did he say what gun he used?

The .22 with the silencer.

And he told you he used that gun?

He used his .22. He liked that .22. From there he left. He said he left her car at the airport, and then didn't tell me he picked his car up. He just said he left the car at the airport. And that's how he explained the murder in detail.

Did he ever say anything about the car Jon Emr was driving?

It was a Lincoln.

Did that aggravate him?

He said that it, yeah, yeah, I should have told you that.

Yeah, but is that true, though?

Yes. The Lincoln was a new model Lincoln, the big kind, like my wife likes also. He said that when he saw that, Jon Emr must have gotten some money.

Did he ever say he tried to ask him for money before killing Jon?

He didn't tell me that he contacted him at all.

Did he say anything to Jon Emr before he shot him?

No, just that he started shooting, the windows were down, which I thought that was kind of weird for a Lincoln. And he started shooting at them.

What did he say he did after the murder besides dropping off Susan's car?

He went back to the hotel or wherever he was staying.

Did he say where?

I didn't know where he was staying at this time. He purposely did not tell me that. I don't know why. He told me everything else. And then he, of course, he called me.

Did he say how he got to Jim's Burgers?

No. The only thing that I asked him was where was the car? He said he dumped it already. All he had was his blue shorts, white shirt, white tennis shoes, and a black bag.

A small black bag?

It was one of them, like—

Duffel bags?

Like a footlocker-type bag. Pretty good size.

And then where did you go from the hamburger place?

From there he said he wanted to get either on Amtrak or a bus to take him out to the Twentynine Palms [California] area. That would be close enough. From there he could walk the rest of the way. The desert area, basically.

Did he say the Twentynine Palms area?

Yeah, the area of Twentynine Palms.

And that he could walk the rest of the way?

He could either walk or hitchhike the rest of the way.

And that would be to go to Susan's body?

So he could finalize his last plan.

Okay, which would be killing himself.

Yeah, so I'm taking him down Imperial Highway, I was taking him to the Amtrak in Fullerton. And then he said, well take me to Disneyland. So, I headed towards Disneyland. He said, I wanna go to Disneyland one last time. Just before we got to Disneyland there was a hotel on the right. He said, Let's go here. He got a room which was upstairs, which is unnormal for Rob. He always went downstairs. This time it was upstairs and he put his black bag there. He never once let me look in the black bag. I think there would have been a lot of answers for me in that black bag.

When he came out he said, Let's go to Disneyland. When we were on the train ride, he made a joke. He said, "Hey Rob! you've just killed the Emr family. What you gonna do?" He says, "I'm going to Disneyland." He said this around everybody. I just hoped they thought he was a tourist and that he flipped out or something. I wanted to crawl under a rock. We did all the fast rides. When we were done he gave me two day passes. He said, "You and Jenny can come here anytime. Think of me when you come here."

When we got to the hotel, he said, "I'll just say my good-byes out here." He hugged me and he said, "Give hugs and kisses to the babies. Don't tell the cops my location. Do that one last thing for me. Be a good friend. I'll see you in the afterlife."

Did he say when he was planning on going to the desert?

He was going to do it on Monday or Tuesday. But he wanted to see if there was going to be any news on TV first.

About Jon Emr?

About the killings. And then Sunday morning I couldn't go to church. I felt I'd done something that wasn't right and I was ashamed. So, instead I went and got the L.A. paper. I saw a small article about Jon Emr being killed Mob-style. And that's exactly the way he told me about it. And, so I called the pager and I said, "*L.A. Times*, Rob." Then I hung up. I didn't think I should talk long.

You've never heard from him again?

The only dealing I had was Tuesday afternoon around 2:00. I was driving a truck and I felt a shuddering all over. I felt like maybe he was dead.

Do you think that he eventually thought you'd want to talk to the police?

No. I think that he eventually thought I was going to stay with him.

By not saying anything?

By getting myself so deep that I couldn't go back to the right way and become his . . . what is the word, like "criminal"?

Accomplice?

Yeah, like Bonnie and Clyde.

Okay, if you remember anything else, contact me.

Well, I want you to understand that I want to cooperate with you in every possible way. I'm hiding nothing. I might have forgot but I'm hiding nothing on purpose. The lie detector proved it. And that's what I want to say.

Okay. This interview is terminated at approximately 7:30 P.M.

The James Dean Con:
Late June–July 11, 1991

I don't think we're in Kansas anymore, Toto.
—Judy Garland in the *The Wizard of Oz*

In late June, Max Caulfield received a call from his former boss Robert Suggs. For the first time, Suggs seemed to Caulfield to be weak and broken. He was calling from his apartment building, where all that was left was the phone that he was now using. He tearfully told Max that his girlfriend, Susan, the absolute treasured love-of-his-life, had left him. The final straw was the fact that he had been evicted. He also confessed that he had to leave Jon Emr, who he was now convinced was a two-bit hustler.

None of this was a surprise to Caulfield. Like everybody else who had been close to him, including Susan, he had warned Suggs that Jon Emr could not possibly be anything more than a con artist. He had assured Suggs that one day Emr would bring him to his knees and, for certain, Rob had no future in the film industry . . . certainly not riding *this* guy's coattails.

The purpose of Suggs's call was to explain to his old pal that, in no uncertain terms, his entire financial world had collapsed around him as a result of his relationship with Jon Emr. He had nothing left. *Nothing.* He had used Susan's credit cards to the max, and now she was about to have her car repossessed and was blaming him for it. They owed three months' back rent. He had already sold all his appliances, including his beloved big-screen television. He had even pawned his guns in Arizona.

What Robert wanted to know was whether or not Max would want to buy off his private-eye equipment, including the Maxitrack radios and surveillance equipment. Max considered the option for a few minutes.

He certainly did not feel warmly toward Robert, who he felt still owed him a great deal of money. Then there was the matter of Rob endangering his life and his family's life. A couple of months earlier, Rob had taken it upon himself to explain to Jon that his old friend and "partner" Max Caulfield was in the Witness Protection Program. Rob's intentions had been good. He had felt that Max's story might make a great movie. But publicity was not why Max was in the program.

Would he help Rob? Well, after all, they had been a part of each other's lives and they did share some history together. Max offered Suggs $700 for the equipment, which had an actual value of over $4,000.

Suggs accepted the offer. When he received the cashier's check from Max, Suggs had enough money to get his guns out of the Scottsdale pawnshops he had left them in.

If there was any one dynamite reason why Jon Emr so flippantly blew off Nicholas Karino, it was because he thought that Nicholas simply had no cash and was a typical Hollywood blowhard. In fact, Jon was now telling anybody who would listen that Nicholas Karino was a Mafia chieftain. And then there was the matter of the *other* investor. The real one, or so Emr thought. His name was David Jackson. He had come into the picture via Kirk Heinlen, the propmaster who had obtained for Emr the preproduction money used to buy the James Dean rights, and his friend Jim Etter. Etter was a veteran lighting technician on film sets. Like most people in the industry, Jim had always wanted something just a little better, a step up the cinema showcase ladder. For Jim Etter, that meant making movies, even if they were nonunion cheapos.

In 1991, Jim was producing a film called "Medium Hot," which cost about $250,000, a mere flyspeck when compared to budgets on most Hollywood films. In the project was a young, attractive waitress-turned-actress named Marian Hahn. For a whole series of reasons, Etter disliked Hahn. For the most part, he found her unpleasant and disruptive.

One day, Hahn told Etter that she was going to be making it big in the movies, playing one of the lead roles in the new film about James Dean. In truth, nobody had hired Hahn, not Alan Hauge and not Jon

Emr. All she had done was send in several head shots to the studio. By coincidence, Jim Etter knew one of the investors in the Dean project, one of those people that Kirk Heinlen had brought in to help buy the rights from the Dean family.

Etter wanted to warn the investor about this Marian Hahn. Etter was turned over to Jon Emr and, in *Casablanca* parlance—it was the beginning of a beautiful friendship. Emr, as he did with just about everybody, promised Jim Etter a piece of the James Dean pie *if* he could help bring in the financing.

Etter, it seems, took the matter very seriously indeed. By June, he had rounded up about twenty people who were seriously considering investing in the project. One of them was David Jackson.

Jackson introduced himself to Emr as a producer who was trying to buy a small studio in Burbank called World-Wide Studios. Jackson said he hoped to turn it into a postproduction house. He said that he personally had Texas investors who wanted to fund the studio complex and "James Dean: The Legend" at the same time. Both he and these Texans were thrilled with the screenplay that Hauge had written.

Contracts were sent back and forth between Emr's attorney, Doug Smithers, and Jackson's lawyers. Eventually, Jon approached Hauge and told him that he wanted him to read the final contract that had been agreed upon by him and David Jackson. Hauge took the contract and went to the farthest office at GMT Studios to study it.

As he was reading it, Alan became pale and angry. The contract was exclusively between Jon and David Jackson. It called for a $3 million deposit. As collateral, Jon Emr had put up Alan Hauge's original screenplay. Hauge searched and searched for where in the contract he received anything. Three times, Jon knocked on the door and poked his head in. "Hey, how we doing?" he'd ask. It was as if Jon knew that Alan was going to get upset.

A half hour later, Alan went to Jon's office holding the contract over his head. "This is not real, right?"

"What's wrong with it?"

"You've gotta be kidding me." Hauge slapped the script on the table. "You are using my screenplay as collateral? You're promising them the rights to my script!"

Jon smiled. "Alan, Alan. That's the only way that I can get the money."

"Well, why the hell didn't you ask me for permission? This is my screenplay."

Jon nodded, his face full of understanding. "I see your point. I guess that we'll have to change that."

"That's right, you will. There's another problem." Hauge moved to the last page of the contract. "You have American Icon here as having complete control. That means *you* get complete control of the money."

The smile that had been on Jon's face for the past couple of minutes was still there. "We'll change that as well. I'll send these over to Doug Smithers."

"Damn right you're going to change it," Hauge said as he stormed off.

One morning toward the end of June, the phone rang to wake up Max Caulfield and his wife. Christine handed the phone over to Max. "It's Rob," she said.

"How are you doing," Max said sleepily.

"Fine. I want to ask you two things."

"Okay."

"I need your help on a job, a couple of jobs. It can only be you. It's gotta be you. You can't tell Christine about it. I'm not even telling Susan. There is one other person involved, but that's it."

"Well, let's hear about it."

"Here it is. I have a client who is a Mexican national. He has a kid in Arizona who he lost custody of. He wants me to go and get the kid and bring him to Mexico."

"Jesus, Rob. Kidnap the kid?"

"Whatever. I want you to help me out. I can pay you fifty thousand."

Max didn't even stop to consider the option. "No, Rob. I can't do that, not for any amount of money. That's kidnapping, and you shouldn't do it either. You're going to go to jail. You've got no paperwork, right?"

"That's right. The guy lost custody but he's rich and he really wants the kid."

"Rob, this is no good. It's like the Lindbergh kidnapping. It does not matter what the motive is."

There was a pause. "Well, yeah, I guess you're right. Okay."

Max was happy that Rob seemed to have come to his senses. "Okay, there were two things. What's the second thing?"

Rob laughed. "I don't even want to ask you. You're not going to do it if you won't do the first."

After he hung up with Rob, Max told Christine, "Jesus, I think that Rob is planning to whack somebody."

That same day, Rex Ravelle, who had been conned by Jon Emr in the early eighties, received a phone call from Robert Suggs. He told Ravelle that he knew that he was enemies with Jon Emr and that he (Suggs) was planning to have Emr "taken care of." He wanted to know if Rex might want to donate some much-needed cash to the cause. Rex turned the offer down. He had no money, he said.

None of Jon's other enemies say that they were contacted by Robert Suggs. Scott Barnes, however, did receive a package from Suggs at his post office box. It included a note from Suggs apologizing for their feud.

It also contained several documents from GMT Studios. "Have a field day," Suggs wrote to Barnes.

On July 7, for some reason, a terrified Jon Emr contacted his longtime ally Brian Barnes. "Look," he said. "We had to lay off Robert Suggs. The guy is nuts. He's threatened me. He's got a gun and he's carrying it around. What can you do for me?"

"Let me make a couple of calls," said Brian, who, if for anything, was known for his calm.

Brian hung up and contacted the Hermosa Beach Police Department. He knew that Rob had been living there with Susan, but was clueless to the fact that he and Susan had broken up. He told them all about Suggs. He told them that Suggs was carrying around a concealed weapon. He told them about all the weapons that he knew Suggs owned. He told them about the AR-15, the fully automatics, the semi-automatic pistols, the 9-millimeters, the .45s; the German shepherd attack dog named Joe.

The police told Brian that there was really nothing that they could do. At all.

Jesus, Brian thought to himself. Then he gave them Jon's phone number and Robert Suggs's phone number. The police took the information down and then reiterated that there was simply nothing that they could do.

Brian had no better luck when he contacted the Culver City police. "There's nothing that we can do until he takes that pistol out and threatens the guy," the police told Brian.

Brian contacted Jon. "There's nothing I can do," he told his flustered boss.

"Of course there is. Think," Jon growled. "There must be something."

"Jon, I think that you should call Rob yourself. You talk to him in a professional manner. Try to iron things out."

"Look, that's not going to work," Jon said softly. "It's too deep."

Sometime in the first week of July, Alan Hauge approached Jon to have a heart-to-heart talk with him. Over the past couple of months, things had gotten pretty damn hairy around the office. Jon had clearly brought some pretty intense karma with him when he moved in. The problems were not just related to phone calls from Scott Barnes, or dubious investors that always managed to disappoint, or the Nicholas Karino affair, which Jon was now claiming was Mafia related, or the gay men and women lining up around the corner to apply for work in GMT porno films, or even the major blowup with Robert Suggs.

What really, really annoyed not only Hauge but also his partners and the secretaries and other employees at GMT was Jon's basic demeanor, his flamboyance, his incessant cursing. He was an embarrassment and that's all there was to it.

Alan Hauge told Jon Emr that he needed to cool his attitude down a bit, that he needed to be less boisterous and that he certainly needed to tone down his language, which the female employees found especially offensive.

Jon was not particularly hurt. He smiled and said, "Well, I can't just change the way that I am. This is my nature, it's my style. Maybe I should just change offices."

Alan was very quick to agree and happy that Jon was not putting up a fight. "I think that's a good idea, Jon," he said. "If you can't stop acting like that, you certainly will need to move to a new office."

What Alan had no way of knowing was that Jon had already planned to move out. Only he wasn't planning to move to a new office in the neighborhood, or even Los Angeles, or, for that matter, even the state of California. Emr told at least one woman he was romancing (not his girlfriend, Sue Fellows) that he was moving out of the state.

For a week, Jon spent time clearing out his office, putting everything away in filing boxes. He promised Alan Hauge that the minute the investment dollars from Mr. David Jackson started to come in and were deposited in the American Icon account, he was out of there and into a brand-new office. Every time he heard that, Alan was happy. So were all the rest of the employees at GMT.

The following day, Alan Hauge's wife, Lanette, walked into the office and she found Renee and Jon sitting comfortably at the desk. There was not one sheet of paper in the room. It was nearly empty. Lanette smiled. Jon was infamous for being sloppy and disorganized. The only thing that seemed to have remained was Jon's desk calendar, and even that was still laid out to February. "My goodness, it looks like we've been robbed."

Jon and Renee turned to one another and began to laugh.

At that point one of the secretaries stuck her head in the door. "Jon, I'm going to the store to get some cases of Pepsi. Would you like some?"

Jon waved her off with a smile. "Nah, I'm going to be gone as of next week anyway."

On July 10, 1991, Jon announced that the contract with David Jackson would be signed the next day.

On July 11, 1991, Alan Hauge did not arrive in his offices until after lunch. True, this was to be the big day. The day when the cash from David Jackson was allegedly set to get the Dean project rolling. Finally. Today was also when Los Angeles would get to see a rare eclipse. On the news, Hauge had heard that the moon would be blocking out the sun at 11:45. He was home, at the ready, with his trusted telescope.

When Hauge finally did arrive at GMT, Jon assured him that absolutely everything was a go. He told him that the contracts were now complete and ready to be executed. He would be meeting with David Jackson and his attorneys that night. Of course, Alan was more than welcome to be present for the great moment. Within twenty-four hours, the project itself would be millions of dollars richer and that much closer to going before the cameras. Everybody's dreams were about to become a reality. That was something that Jon Emr had been promising all along.

Hauge tried to remain collected. In fact, he even allowed a bit of his skepticism to eke out. "Let me tell you, Jon, I'm warning you in advance, if that contract looks anything like it did when you showed it to me last week, you won't have me or the screenplay." Hauge was referring to the fact that Jon had originally wanted to put Hauge's script up as collateral and had arranged it so that Jackson's funds would be deposited in a bank account that Jon exclusively controlled.

"Don't worry about it," Jon said. "I've already told you that. Doug Smithers handled all of that."

Hauge took Jon's word for it. If anything, he trusted Smithers, who was the attorney for the James Dean project. Alan told Jon that he had a number of appointments but that he would certainly be back in time to meet with the mysterious but apparently very wealthy David Jackson.

At 2:00 in the afternoon, Alan Hauge went to Century City to meet with his attorney. An hour later, Hauge strolled out of the law offices and rode the elevator down to the lobby. He went to a pay phone and called the studio. Coincidentally, Jon picked up the line. Hauge wanted to make sure that the meeting with Jackson was still set to go, that there had not been any last-minute glitches.

"Well, we do have kind of a problem," Jon said. "There's one more thing that these fucking attorneys want changed. There'll be no meeting tonight. We're going to do it tomorrow night. Don't worry about coming back here. I'm just going to get some dinner and then go home."

"What is the change in the contract?"

"Nothing that concerns you, really," Jon said. Hauge didn't know what to make of that comment. Wasn't everything about this film supposed to concern him? He would bring up the matter with Jon later that day.

Hauge would later say that, at the very moment that he was hanging up the phone, God told him not to return to the studio. It was not a message that was fearful or filled with anxiety, just a simple and quiet admonishment. Hauge rode the escalator down to the deli that was in the basement of his attorney's high-rise. For lunch, he ordered a small salad. Later, as he drove out of the parking lot, Hauge says he got his second message from God not to return to the studio.

Hauge drove down Century Park East, took a right on Pico, and then a left on Motor Avenue. He got to Washington Boulevard and stopped at a sign shop where he had ordered a neon "GMT." At 4:15, Hauge was back in his car. Now, for a third time, he felt that God was telling him not to return to the studio.

At about 4:10 in the afternoon, Jon Emr left his office at GMT Studios. With him was his girlfriend, Sue Fellows, who had been serving as his secretary, his young son Roger, who was visiting during his summer break from Murray State University, and, naturally, his mother, Renee. In the trunk of the car, one of the passengers had placed some documents, mostly relating to the James Dean project. The two women climbed into the backseat of the white Lincoln that Jon had rented from Budget Rental. Jon moved into the passenger seat. In his arms was a small poodle with a tiny cast on its leg. His son Roger moved into the driver's seat. Jon had not been feeling particularly well and had even been scheduled to have some heart surgery in Arizona. In the fanny pack he wore around his waist was a vial of nitroglycerine and a .38 pistol.

Roger pulled out of his parking space, and drove out to Buckingham Parkway and then took a right on Slauson Boulevard. Nobody seemed to notice that a white Toyota had pulled out immediately after them.

After a few blocks, Roger came up behind a Blue Mercedes that was at a stoplight at the Sepulveda Boulevard intersection. Jon, whose window was rolled down, all of a sudden said, "Hi!" and gave a little wave to the man in the white Toyota who had now pulled up next to them. At first, it was difficult for anybody in the Lincoln to recognize Robert Suggs. His hair had been shorn down to a crew cut. They had never seen his hair quite like that.

Seemingly out of nowhere, Suggs pulled out a Ruger that had a silencer attached to it. *Piff.* The first shot was probably to Roger's head, one bullet, which was followed by several more. Suggs had to take out the driver first because Roger might otherwise have tried to escape after the initial bullet had been fired.

Both women started to scream. Sue Fellows ducked for cover.

As Suggs kept shooting with deliberate calmness, Jon's body flailed with the impact of each bullet. Suggs had only one apparent miss. That bullet went through Jon's chair, into the back, and blew off a small part of Sue Fellows's cheek.

When Suggs was convinced that Jon and his boy were dead, he moved the aim of his Ruger to Renee Emr, who sat in stunned horror in the backseat. He slowly pulled the trigger. *Click.* He was out of bullets. He smiled briefly, the way one does to acknowledge an opponent's excellent tennis ace, and then screeched the car to the right, heading north on Sepulveda.

The Mercedes that had been in front of the Emrs' white Lincoln had long since gotten the hell out of the way. The impact of the bullet to his skull had forced young Roger to take his foot off the brake. The Lincoln started to roll down the street, hopelessly out of control. Sue Fellows reached her whole body over Roger's and tried to gain some control of the steering wheel. Within a few seconds, she could see on her right a traffic cop issuing a speeding ticket.

Had Alan Hauge traveled his normal route to get to the YMCA where he was scheduled to play racquetball, he would have driven along Sepulveda and run into the traffic congestion created by the murders. Instead, for some reason, he decided to take the 405 highway. He had no way of knowing it, but he drove directly over the murder site. He was informed of the murders when somebody from his office called him at the YMCA.

Scott Barnes claims that he was in the Caribbean islands at the time that Jon Emr was murdered. Nevertheless, he certainly managed to find out about it within a couple of hours, calling many of those people who knew and hated Emr to tell them the "good news."

Where was Roy Ashton, the convicted killer who felt that Jon Emr owed him several thousands of dollars for bringing in the investor Aubrey Brothers, when the murder took place? Nobody seems to know. As of the publication of this book, Ashton was back in a Louisiana prison for attempting an armed robbery for which he was later convicted.

A few hours after the murder, Alan Hauge admitted the police into Jon's offices at GMT, where they confiscated several boxes. One of the things that they left behind was the contract that Jon was to sign with David Jackson. Hauge looked it over. Jon had changed nothing. It was clear to Alan that Jon was simply going to take Jackson's money and run with it.

THE TRAIL OF THE ASSASSIN: EIGHT

As far as Hank Davies was concerned, Benny was simply too stupid to have "beaten" any polygraph machine. He did not have the calculated pathology that Hank attributed, say, to a Scott Barnes. That is why Hank Davies was absolutely convinced now that Robert Suggs, also known as Robert Allen, was the killer of all three Emrs. At this point, Hank felt that he had nailed down all the events leading to the murder, the murder itself, and the Saturday when Suggsy met up with Benny and the two of them bonded one last time on Space Mountain in Disneyland.

What was still bothering Hank was what happened on the Friday following the murders and before the Disney trip.

On September 6, 1991, at 10:00 P.M. Hank Davies was relaxing at his new home in Los Angeles. He was scheduled to be married the next morning. Several of his friends, all of them his ushers who had flown in from all over the country, had taken Hank out for his last drinks as a bachelor. That day had been his first day off since the murders and he was going to be taking a full week to spend on his honeymoon.

Davies was not feeling particularly guilty. The murder investigation had slowly metamorphosed into a manhunt. Although there was some circumstantial evidence that Suggs might have been part of a larger conspiracy, there was nothing solid. Not even on Scott Barnes, who everybody—everybody—had pointed an accusing finger at over the past two months. If Suggs was dead, as he believed, then there was really nothing to do now but wait for some hiker to find the body. Realistically, Hank Davies's job was over.

This is why he was more than a little annoyed when he got paged and noticed the phone number of Robert Sahimbas, a good friend of Suggs, digitally scrawled across his beeper. He didn't like Sahimbas. He had interviewed him once before and had been given no information other than that Suggs had him send a package to his mother right before the murders. Even back then he could sense that Sahimbas was full of shit, protecting his buddy. It had particularly irked Davies that Sahimbas was a cop, albeit a low-level one.

"Yeah, Robert, what is it?" Hank said, straining over the obnoxiously loud voices of his pals.

"Hank, me and Ellen been thinking and we need to see you. There are some things that we need to get off of our chests."

Jeeeeesuuuusssss! "Robert. It's late."

"Hank, this is important."

"Look, I'm not going to drive out there right now."

"That's okay. We'll come to you. What's your address?"

"I'll meet you in the lobby of the Hilton hotel by the airport. Do you know it?"

"We'll be there."

Hank left his friends and told them that he'd be back after midnight. They proceeded to play poker without him.

Robert and Ellen Sahimbas were the only ones sitting in the lobby when Davies got there. He sat down next to them and pulled out a notebook. "I don't know why you waited until now to call me."

Ellen started to speak, but Robert beat her to it. "We thought that Suggs might have some people after him. He talked to us about thugs and things."

Thugs and things. This might be a long one, Hank thought. "Look, guys. Just tell me what you know."

And so they did.

In mid-morning of July 12, a day after Jon Emr and his boy Roger were swarmed with bullets, Robert Sahimbas's wife, Ellen, picked up the phone in her home. It was Robert Suggs on the line. "Hello, Ellen." He sounded despondent. There was a section of his voice that was dead. Ellen recognized it right away and it scared her. "I need you guys to pick me up. Put the kids with a sitter."

"Is something wrong, Rob?"

"Yeah," he responded. "Something's wrong. Real wrong. I gotta meet with you guys. Don't tell anybody."

This sounded a bit melodramatic. "C'mon, Rob. Who would I tell?"
"I don't know. Just don't. I'm waiting."

"Take me to the public library."

Somehow Robert and his wife knew better than to ask questions. They simply rode in silence to the library. When they got there, Rob told them that he'd be right back and hopped out of the car. When he came back he had the first smile of the day on his face. He put his head back on the seat. "Okay," Rob said, "things are in motion."

"What are you talking about, Rob?" Robert asked him.

"I'll tell you later." He paused. "I'm pleased. Very pleased."

"About what?"

"Let's talk about it over lunch."

Robert was slightly irritated. Maybe the cloak-and-dagger bullshit was going just a bit too far for his taste. "Where do you want to eat?"

"How about Red Lobster? Can we go to the Red Lobster?"

"Whatever you want, Rob."

Ellen peered over her seat. "Rob, where's Susan? They're going crazy looking for Susan."

Suggs did not answer right away. "Okay. I'll tell you about that over lunch. Let's just talk about it over lunch."

At the restaurant, Rob ordered shark, which Ellen thought was disgusting and had no problem telling Robert Suggs. She and her husband both ordered whatever was on special that day.

Suggs launched into it. "You were right, my friend. You were right."

"Right about what?"

"You were right about Jon Emr. I should have gotten out of it a long time ago."

"You see?"

"I'm at a point of no return. No fuckin' return. Everything has come undone. It's just goddamn unraveled."

"You're just talking silliness, Rob."

Rob's voice became pallid. "It's time. Time to disappear."

"Disappear?"

"I told you that someday this would happen. Someday I'd have to disappear forever. After today, we'll never see one another again. That makes me very sad."

Ellen cut in. "What are you saying, Rob?"

"I told you that someday I would have to write a book about all of this shit that has gone down. It's time to write the book." He thought for a second. "I think that I will call the book 'The Ambitious Young Man and the Distinguished Gentleman.' " He smirked. "Catchy, huh?"

As the waitress brought the food to the table there was an awkward silence. When she left, Rob took a few bites of his shark and then continued. "Here is the story. There was once an Ambitious Young Man who wanted to make something of himself. He wanted to get into the movie business. So the Ambitious Young Man and his beautiful girlfriend sold everything that they had, gave up everything, just so that they could make this dream happen. The reason why they were so confident is because the Ambitious Young Man had met up with a Distinguished Gentleman, who was very dapper and very charming and convinced him that he could make the dream happen."

Robert got in. "And who is who, Rob?"

"Please just listen to the story." He continued. "Things were going well for a while. The Ambitious Young Man was not getting the money that he was promised, but the Distinguished Gentleman talked a good game. But then the Ambitious Young Man began to look into the background of the Distinguished Gentleman and he didn't like what he discovered. But he kept quiet. In the meantime, the Ambitious Young Man was losing money, losing everything, maybe even his girl.

"One day, after the Ambitious Young Man was totally broke and had hit rock bottom, he discovered that the Distinguished Gentleman was nothing more than a con man. I mean, he knew it for sure. Found the evidence." He leaned forward. "So the Ambitious Young Man was very pissed off and he began to make threats against the Distinguished Gentleman. He was making life very tough. So the Distinguished Gentleman, who had connections to some thugs, tried to have the Ambitious Young Man eliminated."

Robert's eyes opened wide. "You mean killed?"

"Yeah, I mean killed. So, the Ambitious Young Man had no choice. He had to destroy the Distinguished Gentleman before the reverse happened. He drove to another state with a friend of his, a friend who had many, many kids. First, he killed the father of the Distinguished Gentleman. That would be the only thing that the Ambitious Young Man would regret. The father didn't do anything, but he put a bullet in his head. Then the Ambitious Young Man told his friend a bunch of things. Many of them were bullshit, designed to steer the police in the wrong direction. He loved his friend but knew that he would crack and speak to the cops.

"Then the Ambitious Young Man drove to Culver City and drove up along the Distinguished Gentleman and his son, who was driving. He had to kill the son because otherwise he would drive away as soon as the first bullet was fired. It was a necessity. Then the Ambitious Young Man fired ten more shots and killed the two of them. Now, the Ambitious Young Man had to disappear."

The Sahimbases were quiet. They were not sure what Suggs was telling them because they had not yet gotten word of the murders two days prior. Ellen said slowly, "My God. Where is Susan?"

Suggs nodded his head slowly. "She's fine and she's in a safe place." Another pause. "You may hear that she's dead. But she is okay."

In silence, they drove Suggs to a phone booth and they hugged for several minutes. Somehow, both of them knew that they would never see one another again. "Call me," Robert Sahimbas said. "Don't just disappear."

Suggs shook his head. "If I call you—if you try to reach me—if you try to help us—if you do anything—you will get Susan and me killed."

"Look, Rob, you have my pager number—"

"I do."

"If you want to signal us that everything is all right, then give us a series of ones. If one of you is injured, then give me twos. If she is dead, give me threes. If you want to come in from the cold, then give us fours."

Robert nodded. He understood. Then he kissed Ellen good-bye for the very last time.

Epilogue:
Christmas, 1992

The horror!
—Marlon Brando in *Apocalypse Now*

Variety, Hollywood's daily trade paper, was the first publication to offer an account of the executions of the Emr family. Reporter David Robb indicated that Emr was indeed a movie producer and that his murder and those of his son and father just might have been connected to the way that he did business. If that was true, it would have been a first. Hollywood had seen its share of spectacular homicides. There were the Manson murders. The Cotton Club murder. The stalking that led to the death of Rebecca Schaeffer. The Menendez murders. Even the murder of Sal Mineo. There had been many murders connected *with* the film business, but none *over* business.

Intrigued by the Robb article, my editor at *Entertainment Weekly* contacted me about investigating the concept that Emr had died over the making of the James Dean film. What began as a fairly routine crime story metamorphosed into something much more labyrinthine. Within a couple of weeks, it became clear that the story of Jon Emr and his career was too long a tale to tell for *Entertainment Weekly*, which could give it only 750 words. The story bounced to *LosAngeles Magazine*, known for longer-format stories and a penchant for investigating Hollywood.

Jon Emr, on the most primary level, was indeed a "player." That simply meant that while he was alive he was in motion, still "developing," that he had not yet given up on the business and moved back to New Jersey, where he came from. He had a business card identifying him as a producer, dusty scripts under his arm, and a video camera on his shoulder. Apparently, that was enough.

True, Jon lived in Torrance and nobody expects communities like Torrance to be even peripherally involved in the American entertainment industry. And, to be truthful, they are not. Yet, these are towns that are made of an uncommon hubris. Torrance and its ilk—call these towns the Hollyburbs—are crammed with producers, actors, screenwriters, directors, cinematographers, editors, you name it. To them, actual entry into the industry is just one fax or phone call or blow job away. "In the works" is one of the most common phrases in the industry. If a major deal is not going to happen "any second now," then it's "tomorrow," or "next week," or "in the works."

Emr was the master of "in the works." Is it so hard to understand why so many people believed that Emr was just that one signature away from being the next Samuel Goldwyn? Emr had the quality, or, as it turns out, the misfortune, of understanding not only his own nature but the nature of all human beings. From firsthand experience, he understood the complex lure of Hollywood. This was a man who realized that the access to Hollywood glamour could be used as a bear trap. Jon Emr understood that once you controlled a man's dreams, his soul would soon be yours as well. And if not his soul, then maybe his wallet.

From the outside looking in, Hollyburb to Hollywood, one sees only the successes. One sees the Oscars, Spago's, Nicky Blair's, cleavage, Heidi Fleiss, limos, Aspen vacations, billboards with your face on them, Beverly Hills teardowns. The Hollywood game can be festive and almost spiritual, but it can also be, and usually is, frustrating and disengaging. It is a sometimes violently intense game with towering financial stakes, one in which the gamesmen influence the lives of legions of people.

The murder of Jon Emr, I came to realize, did not so much represent the death of a man. Instead, it represented the logical resolution to a life of deception and manipulation. It represented the quashing of dreams. It represented the rage of the meek, of the Hollyburbs. It represented the tragedy of Hollywood and the curse of James Dean. But, most of all, it represented the lie of the pipe dream.

Among cineasts and film students there is a term known as the "suspension of disbelief." Simply stated, the term refers to a collusion between the filmmaker and his audience to pretend, even though everybody knows better, that what is happening on-screen is reality, the only reality, for the time being. When audiences believed that Willem Dafoe was Christ, that screen couples are actually making love, that dinosaurs roamed the modern earth, all of that, in a very real sense, was a suspension of disbelief.

In a way, Jon Emr was a walking, talking embodiment of the very concept of the suspension of disbelief. As we examine Jon Emr's claims, as we revisit their credibility, it is easy for us to slap our heads in that very disbelief. What Jon Emr promised was so ludicrous, so out in left field, so crammed with inconsistencies, that it seems an impossibility that so many people fell for his cons. Yet they did. They believed him. Because they wanted to. Because they had to. It was their only shot at The Dream.

In October of 1991, *LosAngeles Magazine* printed my roughly five-thousand-word article about the life and murder of Jon Emr. My editors called the piece "Pop Goes the Weasel," a harsh but nonetheless appropriate title. Naturally, Renee Emr and her surviving grandson, Bobby, took tremendous exception to both the title of my piece and its content. In a letter to me, Renee figured that 90 percent of my piece was fallacious.

Renee did not cooperate with me on this book. She also encouraged several of Jon's friends, people who no doubt would have given me positive information about Jon, not to speak with me. There is no doubt that most of the information about Jon contained in this book comes from the point of view of his enemies. Of course, I sought confirmation of their stories and allegations. Nevertheless, what nagged at me was that Renee refused to defend her son in an on-the-record conversation (I had interviewed her twice for my magazine article). I had spoken to her on the phone in an unofficial capacity several times. She was predictably hostile and almost hysterical in her attempts to shoot down the various bits of information I had uncovered about Jon.

What Renee Emr did do was send out several letters. One to me, one to my publisher at *LosAngeles Magazine*, and two to my book publisher. In the letters, Renee spells out her defense not only of her son's behavior but of her own as well. It essentially boils down to this: everybody who has ever said anything negative about Jon Emr is a liar. *Everybody.*

I have tried wherever possible to include Renee's retorts, regardless of what weight I place on their credibility, in footnotes throughout *Once Upon a Time in Hollywood.*

In any case, Renee Emr did everything she could to get her "side" of the story out on her own. She hired an attorney to try to pitch her "story" to various film companies, never to any avail. In 1994 she began contacting journalists in the hope that another Emr story, one that would cancel out "Pop Goes the Weasel," would be written. Nobody bit. She would instead have to deal with an article by Fred Schruers of *Premiere* magazine, who had his own problems with the way that Jon Emr did business.

As of the writing of this book, Renee was living in a secret location in Arizona with her sister and surviving grandson.

On Christmas Eve, 1992, the Culver City Police Department called a press conference to make what they described as a pair of "significant announcements." Word spread through media circles that Robert Suggs, the man whom the police and the FBI had spent well over a year searching for, had finally been found. No details about his condition or the whereabouts of his girlfriend, Susan Lynn Calkins, were made available before the press conference.

The briefing room at the police station was crammed with wall-to-wall reporters, representing print and television and radio. Hank Davies, flanked by two members of the FBI, was sitting at a fold-out table in the front of the room. Behind them were some sparse Christmas decorations. To their right was an easel holding up a poster board. On it were the now familiar photos of Jon Emr, his boys, Sue Calkins, and, of course, Robert Suggs. Also on the poster board was a huge photo of James Dean. The Culver City police knew their selling point.

Chief Ted Cooke came out in front of the audience. He was dressed almost completely in black. His shirt, jacket, and pants were all coal. His only off color was red. That was in his tie and his pocket square, which was, for some reason, stapled to a piece of cardboard. Cooke was smiling and animated when he began the press conference.

He announced that, indeed, Suggs had been found. Some hikers had found his remains in the Mojave desert, off Route 62. Actually, the "remains" in this case were just bones. Actually, it was just the jawbone with a few teeth attached. Dental records obtained from the Air Force showed that, sure enough, it was Suggsy. And there was more news. The bones of Susan Lynn Calkins were also found at the site. In addition, the remains of Suggsy's German shepherd, Joe, were discovered.

Some of Susan's other remains were found as far as twelve miles away from the site. Coyotes had probably dragged the bones away. The conclusion of the police and the feds was that this was a murder-suicide. Suggsy had killed the girl and then put the gun in his mouth and blown his head clean off.

Cooke then went into an explanation of the events that led up to the murder. "The fact that the film actor James Dean is involved makes this real interesting for you folks," Cooke explained. "You see, there were two competing interests for the rights to the James Dean story. They clashed and that led to all the bitterness that led to this murder."

He then went on to describe the actual murder of Jon Emr. Cooke made several factual errors, the most dramatic being that Renee Emr was Jon Emr's wife. Cooke ended his statement by saying, "As far as I am concerned this case is closed. All the loose ends have been tied up."

Then he took questions.

"Was Suggsy's car found there?"

No, it was not.

"Was the murder weapon found?"

Yes, in fact it was. Two guns were found in the same area next to a duffel bag that they determined belonged to Suggsy.

"How do we know that he committed suicide?"

There was a suicide note.

"What do you mean when you talk about the competing interests for the James Dean movie?"

The Chief finally came to the conclusion that he was in way over his head. Hank Davies took over.

Davies adjusted his dark blue sports coat and moved to the podium. He briefly discussed the nature of the James Dean deal and how it figured in the murders. "Basically, I think that Robert Suggs blamed Jon Emr for his financial problems and for the loss of his girlfriend. He just snapped."

"Was there the possibility that there might have been a conspiracy to kill Jon Emr?"

Davies conceded that they had uncovered a great deal of circumstantial evidence that there might have been more people involved than just Suggsy. But, unfortunately, there was absolutely no concrete evidence.

"Can you give us the name of the man who traveled with Suggsy when he killed Art Emr?"

Davies said that information was not being offered to the press.*

Then, just before he sat down, Davies had to correct the Chief on one issue. The guns were not found *next* to the duffel bag. They were found *inside* the bag. Also included in the blue vinyl bag was a can of Mace, a water bottle, and a photograph of the Sahimbases' children. In the vicinity of the blue duffel were blue thongs, a yellow-colored blanket, one knife, three cans of Mace, a small shovel, and Jockey shorts.

The same day, in Paradise Valley, Detective Alan Laitsch was also meeting with a group of journalists. This marked the first time that Laitsch would be making an appearance on television in connection with the Emr case. He made it very clear that, as far as he was concerned, this case was wide open.

And he had reason. Here are just a few of the loose ends that Culver City police chief Ted Cooke said did not exist:

- If Suggsy committed suicide, how did the guns get back into the duffel bag?
- How did Suggsy get out into that spot in the desert? No car was found in the vicinity. Even if he hitchhiked along Route 62, it was a long walk. Was it conceivable to have made that trudge in the desert sun of summer?
- If the note that Kathy Calkins found was a suicide note, then why was Suggsy writing it to the same person he planned to kill?
- Almost every suicide victim wants to be found. Why did Suggsy go through such an effort to keep the bodies hidden?
- If Suggsy was going to kill himself, why did he create a series of red herrings that he knew Benny would then feed to the police?

After the murders, Renee Emr still claimed that she owned the rights to the James Dean project. That left Alan Hauge in a bind. Several investors were still interested in the movie but were refusing to play ball if Renee, or any other Emr, was still involved. Hauge made her an offer

---

*In December of 1993, Benny was finally arrested and charged as an accessory to the murder of Arthur Emr, Sr.

of close to a half-million dollars to bow out. She refused. She not only wanted more money, she wanted something that made people at Curtis Management and Hauge ill.

She wanted the film to be dedicated to Jon Emr. The producer. Her son.

The issue of who owned the rights to James Dean was settled in an arbitration. When it was all over, Renee Emr was left with absolutely nothing. One of the reasons for her dismissal was that her son Jon Emr had sullied the image of James Dean. The image of Hollywood.

AUTHOR'S NOTE

O *nce Upon a Time in Hollywood* is a true story. It is neither a fictionalization nor what has commonly been referred to as a "nonfiction novel." No scenes have been created from my imagination in order to achieve a novelistic effect. At times, I attempted to re-create the thoughts of some of the principals. In cases where the person was alive, those thoughts were described to me by the character in question.

Because many of the principal characters in this book had a propensity for tape-recording phone calls and/or writing affidavits about their conversations, my effort to present dialogue close to its original form was made easier. In some instances, dialogue was re-created when two or more people offered identical versions of the same conversation. In other limited cases I relied on the credibility of at least one of the participants in the conversation.

In a number of cases, it was necessary to change the identity of a character. First, as a condition of the interview. Second, to protect the privacy of the individual in question. Third, for other legal concerns.

Benny (not his real name) did not wish to be interviewed for this book but he had previously given a detailed statement to the police. In "The Trail of the Assassin" chapters, I have re-created conversations and feelings based on the information in Benny's statement to the police and other information provided to me by reliable sources.

Once Upon a Time in Hollywood is based on court records, police reports, interrogation proceedings, tape recordings, published works, videotapes, scripts, photographs, autopsy reports, legal contracts, diary entries, and the cross-checked memories of well over one hundred interviewees.

Almost every character who was alive during the research process of this book was given an opportunity to offer his or her input to the author. The vast majority seized that opportunity. A few people elected not to be interviewed for various reasons. I formally spoke with Renee Emr twice. Once on the phone a couple of weeks after her son was murdered and then, again, at the Ontario Hilton a few days after. I spoke to Renee informally several times thereafter on the phone. She has written me, my magazine editor, and my publisher in order to "set the record straight."

This is a story about conflict. Indeed, there were often two, sometimes three or four, sides to the events recounted in this book.

In each case, I weighed the documentary and testimonial evidence, general credibility of the source, and my own common sense before coming to my own educated conclusion about the truth. Where the versions of events differ dramatically, I have included footnotes in order to present both sides.

There are a number of people to whom I am enormously grateful: Hank Davies of the Culver City Police Department, who put up with three years of incessant phone calls and badgering, Alan Laitsch of the Paradise Valley Police Department, Alan Hauge, Earl Rutledge, Aubrey Brothers, Yoko Wright, Chuck Norris, Mark Roesler, Randy Pike, Audrey Gillette, Steve Yoshida, Tim Johnson, Jean Johnson, Vern Nobles, Jane Favor, Brian Barnes, Michael Douglas, Ira Miller, Jerome Landau, Randy Collier, George Lewis, Art Lord, Deborah Pettit, Mark Smith, Jack Bailey, Mark Wilson, Ed Gold, Kirk Heinlen, Carol Casey, Max Caulfield, H. Ross Perot, Michael Trihey, Rex Ravelle, Stan Esecson, Janine Swann, George Gugas, Lanette Hauge, Ruth Charney, Anthony "The Bunny" Costello, Helen Vardi, Damian Chapa, and Scott Barnes.

For their wise counsel and continued support throughout an arduous four-year process, thanks are due to my agent, Ed Novak, and my attorney, Jerry Bregman. Of course, this trek essentially began at *LosAngeles Magazine*, under the expert eyes of my slew of editors: Lew Harris, Rodger Claire, and, especially, Ed Dwyer. My editor at Pantheon, Erroll McDonald, has been especially generous with his patience and expertise. Finally, there is my family: my parents, Tamar and Ranan, my brother, Barry, my sisters, Danielle and Daphne, my son, Hunter, my daughter, Paige, and, most significant, my wife, Gretchen. Without them, nothing would be possible.

Rod Lurie
Pasadena, California

INDEX

ABOUT THE AUTHOR

The reporter who exposed the news-gathering techniques of the *National Enquirer*, Rod Lurie is the host of a KMPC-Radio morning talk show in Los Angeles and is the film critic for *LosAngeles Magazine*. Lurie graduated from the U.S. Military Academy at West Point.